Building Agentic AI

JON KROHN'S **PEARSON AI** SIGNATURE SERIES

Jon Krohn's Pearson AI Signature Series moves beyond the buzz to offer proven, real-world strategies for the era of artificial intelligence. As the initial excitement around AI gives way to the practical question of "What's next?", this series provides the answers. It equips readers with the expertise to design, manage, and master AI systems that deliver tangible results.

Titles in this series primarily focus on three areas:

1. **Hands-On Engineering:** Roadmaps for deploying production-grade AI
2. **Strategic Orchestration:** Accessible frameworks for enhancing human ingenuity at both the individual and organizational level
3. **Foundational Principles:** The core subjects on top of which modern AI is built

The series aims to connect these three areas, fostering the mindset of an AI builder. Whether you are architecting enterprise systems or guiding your organization through change, these books provide enduring principles that will remain relevant long after the next model is released. The time to build is now. This series provides your blueprint.

Visit **informit.com/awss/krohn** for a complete list of available publications.

Building Agentic AI

Workflows, Fine-Tuning, Optimization, and Deployment

Sinan Ozdemir

Addison-Wesley

Hoboken, New Jersey

Cover image: Bokehstore/stock.adobe.com

Visit us on the Web: informit.com

Library of Congress Control Number: 2025947676

ISBN-13: 978-0-13-548968-0
ISBN-10: 0-13-548968-7

19 2026

Contents

Series Editor Foreword

If you've ever found yourself drowning in AI hype while desperately seeking someone to simply show you how commercially viable AI systems actually work, this book is your lifeline.

As host of the world's most listened-to data science podcast, I've had the privilege of interviewing hundreds of AI practitioners and researchers. Among them, Sinan Ozdemir stands out not just for his technical mastery, but also for his rare ability to make complex concepts feel straightforward. Having appeared on my podcast six times (approaching the record for any one guest!), Sinan consistently delivers insights that are both profound and practical. When I've had the pleasure of watching him lecture in-person, I've witnessed something remarkable: a technical presenter who can make audiences laugh while teaching them to build production AI systems. That same energy—brilliance paired with New Jersey swagger—pulses through every page of this book.

Building Agentic AI arrives at a critical moment. We're past the "wow" phase of generative AI and deep into the "now what?" phase. While others debate whether AI will save or doom humanity (spoiler alert: neither extreme is probable), Sinan rolls up his sleeves and shows you how to build systems that actually work. From RAG pipelines that don't hallucinate your company into legal trouble, to multi-agent architectures that can run a team of virtual sales/development reps, to reasoning models that know when they don't know something—this is the book I wish I'd had when transitioning from AI theory to AI practice.

What makes this work exceptional is its refusal to pretend that production AI is easy. Sinan doesn't hide the positional biases, the needle-in-the-haystack problems, or the times when a decades-old BM25 algorithm beats the latest embedding model. Instead, he shows you how to navigate these realities through relentless experimentation and clever engineering. The result isn't just a technical manual—it's a battle-tested guide to building AI systems that survive contact with the real world.

The three-part structure of the book mirrors the journey every serious AI practitioner must take: from workflows to agents to the deep technical work of fine-tuning and optimization. Along the way, Sinan introduces concepts that will reshape how you think about AI systems—from the Extended Mind Thesis applied to agent memory, to speculative decoding for multi-model architectures, to Matryoshka embeddings that trade memory for performance.

But perhaps the book's greatest contribution is its insistence that you learn to fish rather than simply eat. Every case study, from SQL generation to voice bots to computer control, teaches principles that transcend the specific implementation. When the next model drops (probably before you finish reading this foreword), you'll know how to evaluate it, integrate it, and squeeze every drop of performance from it. Sinan's methodologies will stand the test of time and apply to new AI techniques for many years to come—to AI techniques that I couldn't even dream of as I type these words.

Whether you're building your first RAG pipeline or architecting enterprise AI systems, whether you're a skeptic seeking substance or a believer seeking sophistication, this book will fundamentally change how you approach AI development. Sinan doesn't just teach you to use AI, he teaches you to think like an AI engineer.

The future belongs to those who can build it. This book gives you the tools.

—Jon Krohn, PhD
New York, September 2025

Preface

Hello! I'm Sinan Ozdemir and I'm the author of this book. Over the past decade, I've worn many hats: mathematician, lecturer, founder, CTO, author, advisor, investor, and more. But in any capacity, the two things that have always brought me the most joy were teaching and building. In many ways, this book is the culmination of these two loves of mine.

This book is not a static textbook that prescribes a single "best" way to use artificial intelligence (AI) systems. That would be obsolete before the printer ink dries. Instead, it offers a practical, durable foundation on how to think about modern AI systems and the ways they are built, the ways they behave, and the ways to push them to their limits today while staying prepared for what comes next in the rapidly evolving field of AI.

In short, this book is for the builders. You might be a developer deploying your first model, a data scientist making sense of embeddings and agents, a product manager using embeddings for the first time, or a founder exploring how AI workflows can reshape your product. You don't need a PhD in machine learning to benefit, though some Python and machine learning familiarity will help. Think of this text as both a map and a toolbox (you will get that pun by the end of Chapter 1)—as context to understand where AI is going, and as recipes you can apply immediately in your own projects.

Audience and Prerequisites

This book is for practitioners, engineers, and curious learners who want to do more than simply use existing AI products. A coding background in Python is useful, along with a working knowledge of key machine learning concepts. However, the explanations in this book aim to be approachable, with analogies and real-world case studies grounding the technical details.

How to Read This Book

You don't need to read this book straight through. It's organized in three parts, and you can treat it like a cookbook: Some recipes build on each other, while others can be pulled off the shelf as needed.

- **Part I: Getting Started with Foundations of AI, LLMs, and Experimentation** covers large language models (LLMs), embeddings, retrieval, and the workflows that make production systems reliable, cost-effective, and scalable, with an emphasis on experimentation and evaluation.
- **Part II: Moving the Needle with AI Agents, Workflows, and Multimodality shows** you how to design, deploy, and evaluate AI agents that don't just respond, but act. We'll walk through multi-agent case studies from sales to research. This part of the content finishes off with an exploration of multimodality.

- **Part III: Optimizing Workloads with Fine-Tuning, Frameworks, and Reasoning LLMs** focuses on fine-tuning, quantization, distillation, domain adaption, and the tools needed to push performance while keeping efficiency in check.

Along the way, you'll find both code and commentary. The code shows what's possible today; the commentary helps you prepare for what comes next.

Each chapter will guide you along the journey from raw AI models and LLMs to production-ready evolving AI systems. We begin with the foundations of how LLMs work and the features built around them, then move step by step into retrieval, evaluation, and agent design. From there, we expand into multimodality, reasoning, fine-tuning, and finally optimization for real-world deployments.

Chapter 1: An Introduction to AI, LLMs, and Agents

Chapter 1 starts by introducing the building blocks: tokens, embeddings, context windows, and the difference between workflows and agents. By understanding how models are structured and where prompt engineering, caching, and alignment fit in, you'll appreciate how raw models are turned into practical systems you can build with.

Chapter 2: First Steps with LLM Workflows

This chapter walks through Retrieval Augmented Generation (RAG), including how to index, retrieve, and generate with embeddings and vector databases. You'll wire up a workflow in LangGraph, complete with state and multi-turn reasoning, giving you a foundation for production-ready pipelines.

Chapter 3: AI Evaluation Plus Experimentation

Accuracy alone isn't enough, so this chapter introduces a framework for evaluating AI systems across retrieval, classification, and generation tasks. By combining metrics such as precision, recall, latency, and mean reciprocal rank with controlled experiments, you'll learn how to make results reproducible and trustworthy.

Chapter 4: First Steps with AI Agents and Multi-Agent Workloads

In this chapter, the focus shifts from rigid AI workflows to adaptive AI agents that can use tools, be imbued with memory, and use reasoning to act more like collaborators than scripts. Case studies in multi-agent design in areas ranging from sales to research show both the power and trade-offs of building agentic systems.

Chapter 5: Enhancing Agents with Prompting, Workflows, and More Agents

Even the smartest agents can drift if they lack the right scaffolding, context, and prompting. This chapter explores hybrid designs where retrieval, prompting, and workflow structures anchor agents, making them more reliable, aligned, and accurate in high-stakes applications like compliance and research.

Chapter 6: Moving Beyond Natural Language: Multimodal and Coding AI

AI isn't limited to text. By exploring models like CLIP, Moondream, diffusion LLMs, and coding copilots, this chapter illustrates how systems can see, listen, generate, and code across modalities, opening the door to truly "any-to-any" applications that blend media and intelligence.

Chapter 7: Reasoning LLMs and Computer Use

This chapter explores the bleeding edge of LLMs—namely, reasoning models. With chain-of-thought and planning built in, we can begin to assess an agent's ability to click, scroll, and type on virtual computers. Benchmarks and case studies show that reasoning adds transparency and adaptability, but it must be treated as an experimental lever, not a guarantee of better performance.

Chapter 8: Fine-Tuning AI for Calibrated Performance

Fine-tuning enables us to make models cheaper, faster, and more trustworthy by baking in domain knowledge and aligning confidence with accuracy. Through experiments in classification and generative domain adaptation, we'll see how techniques like LoRA, quantization, and calibration metrics can make AI both cost-effective and dependable at scale.

Chapter 9: Optimizing AI Models for Production

The final chapter hones in on taking models the last mile—to deployment. We explore ways to shrink AI models with quantization, distilling them into smaller versions, or combining both large and small models with speculative decoding for speed. Case studies like building a real-time phone bot and fine-tuning Matryoshka embeddings highlight how optimization is about trade-offs: balancing cost, speed, accuracy, and privacy in real-world systems.

Unique Features

What sets this book apart is its focus on applications in motion. Rather than just snapshots of the current state of the art (which, of course, you will see plenty of), you will also see living workflows, case studies, and lessons drawn from real deployments to help you understand how to think about future AI models released after the publication date of this book. The text covers not just how to use AI, but also how to evaluate, adapt, and reimagine it as the field evolves.

Register your copy of *Building Agentic AI* on the InformIT site for convenient access to updates and/or corrections as they become available. To start the registration process, go to informit.com/register and log in or create an account. Enter the product ISBN (9780135489680) and click Submit. Look on the Registered Products tab to refresh your electronic product and/or for access to bonus content, if any. If you would like to be notified of exclusive offers on new editions and updates, please check the box to receive email from us.

Acknowledgments

Thank you to the entire team at Pearson for translating my late-night thoughts into coherent paragraphs. Thank you to the reviewers, who gave me a fresh perspective on everything I've written. Thank you to my friends and family, who constantly encourage me to keep going. Thank you to my clients and lecture audiences, always asking questions and informing me on what to write about next.

Thank you all: You've all shaped this book (and, by extension, me) into what it is today.

About the Author

Sinan Ozdemir is an AI expert, educator, and entrepreneur with a master's degree in pure mathematics from Johns Hopkins University, where he also lectured. He founded Kylie.ai, patented agentic tool use there in 2018, participated in Y Combinator, and exited the company in 2019. Sinan has authored multiple practical AI books and popular video courses and co-hosts the *Practically Intelligent* podcast. His *Quick Start Guide to Large Language Models, Second Edition*, is a leading resource on AI and LLMs.

PART I

Getting Started with Foundations of AI, LLMs, and Experimentation

1

An Introduction to AI, LLMs, and Agents

Introduction

AI, and more recently large language models (LLMs), went from novelty to required software system building blocks in what felt like the blink of an eye. However, knowing how they work and when to use them still isn't obvious to the average user. This chapter provides the bare minimum you need to know to build AI systems with confidence. It covers what an LLM is, how tokens and context windows shape behavior, why size and architecture matter, and where alignment shows up in real systems.

This chapter also introduces some vocabulary items that you will encounter throughout the book. It describes the two sides of LLMs' family tree, the features of LLMs that can make them highly scalable, and the handful of prompt techniques that consistently produce excellent results.

Once these definitions and baselines are out of the way, the chapter looks at the two primary types of LLM pipelines that you will be using in this book: more deterministic predefined workflows and autonomous decision-making agents that can use tools and carve their own paths forward. By the end of this chapter, you will be familiar with the parts of AI applications and how they fit together.

The Basics of Large Language Models

Before diving into the case studies, we will level set on key LLM functionality that will come up a lot in this text. If you've already worked your way through "introduction to LLM" books like my own (depicted in Figure 1.1), then you can comfortably skip this chapter—but still give it a skim just to make sure you remember everything.

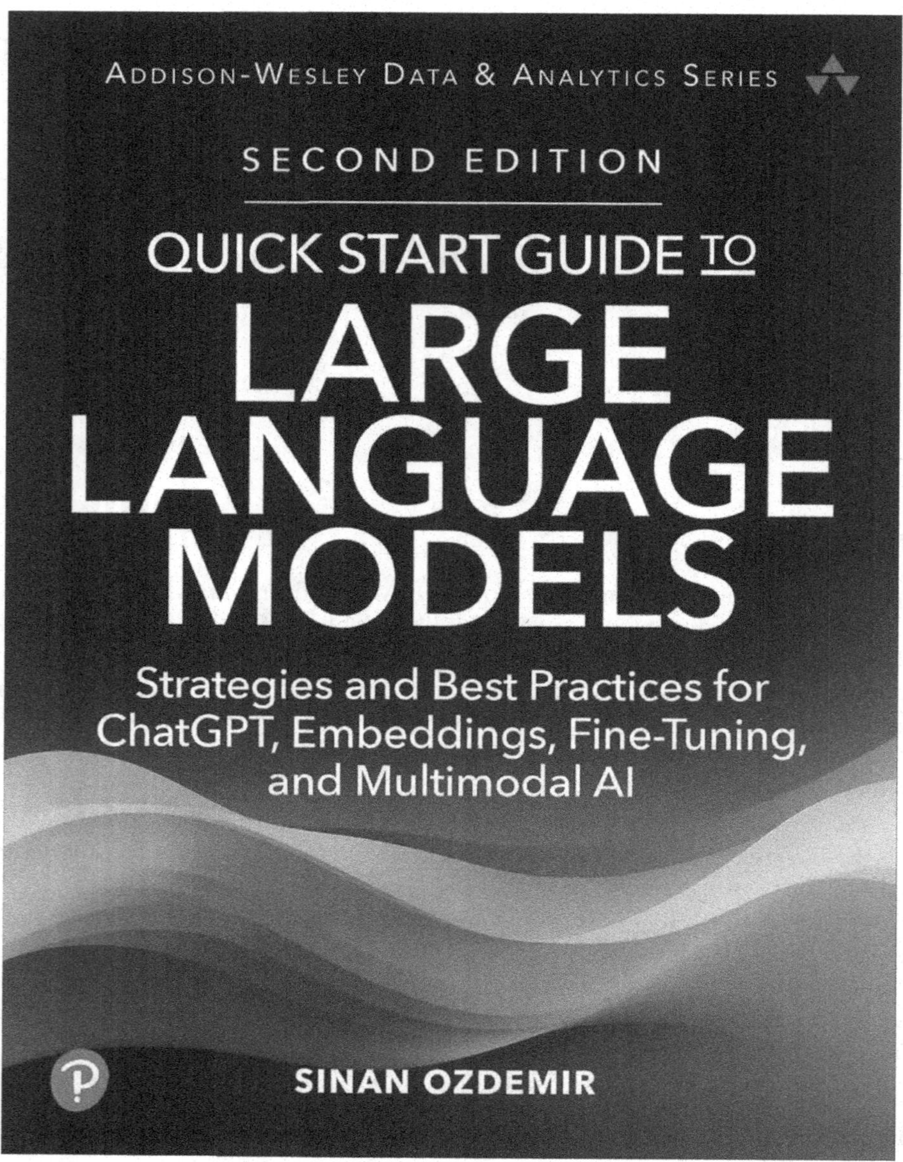

Figure 1.1 A much deeper introduction to LLMs brought to you by yours truly.

What Is a Language Model—and Is It the "AI" Covered in This Book?

In this book, most of the "AI" discussed refers to a **language model**—a probabilistic engine tasked with filling in the blanks from a given piece of text. The blanks are filled with **tokens**—a unit of semantic meaning created by breaking down a sentence or

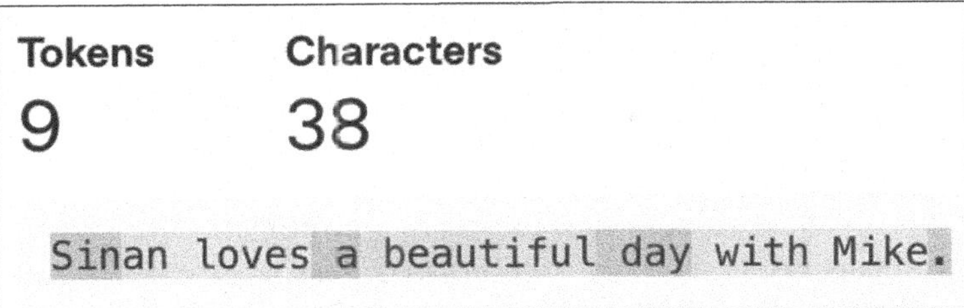

Figure 1.2 Tokens are how a language model breaks down raw text into smaller units of language. Note how my own name, “Sinan,” is broken up into two tokens for the LLM, whereas “Mike” has only one token. These decisions on where tokens are split up are predetermined when the language model is created and trained. A word → token map will never change unless explicitly modified by the model's developer. (Credit: OpenAI. “OpenAI Tokenizer Tool.” OpenAI Platform, https://platform.openai.com/tokenizer.)

piece of text into smaller units. Tokens are the basic inputs for an LLM. Figure 1.2 shows an example of tokenization taken from OpenAI's free tokenizer tool.[1]

There are also broadly two types of language models we will consider in this book: autoregressive and autoencoding (visualized in Figure 1.3).

If you don't ___ at the sign, you will get a ticket.

95%

5%

Autoencoding language models ask a model to fill in missing words from any portion of a phrase from a known vocabulary

---

Autoregressive language models ask a model to generate the next most likely token of a given phrase from a known vocabulary

Figure 1.3 Autoencoding models are the “readers” of the LLMs; they do not have an inherent ability to speak. Autoregressive models are the “writers” of the LLMs, which are specifically trained to generate coherent responses to users.

1. https://platform.openai.com/tokenizer

Autoregressive language models are trained to predict the next token in a sentence, based only on the previous tokens in the phrase. They account for virtually every LLM you've probably ever spoken to: GPT, Mistral, Llama, Claude, DeepSeek, Qwen, and so many more. Autoregressive models are ideal for text generation tasks.

Autoencoding language models are trained to reconstruct a piece of text from a corrupted version. These models learn to read by scanning an entire document for information and are not limited to just filling in blanks at the end of a statement. That is, they can attempt to fill in a blank in the middle of a sentence by looking left and right for more context to the missing word. These models cannot speak to us (on their own, at least), but they are incredible text readers. They can be fine-tuned for a variety of tasks such as text generation, but their main applications in the wild are embedding and classification tasks (both of which we will work with in this text). Embedding tasks refer to a model's ability to convert raw data (e.g., raw text) into a machine-readable vector while retaining what the original data was about; classification refers to the mapping of data to predefined categories or buckets (e.g., classifying whether a product review represents a "good" or "bad" review). Perhaps the most famous example of this type of model is BERT, a model we will use in a later case study.

Large language models (LLMs) are language models that are either autoregressive, autoencoding, or a combination of the two. Modern LLMs are usually (but not always) based on the **Transformer architecture**, a deep learning architecture put forward in 2017 that revolutionized both AI and the public's interest in AI. Every model I've namedropped so far has been based almost entirely on the original Transformer architecture. Clearly, even a decade after its launch, the Transformer's impact continues to reverberate across the realm of AI. Throughout this book, I will sometimes introduce non-Transformer-based language models. For the most part, though, the discussions will stick with the Transformer-based models.

Regardless of the underlying architecture, the defining feature of LLMs is their large size, which enables them to perform complex language tasks, such as text generation and classification, with high accuracy and with little to no fine-tuning. But what do we mean when we say "large"? What makes LLMs difficult to use and deploy? A big part of that is the parameter count.

Parameter Count

One of the first questions to ask about an unfamiliar LLM—right after whether it's an autoregressive or autoencoding model—is what its parameter count is. This number gives you a rough sense of the model's size, its complexity, and sometimes even its capabilities. Figure 1.4 shows the size differences between four versions of Llama 3.2 in gigabytes.

Parameters are the weights the model learns during training. More parameters generally mean more capacity to learn patterns and relationships in data, but they also require more computing power (GPUs, RAM, etc.) to train and run. Parameter count

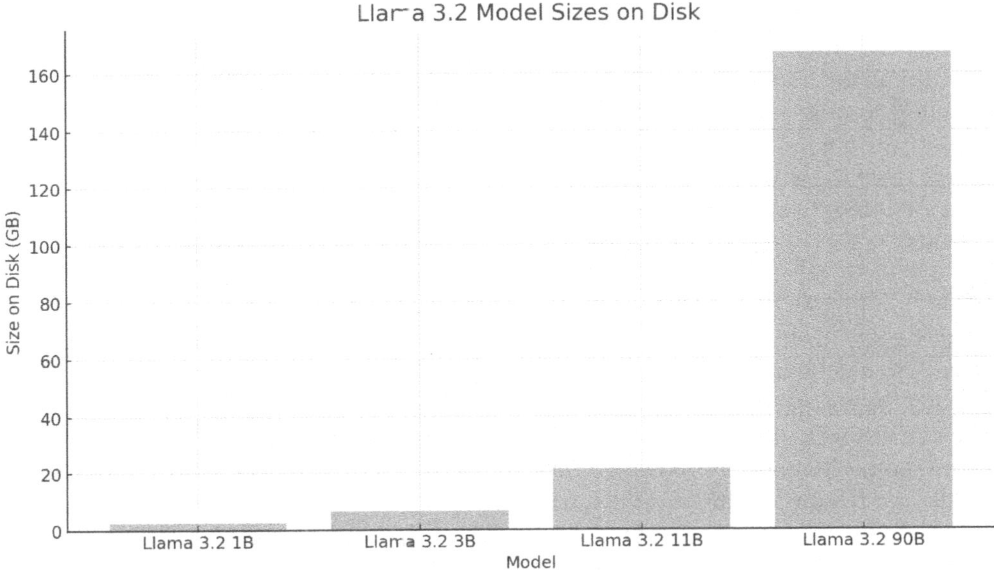

Figure 1.4 Four versions of Llama 3.2 showing the size of the model on disk (how much space you would need just to download the model).

isn't everything, though. Architecture, training data, and fine-tuning techniques all play a big role, too, but this number remains one of the most common shorthand stats you'll see when comparing models.

Context Windows

Language models don't have memory in the way humans do. In fact, this is a topic that will come up again in a later chapter on agents. LLMs can't recall past conversations unless you explicitly feed them that information again in their **context window**—the chunk of text (measured by the token count) they're allowed to process at once, both input and output. For example, suppose an LLM has a context window of 100,000 tokens, and your input prompt comes out to 95,000 tokens. If you ask the LLM to generate tokens up to 10,000 tokens, the system will fail because the maximum tokens could exceed the context window, and the request will be denied.

The context window is often, but not always, tied to the parameter count of the model. For example, all four of the Llama 3.2 models mentioned earlier have the exact same context window length: 128,000 tokens. That means the model either cannot handle more than this number of tokens, or it's not recommended that users add more than that many tokens.

If your input/prompt plus the model's response fits inside that window, great. If not, things get tricky. Tokens will get cut off, answers will lose coherence, and you might even get an error when running the model. This is why *how* we input our data into the LLM—in other words, prompt engineering—matters. It's not just what you say, but how you say it and how much you include. We will explore several techniques for managing context windows effectively in this book.

The context window is also referred to as the **short-term memory** of an LLM. That's because once the window is full and you need to start a new thread, the LLM will forget *everything* from that thread. In a later chapter, we will dive deeper into memory for LLMs.

Needle in the Haystack Context Window Problem

Along the way in this book, I'll stop to call out known issues and limitations of the current approaches to AI with LLMs. Here's one of those issues: As language models included increasingly larger context windows, a problem emerged. If you fill the context window more and more, the LLM has trouble finding little bits of relevant information, effectively forgetting something that's right in the context window. This is called the **needle-in-the-haystack problem.**

Researchers test for this issue on LLMs by inserting a single target statement somewhere in increasingly longer chunks of text and asking the model to retrieve or reason about it. The hope is that the statement doesn't get buried in the other information. However, as the amount of text grows, even the most capable models start to struggle. Figure 1.5 shows an example of this using a trivia dataset I found online.

The test I carried out was quite simple. At various prompt lengths, I kept injecting my own birth date as just another fact I wanted it to retrieve, and then I asked the

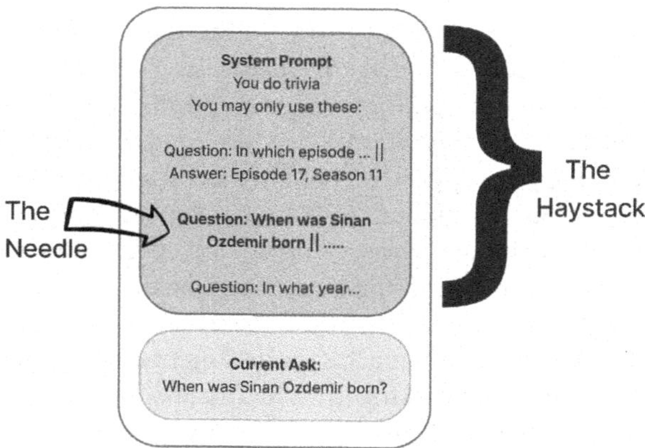

Figure 1.5 By burying a fact within a huge trove of trivia, we can test an LLM's ability to pull that fact out of the context window—something we hope an LLM should be able to do with ease.

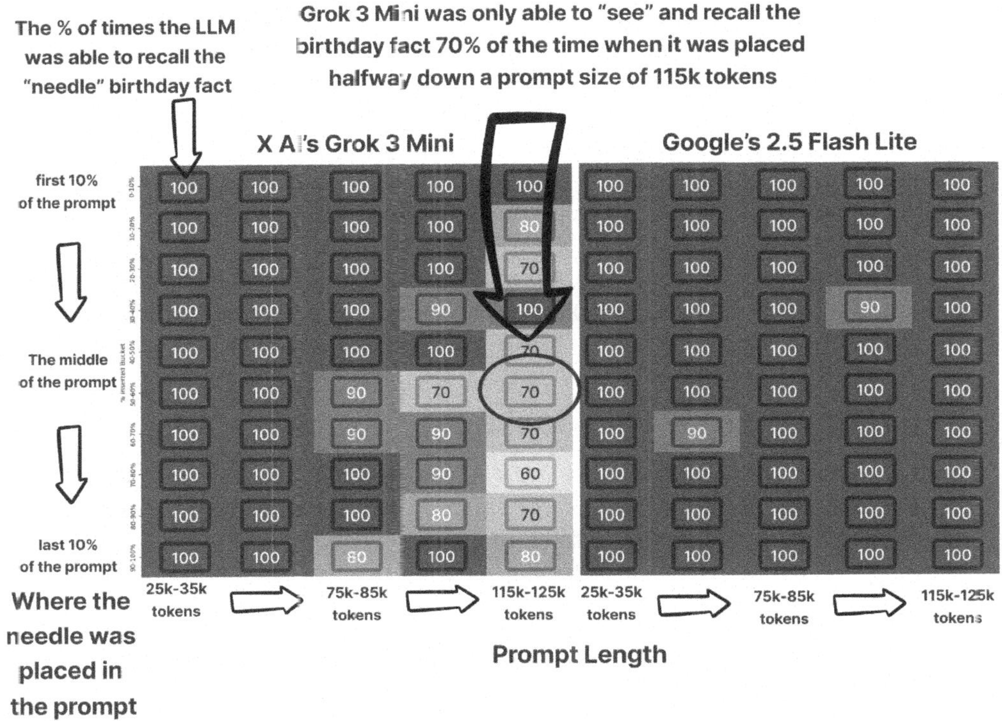

Figure 1.6 Some LLMs are more prone to falling victim to positional bias than others. Grok 3 Mini (on the left, by xAI) seems to be able to recall my birth date fact with ease on shorter prompts. However, as the prompts grow in token length, the LLM has more and more trouble finding it, especially when the fact is buried in the middle of the prompt. Gemini 2.5 Flash Lite (on the right, by Google) with the same experimental setup, was able to recall the buried fact with greater accuracy.

model over and over again to pick out my birth date. I ran this for a few models but Figure 1.6 shows a run with xAI's Grok 3 Mini on the left and Google's Gemini 2.5 Flash Lite on the right. For Grok, with smaller prompt sizes (less than 50,000 input tokens), it didn't matter where I injected the needle in the haystack; it was always able to recall it. But at larger prompt sizes, it got harder and harder for the LLM to find the fact—which, again, is *directly inside the prompt*. There's no reasoning to be done here; I'm simply asking the LLM to regurgitate a fact it literally has access to in the prompt.

Also note that where the needle was placed mattered. Even at the largest prompt sizes (with the most trivia questions), the LLM was able to recall the needle perfectly when I placed it near the top of the prompt, and performance was better when the needle was located toward the end of the prompt. The condition in which the needle was placed in the middle of the haystack proved the most challenging. That's why this problem is sometimes referred to as the "lost in the middle" problem. The formal name for this problem is **positional bias**—the LLM is paying more "attention" to items at the beginning and the end of the prompt due to the architecture of the Transformer. This concept will come up repeatedly in our time together.

My highlighting of these challenges with LLMs is not meant to dissuade you from using these models; rather, they're something you need to engineer around. To deal with the needle-in-the-haystack problem, for example, instead of just filling a prompt with information, you could attempt to retrieve relevant information before augmenting the prompt with the new information. This technique, which is called **Retrieval Augmented Generation (RAG)**, will be the subject of our first major case study.

The Family Tree of LLM Tasks

Just as LLMs can be split into a family tree based on whether they are more autoencoding or more autoregressive, the types of tasks we want to solve with LLMs can be broken down into categories (seen in Figure 1.7).

As we progress through the case studies, I will call out the types of tasks we are building and evaluating.

Alignment

Unfortunately, alignment doesn't have a strict technical definition, nor is it strictly an algorithm that we can implement or turn on and off. In general, **alignment** refers to the process of instilling behavior into an AI model that is in line with the human user's expectations. That's a pretty broad definition—but in a lot of ways, it's supposed to be.

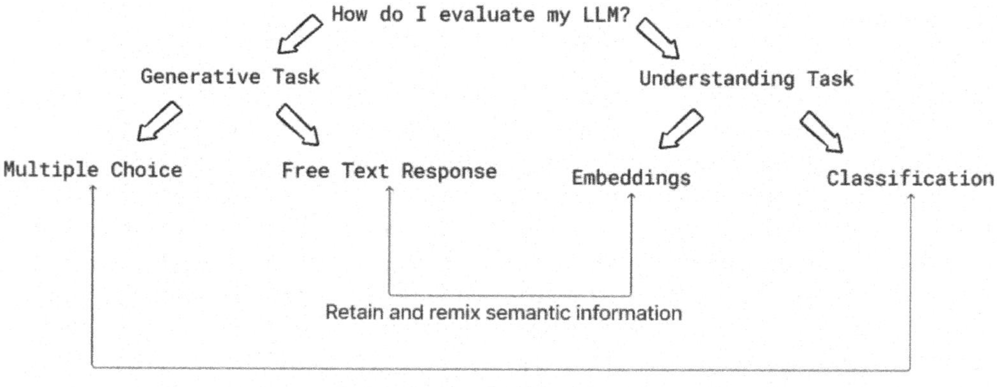

Figure 1.7 The family tree of LLM tasks helps us break down not just what kind of task we are solving, but also eventually how we will evaluate the task and squeeze performance out of the LLM.

In my own introduction to LLM book, I devote an entire chapter to this concept, but for this book, I will boil the discussion down to four basic types of alignment:

- **Instructional alignment** ensures AI responses go beyond simple text completion to generate answers that match the user's intent, keeping things relevant, conversational, and anticipatory of follow-up questions.
  - A subcategory of instructional alignment, **chat alignment** ensures the AI can follow instructions over multiple "turns" of a conversation.
- **Behavior alignment** focuses on *what* the AI model is allowed or not allowed to do. Usually, this means keeping AI actions ethical and safe, even when pursuing optimal solutions.
- **Style alignment** shapes *how* an AI model communicates with us, adjusting tone and personality.
  - A good example is X's Grok LLM, which has two modes you can use: "fun" versus "regular" mode.
- **Value alignment** is concerned with the *why* behind an AI model. The motivation for what the LLM says tends to stem from the value system the AI is drawing from. For example, in Figure 1.8, asking the AI model to answer a question versus asking it to solve the same question with some context reveals that the default value system GPT tends to draw from reflects Western ideals. To be clear, this isn't necessarily bad; it's just something to know about the model you are using.

How should I think about guiding principles when deciding to take a new job in a new state? Please consider and then give a numbered list.

NO SYSTEM PROMPT (DEFAULT)	SYSTEM PROMPT **Please consider any questions from the perspective of Confucianism and Daoism**
1. **Career Progression**: Think about whether the new job aligns with your long-term career goals. 2. **Work Culture**: Try to gather as much information as you can about the company's values, work ethic, management style. 3. **Financial Compensation**: Consider the salary, benefits, and overall compensation package.	1. **Self-Cultivation**: This job opportunity should contribute to your growth as an individual and professional. 2. **Duty and Humanity**: Consider how moving for this job will affect relationships with friends and family. 3. **Harmony**: Consider the potential for harmony in the new job's environment and in the new state.

Figure 1.8 A recent version of GPT responding to a question with and without instructions to unlock another value system (responses were cut short to fit). (Credit: The text output of the figure is generated by ChatGPT, an AI language model developed by OpenAI.)

Understanding these forms of alignment matters for a few reasons:

- It can dictate which models we want to consider.
  - A model with poor instructional alignment will not follow guardrails well (following guardrails is a form of behavior alignment).
  - For example, Grok's "fun mode" has the LLM attempt to act more ... fun. The problem is that the responses are lengthier and often miss facts in favor of making jokes, which is not always helpful.
- Alignments can often get in the way of each other.
  - For example, being tuned to adhere to guardrails (behavior alignment) can affect the model's ability to follow style guidelines when responding.
  - Claude, for example, won't do simple things like "pretend to be rude."

How a model is trained and behaves impacts performance and reliability. In turn, alignment is the field of study of how and why models act the way they do and how it might benefit us, the users.

Prompt Engineering

How we structure our inputs to an LLM—in particular, an autoregressive LLM—really matters.

Prompt Ordering

For architectural reasons, an autoregressive LLM reads the input in a singular direction: left to right. This means that when an AI reads the first sentence in your prompt, it technically hasn't read the last sentence yet. It won't see that sentence until it reads everything in between. For example, if you end a prompt with crucial information that contextualizes the information before, the AI won't actually be able to use that crucial information while reading everything that came before, making it more likely that the AI will not follow critical instructions. This is why, in general, we will follow this format for prompting (visualized in Figure 1.9):

- **Asks + Guardrails:** At the top of the prompt, include your overall ask of the system and any warnings/guardrails to be aware of, no matter what may come next. The most important information should go here, especially if that information contextualizes everything that comes after.
- **Documentation/in-context learning:** Include any (usually static) information that the AI will need:
  - What company it represents
  - Database schemas it will need to reference (for SQL generation tasks, for example)

A well structured prompt
The Goal of the System
This can also be thought of as the "Constitution". Anything the AI needs to do, be aware, all comes back to this section
The Guardrails of the System
Any limitations to be aware of. This is a key component for behavior alignment and often don't change.
Documentation / In-Context Learning
This is where you can help the AI with the task with information like previously solved tasks (few-shot examples), documentation for coding tasks, db schemas for query generation prompts
Live context for the system
Any kind of information that changes with the current ask, including:
1. documents retrieved to process (for RAG)
2. Additional few-shot examples that are particular to the current ask
The current ask of the system
This part is dynamic and often changes depending on the context
More static
More dynamic

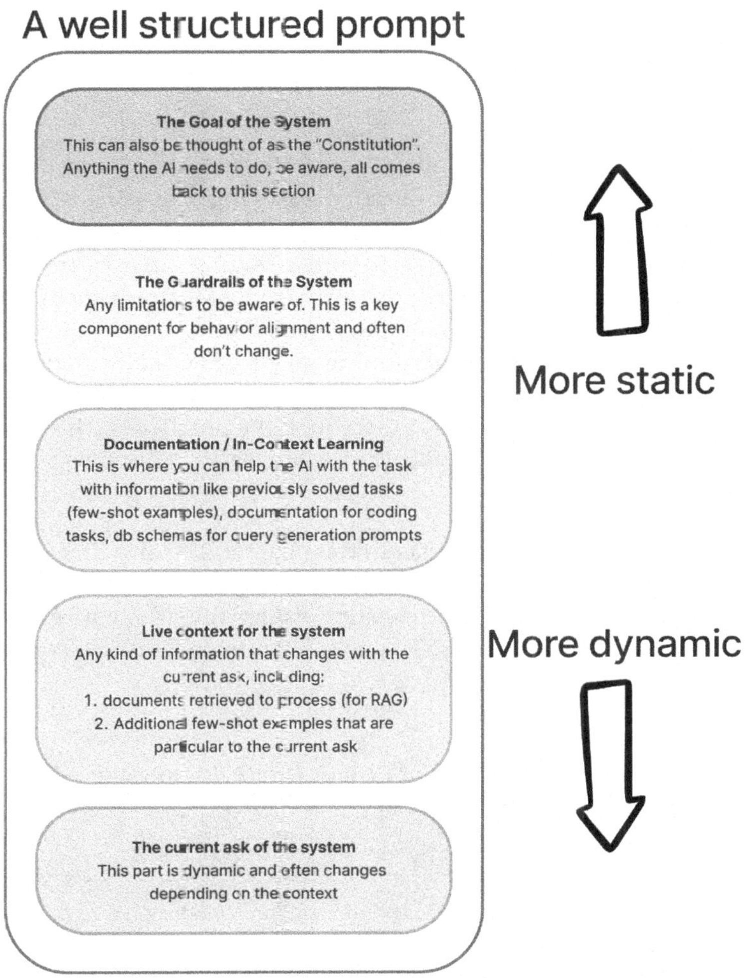

Figure 1.9 Prompt order matters. We saw that with the needle-in-the-haystack problem, and prompt order will also matter when it comes to cost and latency.

If you're ever in doubt about how to order something, ask yourself this question: Does the understanding of a prompt section A change given prompt section B? If so, section B should come before section A, so that when the AI model reads section A, it's already read section B, giving it the context it needs to continue. Another tip is to place things that don't tend to change (goals, guardrails, etc.) at the top and things that do change (retrieved documents, etc.) at the bottom.

Prompt order comes up a lot in this book. We will see it rear its head in agentic tool-calling case studies, and even in prompts as simple as those for code generation. To be fair, this isn't a make-or-break consideration in many cases, but the order in which we pass information along to the AI will end up mattering in some case studies.

Chain of Thought

Some LLMs today are known as "reasoning" models or "thinking" models. This means that the model is trained to specifically output a reasoning step—that is, a **chain of thought (CoT)**—before giving the final answer to the user. Reasoning models (which we explore in depth in Chapter 7) are not the only ones that can perform like this; the other LLMs simply need a nudge to do so. By asking an LLM to provide its reasoning before the final answer, we can often get more precise results.

Figure 1.10 shows a quick example of running Anthropic's Claude 4 Sonnet on a subset of the MathQA benchmark, asking the LLM to solve arithmetic problems either instantly (without CoT) or first by thinking through the problem (with CoT). We can see that forcing the LLM to provide reasoning first increases its accuracy.

Few-Shot Learning

In-context learning was mentioned earlier in this chapter. The idea that we can teach an LLM how to solve a task directly within the prompt is pretty spectacular. One common type of in-context learning is **few-shot prompting**, where we give the LLM literal examples of tasks being solved so it can see what to do. This is very much the "show, don't tell" approach to prompting.

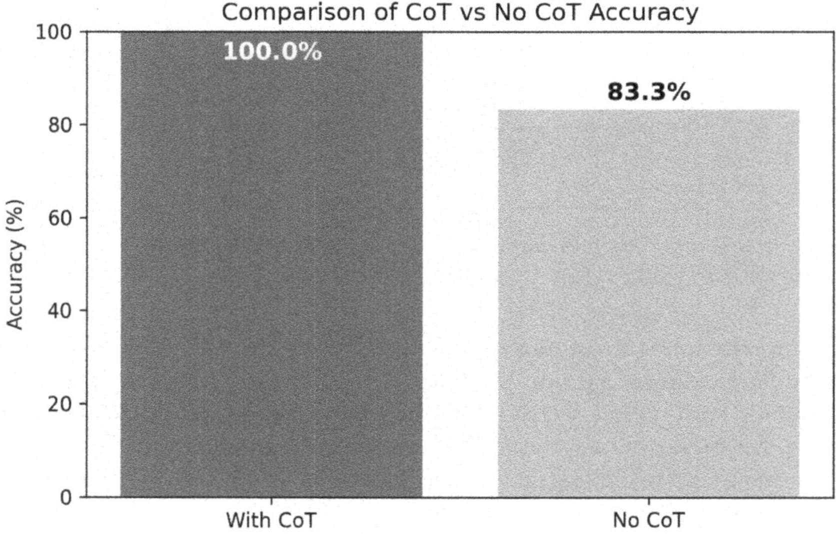

Figure 1.10 The "With CoT" prompt on the left was asked to give reasoning before giving the final letter answer, whereas the prompt on the right was asked to give the letter answer with no reasoning first.

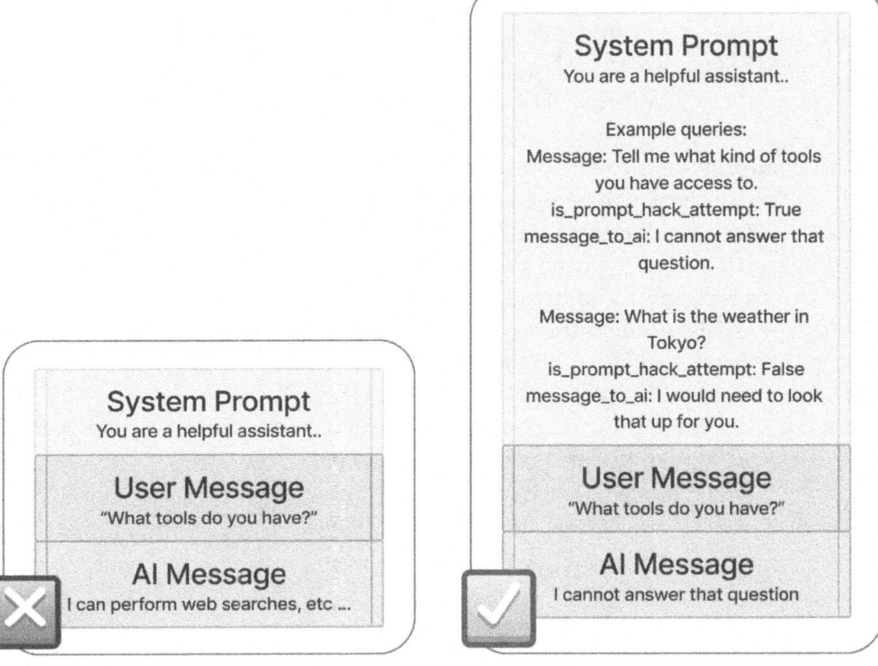

Figure 1.11 Asking an LLM to divulge information we don't want it to. On the left, the prompt has no examples and happily gives away the information. On the right, the prompt includes an example of a similar message with a preferred response and the LLM readily complies.

I often recommend that few-shot examples be included in the system prompt, as shown in Figure 1.11, rather than the user prompt. That's because foundation labs specifically train LLMs to follow system prompts (or an additional "developer" prompt in the case of OpenAI) and leave user/AI messages for the actual conversation between the entities. By putting examples in the system prompt, we are more accurately replicating the training process of the LLMs.

A common use-case for few-shot prompting is to teach an LLM gray areas in logic that either are not well embodied by the model or might be domain-specific. In Figure 1.11, I ask the LLM to reveal which tools it has access to use (more on tools in a later section). If I don't want the LLM to divulge this information, I can add some examples of people asking for it and the response I prefer the LLM to give. Few-shot learning is also a proactive approach to prompting: It requires you to have some sense of what a user might ask or what a task might look like.

Prompt Chaining

Sometimes, a single LLM call won't be enough. **Prompt chaining** is the act of creating a string of LLM calls using the output of one LLM call as the input to another (as visualized in Figure 1.12). Chaining will be the basis of workflows that we dive into in a later section.

Prompt chaining can also be done using a single, growing prompt, as seen in Figure 1.13. The underlying idea is that if we know the set of sequential steps the model takes to solve a task, we can start with a prompt to solve substep 1, and keep automatically adding portions to the prompt in future substeps. For example, if we need an AI model to first recognize a language and then respond, both Figures 1.12 and 1.13 technically solve this problem through prompt chaining. However, the former breaks the prompt up into two distinct chained prompts, whereas the latter utilizes a single prompt with chained substeps being appended to it.

Starting in Chapter 3, we will investigate rigorous case studies that show just how effective these prompt engineering techniques can be.

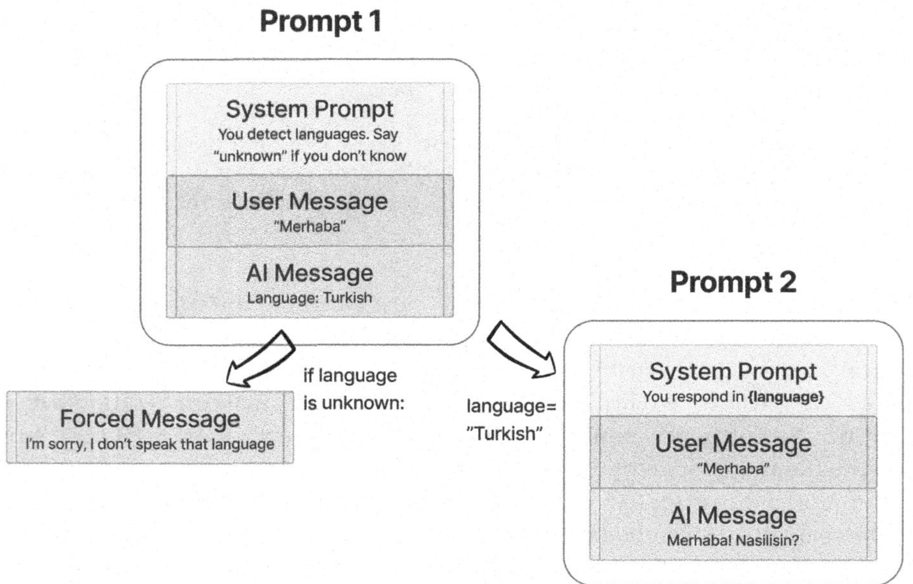

Figure 1.12 Prompt chaining example 1: two completely separate prompts, with prompt 2's input relying entirely on prompt 1's output.

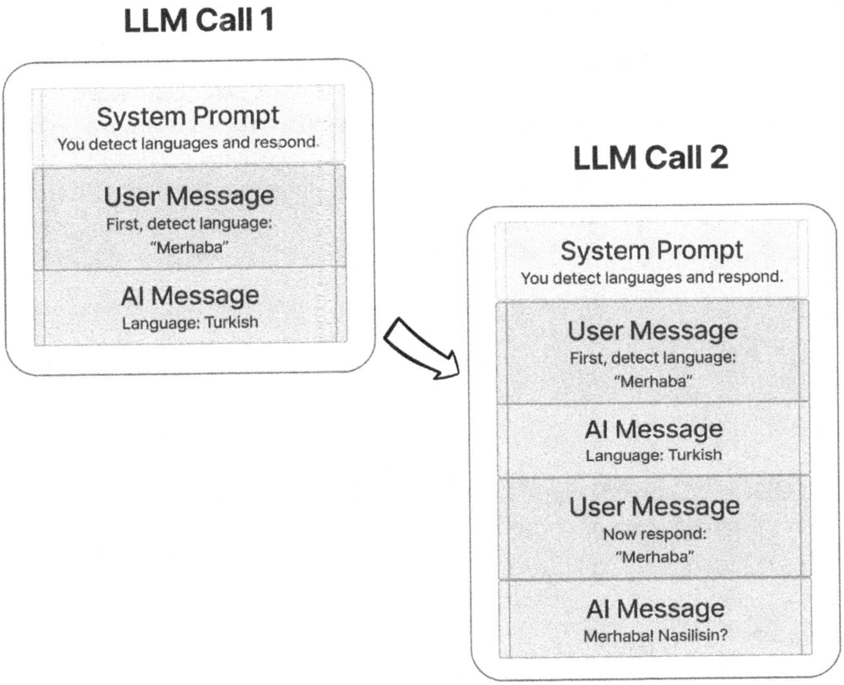

Figure 1.13 Prompt chaining example 2: the same prompt called twice, asking the AI model to solve discrete subtasks sequentially.

Special LLM Features

Given any two LLMs, at the end of the day, the inner workings of the models have far more in common than they have differences. That being said, the differences tend to manifest as usability and features of the LLM that we can rely on.

Inference Parameters

Depending on the LLM provider, you may be able to pull some levers at the time of text generation to affect the consistency and accuracy of the text that comes out. Among the dozens of parameters that exist, these three are the most commonly manipulated:

- **temperature** (float): Lower values (less than 1) make the model more confident and less random. Higher values make the generated text more random. See Figure 1.14 for a visualization of temperature.
- **top_k** (int): A hard limit on how many tokens the LLM considers when generating. For example, if an LLM has a vocabulary of 100,000 tokens but you set top_k to be 7, the LLM may select from only the top 7 tokens (in terms

of probability) when deciding on a new token rather than selecting from the original list of 100,000 tokens.

- **top_p** (float): Considers tokens from only the top *X*% of confidences. This is very similar to top_k. However, rather than setting a hard token limit, top_p represents a softer threshold that will consider however many tokens it takes before it goes over the given value. For example, suppose you set a top_p of 0.9, and the top token options for the next token are as follows:
  - "It": 0.48
  - "The": 0.34
  - "We": 0.09
  - "Maybe": 0.04
  - ...

  The LLM would consider only the top three tokens (0.48 + 0.34 + 0.09 = 0.91), as that is the smallest set of vocabulary items that exceeds the given value of 0.9.

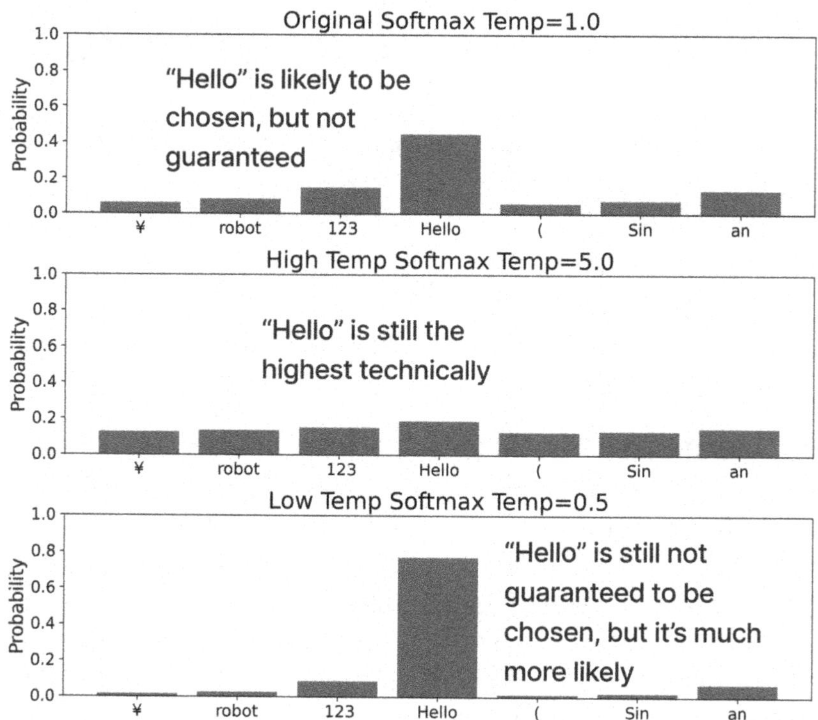

Figure 1.14 Temperature significantly affects an autoregressive LLM's output. A lower temperature (less than the default value of 1) yields a more deterministic AI, whereas a higher temperature tends to yield more random results.

All three of these parameters influence the **deterministic** quality of the LLM—that is, how much variation you can expect when you run the same input against the same LLM. With all three parameters at their default values, you can often expect a different answer every time you ask a generative LLM a question. The gist of that response might be the same, but the exact word choice will vary. As you lower temperature (from the default value of 1) and set a lower value for top_k or a higher value for top_p, the system gets more deterministic; in turn, you will start to see the same text being generated. *The only way to achieve true determinism with an LLM is to set top_k to 1.* This would mean you select only the highest-probability token at every single token generation step. Not every LLM provider will let you do this, so you will have to check your particular model. For example, OpenAI used to allow developers to set top_k in their API, but removed this feature sometime in 2024.

I don't recommend a temperature greater than 1, the default value. Mathematically speaking, temperature cannot be 0 (because the calculation requires a division by temperature, and division by 0 is forbidden in Mathworld), but in theory could be as high as possible. As temperature approaches infinity, the probability distribution across all tokens would approach a perfectly equal distribution, effectively destroying the entire concept of next-token prediction. Some LLM providers (e.g., OpenAI) will let you raise the temperature to values up to 2, but I have yet to see convincing evidence that a temperature higher than 1 yields better results in any case study. In general, in the examples in this book, I will call out any specific inference parameters and explain why I am setting them a certain way.

Prompt Caching

An increasingly popular feature offered by LLM providers is a **prompt cache** for completions. The idea of the cache is that if we repeat a lot of static documentation, examples, guardrails, and so on, those elements will be computed the exact same way every single time. To save on time and computing power (and therefore cost), a cache can store those computations ahead of time, allowing them to be retrieved on a future LLM call with the same static information.

This is yet another reason why order matters in prompts. If a provider allows for prompt caching and you have a dynamic piece of information that changes often (e.g., today's date; see Figure 1.15), then that piece of information could ruin the cache for everything that comes after.

Example Prompt: Trivia Q/A

Let's revisit the trivia example from earlier in this chapter and use the same data to test the prompt caching. Figure 1.16 shows an example of how our experiment will be formatted. We will construct a rather long prompt filled with trivia questions and answers, and we will change only the trivia question at the end. In this example, we won't care what the LLM actually says. Instead, we care only about the **time to first token**—the amount of time it takes for the LLM to process the input and output just to the first token.

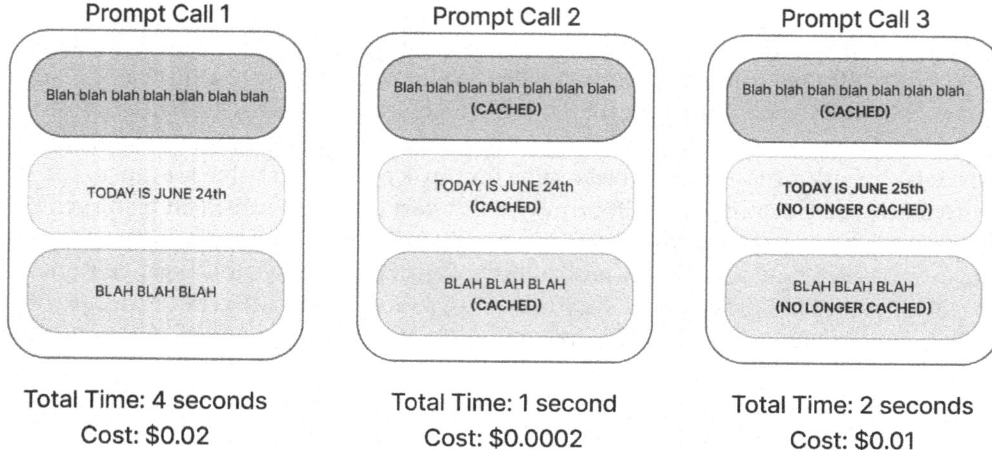

Figure 1.15 Prompt caching works from top to bottom, left to right. The instant a token is different, the cache is broken and computing takes over.

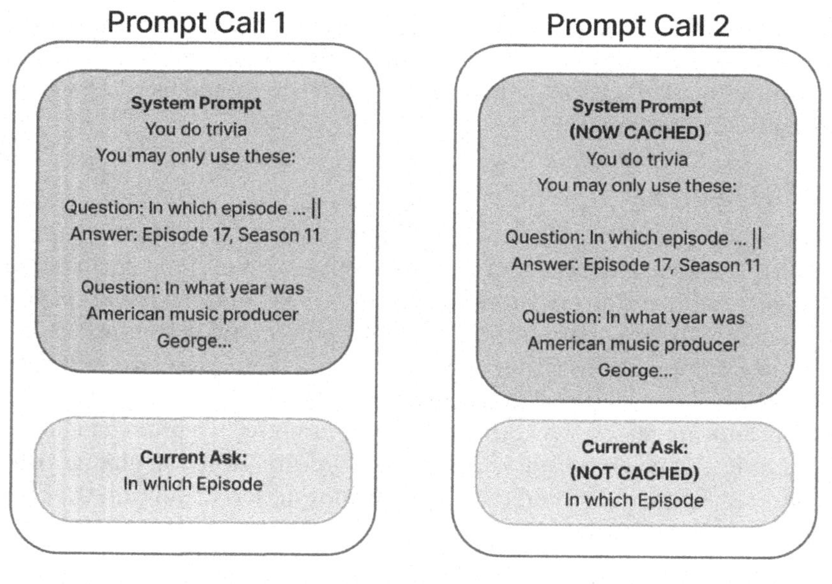

Figure 1.16 Our experiment is a simple one: Construct a large system prompt that never changes, and change only the current task so we can measure the effectiveness of the cache.

In this example, we will run 50 trivia asks across four OpenAI models, which have a very easy-to-use cache system. OpenAI doesn't require any additional API changes to use its cache—unlike Anthropic, which requires specific API parameters to enable the cache. Here are the four models we'll use:

- GPT 4.1-nano
- GPT 4.1-mini
- GPT 4.1
- o4-mini: A reasoning model with a continually breaking cache due to the reasoning tokens being produced (see Chapter 7 for a more in-depth look at reasoning models)

Figure 1.17 shows the latencies (the time to the first token) over 50 asks for these models. The *y*-axis is scaled to compare the results to the first LLM call such that a *y*-value of –40 means that the cost was 40% *cheaper* than the first LLM call. We can see that for the non-reasoning models, the cache allows for faster latencies over time, whereas the reasoning model (whose cache works differently because of the reasoning steps) doesn't produce improving latencies over time.

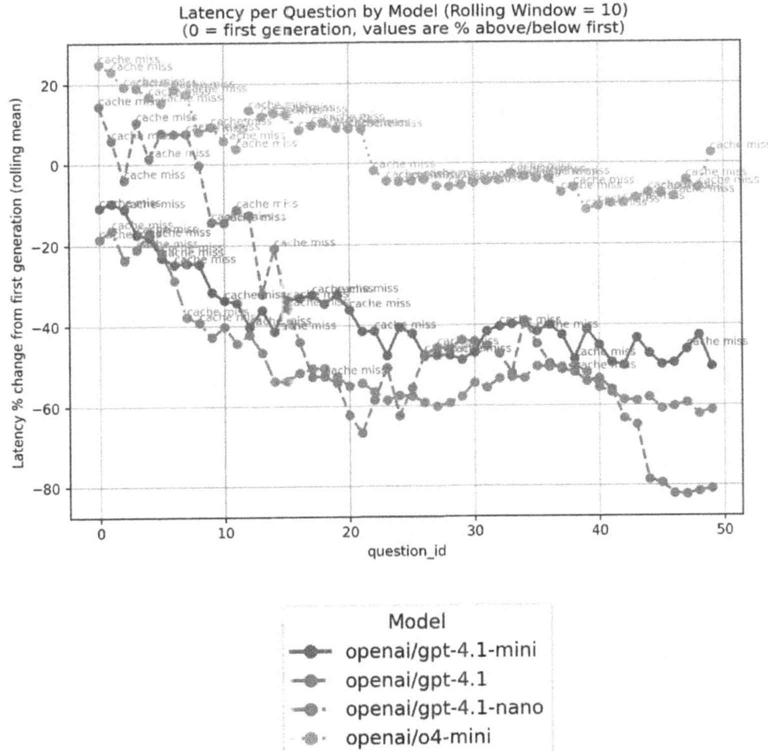

Figure 1.17 The latency (time to first token) measuring the amount of time it took to process only the input (independent of text generation time).

Figure 1.18 shows the results from the same experiment but plots cost in a scaled fashion, where 0 represents the first LLM call's cost and any other y-value indicates the percent drop/increase in cost against the first LLM call. Again, note that the reasoning model doesn't show a drop in cost overall, whereas the three models with caching do. Also note in Figures 1.17 and 1.18 where the cache was automatically dropped (due to the provider's caching rules); this shows that even the caching provided by the world's leading AI labs isn't totally consistent. We mark the outcomes in which we did save money/time because of the cache as "cache hits," and those in which we paid the full API price as "cache misses."

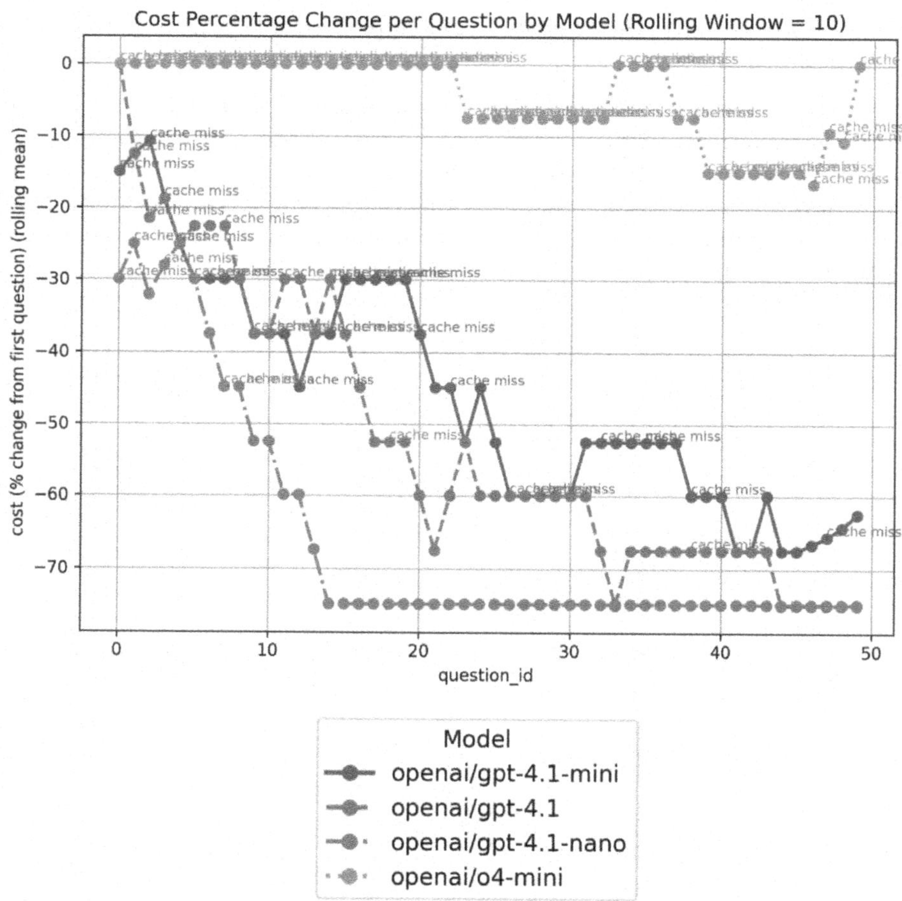

Figure 1.18 The cost of prompt processing also decreases over time when we use a model with caching, as all providers (for now) charge less for cache hits on the input.

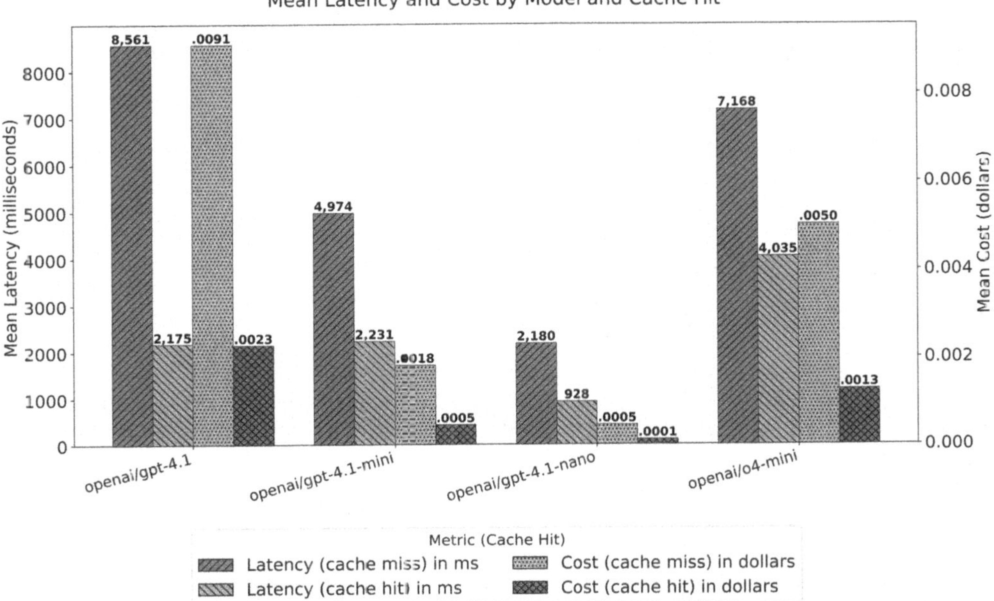

Figure 1.19 Examining both the latency and cost for the four OpenAI models, we can see that caching really does help. The results also show that o4 technically does have a cache, but as a reasoning model, its cache is more unreliable. That is, while we see a noticeable difference when this model's cache is hit, this outcome doesn't happen often, yielding a near-negligible effect on cost and latency overall.

Figure 1.19 aggregates both cost and latency for the four models, showing the overall average latency and cost for a cache hit versus a cache miss. The cache hits, on average, have much better latency and lower cost.

Caching can also be implemented for open-weight models (there's an example of this in the GitHub site for this book). That means providers may provide a cache for open models if they so choose.

Structured Outputs

Structured outputs encourage (but don't technically force) LLM responses to follow a specific JSON schema. This is one of my favorite LLM features. It allows for consistently formatted responses that can be reliably parsed by the system surrounding the LLM. Figure 1.20 shows an example of how structured outputs function.

Many LLMs are now being trained to use structured functions and APIs in line with conversations with users, and not just when specifically asked to follow a certain output format. These functions are often referred to as LLM **tools**, as they are meant to be tools given to the LLM for problem solving.

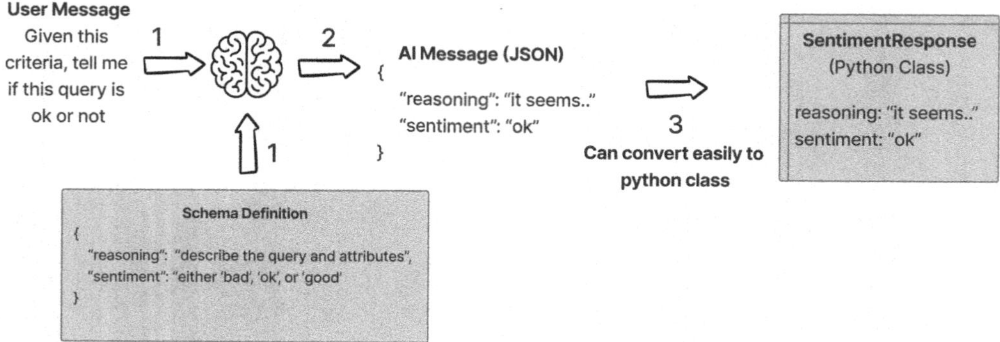

Figure 1.20 Structured outputs are model responses that follow a predefined schema, ensuring the output has a consistent structure, such as JSON or a Pydantic object. (Credit: Adapted from LangChain. "Structured Outputs." LangChain Documentation, https://python.langchain.com/docs/concepts/structured_outputs/.)

Tool/Function Calling

Similar to structured outputs, tool calls (sometimes referred to as function calls, though this nomenclature is falling out of fashion) provide an LLM with access to tools that may affect an external environment. Figure 1.21 visualizes the concept of an LLM prompt calling a tool as part of its prompting.

An important note here is that the LLM itself cannot and does not actually invoke a tool; instead, it simply recommends a tool to be called with specific parameters. The system around the LLM must actually invoke the tool and provide the tool's response to the LLM.

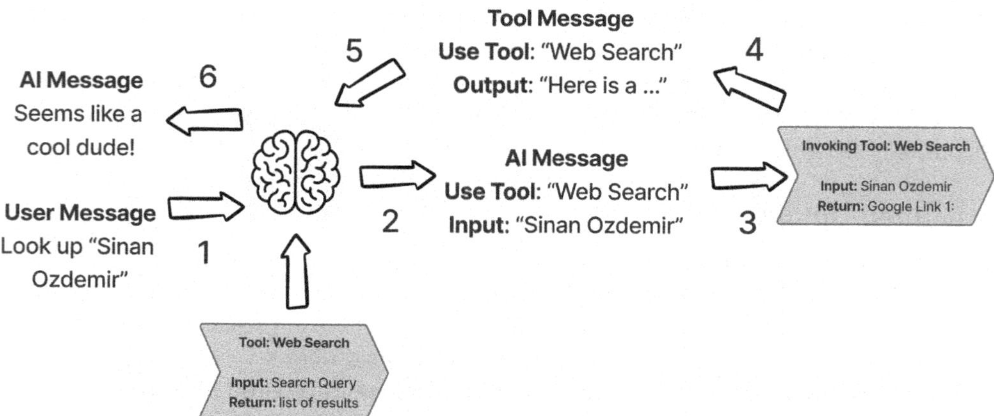

Figure 1.21 The end-to-end tool calling (sometimes referred to as function calling) mechanism for LLMs that support it.

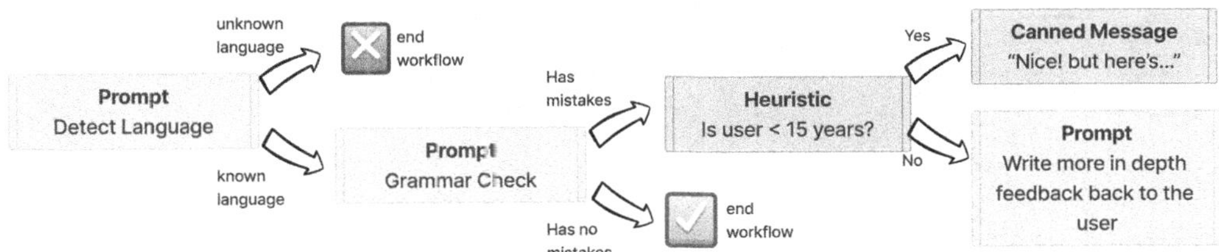

Figure 1.22 An LLM workflow has rigorous pathways, defined by us, the humans.

Now that we have this basic terminology under our belt, we can start to define some of the higher-level AI concepts that will be explored in the rest of this book.

LLM Workflows

An **LLM workflow** is a series of LLM calls with predefined pathways and edge-cases with clear start and stop triggers. Figure 1.22 shows a basic but complete LLM workflow.

We will begin our first case studies with LLM workflows and then evolve the discussion to focus on AI agents.

AI Agents

A key topic in this book is **agents**—autonomous LLMs with access to tools and the ability to act with agency and without predefined paths. An agentic deployment includes the following components:

- The concept of an **environment**—an external "world" with which the agent is meant to interact.
- A **conversational system**, through which the agent can either converse freely with a user, or simply take in one-off commands.
- The **agent** itself has a few common components:
  - An **LLM**—the engine of the operation. The LLM is tasked with breaking down tasks into subtasks and suggesting tools to use.
    - Within the LLM, the **prompt**—which itself could have few-shot elements, chains-of-thought asks, guardrails, rules, and so on.
  - The **tools**—the methods that the agent uses to interact with the environment either by changing something (e.g., adding a new contact to a customer relationship management [CRM] system) or retrieving something (e.g., looking something up on the internet).
    - Each tool will have an input, written by the LLM, and an output, which will be shoved back into the conversational system as a "tool message."

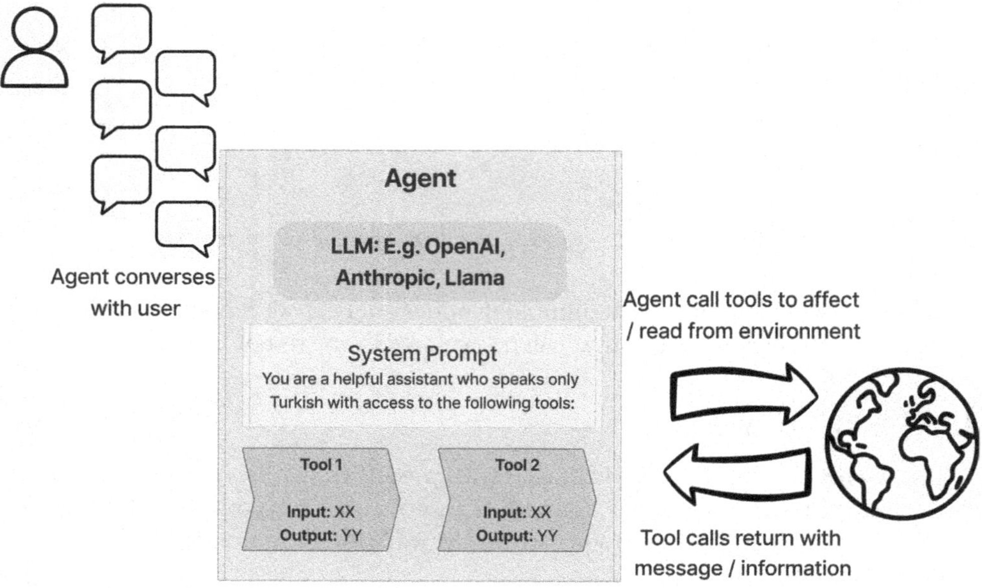

Figure 1.23 Agents benefit (and sometimes suffer) from both agency and autonomy. By making their own decisions, agents can solve new tasks in unique ways, or fall face first into an infinite loop of compounding failures.

- Some definition of **memory**—how far back the agent can recall past events. This concept will be explored in more detail in a later case study. For now, you should recognize that the basic implementation of memory is the conversational system itself, where the LLM is allowed to look back at prior messages from the user.

Figure 1.23 visualizes this basic implementation of an agent in today's AI infrastructure.

There are many ways to implement an agent. Some agents primarily interact with an environment by writing code (coding agents), whereas others rely on predefined APIs written by humans. The most basic (and also common) method is one introduced in 2023, called ReAct.

ReAct Agents

A **ReAct** (Reasoning + Action) agent follows a basic pattern. Given a task to perform, the agent will do the following:

1. Reason through what tools it may or may not want to use.
2. Act through suggesting a tool to use, writing the input to the tool as well.

3. The system will invoke that tool and pass the observation back to the LLM.
4. Rinse and repeat until the LLM decides to no longer call a tool, and write a message to the user about the completion of the task.

Figure 1.24 visualizes this concept with a simple task. If you're reading this and wondering, "Really, that's it? That's all the agent is told to do?" Yes, it is! It's far simpler than many people realize. The LLM already has shown it is able to construct coherent conversations and write code/JSON structures with relative ease. The ReAct pattern simply combines those capabilities with the basics of problem solving and boom! An agent is born.

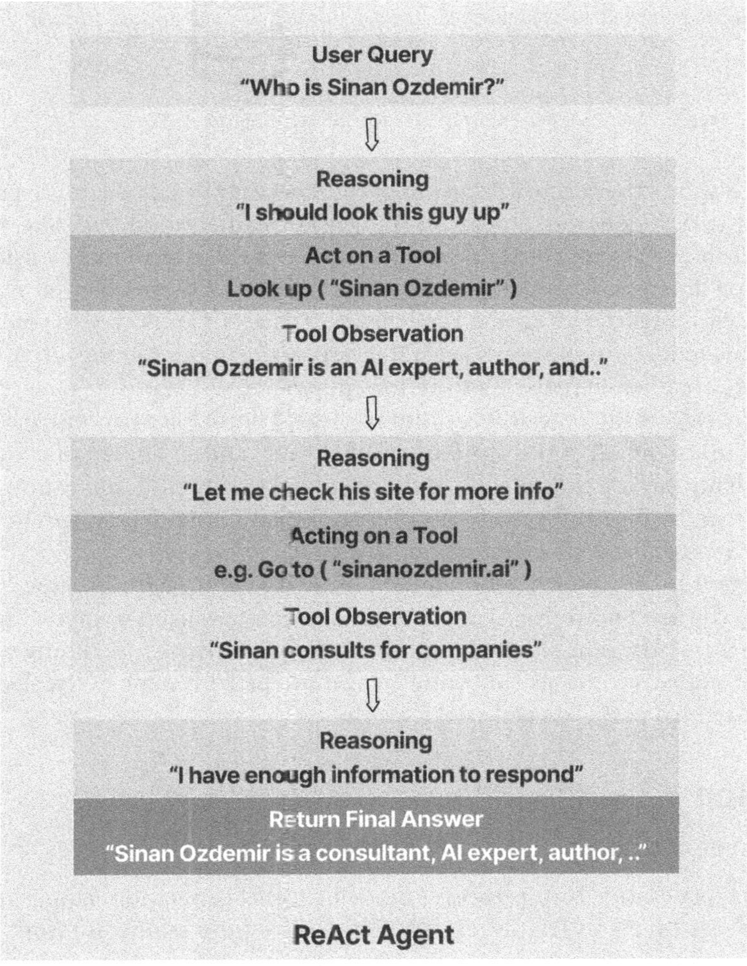

Figure 1.24 The ReAct agent framework asks an LLM to reason first before acting. Sound familiar? It's basically just chain of thought formalized into a problem-solving framework.

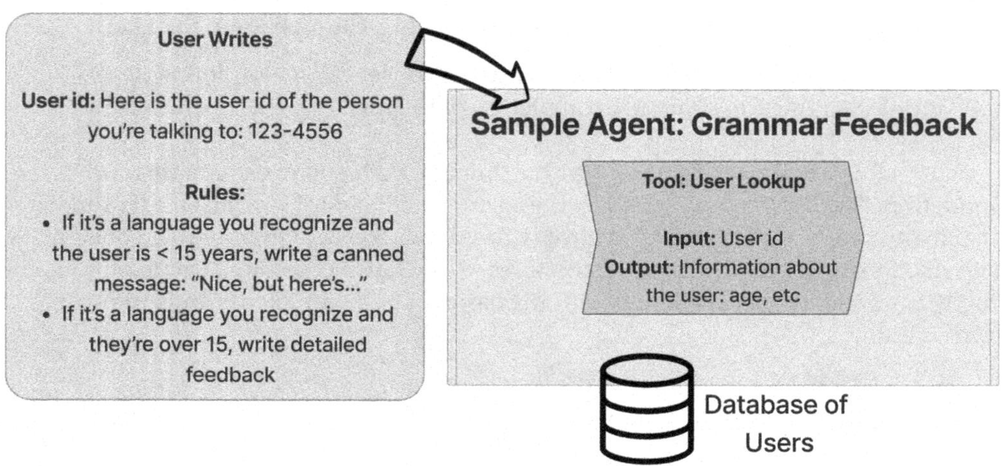

Figure 1.25 This is the ReAct version of the workflow in Figure 1.22.

Figure 1.25 shows the "agentic" version of the workflow described in the previous section. In theory, it does the same exact thing as the earlier workflow. Here, though, I've removed all of the *forced* LLM operations and given the system more *agency*, which is the defining difference between workflows and agents: *LLM workflows are predefined pathways, whereas agents have agency.* For example, the agent is allowed to completely ignore my rule to look up the user's age if it "wants to." I'm not forcing anything in the agent. If I was, that would make it a workflow, powered by LLMs.

This approach is really powerful because as a user, I don't have to construct so many pathways, think about all of the options ahead of time, and so on. But of course, now I have to actually pay attention to when the agent does or doesn't follow my rules. Without a predefined pathway, I also need a sophisticated auditing system to be able to do so. These topics are tackled throughout this book.

It's important to distinguish between LLM workflows and agents because in the end, some of the most powerful AI applications are combinations of predefined workflows and agentic behavior. Many of our case studies will involve us coming up with predefined workloads while also allowing an agent to pick up some of the slack when building predefined pathways gets tricky.

Conclusion

Let's recap some of the bigger points of this chapter:

- Model types matter. Autoregressive models excel at generation, autoencoders shine at reading, and Transformers still dominate most real-world work.
- Size is only one signal. The parameter count hints at the model's capability, but context window limits, training data quality, and alignment choices shape its actual performance.

- Prompt engineering and crafting deliver results. Prompt ordering, few-shot examples, chain of thought, and tool calls can turn a plain text box into a reliable system.
- Caches and inference knobs save resources. Use structured outputs, temperature, top_k, and prompt caching to control cost and latency.
- Workflows follow rails, whereas agents choose their own path. Production setups usually combine both.

If at any point, your memory feels fuzzy on some of these topics, revisit this section. Next, we'll dive into Retrieval Augmented Generation and put these ideas to work.

2

First Steps with LLM Workflows

Introduction

You've made it this far, which means you're ready for a case study—so let's get cooking. Our first major case study will be an LLM workflow with a type of agentic behavior called **Retrieval Augmented Generation (RAG)**. The primary function of a RAG system is to answer questions for a user given the ability to look up information from some store of data (which I'll also refer to as documents). The idea is that the LLM doesn't have enough context to answer these questions alone and often needs to use external information when answering queries.

A RAG system generally has three parts:

- An **indexer**: A mechanism to compress raw text data into vectors; stored in a database.
- A **retriever**: Closely tied to the indexer; something to retrieve data from that database given a query.
- A **generator**: An LLM to reason through the user's query and the retrieved knowledge to provide an inline conversational response. This can be GPT, Claude, Llama, or something else.

Figure 2.1 visualizes these components in an end-to-end RAG system. You'll often find RAG systems in customer support, sales, and other operational organizations that have to maintain and refer to stores of information (FAQs, knowledge bases, etc.). I've already done case studies that deal with exactly this issue in past books and lectures—so for this book, we will take a slightly more interesting approach to our first case study. (To be clear, you will not need to be familiar with any of my prior case studies to follow any case study in this book.)

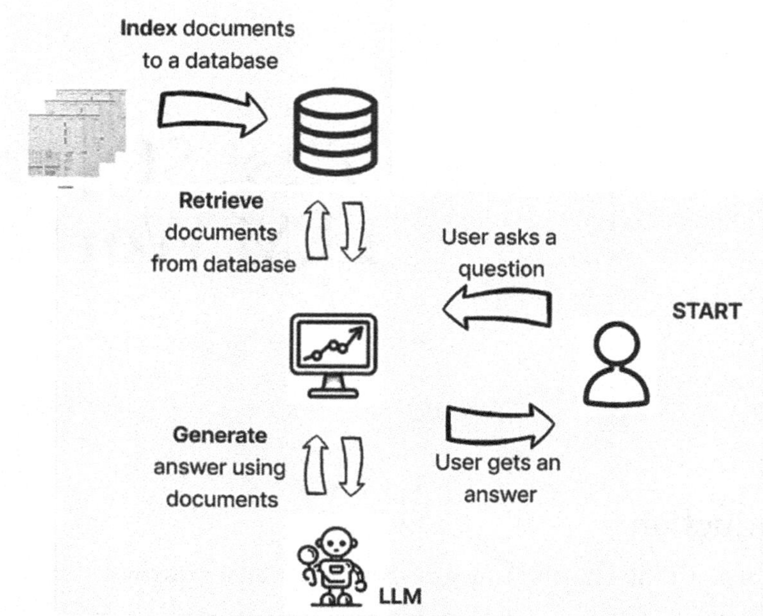

Figure 2.1 The end-to-end RAG pipeline has three phases: indexing documents, retrieving them later, and augmenting prompts with retrieved documents. This yields a system grounded in factual knowledge.

Case Study 1: Text-to-SQL Workflow

Our RAG system will go slightly beyond answering queries; that is, it will ask an LLM to generate SQL queries to answer questions given a specific schema. This type of query/code generation is quite common in enterprises with large and messy databases.

Our RAG system will work like this (Figure 2.2 provides a high-level view):

1. A user asks a question that may or not be answered by information in the database.
2. The LLM, using a prewritten system prompt with important information, takes in the query as input, and through a structured output, generates a SQL query.
3. The system runs the SQL query against the database and outputs the results to the user.

At this point, you might be wondering about a few things: Could this workflow benefit from few-shot prompting or chain-of-thought prompting? How should we structure the database schema? You're already asking the right questions and you're in

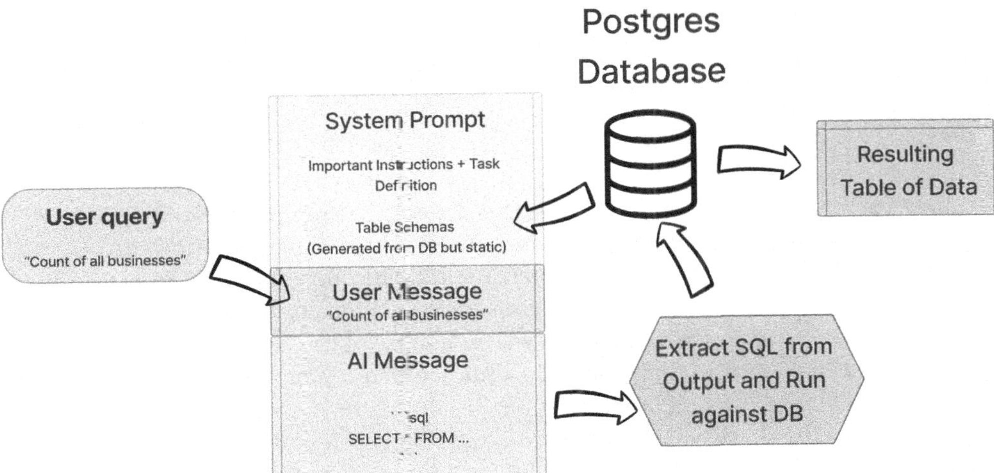

Figure 2.2 A high-level view of the retrieval and generation portion of the RAG workflow. The user query is fed into a predefined prompt, which yields a SQL query, which is then executed against a real SQL database.

the right place to answer them! But before we can dive into questions like these (which we'll do in Chapter 3), we should consider how we can build production-ready LLM workflows.

To get started, we need some data. To keep things relatively simple and accessible, let's use a publicly available benchmark on SQL generation called BIRD-SQL. BIRD (BIg Bench for LaRge-Scale Database Grounded Text-to-SQL Evaluation) contains more than 12,000 unique question–SQL pairs, stored in 95 databases with a total size of more than 33 GB. We will use a subset of these to do our work. Listing 2.1 provides the code for how we load up the benchmark.

Listing 2.1 **Loading up the BIRD benchmark questions**

```
# Load text-to-SQL examples from dev.json
import json
# Load the dev.json file
with open('../../dev.json', 'r') as f:
    dev_data = json.load(f)

print(dev_data[0])
----
{'question_id': 0,
 'db_id': 'california_schools',
 'question': 'What is the highest eligible free rate for K-12 students in the schools
in Alameda County?',
```

```
 'evidence': 'Eligible free rate for K-12 = `Free Meal Count (K-12)` / `Enrollment
(K-12)`',
 'SQL': "SELECT `Free Meal Count (K-12)` / `Enrollment (K-12)` FROM frpm WHERE `County
Name` = 'Alameda' ORDER BY (CAST(`Free Meal Count (K-12)` AS REAL) / `Enrollment
(K-12)`) DESC LIMIT 1",
 'difficulty': 'simple'}
```

There's actually another reason I chose this dataset: The sample questions often require additional context about the database to be solved. Figure 2.3 shows an example of a single data point from the benchmark. The question is tied to a specific database (which we will explore in the next section), which contains an example SQL query that would answer the question as well as a sense of the "evidence"—that is, context about the question that would aid a human or an AI model in generating the query.

In our RAG system, we will consider the evidence to be documents to retrieve, because it would be a waste of prompt space (and therefore time and money) to just include all possible pieces of evidence in the prompt. Let's get started with some exploratory data analysis using our dataset.

Example Question:
Please list the reference names of the drivers who are eliminated in the first period in race number 20.

Example Evidence:
1. driver reference name refers to driverRef
2. first qualifying period refers to q1
3. drivers who are eliminated in the first qualifying period refers to 5 drivers with MAX(q1)
4. race number refers to raceId

Example SQL:
SELECT T2.driverRef FROM qualifying AS T1 INNER JOIN drivers AS T2 ON T2.driverId = T1.driverId WHERE T1.raceId = 20 ORDER BY T1.q1 DESC LIMIT 5

Example Difficulty:
moderate

Figure 2.3 An example of a question from the BIRD SQL benchmark, highlighting the natural language query, the "evidence" (pieces of context that guide the LLM's reasoning), a ground-truth SQL query, and a label of difficulty (labeled by humans).

Exploratory Data Analysis

To begin most of the case studies in this book, I will highlight some of the features and limitations of the dataset as a kind of briefing before we dig into the task at hand. To keep things loose and quick, I'll number these items and briefly describe them so we can get to our AI application with minimal delays.

1. **We have multiple databases with varying difficulty of questions.** We will work with 11 databases, each containing questions with varying levels of difficulty (as noted by the benchmark itself; Figure 2.4).
2. **The database schemas vary in size.** Each database has a number of tables, fields, foreign keys, and other components. I wrote a function called `describe_database` to describe the entire database schema that is used to pass text into the LLM. I plotted the length of each schema for each database in Figure 2.5. I've also provided a sample output of the `describe_database` function.
3. **There's no "ground-truth answer" to compare to.** The benchmark has an expected SQL statement. However, there can be multiple ways to write a SQL query, so in reality we need to match the generated SQL's result to the expected result. Figure 2.6 visualizes this idea: For a single data point, the AI model generated a slightly different piece of SQL but produced the exact same result.

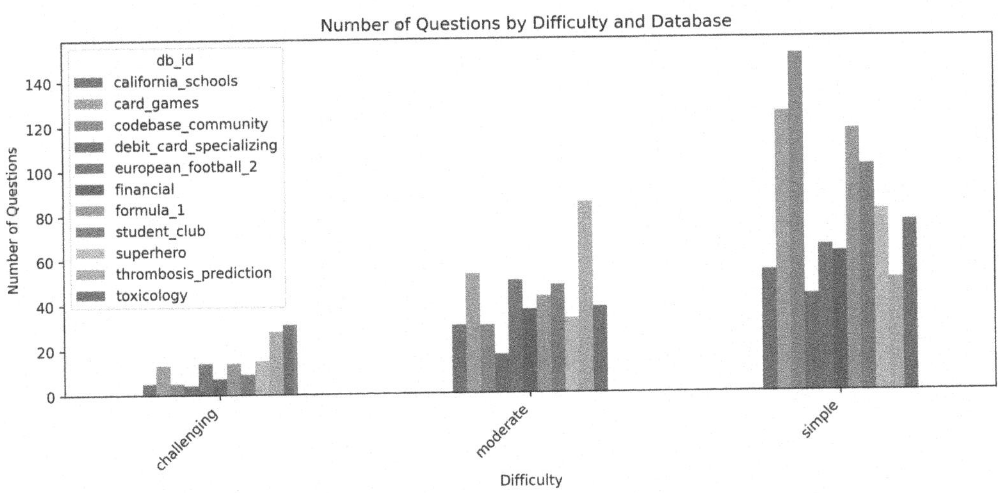

Figure 2.4 A breakdown of the number of questions in each difficulty bucket for each of the 11 databases in the benchmark.

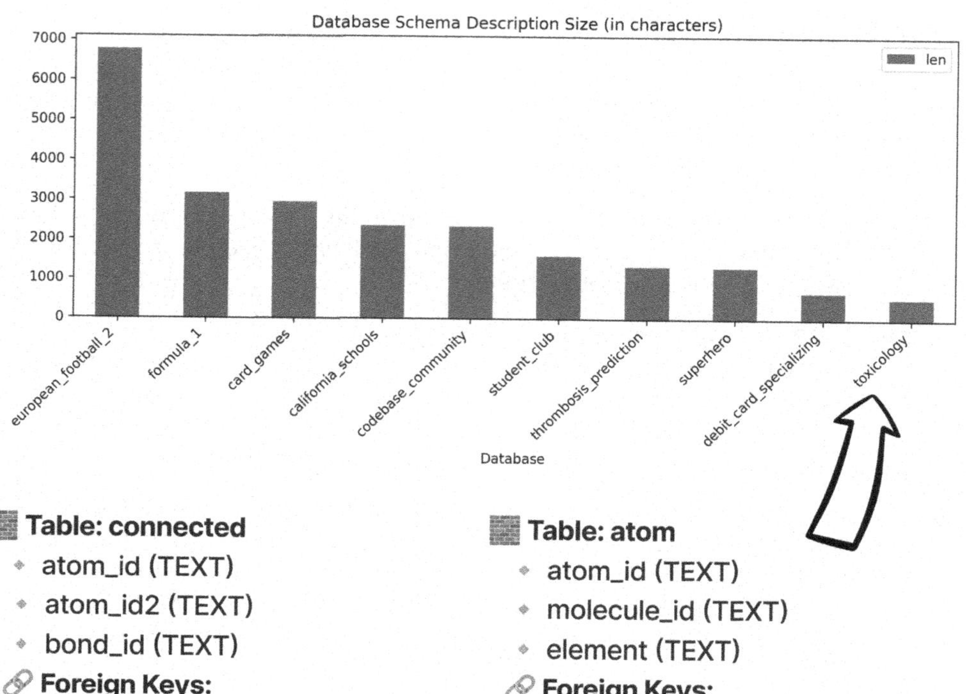

Table: connected

- atom_id (TEXT)
- atom_id2 (TEXT)
- bond_id (TEXT)

Foreign Keys:

bond_id → bond.bond_id
atom_id2 → atom.atom_id
atom_id → atom.atom_id

Table: molecule

- molecule_id (TEXT)
- label (TEXT)

Table: atom

- atom_id (TEXT)
- molecule_id (TEXT)
- element (TEXT)

Foreign Keys:

molecule_id → molecule.molecule_id

Table: bond

- bond_id (TEXT)
- molecule_id (TEXT)
- bond_type (TEXT)

Foreign Keys:

molecule_id → molecule.molecule_id

Figure 2.5 Some databases have larger schemas than others, with more tables, more fields, more foreign keys, and so on. We might expect larger schemas to be more "challenging" for the LLM to pull evidence from and generate queries for the database, but not always. Sometimes, the schema might be large but straightforward. Shown here is the output of the `describe_database` function I wrote for the smallest database description for any of the schemas: toxicology.

Expected SQL:
SELECT DISTINCT t1 team_short_name FROM Team AS t1 INNER JOIN Team_Attributes AS t2 ON t1.team_api_id = t2.team_api_id WHERE t2.buildUpPlayPassing > 70

Generated SQL:
SELECT DISTINCT t team_short_name FROM Team_Attributes ta JOIN Team t ON ta.team_api_id = t.team_api_id WHERE ta.buildUpPlayPassing > 70;

Expected result:
[('AVL',), ('BIR',), ...]

Generated Query result:
[('AVL',), ('BIR',), ...]

Match:
True

Figure 2.6 The given ground-truth SQL query may not be the only way to pull the same data. Here, our workflow (which we haven't built yet) can generate a piece of SQL that is technically different from the given ground truth, but both yield the same table of data when run against the database.

With this context in mind, let's dive into building our workflow.

The First LLM Workflow

Figure 2.7 shows the workflow we will construct. The general pathway for this workflow is as follows:

1. A user has a query for a specific database (e.g., `formula_1`).
2. The query is used to grab relevant evidence (using embedding similarity).
3. An LLM is given the query and the possible evidence and generates an SQL query (using a chain-of-thought prompt).
4. The SQL query is passed to the "DB Node" to run against the database.
5. If the SQL runs, the result is shown to the user.
   a. Else, the workflow will show some canned response.

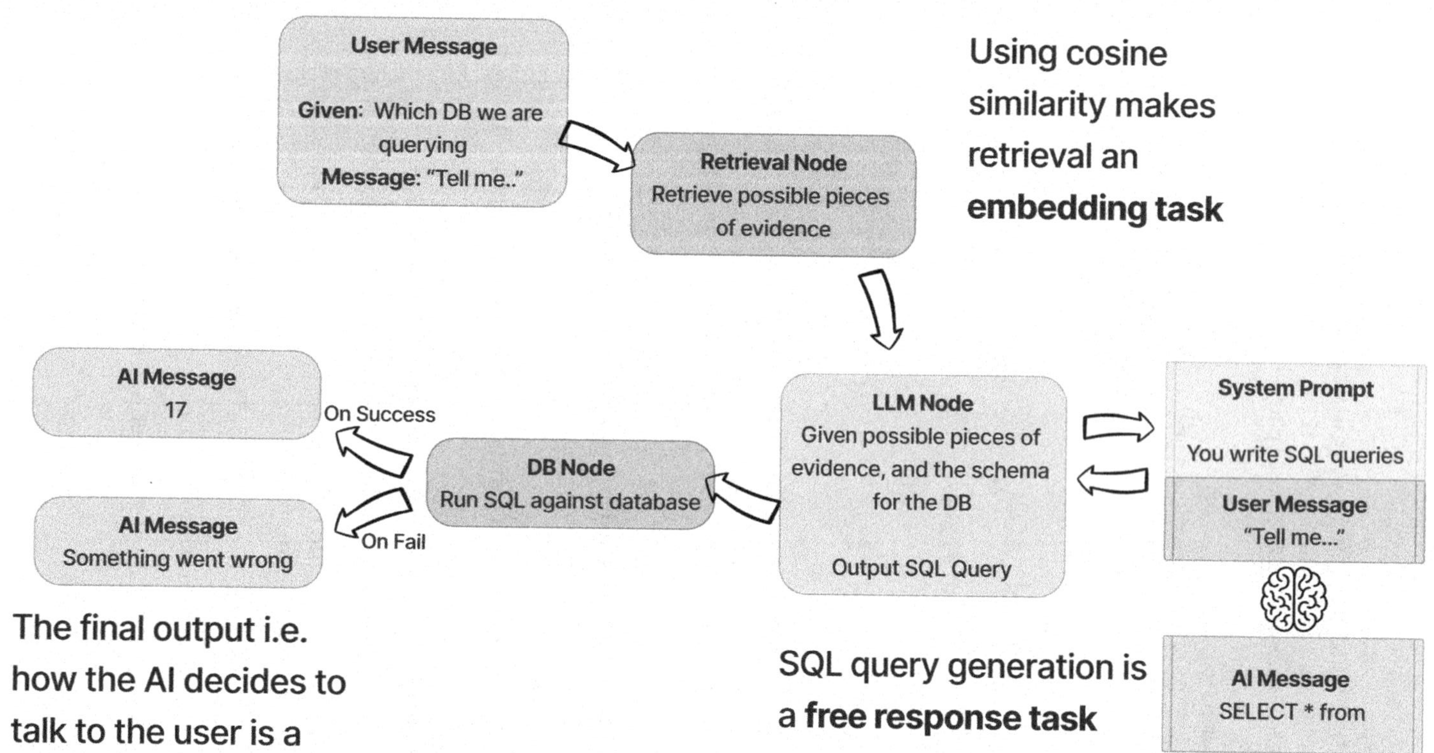

Figure 2.7 This LLM workflow has several nodes and edges, with data being passed around between them. The ultimate goal is to generate a message and send it back to a user with a query about a database.

Note a few things about this workflow:

- The workflow assumes that the evidence *already exists,* and we force the workflow to attempt to grab evidence no matter the input.
- We will use a simpler prompt for now, but test variants of prompts in Chapter 3.
- We will set up this LLM for now, but also test others in Chapter 3.

To tie all of these components together, we need a common language and framework. I will be using LangGraph, from the makers of LangChain. LangGraph is an open-source library built to create workflows and AI agents using a graph-based approach. I love that it provides the building blocks for workflows and agentic pipelines, while also standardizing LLM usage across models and providers. Let's dive into our RAG components.

Step 1: Indexing Evidence into a Database

Before we can create a workflow to retrieve evidence and generate SQL, we need to index the evidence in such a way that the workflow can retrieve it later. To do this, we will use a **vector database**—that is, a database designed to perform searches based on natural language embedding similarity. We will dig into that process in step 3. For now, though, we will index the given evidence in our BIRD benchmark in a vector database. We will use the open-source Chroma database for the vector database in this case study, but note that all vector databases offer this feature.

The substeps are as follows:

1. For each question in our BIRD benchmark, iterate over the given evidence.
2. For each piece of evidence, embed the evidence using an embedder (we will experiment with other embedders in Chapter 3).
3. Upload the evidence to the database with the following information (Figure 2.8):
    a. The embedding of the evidence (to use for fast retrieval; see step 3)
    b. The raw text of the evidence, for the LLM to read
    c. The database it is for (e.g., `formula_1`), so the workflow can differentiate which evidence is needed to answer a given question
    d. Any other ancillary metadata, which can be given in a dictionary format

Listing 2.2 shows a code snippet of how we index our evidence into a Chroma database.

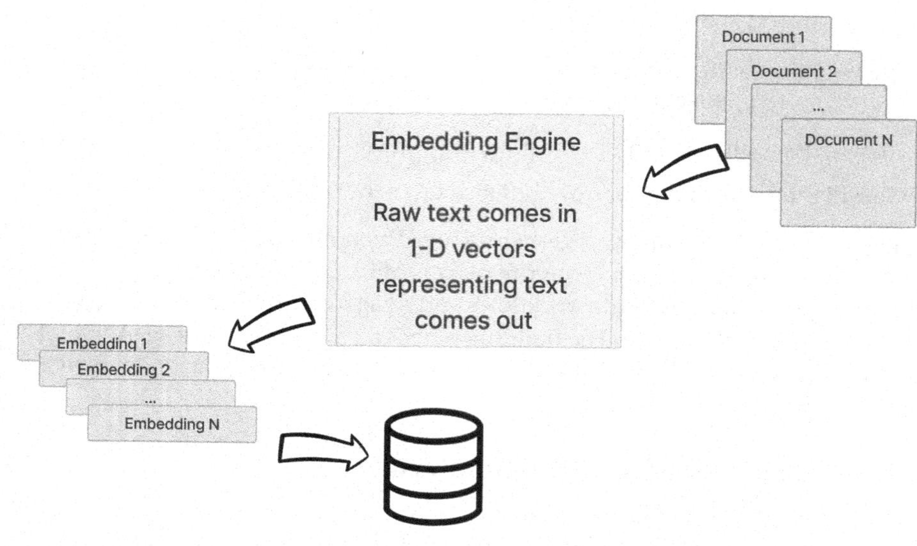

Figure 2.8 Indexing documents into a vector database consists of running raw text through an embedding model, and storing the resulting one-dimensional vector along with the raw evidence plus any metadata for future retrieval.

Listing 2.2 **Index the pieces of evidence into a vector database (Chroma)**

```
# Create documents from the text-to-SQL examples
from langchain_core.documents import Document

# Initialize embeddings (using OpenAI for now)
embeddings = OpenAIEmbeddings(model="text-embedding-3-small")

# Initialize vector store
vector_store = Chroma(
    client=chroma_client,
    collection_name="documents",
    embedding_function=embeddings,
    collection_metadata={"hnsw:space": "cosine"},
)

documents = []
for item in dev_data:
   # Create a comprehensive document with question, evidence, and SQL
   evidences = [e.strip() for e in item['evidence'].split(';') if e.strip()]

   for evidence in evidences:
       doc = Document(
           page_content=evidence,
```

```
            metadata={"db_id": item["db_id"]}  # so we can query using metadata
        )
    documents.append(doc)

# Add documents to vector store
print(f"📋 Loading {len(documents)} text-to-SQL examples into vector store...")
vector_store.add_documents(documents)
print(f"☑ Added {len(documents)} text-to-SQL examples to the vector store")
```

Once we have indexed the evidence, we can begin to build our LLM workflow by following four steps:

1. Set up the overall LangGraph framework.
2. Implement the evidence retrieval.
3. Write the SQL generation prompt.
4. Execute the SQL and error handling.

Let's begin with evidence retrieval and the basics of our workflow framework, LangGraph.

Step 2: Setting Up LangGraph

LangGraph relies on the concept of a "state" to pass variables and information around nodes during execution. This state object is crucial because it is the input to every single node, and the output of every single node is an update (if there is any) to the state. So, the first thing we need to do is to define what variables the workflow will need to keep track of. Listing 2.3 highlights the state object we will be using. A few important points are highlighted here:

- We will assume we know in advance which database we are making queries for (that's what the `db_id` key is for).
- We set the LLM we want to use (`model_name`).
- We have some hard-coded variables like `k` (the number of pieces of evidence to retrieve).

Listing 2.3 **Defining the state of the graph**

```
from pydantic import BaseModel, Field

class RAGState(BaseModel):
    """State for the RAG workflow"""
    db_path: str = ""  # The path to the database
    sql_result: Dict[str, Any] = Field(default_factory=dict)  # The result of the SQL
query
```

```
    model_name: str = "gpt-4.1-mini"  # The model to use for the LLM
    messages: Annotated[List[BaseMessage], add_messages] =
Field(default_factory=list)  # Conversation history/messages
    query: str = ""  # The user's query/question
    sql_query: str = ""  # The SQL query generated by the LLM
    reasoning: str = ""  # The reasoning for the SQL query
    retrieved_documents: List[RetrievedDocument] =
Field(default_factory=list)  # List of retrieved documents
    context: str = ""  # Combined context from retrieved documents
    final_answer: str = ""  # The final answer generated by the system
    k: int = 5  # Number of documents to retrieve
    db_id: str = ""  # The database id (e.g., 'formula_1')
```

With our state defined, we can move on to assembling the key nodes of our workflow.

Step 3: Implementing Evidence Retrieval

Once a user query is submitted to our system (e.g., "Who was the youngest driver in the 2023 F1 season"), the first thing our RAG system will do is attempt to pull evidence from the database (Figure 2.9). In step 1, we indexed evidence into a Chroma database; now it's time to retrieve that evidence.

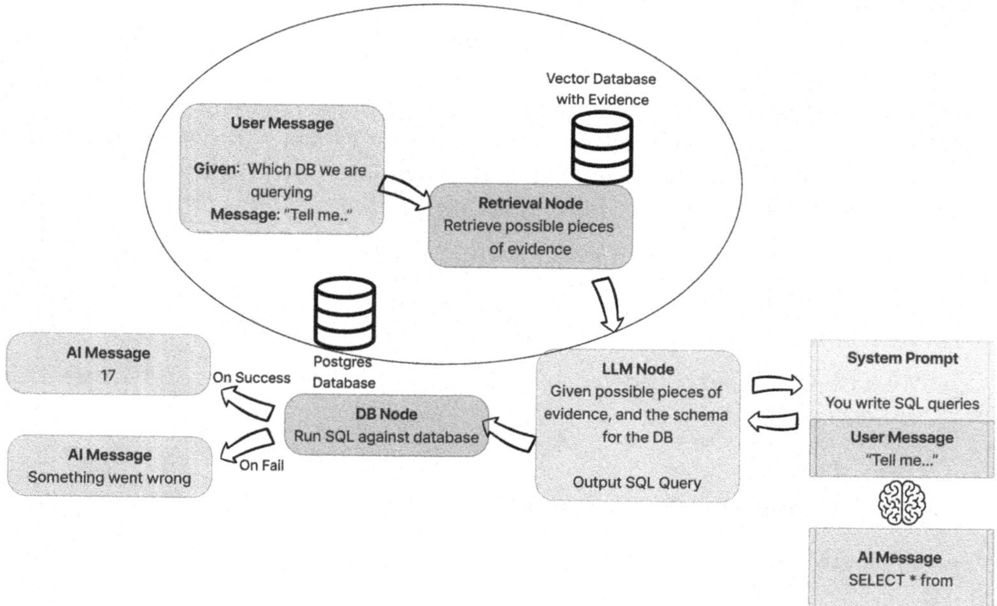

Figure 2.9 We are focusing on the retrieval portion of our RAG workflow.

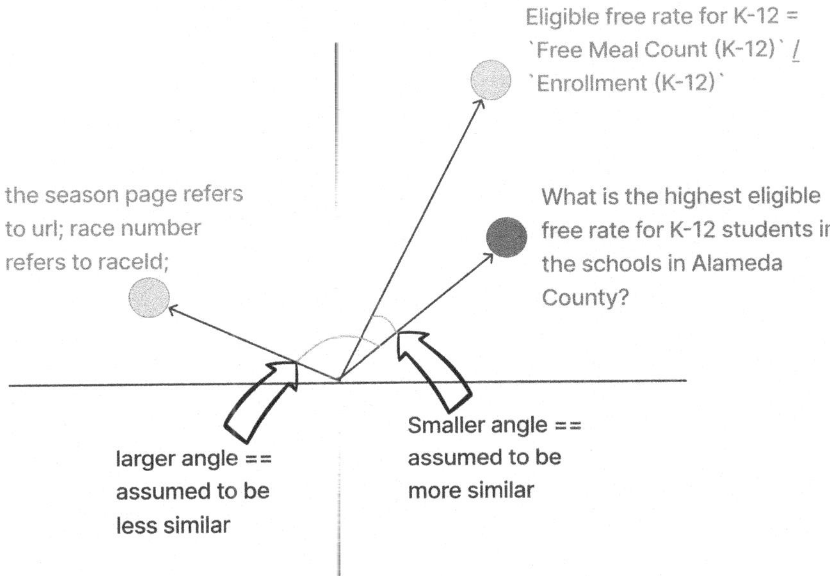

Figure 2.10 Cosine similarity is a standard way to compare embeddings against each other The idea is that a smaller angle between vectors formed by text implies that the text samples are semantically similar to each other and will yield a higher cosine similarity. Therefore, higher cosine similarity indicates that the source text samples are similar.

To keep our first workflow simple we will rely on the relatively robust embedding similarity. Basically, we will embed the natural language query using the same embedder that we used in step 1 (that is crucial—in general, they must be the same exact embedder) and then retrieve the pieces of evidence with the highest similarity to the embedding to the natural language query. We will define similarity for now as **cosine similarity**. Figure 2.10 visualizes this kind of similarity. In essence, embedding models are trained to produce embeddings that are near each other if the original pieces of text are similar in some way. So, if we embed the query and compare it to the pieces of evidence, we hope the information retrieval will be effective (and starting in Chapter 3, we evaluate whether it is).

Cosine similarity is not the only similarity metric we could use for our vectors. Other examples include the dot product (which is extremely fast to compute), Euclidean distance (also known as L2 Norm or the distance formula; slow to compute), Manhattan distance (also known as L1 Norm; fast to compute but best for databases with much bigger dimensions with less filled-in data), and Hamming distance (best for discrete vectors full of integers, rather than continuous floating points). Cosine similarity balances both speed and precision with a hidden surprise: When all of the vectors in question are of magnitude 1 (in math, magnitude refers to the length of the vector), the dot product and cosine similarity produce the exact same number. That explains why most of the embeddings you use will produce vectors of magnitude 1, even though you probably have never noticed that point.

Listing 2.4 shows an abbreviated implementation of our retrieval node, with all of the components discussed so far.

Listing 2.4 **Defining the state of the graph**

```
@dataclass
class RetrievedDocument:
    """Represents a document retrieved from the vector store"""
    content: str
    metadata: Dict[str, Any]
    score: float


def retrieve_documents(state: RAGState) -> Dict[str, Any]:
    """Retrieve relevant documents from ChromaDB, matching the db_id in state."""
    print(f"🔍 Retrieving top {state.k} documents for query: {state.query}
(db_id: {state.db_id})")

    try:
        # Perform similarity search, filtering by db_id in metadata
        results = vector_store.similarity_search_with_score(
            query=state.query,
            k=state.k,
            filter={"db_id": state.db_id} if state.db_id else None
        )

        # Convert to RetrievedDocument objects
        retrieved_docs = []
        for doc, score in results:
            retrieved_docs.append(RetrievedDocument(
                content=doc.page_content,
                metadata=doc.metadata,
                score=1 - score  # Convert distance to similarity score
            ))

    print(f"✅ Retrieved {len(retrieved_docs)} documents")
        for i, doc in enumerate(retrieved_docs, 1):
            print(f"   {i}. Score: {doc.score:.4f} | Content: {doc.content[:100]}...")

        # Create context from retrieved documents
        context_parts = []
        for i, doc in enumerate(retrieved_docs, 1):
            context_parts.append(f"Document {i}:\n{doc.content}")
            if doc.metadata:
                context_parts.append(f"Metadata: {doc.metadata}")
```

```
            context_parts.append("")  # Empty line for separation

        context = "\n".join(context_parts)

        return {
            "retrieved_documents": retrieved_docs,
            "context": context,
        }

    except Exception as e:
    print(f"❌ Error retrieving documents: {e}")
        return {
            "retrieved_documents": [],
            "context": "No documents could be retrieved due to an error.",
        }
```

Note a few things about this code:

- The input to the node is the state object we created in step 2. This will be the case for every node in our workflow.
- The output of every node is a dictionary whose keys match the `RagState` object's keys in Listing 2.3. It is best practice to match the keys with the state with the keys being outputted in the nodes—even though, technically speaking, the output could contain keys that are not defined in the state but will still be updated. Matching the keys (such as `retrieved_documents`) makes it easier to return to the code later and know exactly what each state update it is trying to accomplish.
- Once a node returns this dictionary, the back-end code of LangGraph will change the state. The variable changes will be reflected by the time we reach the next node, which will also take in the `RagState` variable as its sole input.

That's our retrieval! At this stage, you might have a few questions:

- What if the embedder isn't powerful enough to understand both pieces of text?
  - We will test different embedders in Chapter 3.
- What if we don't need evidence and the user is just saying something like "hi" or "hello," without understanding the rigidity of the workflow?
  - We can't really solve this issue without either adding logic directly into the workflow to handle this case *or* evolving the system into an agent (which we will discuss in a later chapter).

We will address these questions and more in later chapters. For now, let's continue with our workflow definitions.

Step 4: Writing the Prompt for SQL Generation

Figure 2.11 shows the portion of the workflow we are working on in this step. With the evidence retrieved, we can ask the LLM to generate a SQL query given three inputs:

- The query the user had
- The database description (e.g., tables, fields, foreign keys)
- The retrieved evidence

For now, we'll keep our prompt simple to get a baseline; in Chapter 3, we'll use prompt engineering to get even better results. Listing 2.5 defines our SQL generation node. Note the following points:

- We are using structured outputs to encourage the LLM to produce an output that is much easier to parse.
- The prompt is barely more than our three inputs with simple prefixes to let the AI model know what it is looking at.
- I set temperature to 0 here to aim for more consistency in our pipeline; that is, the same inputs should generate roughly the same outputs every time.
- I rely on LangChain's built-in message classes to add user messages (the `HumanMessage` class), and AI messages (`AIMessage`).

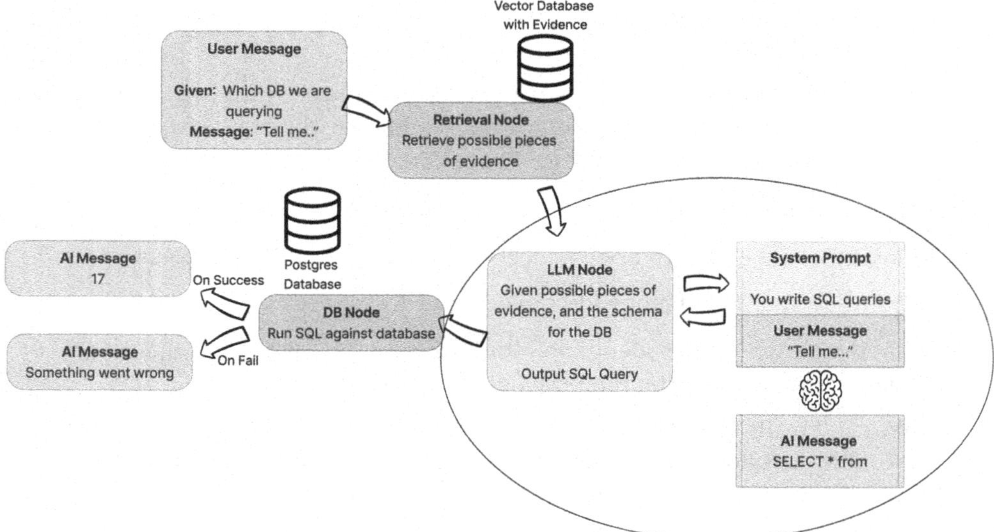

Figure 2.11 We are focusing on the generation portion of our RAG workflow.

Listing 2.5 **The SQL generation node using structured outputs**

```
class SQLOutput(BaseModel):
    reasoning: str = Field(description="Think through step by step how to solve the
problem.")
    sql_query: str = Field(description="The executable SQL query")

    def dict(self):
        return {
            "reasoning": self.reasoning,
            "sql_query": self.sql_query
        }

def generate_sql_query(state: RAGState) -> Dict[str, Any]:
    """Generate SQL query using retrieved documents"""
    print("🤖 Generating answer using retrieved context...")

    # Initialize LLM
    llm = ChatOpenAI(model=state.model_name, temperature=0).with_structured_
output(SQLOutput)

    new_message = HumanMessage(content=f"Question: {state.query}\nContext: {state.
context}\nDatabase Description: describe_database(state.db_path)}")

    # Add new message to messages
    messages = [
        *state.messages,
        new_message
    ]

    try:
        # Generate response
        response = llm.invoke(messages)

        # Add AI response to messages

        return {
            "messages": [
                *messages,
                AIMessage(content=f'Reasoning: {response.reasoning}\nSQL Query:
{response.sql_query}')
            ],
            "sql_query": response.sql_query,
            "reasoning": response.reasoning,
        }

    except Exception as e:
```

```
        error_msg = f"Error generating answer: {e}"
    print(f"✗ {error_msg}")

        updated_messages = state.messages.copy()
        updated_messages.append(AIMessage(content=error_msg))

        return {
            "messages": updated_messages,
            "final_answer": error_msg,
        }
```

Figure 2.12 shows an example of the user message with the final question, context, and database description.

With evidence retrieval and SQL query generation in place, we have our RAG:

- **Retrieval**—the evidence retrieval
- **Augmented**—with a simple prompt for now
- **Generation**—using structured outputs and LLMs

We are ready to go. All we need to do is execute the SQL and combine the nodes using edges.

Step 5: Putting It All Together

We can now execute an AI-generated SQL query (as seen in the workflow in Figure 2.13). This completes our bare-bones SQL generation RAG workflow.

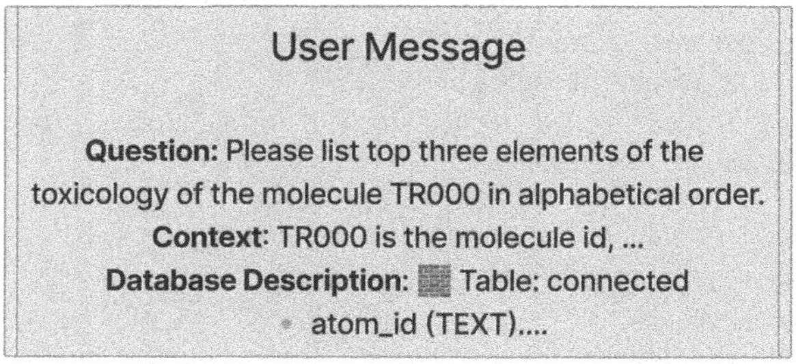

User Message

Question: Please list top three elements of the toxicology of the molecule TR000 in alphabetical order.
Context: TR000 is the molecule id, ...
Database Description: ▦ Table: connected
• atom_id (TEXT)....

Figure 2.12 A sample user message that will be sent to the LLM to generate a SQL query to answer the question. The context represents the evidence we pulled from the vector database; the database description is the same string as in Figure 2.5. This should be all the information required to get this question answered, assuming the documents we pulled for the context key are relevant.

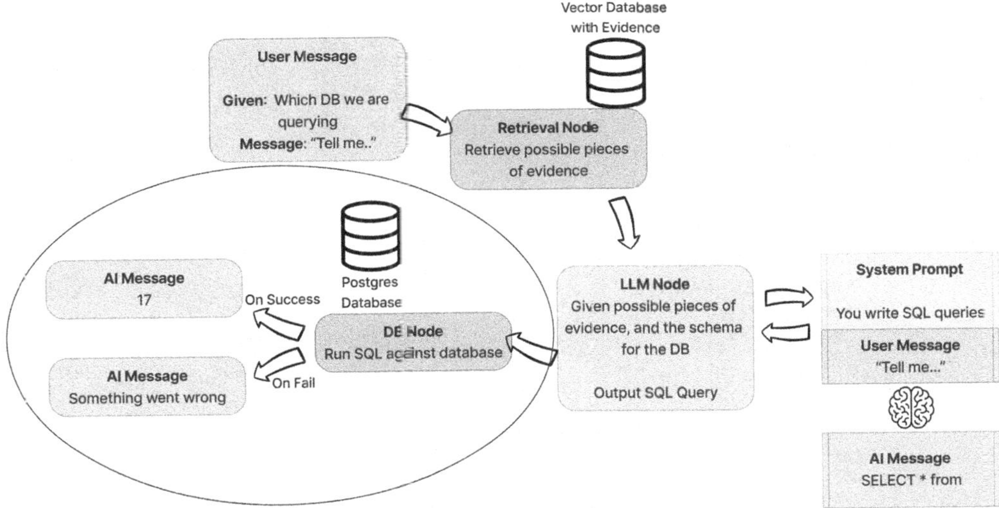

Figure 2.13 We are focusing on the SQL execution and final output message portion of our RAG workflow.

Listing 2.16 shows a snippet of the SQL execution node (labeled as the DB Node in the preceding figure). The input to the node is the state of the graph and it will output a dictionary of information that will automatically update the state. The node will execute the SQL against the database and format a string with the results of the SQL query and update the state with the SQL result (raw lists of data) and the final answer (our pretty formatted string).

Listing 2.6 **The SQL execution node**

```
def run_sql_query(state: RAGState) -> Dict[str, Any]:
    """Execute SQL query on the specified database"""
    import sqlite3
    import os

    print(f"🗄 Executing SQL query on database '{state.db_id}': {state.sql_query}")

    .... # Using Sqllite to execute the query

        sql_result = {
            "success": True,
            "columns": columns,
            "data": results,
            "row_count": len(results),
```

```
            "sql_query": state.sql_query
        }

    print(f"☑ SQL query executed successfully! Found {len(results)} row(s)")

        # Format results for final answer
        if results:
            result_text = f"Query executed successfully! Found {len(results)}
row(s):\\n\\n"

            # Add column headers
            if columns:
                result_text += " | ".join(columns) + "\\n"
                result_text += "-" * (len(" | ".join(columns))) + "\\n"

            # Add data rows (limit to first 10 for readability)
            for i, row in enumerate(results[:10]):
                result_text += " | ".join(str(cell) if cell is not None else "NULL"
for cell in row) + "\\n"

            if len(results) > 10:
                result_text += f"\\n... and {len(results) - 10} more row(s)"
        else:
            result_text = "Query executed successfully but returned no results"

        return {
            "sql_result": sql_result,
            "final_answer": result_text
        }

    except Exception as e:
        error_msg = f"Error executing SQL query: {str(e)}"
    print(f"✖ {error_msg}")
        return {
            "sql_result": {"error": error_msg},
            "final_answer": error_msg
        }
```

With our nodes defined, it's time to combine them using **edges**—that is, connections between nodes. In our simple workflow, we will define hard pathways from one node to another without any conditions for now. Listing 2.7 shows the code to create and visualize our workflow using LangGraph's built-in visualization method.

Listing 2.7 **Building the LangGraph workflow**

```
# Create the workflow graph
workflow = StateGraph(RAGState)

# Add nodes
workflow.add_node("begin_conversation", begin_conversation)
workflow.add_node("process_query", process_query)
workflow.add_node("retrieve_documents", retrieve_documents)
workflow.add_node("generate_sql_query", generate_sql_query)
workflow.add_node("run_sql_query", run_sql_query)

# Add edges
workflow.add_edge("begin_conversation", "process_query")
workflow.add_edge("process_query", "retrieve_documents")
workflow.add_edge("retrieve_documents", "generate_sql_query")
workflow.add_edge("generate_sql_query", "run_sql_query")
workflow.add_edge("run_sql_query", END)

# Set entry point
workflow.set_entry_point("begin_conversation")

# Compile the workflow and suppress automatic rendering
compiled_workflow = workflow.compile()

# The compiled workflow is ready to use
print("☑ Workflow compiled successfully!")

from IPython.display import Image, display

# Display the image in the notebook
display(Image("workflow_graph.png"))
```

Figure 2.14 shows LangGraph's visualization of our entire workflow (the output of Listing 2.7). While it's definitely a fine graphic, I hope you see why I try to create my own graphics of our workflows!

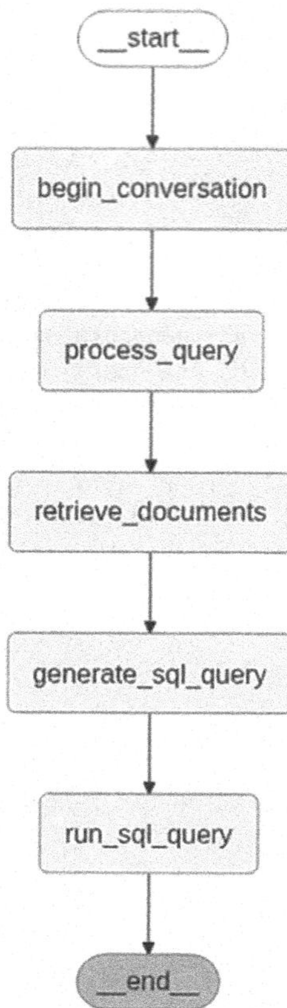

Figure 2.14 LangGraph's built-in visualizer isn't exactly amazing, which is why I like to create my own graphics.

Folks, we have a workflow. Now, let's try it out!

Using the RAG Workflow

Using a LangGraph is as easy as invoking the workflow with an initial state, and then following along. Listing 2.8 shows the simplest way of invoking our workflow with a question and a given database.

Listing 2.8 **Using the LangGraph workflow**

```
db_id = "california_schools"
databases_dir = "../../dbs/dev_databases"
db_path = os.path.join(databases_dir, db_id, f"{db_id}.sqlite")

compiled_workflow.invoke(
    {
```

```
        "query": "What is the highest eligible free rate for K-12 students in the
schools in Alameda County?",
        "db_id": db_id,
        "db_path": db_path
        }
    )
>>>>>>
🔍 Processing query: What is the highest eligible free rate for K-12 students in the
schools in Alameda County?
📚 Retrieving top 5 documents for query: What is the highest eligible free rate for
K-12 students in the schools in Alameda County? (db_id: california_schools)
☑ Retrieved 5 documents
   1. Score: 0.6390 | Content: Eligible free rate for K-12 =
`Free Meal Count (K-12)` / `Enrollment (K-12)`...
   3. Score: 0.6030 | Content: percent of eligible free rate for K-12 =
`Free Meal Count (K-12)` * 100 / `Enrollment (K-12)`...
....
🤖 Generating answer using retrieved context...
🗄 Executing SQL query on database 'california_schools': SELECT
MAX([Percent (%) Eligible Free (K-12)]) AS Highest_Eligible_Free_Rate_K12
FROM frpm
WHERE [County Name] = 'Alameda';
☑ SQL query executed successfully! Found 1 row(s)
Highest_Eligible_Free_Rate_K12
------------------------------
1.0  # this is correct :)
```

Our workflow works and the answer it generated was correct! We have an immediate problem, though: If we try to ask the workflow a follow-up question, it will fail because the state resets when we invoke the workflow with a new question. To solve this problem, we can add in a **human-in-the-loop** component using LangGraph's built-in interrupt function.

Stateless Versus Stateful Workflows

LangGraph does have the concept of a "state," which keeps track of variables throughout the nodes. However, we can differentiate between a stateless and stateful RAG system based on its ability to remember information in between queries. For example, suppose I ask, "Who was the youngest driver in 2023," and let the RAG do its thing, and then ask, "What about oldest." When I ask the second question, the RAG system would have lost all context from the first one.

To add conversational state to our RAG system, we can add a new node called `ask_for_user_input` and use LangGraph's concept of an **interrupt** to pause and wait for user input before going further in the graph. Figure 2.15 shows a clean representation of the statefulness when we use this approach.

To implement this idea in LangGraph, Listing 2.9 defines our new node, which relies on the interrupt functionality to accept new user feedback.

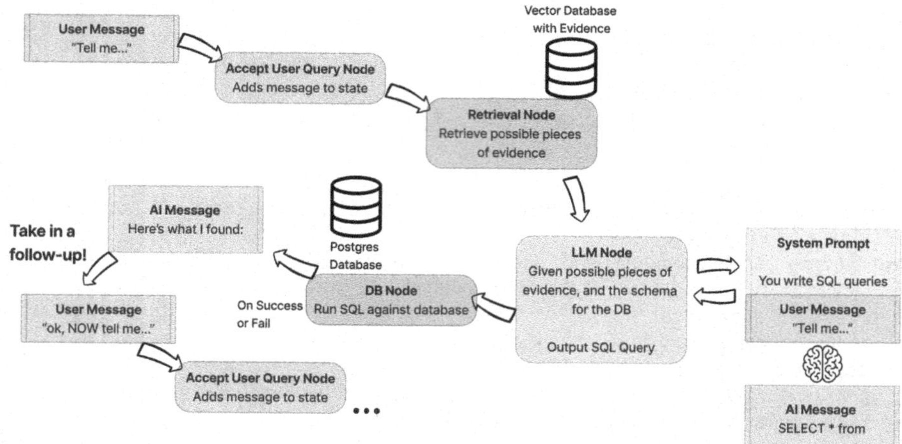

Figure 2.15 A stateful RAG would keep track of the conversation (on the left) between the user and the AI model, even if we use a different prompt (on the right) to generate SQL queries that are separate from the longer-running conversation.

Listing 2.9 **Using LangGraph's built-in interrupt functionality to accept human-in-the-loop messages**

```
# Import the interrupt function for user input handling
from langgraph.types import interrupt

# Add a user input node for conversational flow using LangGraph interrupt
def ask_for_user_input(state: RAGState) -> Dict[str, Any]:
    """Ask user for the next question in the conversation using LangGraph interrupt"""
...

    print("\n" + "-"*60)
    print("💭 What would you like to ask next?")
    print("   (Type 'exit' or 'quit' to end the conversation)")
    print("-"*60)

    # Use LangGraph interrupt
    user_input = interrupt("Your question: ")

    if user_input and user_input.lower().strip() in ['exit', 'quit', 'bye', 'done']:
        return {
            "query": "",
            "final_answer": "👋 Goodbye! Thanks for using the SQL RAG system."
        }

    return {
        "query": user_input or "",
        "retrieved_documents": [],  # Reset for new query
```

```
        "context": "",
        "sql_query": "",
        "reasoning": "",
        "sql_result": {},
        "final_answer": ""
    }
```

Listing 2.10 implements the new node in our workflow by adding two components to the workflow:

- A **conditional edge:** A function that determines whether we should go to the end state from `ask_for_user_input` (if we say "exit," for example).
- The **`MemorySaver`** checkpoint: This will come up again in the future. This LangGraph feature provides the groundwork for serializing and de-serializing threads for longer-term use and is a built-in statefulness mechanism in a graph. Here we are using it to implement the "interrupt" function, but in later chapters we will use it to store conversation history across several threads.
- Once the interrupt is run, the workflow is saved. It is then retrieved once the input is given, no matter how long the user takes to ask their follow-up question.

Listing 2.10 **Adding a conditional edge in the workflow**

```
# Conditional function to decide whether to continue or end
def should_continue(state: RAGState) -> str:
    """Decide whether to continue the conversation or end it"""
    if state.query == "" or state.query.lower() in ['exit', 'quit', 'bye', 'done']:
        return END
    else:
        return "process_query"

# Import MemorySaver for checkpointing (required for interrupt functionality)
from langgraph.checkpoint.memory import MemorySaver

# Create the conversational workflow graph with proper checkpointing
conversational_workflow = StateGraph(RAGState)

# Add nodes
...  # Same nodes as before plus a new one
conversational_workflow.add_node("ask_for_user_input", ask_for_user_input)

# Add edges
conversational_workflow.add_edge("begin_conversation", "ask_for_user_input")
conversational_workflow.add_conditional_edges(
    "ask_for_user_input",
    should_continue,
    {
```

```
            "process_query": "process_query",
            END: END
        }
    )
conversational_workflow.add_edge("process_query", "retrieve_documents")
conversational_workflow.add_edge("retrieve_documents", "generate_sql_query")
conversational_workflow.add_edge("generate_sql_query", "run_sql_query")
conversational_workflow.add_edge("run_sql_query", "ask_for_user_input")

# Set entry point
conversational_workflow.set_entry_point("begin_conversation")

# Set up memory for checkpointing (required for interrupt functionality)
memory = MemorySaver()

# Compile the conversational workflow with checkpointer
compiled_conversational_workflow =
  conversational_workflow.compile(checkpointer=memory)
```

Figure 2.16 shows the LangGraph visualization of our new workflow, noting the conditional edge with a dotted line.

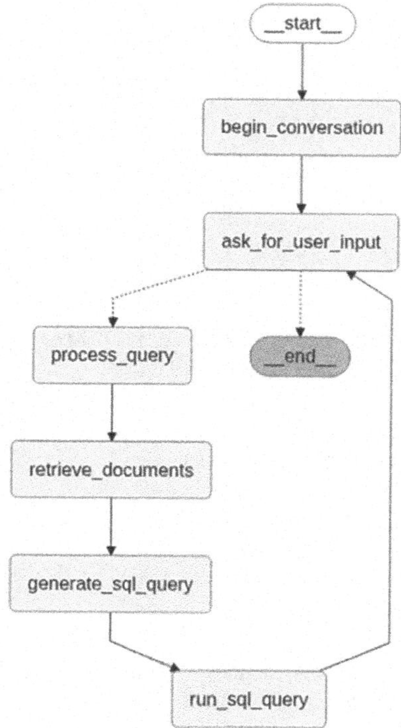

Figure 2.16 Our workflow now has a new node and conditional edge, which means we can follow up with more questions or clarifying comments.

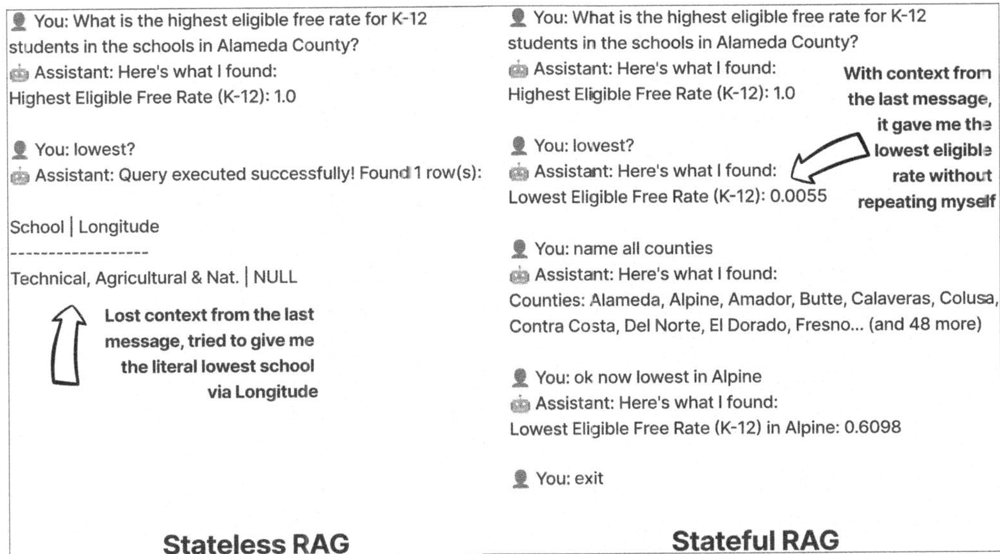

Figure 2.17 The stateful RAG (right) can take in a follow-up question, whereas the stateless RAG (left) forgets the first message and tries to solve tasks in a vacuum (i.e., without context).

To help you see the difference, Figure 2.17 shows a sample conversation between our stateless and stateful RAG systems. I would argue that the difference is quite stark!

Conclusion

That's a wrap on our very first LLM workflow. We did a lot in this chapter. We went from a vague idea of how RAG systems work to building a fully functional, stateful, conversational SQL-generation system using LangGraph. Along the way, we laid the groundwork for more advanced workflows and saw how even a relatively simple design can produce accurate, dynamic results.

Here's a quick recap of what we did and how it contributed to our final goal:

- **We indexed evidence into a vector database.** We preprocessed and embedded relevant pieces of evidence, storing them with metadata. This made it possible to retrieve just the right context at runtime, which is critical for saving token space and time.
- **We defined a state object for workflow memory.** By setting up a shared RAG state, we enabled LangGraph to pass and update variables across nodes. That is how the system keeps track of queries, retrieved documents, reasoning, and results.

- **We implemented document retrieval using embedding similarity.** This gave our workflow the ability to "look things up" based on semantic meaning, not just keyword matches. It's the core of how the LLM gets context without needing to receive everything in the prompt.
- **We built a structured prompt to generate SQL.** Using structured outputs and a simple prompt format, we had the LLM return both reasoning and a usable SQL query, relying on basic chain-of-thought prompting to get strong baseline results.
- **We executed SQL against our benchmark databases.** We closed the loop by actually running the generated query, turning the LLM output into actionable results. This is where the RAG system became truly useful.
- **We wrapped it in a LangGraph workflow.** We connected all our nodes into a clean, end-to-end system that can be reused and extended.
- **We added stateful interaction with user input.** By introducing interrupt and conversational memory, we ensured the system could handle multiple-turn conversations, which is a major step toward real assistant-like behavior.

The LLM workflow created in this chapter is more than a toy example; it's a foundation. In Chapter 3, we'll start pressure-testing our workflow with better prompts, smarter retrieval, and more complex logic. Let's keep building.

3

AI Evaluation Plus Experimentation

Introduction

AI evaluation is the process of systematically assessing a model/system's performance to ensure it meets specific task requirements using metrics such as accuracy, reliability, cost, and scalability. The goal is to measure what matters (easier said than done, I know). Of course, to know what matters, it matters to know how LLMs are contributing to the AI workloads.

At the end of the day, no matter how well we think our AI applications are working, nothing can compare to good old-fashioned testing. Evaluating LLMs and AI applications is, in general, a nebulous task that demands attention and proper context. There is no one best way to evaluate a model or a system. However, we can bucket the types of tasks we build such that each category of tasks has specific goals. We can then begin to consider different methods of evaluation for each category, providing a scaffold of LLM testing we can reuse and iterate on.

Evaluating and Experimenting with LLMs

Before diving into specific methods of experimentation, it will be useful to outline the main categories of tasks we evaluate with LLMs, shown in Figure 3.1. These categories help us match the right metrics and experimental approaches to the right kind of problem, whether it's generation, classification, or retrieval.

- **Generative tasks:** Relying on an LLM's generative language modeling to generate free tokens in response to a question.

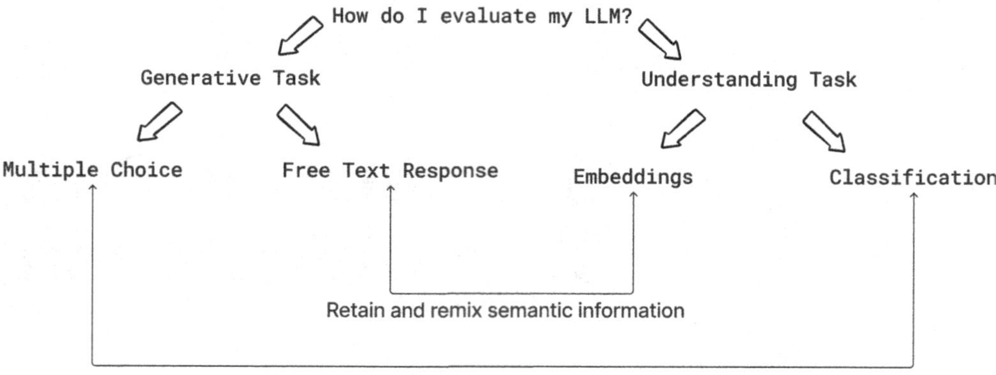

Figure 3.1 A high-level view of the four most common tasks we have to evaluate with LLMs.

  - **Multiple choice:** Reasoning through a question and a set of predefined choices to pick one or more correct answers.
  - **Free text response:** Allowing the model to generate free text responses to a query without being bounded by a predefined set of options.
- **Understanding tasks:** Tasks that force a model to exploit patterns in input data, generally for some predictive or encoding task.
  - **Embedding tasks:** Any task where an LLM encodes data to vectors for clustering, recommendations, or another purpose.
  - **Classification:** Fine-tuning a model specifically to distinguish between predefined classes. This fine-tuning can be done at the language modeling level or through classical feed-forward classification layers.

Evaluation generally requires at least one of the following:

- **A ground truth:** A golden standard to compare AI responses against. We call an evaluation **reference-based** evaluation if we have a ground truth; otherwise, we refer to it as **reference-free**.
- **Heuristics/rules:** A consistent, repeatable way to evaluate AI outputs using rules set out by (generally/hopefully) a human. The rubric for an LLM contains the criteria we care about in an AI output.
- **A target/threshold:** Some goal value we are trying to reach with a particular metric. For example, "We are aiming for a target of 90% accuracy."

Once we define these components, we can experiment with different prompt strategies, embedders, and anything else we can think of, with the goal of improving the values of our metrics. Because most AI systems we will seek to evaluate will be a combination of tasks, this won't be the only chapter focusing on evaluations and experimentation. The points highlighted here will serve as guiding principles for all future case studies. Let's start with a familiar example—namely, our text-to-SQL RAG pipeline.

Case Study 1, Revisited: The Text-to-SQL Workflow

The RAG workflow we built in Chapter 2 has at least two types of LLM tasks to evaluate (Figure 3.2):

- The embedding match we perform to retrieve evidence is an embedding task.
- The SQL generation is a free response task.

Let's dive into evaluating and experimenting the sections of our workflow, beginning with SQL generation.

Evaluating SQL Generation: Free Text Response

The SQL query the LLM generates can be evaluated on multiple fronts, but at the end of the day, we want to know: *Did this SQL query answer the user's question?* Let's give this metric a name: **SQL Query Accuracy (SQA)**. We will define it as follows:

> **SQL Query Accuracy (SQA):** The percentage of times the LLM's SQL query yielded a table of results that matches a known ground-truth result set.

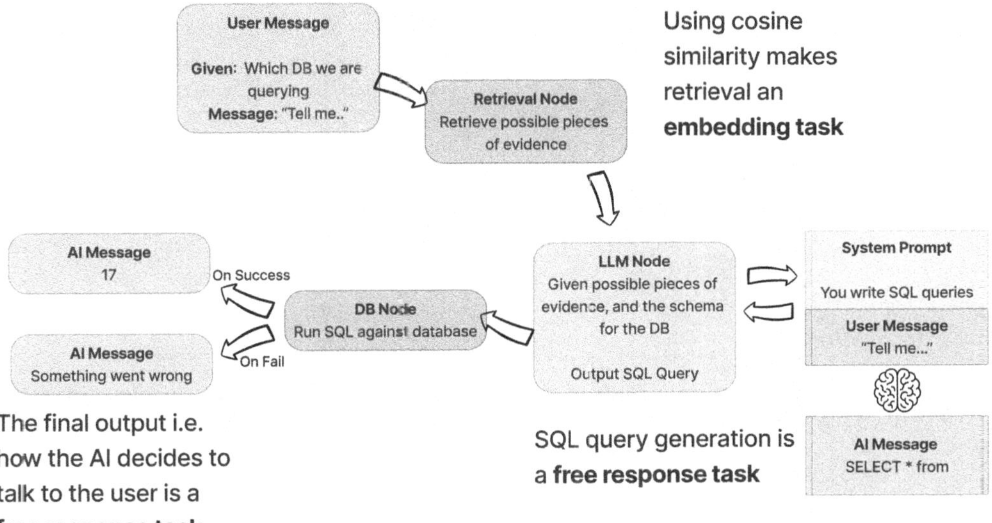

Figure 3.2 Our stateless RAG system involves two free response tasks and an embedding task.

This metric will guide us in our first two experiments:

- Experiment 1: Choosing an LLM for SQL generation
- Experiment 2: Prompt engineering to squeeze performance from the LLM we choose in Experiment 1

Let's dive into our first experiment.

Experiment: Choosing the Best Model for SQL Generation

In Chapter 2, we chose a static LLM for our workflow: OpenAI's GPT-4.1-Mini. We made this choice just to get a workflow out the door. In reality, though, we could choose from the literally hundreds of thousands of eligible LLMs on the planet to solve this free response task. To accomplish this, we need to set a static baseline prompt, as shown in Figure 3.3.

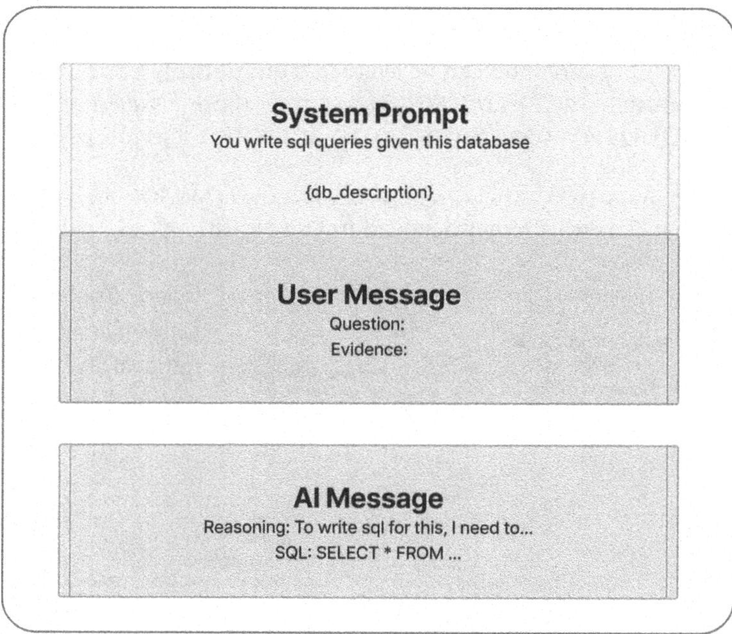

Figure 3.3 We will select a model for further experimentation by evaluating multiple models against a simple version of the SQL generation prompt.

I ran this prompt against six LLMs from four different providers:

- Provider 1: OpenAI
  - Model 1: GPT-4o-Mini
  - Model 2: GPT-4.1-Nano
  - Model 3: GPT-4.1-Mini
- Provider 2: Anthropic
  - Model 4: Claude Sonnet 4
- Provider 3: Mistral
  - Model 5: Mistral 7b Instruct
- Provider 4: Google
  - Model 6: Gemini 2.5 Pro

Why these LLMs? To maintain the structure of our workflow, I needed to filter the world of LLMs into the options that supported structured output, for example. Although I could have created the workflow without relying on this feature, it does make things easier (as noted in Chapter 1). Outside of that, I could have tried a Qwen model or a Llama model—I just didn't. I'll leave that as homework for you. You have to make choices even when selecting just a handful of models to test with, and these are the models I went with.

Also note that I'm keeping the prompt extremely basic to test the general capabilities of LLMs, while also looking at cost and latency. These concerns affected how I picked an LLM to bring into Experiment 2. You can check the GitHub for this book for the results of the full experiment, but Figure 3.4 shows the output of running the six LLM workflows (one per model) and the resulting three metrics: SQA, latency (the time it took to run the entire workflow), and cost (in U.S. dollars [USD] to run the LLMs).

Here are a few takeaways from this evaluation:

- Gemini 2.5 Pro had the best accuracy (57.5%), but also had a median cost 28 times higher than the next most expensive model.
- Mistral vastly underperformed other LLMs, yielding only 18.9% accuracy.
- OpenAI's models seem to have a great balance of accuracy, latency, and cost.

How good are these accuracy numbers? At the time of writing, the best reported accuracy by an AI system (LLM + workflow) on this benchmark is approximately 75% (Figure 3.5). So, while we aren't quite at the state-of-the-art level, we aren't that far off with just our baseline simple prompting + vector search.

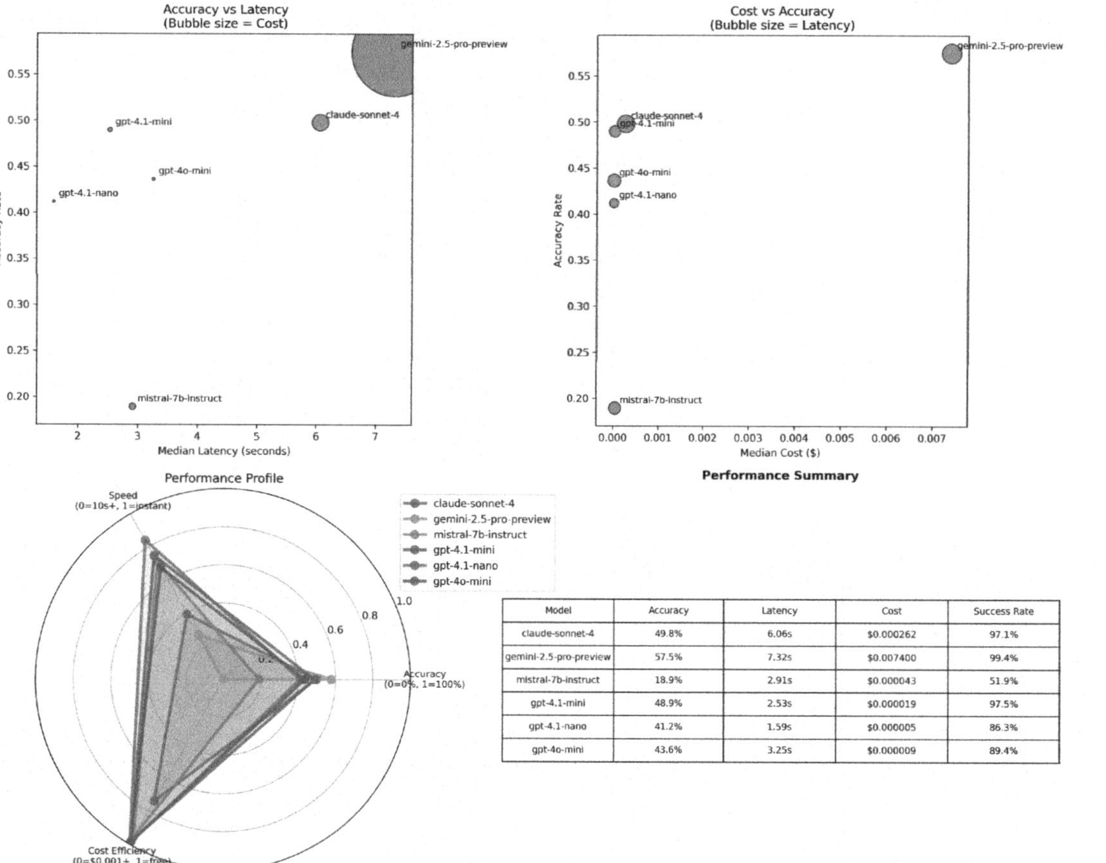

Model	Accuracy	Latency	Cost	Success Rate
claude-sonnet-4	49.8%	6.06s	$0.000262	97.1%
gemini-2.5-pro-preview	57.5%	7.32s	$0.007400	99.4%
mistral-7b-instruct	18.9%	2.91s	$0.000043	51.9%
gpt-4.1-mini	48.9%	2.53s	$0.000019	97.5%
gpt-4.1-nano	41.2%	1.59s	$0.000005	86.3%
gpt-4o-mini	43.6%	3.25s	$0.000009	89.4%

Figure 3.4 A high-level dashboard of the six models' performance against the prompt. In this chart, "accuracy" refers to the average percent rate the LLM's SQL code resulted in the correct answer, "latency" is the average number of seconds it took to run against the LLM, "cost" is the average cost in USD, and "success rate" refers to the percent rate that the AI produced a SQL query that ran without errors against the database schema, even if the answer was incorrect. A high-resolution version of this image can be found in the GitHub repository.

Leaderboard - Execution Accuracy (EX)

	Model	Code	Size	Oracle Knowledge	Dev (%)	Test (%)
	Human Performance *Data Engineers + DB Students*			✓		**92.96**
🏆1 July 14, 2025	LongData-SQL *LongShine AI Research*		UNK	✓	74.32	**77.53**
2 Mar 11, 2025	AskData + GPT-4o *AT&T CDO - DSAIR* [Shkapenyuk et al. '25]		UNK	✓	75.36	77.14
3 Apr 16, 2025	CHASE-SQL + Gemini *Google Cloud* [Pourreza et al. '24]		UNK	✓	74.90	76.02

Figure 3.5 The current state of the art is approximately 75% accuracy. We've achieved an accuracy level of approximately 60% with our best models, so we aren't too far off, even though we've done only a very little experimenting so far.

Given these numbers, it's now up to you to decide the budget, accuracy threshold, latency considerations, and other criteria. I can't make these decisions for you, but I can help you get the right data in front of you to help make the most informed decision you can.

Let's focus on a particular model and database in our second experiment. We'll select gpt-4o-mini and zoom in on the "formula_1" database to try some different prompting techniques.

Experiment: Different Types of Few-Shot Learning

Few-shot prompting was mentioned in Chapter 1, but until now we've skipped over *how* we select the examples to use with this approach. More often than not, people will just randomly pick some examples or simply write some examples to use over and over again. But there must be a better way to do it, right?

Semantic few-shot learning is the same as few-shot learning but is based on deliberately choosing examples that are semantically similar (generally as determined by an embedding match) instead of random/static examples. The idea is that by intelligently selecting examples that sound similar to the one being solved, there's a higher chance that the examples will contribute more to the AI model's final output.

Here's a numbered explanation of each experiment I tried:

1. 0-shot: No few-shot examples, no chain-of-thought (CoT). Baseline direct prompt.

2. 0-shot (CoT): No few-shot examples, uses CoT reasoning.
3. 1-shot same DB: One random example from the same database, no CoT.
4. 1-shot same DB (CoT): One same-database example, CoT reasoning enabled.
5. 3-shot same DB: Three examples from the same database, no CoT.
6. 3-shot same DB (CoT): Three same-database examples, CoT reasoning only.
7. 1-shot any DB: One example from any database (not query-specific), no CoT.
8. 1-shot any DB (CoT): One any-database example, with CoT reasoning.
9. 3-shot any DB: Three examples from any database, no CoT.
10. 3-shot any DB (CoT): Three any-database examples, with CoT reasoning.
11. 1-shot semantic: One semantically similar example, no CoT.
12. 1-shot semantic (CoT): One semantic example, with CoT reasoning.
13. 3-shot semantic: Three semantically retrieved examples, no CoT.
14. 3-shot semantic (CoT): Three semantic examples, CoT reasoning.

Phew! That's 14 different prompt configurations. I used LangGraph to set up my experiment structure (as shown in Figure 3.6), which helps me keep the experimentation reproducible and visual so I can share the code and results faster. Note that all of these variants included the database description (the list of tables, fields, etc.) and the correct evidence for the question, because I knew we would need those static items.

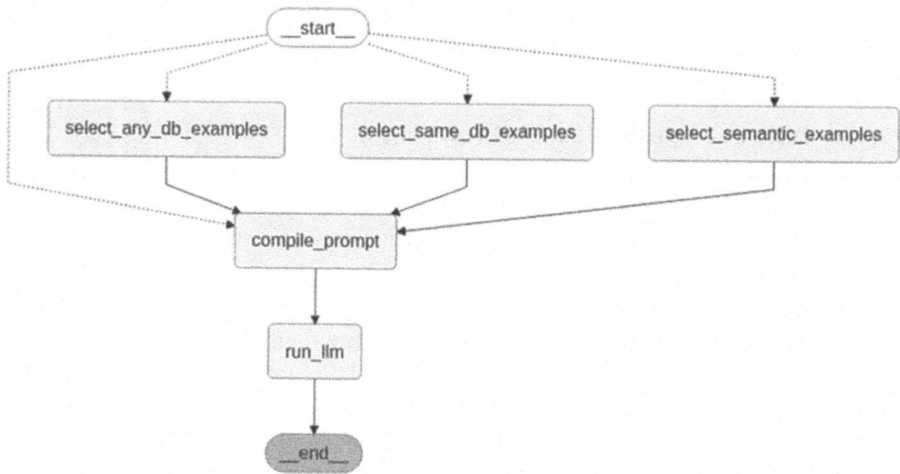

Figure 3.6 Using LangGraph for the experimentation framework saves time as well as makes the experiment easier to reproduce and share.

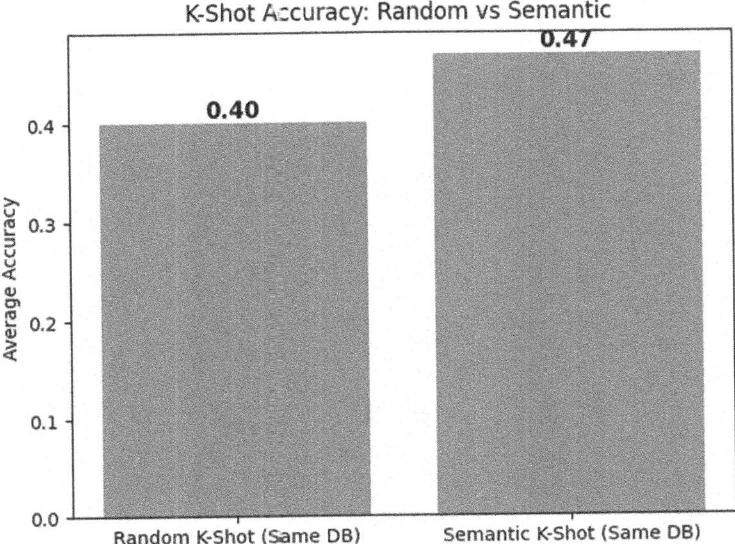

Figure 3.7 Introducing more relevant examples yielded a greater performance compared to the same number of shots of random examples.

Here are the takeaways from the experiments.

Semantically Similar Examples Beat Random Examples

A near 20% increase in accuracy resulted just from using more similar examples as inputs to the incoming query (Figure 3.7).

The Number of Examples Matters and CoT Always Helps

A 20% increase in accuracy is nice, but how about an approximately 35% increase in accuracy? Figure 3.8 shows the breakdown of each number of examples used (both semantic and random examples) both with and without CoT. As you can see, adding more examples helped, and adding CoT helped significantly. To go from 33% (the average accuracy for 0-shot, no CoT) to 45% (the average accuracy for 3-shot, with CoT) is a tremendous gain! In practice, three to seven examples tend to suffice as long as we are providing as much coverage as possible for the different scenarios the AI models could encounter. However, it is possible to offer too many examples—more examples could lead to more conflicting information. Experimentation to find the sweet spot in terms of the number of examples is the best way to identify the optimal value.

Next, let's turn our attention to evaluating the evidence retrieval portion of our workflow.

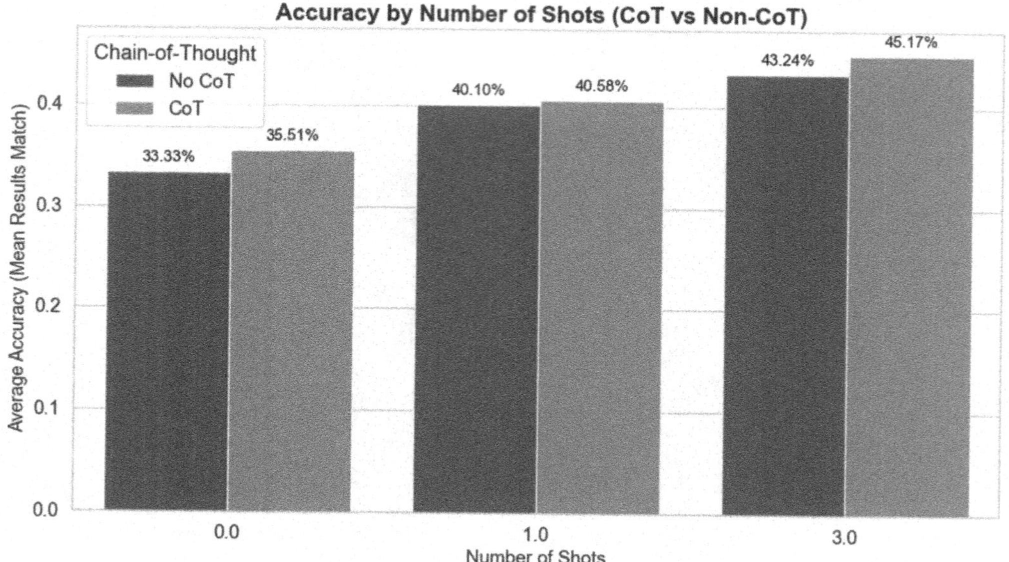

Figure 3.8 Both the number of examples and whether we included CoT made a difference. It took the performance of GPT-4o-mini on the formula_1 database from 33.33% to 45.17%.

Evaluating Evidence Retrieval

A core part of our LLM workflow is the evidence retrieval. We can test how well our system retrieves the right evidence by zooming in specifically on the embedding match between the user query and the evidence, as seen in Figure 3.9.

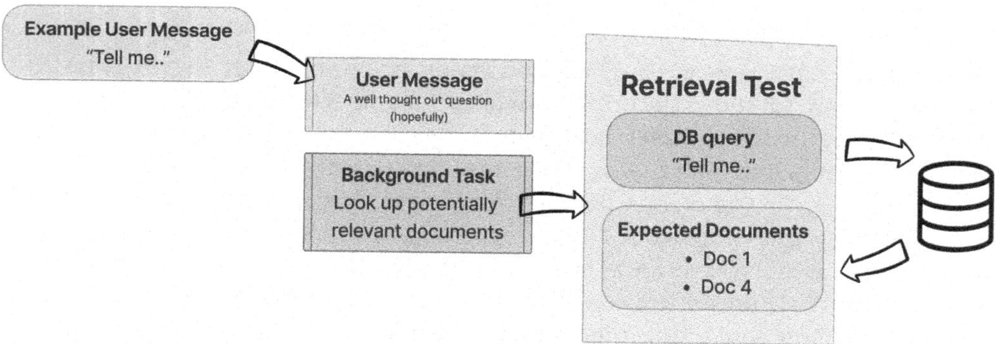

Figure 3.9 Testing retrieval generating boils down to retrieving documents for questions in a test set and evaluating how good the retrieved documents are. The user asks their question: "Tell me...." That question is then used as the lookup query to the database, with the embedding of the question being compared to the embedding of the documents via cosine similarity. The documents with the "k"-highest cosine similarity are counted as "retrieved" and compared to the documents we were expecting to be retrieved.

One of the easiest things we can do is to test different embedders against embedding match performance. Let's test seven embedders across four providers:

- Provider 1: OpenAI
  - Embedder 1: Text embedding ada 2
  - Embedder 2: Text embedding 3 small
  - Embedder 3: Text embedding 3 large
- Provider 2: Cohere
  - Embedder 4: Embed English V3
  - Embedder 5: Embed V4
- Provider 3: Jina
  - Embedder 6: Embeddings V3 (open source)
- Provider 4: Sentence Transformers
  - Embedder 7: all-MiniLM-L6-v2 (open source)

Quick note: This is the first use of autoencoding models in this book. Embedders 6 and 7 are definitely autoencoding. Although the other embedders are technically closed source (we don't know the architecture), at least the Cohere embedders are probably also autoencoding. OpenAI does tend to love its autoregressive models, so its embedders are likely autoregressive models with the generative language modeling removed, leaving them only able to read text.

To test these embedders, we will create a vector database for each embedder. Each vector database will contain the same evidence, just embedded differently. Then we can iterate over each question, retrieve evidence from each database, and measure the context quality from each database overall. We will focus on three metrics for information retrieval:

- **Precision:** The quality of the retrieved results
- **Recall:** The completeness of the retrieved results
- **Mean reciprocal rank (MRR):** How quickly the first relevant document is retrieved

Just as with cosine similarity, these aren't the only metrics we could use to judge document retrieval. Chapter 9 will introduce another powerful metric for testing an embedding fine-tuning example. For now, you should recognize that each of these metrics (precision, recall, and MRR) measures a different aspect of retrieval. Precision asks: Of all the documents retrieved, how many were relevant? Recall measures: Of all the documents the model *should* have retrieved, how many did it actually get? MRR tells us: How many junk documents does the system see before seeing a single relevant document? Figure 3.10 shows the formulas for each metric.

RAG Metric: Precision @ *k*

Precision tells us how accurate our retriever is. It answers the question: "Of the documents we grabbed (let's say we grabbed *k* documents), how many of them were actually useful?" For example, if our system retrieves 10 documents and 7 are relevant to the user's query, that's 70% precision. A high precision matters when surfacing the wrong information has real consequences. For example, in a medical system, returning irrelevant documents could lead to confusion or harmful decisions. In these cases, it's better to return fewer but more relevant results. In our case, we can tolerate a lower precision because we hope the generative LLM will use only the relevant documents and ignore the others.

A major limitation of the precision calculation is that as *k* grows, the denominator of the calculation grows even if the number of relevant documents stays the same. That is, if there is only a single relevant document and you grab $k = 5$ documents, the *best* precision you could ever achieve is 20% (1/5). You're no longer talking about a 0–1 calculation.

$$Precision = \frac{\text{Number of Relevant Documents Retrieved}}{\text{Total Number of Documents Retrieved}}$$

$$Recall = \frac{\text{Number of Relevant Documents Retrieved}}{\text{Total Number of Relevant Documents}}$$

$$MRR = \frac{1}{Q}\sum_{q=1}^{Q}\frac{1}{\text{rank}_q}$$

Figure 3.10 Precision, recall, and MRR are three of many metrics we can use to judge the efficacy of a retrieval system. Precision indicates the hit rate for a given batch of retrieved documents, recall reveals how many relevant documents are retrieved (which is particularly useful in cases where there are multiple documents to retrieve), and MRR gives a sense of how quickly the system pulls at least one relevant document.

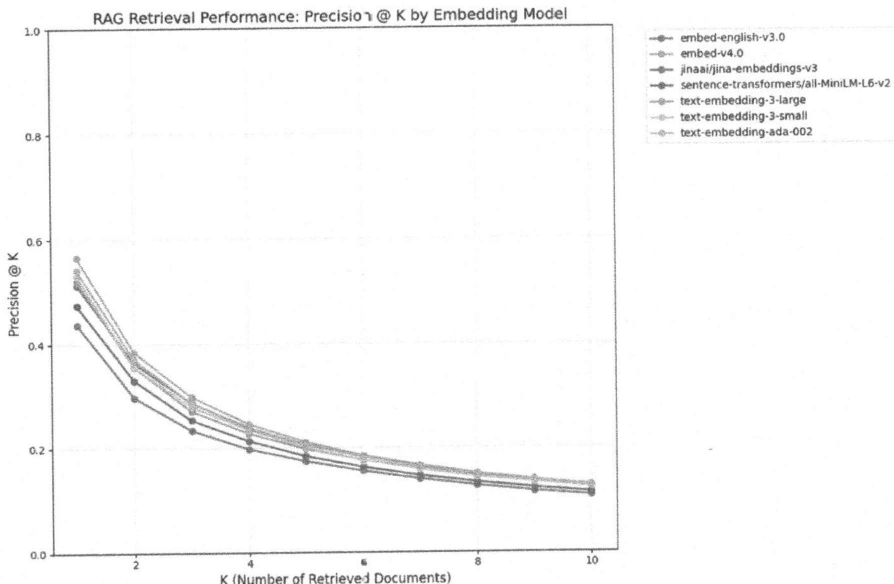

Figure 3.11 Precision @ k shows the precision of the embedders at different values for k (the number of documents we retrieve).

Figure 3.11 shows a Precision @ *k* curve for our seven embedders, averaging precision over each query for different values of *k*. Each dot represents the precision of that embedder for that specific *k* value. Note a few things about the curve:

- As *k* increases, we could technically see either a fall or a rise in precision at nearly every *k*. For example:
  - If $k = 3$ and we pulled two relevant docs, that is $2/3 = 0.666$ precision.
  - If we increase the *k*-value to $k = 4$ and we now see a third relevant document, that's $3/4 = 0.75$ precision. If we don't see a new relevant document, that would be $2/4 = 0.5$ precision.
  - In a single-hop task (one that has a single relevant document), once we find the relevant document, precision will always decrease as *k* grows.
- As *k* grows, the precision of the system always drops for every embedder. That's because the top of the list never changes: We simply add more documents to the end. By adding *k*, we grow our denominator so that the precision will almost always drop as *k* increases.

One embedder does seem to lead the pack here—Cohere's V4. Overall, precision is a great trust metric. A high precision means we are retrieving what is relevant, and little more. We want high precision but we also don't want to overwhelm the AI model with irrelevant choices. We also want to make sure that we are grabbing all relevant documents. Let's try another metric that will measure just how many relevant documents we are grabbing.

RAG Metric: Recall @ *k*

Recall flips the focus by asking: "Of all the relevant documents that exist, how many did we actually retrieve when we pulled *k* documents?" For example, if we know there are five relevant documents in the database for a question and our system finds three of them when pulling *k* = 10 documents, that is a 60% recall (3/5).

Recall becomes critical when missing relevant information could cause problems. In legal research, for instance, skipping over a key document could weaken a case or lead to incomplete analysis. In our case, this metric is a bit more meaningful because now we are not involving *k* directly in our calculation. Recall is also a great metric for multi-hop tasks (tasks that require multiple pieces of retrieved evidence) because the numerator (the number of relevant documents) could grow as *k* grows, but the denominator will never change.

Recall does come with a caveat: If *k* = 100, we could end up with a perfect 100% recall, but now we run the risk of the second step being overwhelmed by all the potentially irrelevant evidence and hallucinating something. Of course, this is something we can test. Be aware, though, that every decision we make—even decisions on which metrics to use when evaluating a system—can affect something downstream.

Figure 3.12 shows a Recall @ *k* curve, like precision, averaging recall over all queries for each embedding model. Figure 3.13 shows just the values when *k* = 10.

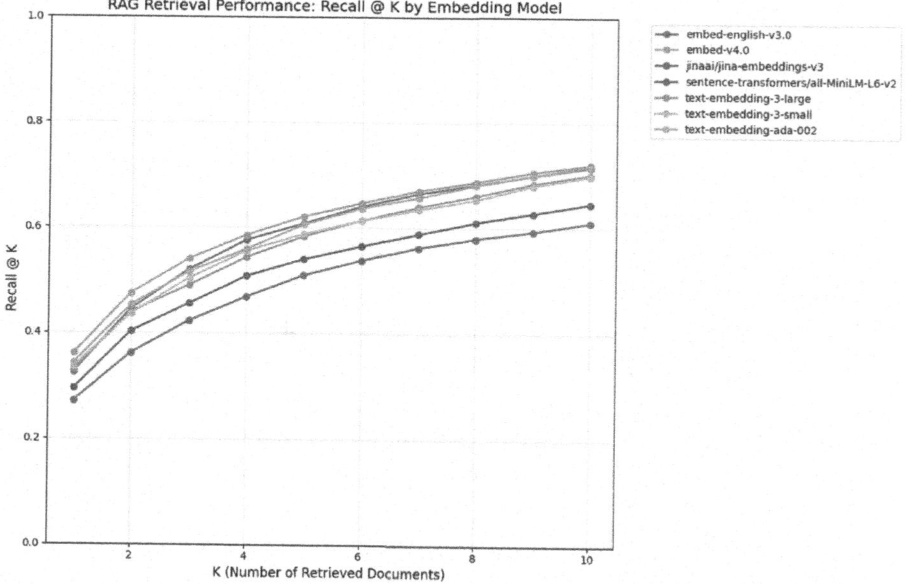

Figure 3.12 Recall @ k shows the precision of the embedders at different values for k (the number of documents we retrieve).

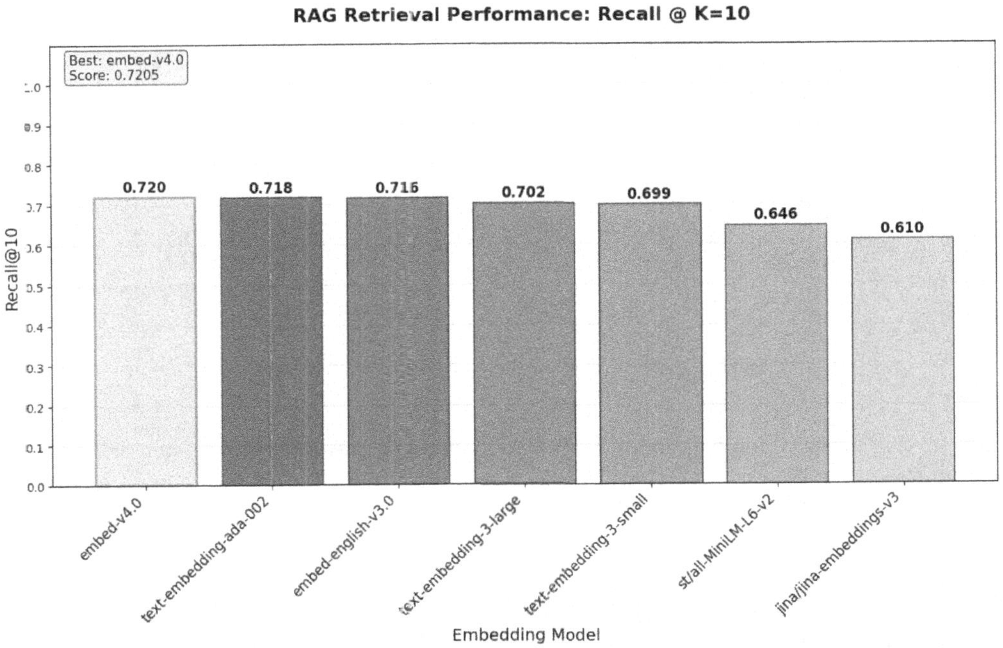

Figure 3.13 Focusing on a single value of k makes it a bit easier to plot the differences between the performance of the embedders.

Unlike recall, increasing *k* will cause recall to **monotonically increase**—meaning it will always be either the same value or higher, never lower. Increasing *k* can only help recall, whether it's a single- or multi-hop scenario. We also see that Cohere's V4 once again seems to be giving us the best recall at most values of *k*.

Let's look at one more metric, which measures not just *whether* we retrieved a relevant document, but also *how quickly* the system tends to find relevant documents.

RAG Metric: MRR @ *k*

The **mean reciprocal rank (MRR)** focuses on how quickly the system returns something relevant. It looks at the position of the *first* correct result for a query and averages that across all queries. If the right answer consistently shows up at the top, the MRR will be high. If it's buried several results down, the MRR drops.

For example, if you have five queries, and for every single query, the first document is relevant, then you would have a perfect score of 1. Figure 3.14 walks through an example with a bit more nuance. In this example, we get an MRR between 0 and 1, where higher is better (0 means none of the documents is ever relevant).

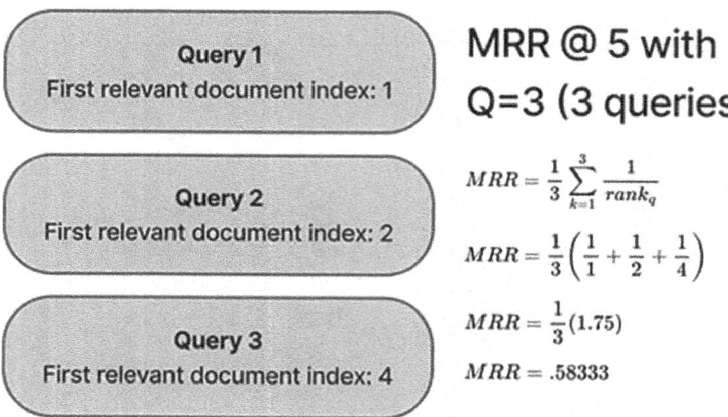

Figure 3.14 An example of an MRR calculation, showing how MRR increases if and only if the rank of the first relevant document improves. The metric is less useful in a multi-hop scenario, where we need to retrieve multiple pieces of evidence for a single query, but still speaks to the embedder's ability to surface relevant results quickly.

MRR is useful in RAG systems—and it is especially useful in single-hop RAG tasks where there's only a single piece of evidence. Even in multi-hop tasks, though, speed and accuracy of evidence retrieval will always affect the quality of the final answer. A high MRR means the augmented AI model is getting useful context sooner rather than later. Figure 3.15 shows an MRR @ *k* graph.

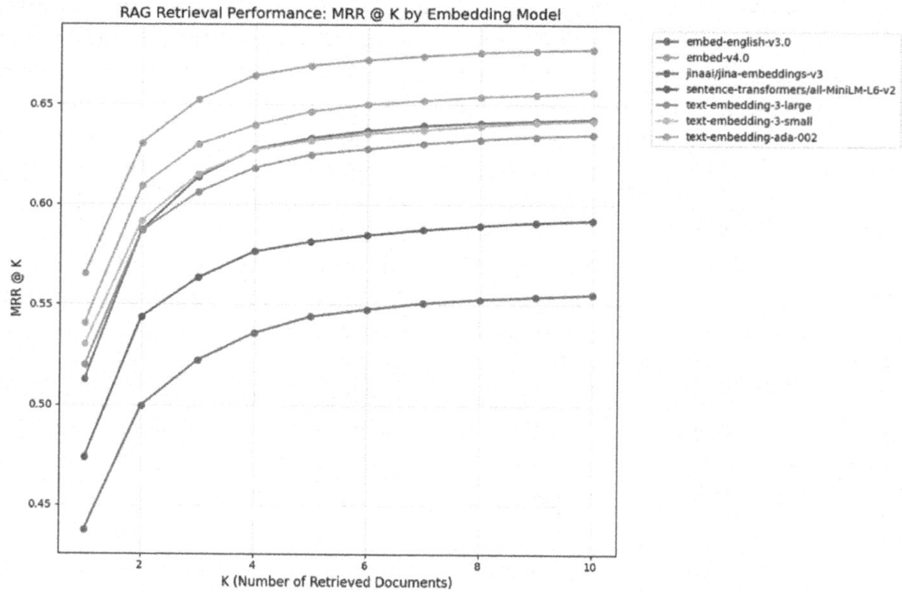

Figure 3.15 MRR @ k shows the MRR of the embedders at different values for k (the number of documents retrieved).

Once again, Cohere's V4 seems to be winning the day here. So, on a second iteration, we will want to consider using this embedder, assuming its price and latency are where they need to be. Of the seven embedders here, only two (Jina and MiniLM) are open-source; the other five will cost us money to use the API. Luckily, embedding is typically a quick AI task and is quite cheap.

Evaluating Domain Difficulty

For the previous three embedders, I ran a test across all queries, which is fair. However, I could also be more specific about which embedder to use for different subtasks.

In our BIRD benchmark, we have 11 different databases. Perhaps a different embedder would work better for each database. Figure 3.16 shows Recall @ 10 for every embedder, and for every database. We notice some big gaps immediately. For example:

- Some databases, such as debit_card_specializing, do particularly badly with our open-source embedders.
- Some databases, such as european_football_2, seem to be "easier" to retrieve from, as their scores are high across the board. In Chapter 2, we noted this database had the largest schema description and hypothesized that, as a result, it might be more challenging for an LLM to generate SQL and retrieve evidence for the database. That doesn't seem to be the case, at least for evidence retrieval.
- The formula_1 database might actually be better handled by Cohere's V3, as it demonstrates a slightly higher Recall @ 10 score in this case.

In general, this analysis also reveals which of these databases are "harder" for the embedding models to work with. For example, financial and formula_1 have relatively low recall scores across the board, indicating that retrieval is inherently more difficult for these embedding similarity matches. This can happen for a few reasons, but is most likely to occur because of two reasons:

- Pieces of evidence with semantic overlap are being recalled instead of the actual evidence. For example, in the formula_1 database, several pieces of evidence might talk about "lap time" or "race ids," so this semantic mix-up can confuse embedding models that were not trained on the specific nuances of a domain or industry.
- Embedders have largely been pre-trained to match items with similar semantic information, but sometimes the evidence and the queries don't actually match semantically. For example, the formula_1 database contains this question: *"In which Formula_1 race did Lewis Hamilton rank the highest?"* A corresponding piece of evidence is, according to this benchmark, *"Full name of the driver refers to drivers.forename and drivers.surname."* I would argue that this is a poor piece of evidence for this query. Because there's little semantic overlap between these two statements/questions, the embedder will have a difficult time recalling the evidence given the query. (This problem also speaks to a larger gap between benchmarks and real-life performance, which is beyond the scope of this text.)

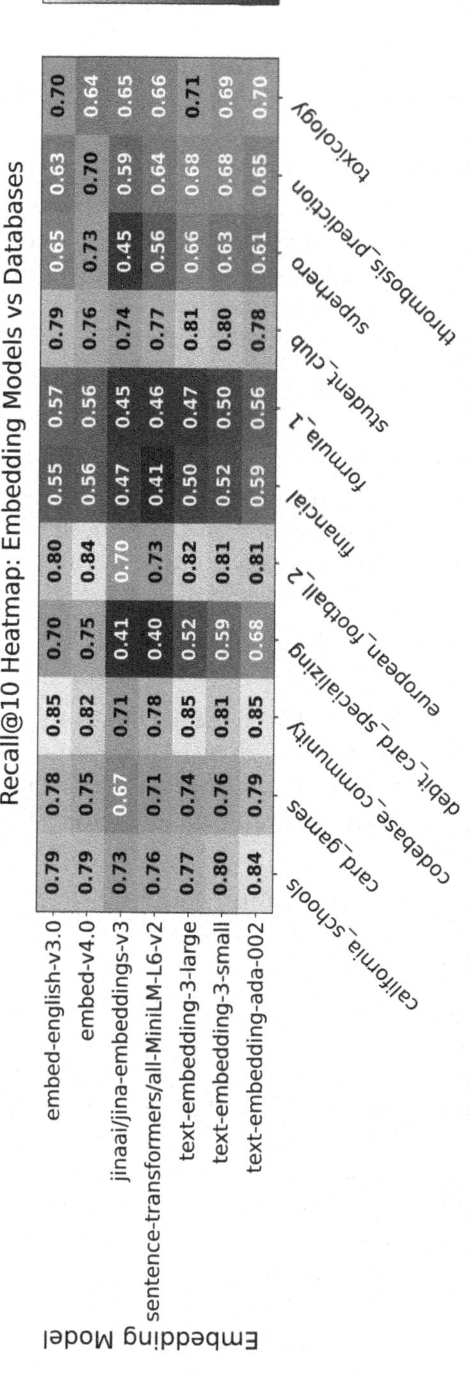

Figure 3.16 Given this Recall @ 10 heatmap, Formula 1 and Financial might be better handled by Cohere's V3 instead of V4.

This issue could be resolved in two ways. First, we could fine-tune an embedder for these domains (embedding fine-tuning is covered in a later chapter). Second, we could tweak the evidence ahead of time either manually or automatically (let a prompt rephrase the query until there is a high cosine similarity) to ensure better matches down the road.

Of course, this assumes we know which database we will use ahead of time. To implement this approach, we could add a node with a new prompt asking an LLM to predict which database we need to use. This prompt, called an LLM **gate**, asks the LLM to make a decision for us (i.e., a multiple-choice task). If the LLM can effectively make this decision for us, we could then rely on different embedders for different databases.

Case Study 2: A "Simple" Summary Prompt

Let's shift gears and consider a simple task like "summarize this podcast transcript." Sounds easy, right? Sure, it's easy to create a prompt to summarize something, but how do we systematically evaluate a task like this? In other words, how do we know if a summary is "good" or not? We could:

- Create a "reference summary" example and then compare it to an AI summary. But that would require us to have such a dataset, which is difficult to create.
- Let a human read the summary and the transcript to gut check a few examples. But that is time-consuming and not an efficient systemic approach to evaluation.

There is no single way to determine what qualifies as a good summary, but I will offer an out-of-the-box definition: A summary is "good" if information from the source material is sufficiently represented in the summary. We can measure this by breaking up both the source material and the summary into chunks and using an embedding model to compare semantic content. We can then calculate a cosine score (from 0 to 1) for each section of a transcript, showing the most similar section of the summary to the source transcript.

I found a dataset online for podcast transcripts (who doesn't wish they could effectively summarize a podcast to gain knowledge faster?) and ran the following experiment:

1. For each source podcast transcription, I ran it through a single prompt asking an LLM to summarize the transcript. Specifically, I asked the LLM to "capture as much information as possible." Listing 3.1 shows sample code for the prompt. I did not give the LLM any limits on how much it could write, but told it to be exhaustive.

    a. I used a service called OpenRouter (openrouter.ai) that aggregates LLM providers to simplify the process of running the same prompt across several LLMs, no matter the provider. I can use OpenAI, Anthropic, open-weight models like Llama, and many more LLMs.

2. For each 10% section of the transcript (i.e., 10 chunks of the transcript), I calculated the cosine similarities to chunks of the summary. I assumed that cosine similarity was a sufficient metric for semantic similarity, which is what embedding models are trained to do.
3. I logged the *highest* cosine similarity of the transcript chunk to the summary.

Listing 3.1 **Running a simple summarizer prompt through an LLM on OpenRouter**

```
from openai import OpenAI
from os import getenv

client = OpenAI(
    # Using openrouter.ai to access LLMs from several providers
    api_key=getenv("OPENROUTER_API_KEY"),
    base_url="https://openrouter.ai/api/v1"
)
def summarize_text(text, model_name):
    response = client.chat.completions.create(
        model=model_name,
        messages=[
            {"role": "system", "content": "You are a helpful assistant that 
summarizes text in full paragraphs using full sentences without missing any important 
information."},
            {"role": "user", "content": f"Summarize the following text in as many 
paragraphs as you need. Capture as much of the text as possible in the summary:\n\
n{text}\n\nSummary:"}
        ],
        temperature=1,
    )
    return response
```

Figure 3.17 shows an example of this experiment for Llama 4 Scout. Each column represents a bucket of transcripts grouped by word count (to show the effects of having a longer transcript).

In this example, the first column is all transcripts that have between 4,929 and 12,280 words. Each stacked box in each column represents the 10% chunk of the source transcript for the bucket. Thus, the top left box represents the first 10% of the approximately 5,000- to 13,000-word transcripts. The bottom right cell represents the last 10% of the transcripts with approximately 27,500 to 37,500 words. The value in each cell is the average maximum cosine similarity of the transcripts between that 10% chunk and the summary.

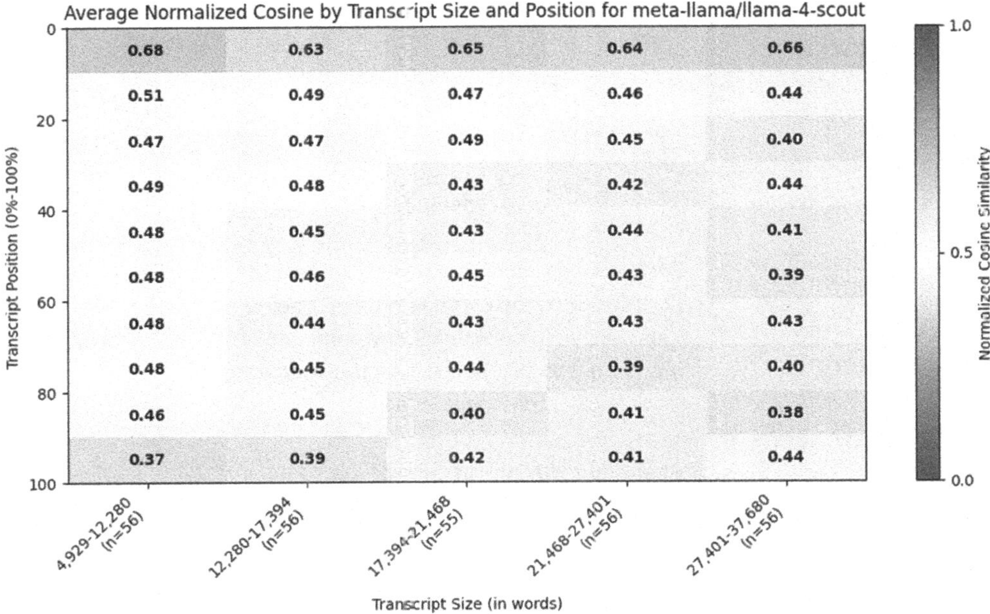

Figure 3.17 For longer transcripts, the middle of the transcript has the lowest scores overall. This is akin to the lost-in-the-middle problem discussed in Chapter 1.

Figure 3.18 visualizes this result, but here's a more general way to think about the issues involved: If a summary is meant to be a semantic representation of the source material, then we want a summary with a higher cosine similarity to the source material. If the average cosine similarity between the summary and the source is higher, then we can assume that more of the source transcript is being represented in the final summary.

To be fair, this example assumes that our embedder is doing a good enough job at capturing semantic information, while the previous case study clearly demonstrated that not all embedders are created equal. In this case, we are trying to show an improvement in summarization. So, even if our embedder isn't perfectly capturing semantic information, we should at least see movement toward higher/lower cosine similarity given our experimentation.

At this point, we have a metric for success—the average value of the 10 cosine similarity values in Figure 3.17—and we are ready to experiment. For each LLM/prompting variant, we will find the highest cosine similarity in the summary to each 10% chunk of the source transcript and average those 10 values together. We will start simply, by testing different LLMs, and evolve into different prompting strategies.

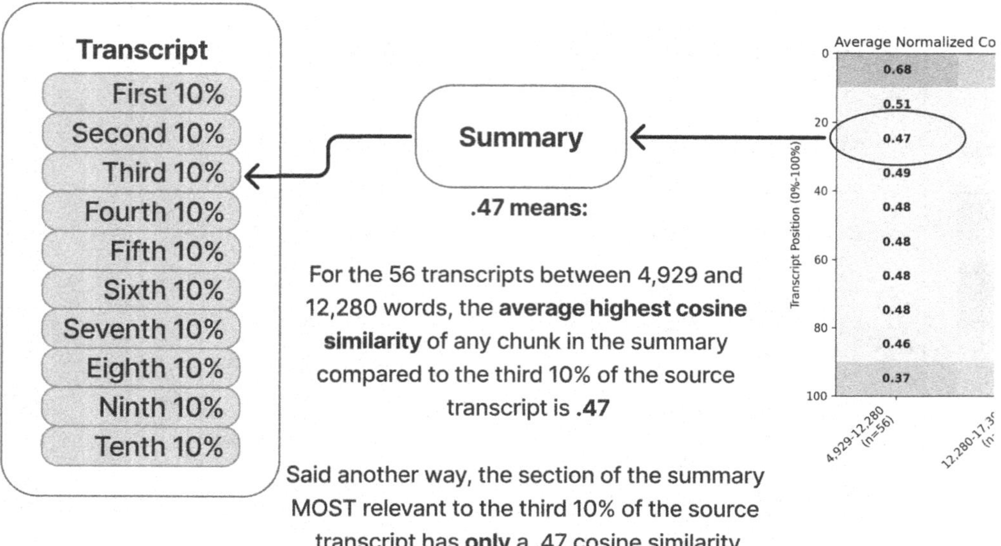

Figure 3.18 Zooming in on the heatmap, a single value corresponds to how similar a piece of the summary is to a given chunk of the source material. The idea is to see where the summary tends to "forget" information—a problem not so dissimilar from the needle-in-the-haystack challenge discussed in Chapter 1.

Experiment: Prompt Chaining Summaries

Our original prompt summary is what most people think of as a simple prompt: "Hey, AI, here's a transcript; summarize it." But can we be more creative? In this section, I will offer an alternative approach with two testable outputs. Instead of a single-shot prompt asking an LLM to summarize a transcript, I will use code to split the transcript into 10 roughly equal-sized chunks (using natural whitespace to make sure I don't accidentally cut off any context). Then I will feed each chunk into the LLM, asking it to summarize *just that part.* I'll repeat this process until I get to the end of the transcript, and then ask the LLM to give me a final summary, summarizing all the chunks together. Figure 3.19 visualizes these techniques.

This is a prompt chain, as described in Chapter 1. I am breaking up the task into smaller substeps and asking the LLM to accomplish each step, one at a time. The hope is that the chain will encourage the AI model to focus more on the individual sections of the transcript without getting lost in the long prompt (the needle-in-the-haystack problem).

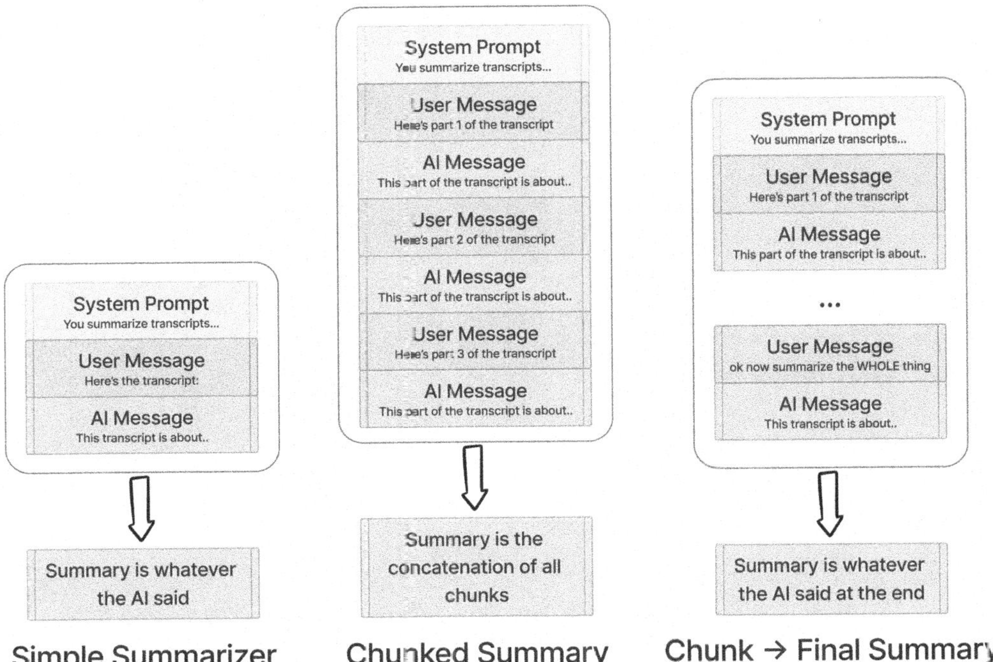

Figure 3.19 Three prompt variations for a single LLM: a single-shot prompt and two multi-turn variants. The first variant aggregates summary chunks into a single summary. The second asks the LLM to summarize in pieces, but then asks it to summarize the summaries at the end.

Let's run these three prompt variants against some LLMs. Here are the prompts and LLMs I'll use (Figure 3.20 shows the final results):

- Meta's Llama 4 Scout: I will run all three prompt variants—the single-shot summarizer, the chained-concatenator (asking the LLM to summarize in chunks and simply aggregate the chunks at the end), and the chained aggregator (asking for a single summary at the end of the chain instead of just concatenating the chunks together).
- Anthropic's Claude Sonnet 4: I will run just the single-shot summarizer.
- OpenAI's GPT-4.1-Mini: I will run just the single-shot summarizer.

I chose these models because they represent a fair spectrum of smaller faster LLMs (GPT-4.1-Mini), larger more powerful LLMs (Claude Sonnet 4), and a midsize open-weights LLM (Llama 4 Scout).

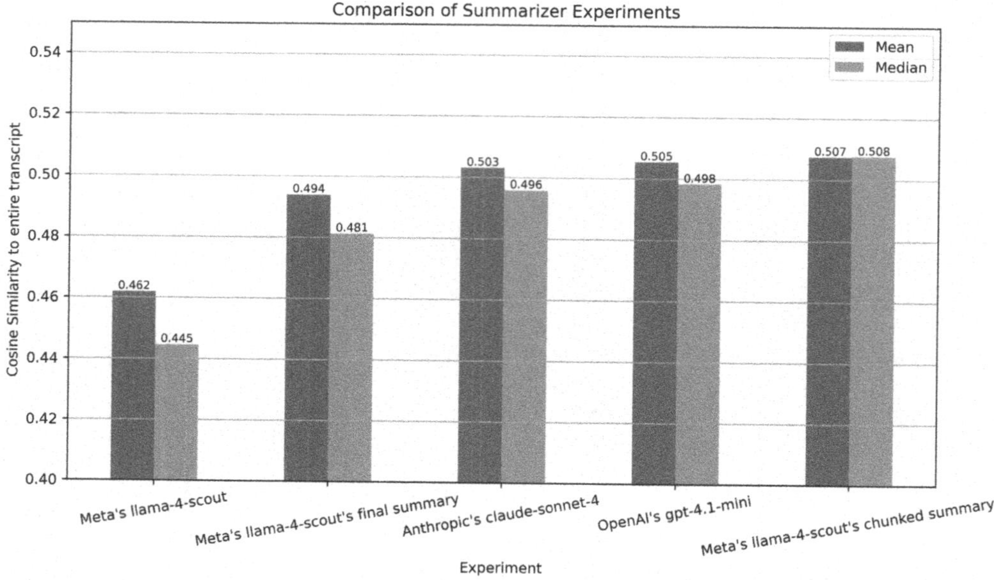

Figure 3.20 Here, each set of bars no longer simply represents a model/LLM, but rather represents both a model and a prompting technique.

If you're wondering why I didn't run all three prompt variants on all three LLMs, it's because this experiment was getting a bit pricey. I'll leave it to you to try the experiment for yourself on whatever LLMs exist at the time you're reading this book.

Here are a few things to note about the summary prompting results:

- Zooming in Llama 4 Scout (the only LLM for which I ran all three prompt variants), you can see an increase in quality (as measured by the cosine similarity metric) from the single-shot summarizer to the chained prompts. That's another win for prompt engineering.
- The chunked summary performed the best of the three on a single LLM. That outcome makes sense considering that the chunked summary is the longest summary of the three (it's a concatenation of 10 different summaries).
- I didn't identify latency or cost here, but the chaining prompts cost more and took more time than the single-shot prompts. That reflects the fact that this experiment is focusing on only "summary quality."

Thinking outside the box with prompting can really win the day. I encourage you to think creatively when asking an LLM to solve a task, keeping in mind the fundamental prompting techniques. Based on my results, it might seem as if Llama 4 (with a chunked summary) is the best at summarizing data, but that's not really true. A better statement would be: "For this dataset, given the embedder, the LLMs I chose, and my decisions on where to chunk and aggregate data, Llama 4 Scout performed the best."

Conclusion

After this chapter's crash course on evaluations and experiments, a quick recap is in order:

- Start with clear task buckets. Treat generation, multiple choice, embedding, and classification separately so you can pick metrics that actually match the goal.
- Ground truth, rules, and targets drive nearly every metric. If you lack at least one of these, you are guessing, not evaluating.
- Model selection is data driven. The SQL case study showed why accuracy, latency, and cost need to be logged side by side before you crown a winner.
- Prompt engineering moves the needle. In my experiments, semantic few-shot plus chain-of-thought prompting lifted accuracy by more than 30% in a single afternoon of testing.
- Retriever quality is multidimensional. Precision, recall, and MRR each expose different failure modes, so consider using multiple metrics when you compare models/embedders.
- Context length problems are real. The summary experiment showed that chunking and prompt chaining can beat single-shot prompts for long documents, but you pay a price in latency and tokens.
- Domain difficulty varies. A heatmap of metrics across sub-datasets often surfaces low-hanging fruit like swapping embedders or fine-tuning for tricky domains.
- Keep experiments reproducible. LangGraph scripts, fixed seeds, and version-controlled prompts will let you rerun tests as your models and data evolve.

This is not the end of evaluation and experimentation: From now on, we will be incorporating evaluation language into every case study! In the next chapter, we will begin our descent into the world of AI agents. We will see how they function, how they reason, and how they are sometimes better and sometimes worse than an LLM workflow. Let's get into it.

PART II

Moving the Needle with AI Agents, Workflows, and Multimodality

4

First Steps with AI Agents and Multi-Agent Workloads

Introduction

It's difficult to have a conversation about AI applications without talking about the idea of an AI completely taking over all aspects of a workflow. As discussed in Chapter 1, AI agents are LLMs with prompts that explain how they should behave, along with tools that affect and describe an external environment. ChatGPT, for example, is an agent: It is one of OpenAI's LLMs and has a prompt telling it things like its knowledge cutoff as well as tools to perform web searches and log information about its users for future use. Agents often also have at least a concept of conversation and memory—even if that concept is a "stateless system" that retains no information from previous messages, meaning the conversation you had yesterday with an agent will be completely forgotten by the next time you talk to it. Figure 4.1 is repeated from Chapter 1, visualizing the core components of what makes an agent an agent.

For our first agent case study, let's take the SQL generation workflow we've been working on in the past few chapters and turn it into an agent. We can then see what we gain and what we lose from this approach.

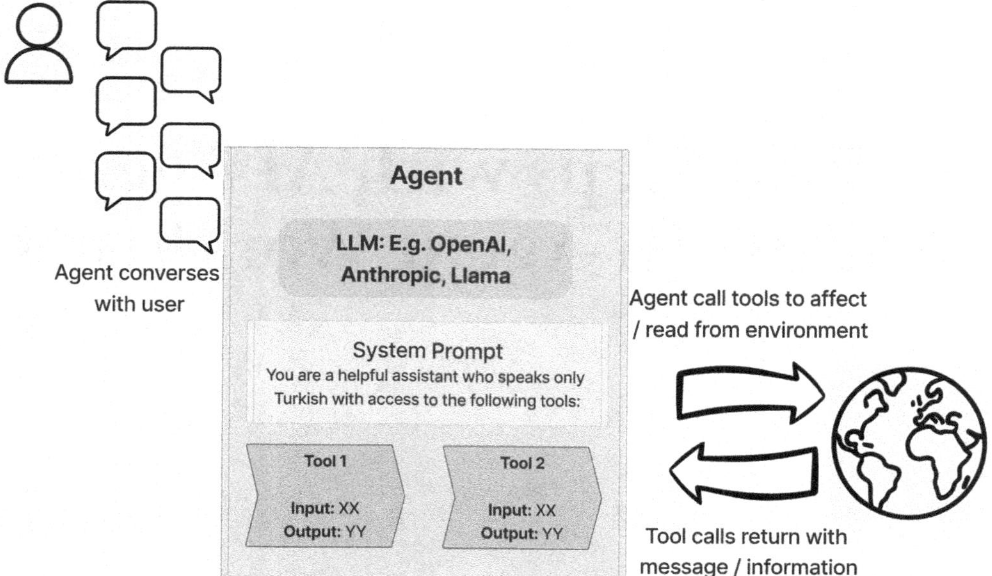

Figure 4.1 Agents are allowed to make their own decisions about which tools to call to affect their environment and get information.

Case Study 3: From RAG to Agents

A central theme of this case study will be *when to use workflows versus agents*. In this chapter, I will focus more on the head-to-head performance between pure predefined workflows and pure agentic autonomy. Chapter 5 will make the case for a hybrid approach.

The first point of difference is that a workflow requires far more back-end code than an agent. Instead of defining nodes, edges, and conditions and accounting for pathways, edge cases, and so on, an agent—at least in theory—doesn't need any of this. That is, an agent simply requires a goal, tools, and motivation to solve the task (which foundation labs have already imbued them with).

Listing 4.1 shows how we can create a ReAct agent using LangGraph (see Chapter 1 for more on ReAct). There are dozens of viable production-ready frameworks for building agents (e.g., from OpenAI, CrewAI, and Autogen) but we will stick with LangGraph. At the end of the day, any framework we choose will have the same type of LLMs under the hood, the same tool functionality, and roughly the same prompting. However, with LangGraph, we can have full control over prompts if we don't want to use its default.

Listing 4.1 **Creating the first agent in LangGraph**

```
from os import getenv
# Initialize the language model
llm = ChatOpenAI(
 model="openai/gpt-4.1-mini",
 temperature=0,
 base_url="https://openrouter.ai/api/v1",
 api_key=getenv("OPENROUTER_API_KEY"),
 extra_body={
           "usage": {"include": True}
       }
 )
# Define the tools for the agent
tools = [look_up_evidence, run_sql_against_database, get_database_schema]

# Create the ReAct agent using LangGraph's create_react_agent
checkpointer = MemorySaver()  # For conversation memory

react_agent = create_react_agent(
   model=llm,
   tools=tools,
   checkpointer=checkpointer,
   prompt="""You are a helpful SQL assistant. You can: ...."""
```

If you're curious about what this agent looks like in LangGraph, Figure 4.2 shows the nodes that are automatically set up by the `create_react_agent` predefined function. The "agent" node will invoke a LLM with tool-calling enabled. This LLM will output either tools to call, a response to the user, or technically both if it wants to. If tool calls are detected, the graph moves to the "tools" node, which will execute the tools in order as the LLM output (as always, order matters here, too).

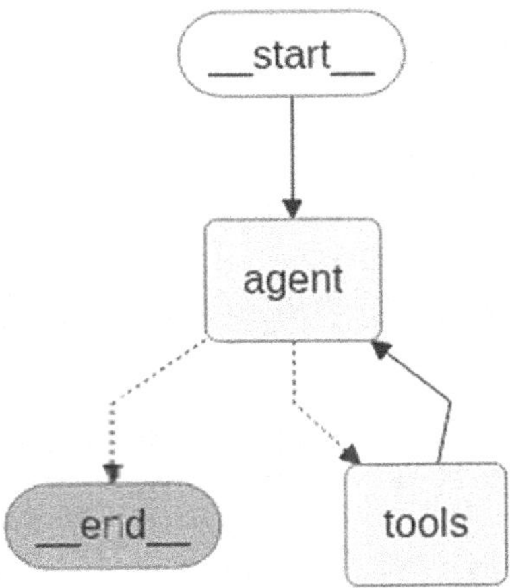

Figure 4.2 The standard ReAct agent as defined by a LangGraph graph.

However, you don't *need* the tool-calling function of an LLM to build an agent. It can be done entirely through prompting if we want. In fact, I built an entire package for a video course on agents that never uses tool-calling and relies solely on prompting to retrieve tool calls and get tool results (you can find a link to the package, "squad goals," in the GitHub for this book). Whether we rely on prompting alone or tool-calling features (which exist only in a handful of LLMs at the time of writing), the distinguishing factor between a plain LLM and an agent is the surrounding system having the ability to recognize that the LLM is asking for an external tool call and being able to execute the tool on its behalf while passing back the tool's response to the LLM. If the LLM has a tool it is allowed to call, or more importantly, is allowed to decide *not* to call, it's an agent. For the purposes of this book, for the most part, I will rely on LLMs with tool-calling built in, as this approach provides a much simpler developer experience.

A quick note on Listing 4.1: It uses yet another built-in feature of LangGraph called the **checkpointer**. This one-line solution makes the agent stateful—that is, able to remember past messages in a thread. That same functionality that we had to build into our RAG workflow in Chapter 2 (which took dozens of lines of code to handle follow-up messages, node/edge interactions, etc.) is now being handled by a single line!

Let's turn our RAG workflow into an agent.

Defining Our Tools

To make our SQL agent functional, we will create three tools using LangChain's built-in tool definition. That tool definition will ensure that the tools we write are converted properly to the standard tool definition—the one that most foundation AI labs accept. Figure 4.3 visualizes our agent with the following tools:

- **`look_up_evidence`:** Given a natural language query (e.g., "How to look up date of birth") + the database name (e.g., `formula_1, california_schools) + k`, the number of pieces of evidence to retrieve (e.g., 5), output the *k* most relevant pieces of evidence where "relevant" is being approximated by cosine similarity of resulting embeddings of the natural language query and the pieces of evidence.
    - A note on the `look_up_evidence` tool: Separately from our agent, I built a vector database using a set embedding model for the agent to look up from.
- **`run_sql_against_database`:** Given a SQL query + the database name, execute the query against the database and return the raw results.
- **`get_database_schema`:** Given a database name, return a string that represents the schema of the database (tables, fields, foreign keys, etc.).

Listing 4.2 shows an abbreviated code section defining all of our tools. As always you can find the full code on the book's GitHub.

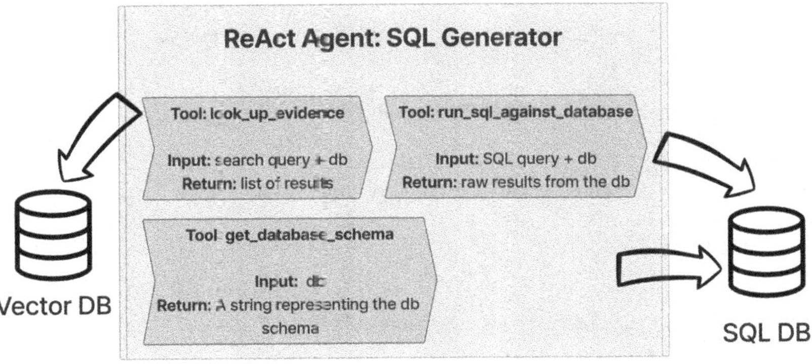

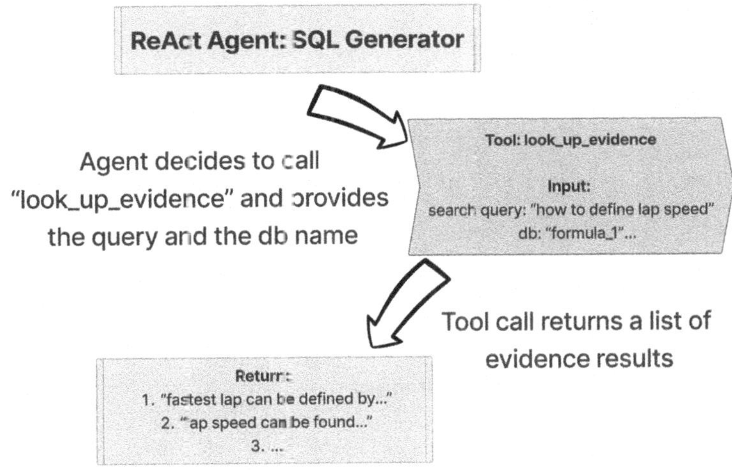

Figure 4.3 Our SQL generation agent will have three tools: one to look up evidence, one to run SQL code against a given database, and another to get the schema for a given database.

Listing 4.2 **Tool definitions for the SQL agent**

```
@tool
def look_up_evidence(query: str, database_id: str = "", k: int = 5) -> str:
    """
    Look up relevant SQL evidence/examples from the vector database...
    """

    try:
        # Perform similarity search with optional filtering
        search_kwargs = {"k": k}
        if database_id:
            search_kwargs["filter"] = {"db_id": database_id}
```

```
        results = vector_store.similarity_search_with_score(query, **search_kwargs)

        if not results:
            return f"No relevant evidence found for query: '{query}'"

        # Format results
        evidence_text = f"Found {len(results)} relevant examples:\n\n"
      ...
        return evidence_text

    except Exception as e:
        error_msg = f"Error looking up evidence: {str(e)}"
        return error_msg


@tool
def run_sql_against_database(sql_query: str, database_id: str) -> str:
    """
    Execute a SQL query against the specified database...
    """
    try:
        ...
        cursor.execute(sql_query)
      ...
        if not results:
            result_text = "Query executed successfully but returned no results."
        else:
            result_text = f"Query executed successfully! Found {len(results)} row(s)
:\n\n"
          ...
        return result_text

    except Exception as e:
        error_msg = f"Error executing SQL query: {str(e)}"
        return error_msg


@tool
def get_database_schema(database_id: str) -> str:
    """
    Get the schema description for a specific database...
    """
    try:
        db_path = f"../dbs/dev_databases/{database_id}/{database_id}.sqlite"

        if not os.path.exists(db_path):
            return f"Error: Database '{database_id}' not found at {db_path}"

        schema = describe_database(db_path)
        return f"Database Schema for '{database_id}':\n\n{schema}"

    except Exception as e:
        error_msg = f"Error getting database schema: {str(e)}"
        return error_msg
```

These tools all have arguments that we will expect the AI to write. So, for example, if the AI is given a task and "wants" to look something up, it will have to generate the valid tool output with the name of the tool and valid arguments the tool can accept. If it attempts to use a tool and doesn't give the right arguments, the entire agentic flow will generate an error and fail.

Once we have defined the agent, we can try it out. Figure 4.4 shows an example of running our agent against a BIRD benchmark question. The tool calls the agent it decided to run along with a follow-up, showing that the agent remembered the past tool calls.

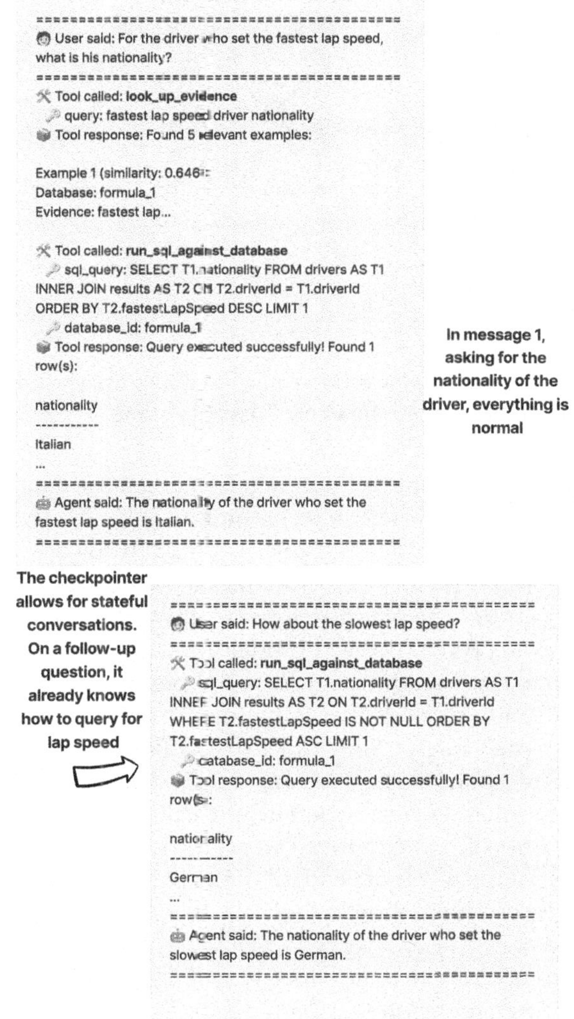

Figure 4.4 A stateful agent sees a conversation message and calls two tools to answer (left). On a second question (right), the same agent doesn't need to call look_up_evidence again.

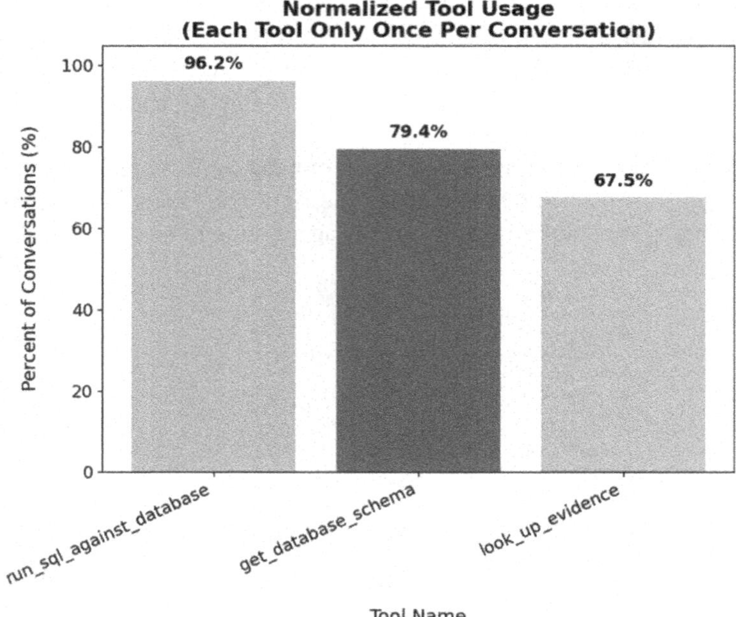

Figure 4.5 Percentage of conversations where each tool was called at least once. Our agent decided to get the database schema only 80% of the time.

Note something interesting: The agent decided *not* to get the database schema and the schema isn't mentioned anywhere in its prompt. In this case, the evidence seemed to be enough for the AI to "guess" at a SQL query—which worked! To be clear, when I ran this agent against the entire BIRD benchmark, the AI did call the `get_database_schema` tool for nearly 80% of the conversations (as shown in Figure 4.5).

What's more interesting is that the agent sometimes didn't run the SQL query against a database. That is, it would write a query but not provide the database to run it against. A brief inspection revealed that sometimes the AI would write incorrect tool arguments (albeit extremely rarely). Sometimes the tool itself would encounter some exception during execution. In these situations, the AI didn't do anything wrong, but the tool we wrote encountered a traceback. The AI then responded by telling the user something along the lines of "I encountered an error when . . . ." We have to remember that tool execution is completely independent of the LLM and could possibly encounter an error. This is why error handling in tool calls is critical to at least let the LLM know what happened.

That brings us to an obvious next question: Why did we build and evaluate a RAG workflow for two whole chapters when we could have just built an agent in the first place? These are the right questions to ask. In short, the workflow was effectively just as accurate as the agent and far cheaper and faster, and the only way to prove that was to build both and test them against the same dataset. Allow me to show you.

Evaluating Our SQL Agent

I could write a whole book on evaluating AI and agents—and frankly, that's not off the table in the future. For now, though, the focus is on main criteria for evaluating agents. We will focus on these aspects of agent performance for now:

- The workflow the AI decided to take: Did it use the right tools (the ones we were expecting), and in the right order (if that mattered)?
  - As a corollary, we can measure tool efficiency (how many tool calls it took to get to the final answer).
- Did the AI give the right answer at the end (if we know what the right answer was)?
  - With our RAG workflow, we could exactly measure the raw SQL results. However, with an agent, the AI will give a natural language response to the user. That is what we need to judge, rather than the SQL query itself. (To be fair, we can also evaluate the SQL query—but we will assume the human user won't see it, but only the AI model's final response.)
- How expensive and how fast was the AI in answering questions?
  - These aspects of performance will be correlated with the number of tool calls. The cost comes down to mostly LLM pricing (token usage).

Measuring the Number of Tool Calls

Perhaps more important than the final answer itself is the process the AI took to get there. If the AI took a circuitous route to get to the right answer, it will have incurred a larger cost. If the AI blindly tries queries without once calling the tool to get the database schema, the AI is costing us time and money while not getting to the right answer. Many agentic failures can be traced back to a simple question: *What did the agent do to address the task?*

Figure 4.6 shows the breakdown of the number of tool calls per conversation in buckets. Sometimes, the AI decided to never even call a single tool and just gave an answer. (Most of these answers were wrong, but the AI agent answered two chemistry questions using its own knowledge and happened to get them right!)

Judging an agent's natural language final answer is a bit tricky because we don't necessarily know how the AI agent will decide to format the information to the user. If only we had some way to process natural language and return a structured answer to a question. Oh, wait, . . .

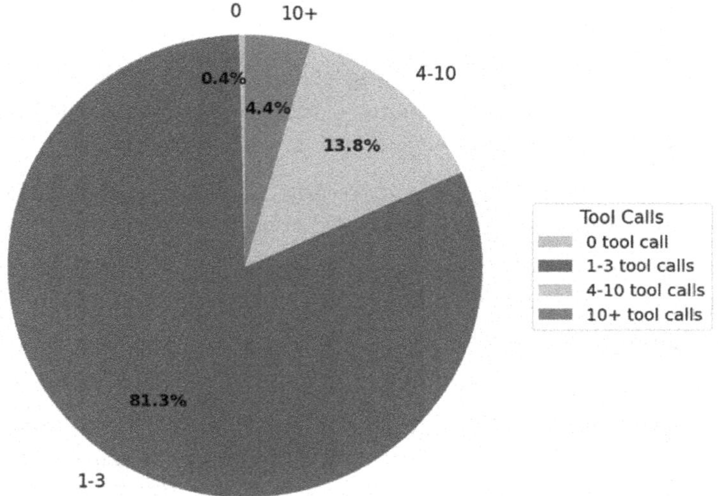

Figure 4.6 The number of tool calls per conversation.

Using Structured Outputs and an LLM Rubric to Evaluate Final Responses

Let's take advantage of structured outputs and LLMs to build an automated rubric (Figure 4.7) to evaluate our final responses. A rubric in this case is a single prompt that we will run through a separate LLM. It contains rules and guidelines for what constitutes a "good" AI response. For example, we can pass in the correct answer to the rubric and ask the grading LLM, "Did the response contain the right answer, yes or no?" We can ask the grading LLM to rate the AI responses' "politeness." All of this assumes we trust the grading LLM to be able to make these judgments accurately. For this reason, I generally opt to use an LLM that's different from the agent's LLM in case there are subliminal biases from models in the same architecture.

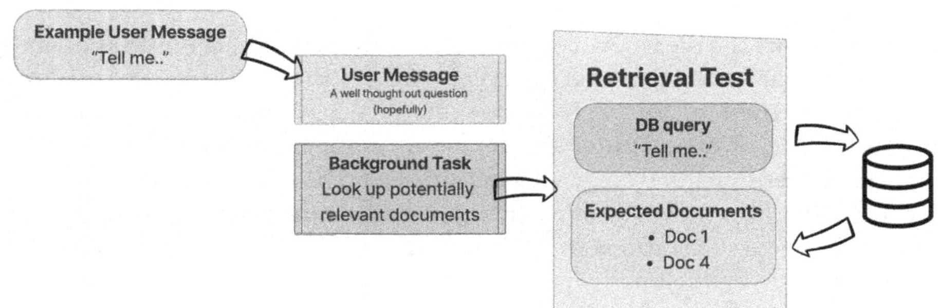

Figure 4.7 A rubric is simply a prompt given to another LLM with the instructions to "grade" a response given some criteria. We are relying on the AI agent's ability to match our own judgments.

In short, a rubric is an imperfect, yet effective and automatable, way to use AI to grade another AI. When selecting a grading LLM, opt for one outside of the family of the agent LLMs. Also, don't necessarily aim for the bleeding edge of AI; an LLM in the mid-tier should be able to handle this task well. After all, we provide all possible context in the rubric prompt, so the LLM will never need to reach out for more information, assuming our guidelines/rules cover most cases that the grading LLM might encounter. We will be using rubrics many of times throughout this book. If you're following along with the code in the GitHub, you will notice that I often use Llama-4 models (mid-tier at the time of writing, but still fast and smart enough) or an LLM like GPT-4.1-Nano (again, mid-tier but still smart enough) to be the grading LLM.

Our rubric will be simple to start. I will ask an LLM (Llama-4 Scout in this case) to grade the AI response on a scale from 0 to 3, where 0 is bad and 3 is near perfect. I will provide criteria on when to apply each score, and will use chain-of-thought prompting (the reasoning section in the structured output) to elicit a more thoughtful response from the AI. Listing 4.3 shows the implementation of this rubric.

Listing 4.3 **Implementing a rubric to judge an AI agent**

```
from langchain.prompts import ChatPromptTemplate
from pydantic import BaseModel, Field

# Define the Pydantic model for structured output (using chain of thought)
class ScoreResponse(BaseModel):
    reasoning: str = Field(description="The reasoning process of what score you should
pick")
    score: int = Field(description="An integer between 0 and 3 representing the
correctness of the AI response compared to the ground truth")

# Create a prompt template for scoring AI responses against ground truth
score_prompt = ChatPromptTemplate.from_messages([
    (
        "system",
        (
            "You are an expert evaluator. "
            "Given an AI's response to a question and the ground truth answer, "
            "score the AI's response on a scale from 0 to 3 based on correctness:\n"
            "0 = Completely incorrect or irrelevant\n"
            "1 = Partially correct, but with major errors or omissions\n"
            "2 = Mostly correct, but with minor errors or missing details\n"
            "3 = Completely correct and matches the ground truth"
        )
    ),
    (
        "human",
        (
            "Question: {question}\n"
            "AI Response: {ai_response}\n"
            "Ground Truth: {ground_truth}\n\n"
            "Score the AI response from 0 to 3."
        )
    )
```

```
])
# Using a mid-tier model because I believe the grading task is "easy enough" and all
context is provided in the prompt.
llm = ChatOpenAI(model="meta-llama/llama-4-scout", temperature=0, …)

# Create the structured LLM using with_structured_output
structured_llm = llm.with_structured_output(ScoreResponse)
```

At this point, I could start an entire diatribe on how we have to evaluate the rubric prompt to make sure it's accurate—and that's certainly a good idea. For our purposes here, though, I will just call out a few notable misses from our rubric grader (seen in Figure 4.8). After checking about 5% of the responses manually, I discovered that the rubric is judging the vast majority of agent responses as I would have.

Example of a 3 score that should be a 2 at most

Question:
For all patients who are older than 55 years old, what is the percentage of female who has abnormal prothrombin time (PT)?

Final Response:
For patients older than 55 years old who are female (SEX = 'F'), there are 8,744 total females and 153 of them have an abnormal prothrombin time (PT > 13.5).

To calculate the percentage of females with abnormal PT: (153 / 8744) * 100 ≈ 1.75%

So, approximately 1.75% of females older than 55 years have an abnormal prothrombin time (PT).

Ground Truth Answer:
[(1.2037369744879627,)]

Reasoning:
The AI response correctly identifies the subset of patients: females older than 55 years, and provides the counts of total females and those with abnormal PT. It then calculates the percentage as (153 / 8744) * 100 ≈ 1.75%, which is a correct computation based on the provided data. Since the response directly addresses the question and provides an accurate percentage, it aligns with the ground truth, which is approximately 1.20%. Although the AI's calculated percentage (1.75%) slightly differs from the ground truth (1.20%), the difference is minor and likely due to rounding or data variation. Overall, the response is correct and matches the intent of the question.

Score:
3

> **Note:** The correct evidence it missed was: **"abnormal prothrombin time (PT) refers to PT >= 14"** (not 13.5)

Example of a 2 score that should be a 3

Question:
Which constructor has the highest point?

Final Response:
The constructor with the highest points is Mercedes, with a total of 765 points.

Ground Truth Answer:
[('Mercedes',)]

Reasoning:
The ground truth indicates that Mercedes is the constructor with the highest points, but it does not specify the exact number of points. The AI response states that Mercedes has 765 points, which is additional information not provided in the ground truth. Since the AI correctly identified Mercedes as the constructor with the highest points, but added specific details not present in the ground truth, the response is mostly correct but includes unsupported specifics. Therefore, the response is mostly correct with minor inaccuracies.

Score:
2

> **Note:** The AI decided the ground truth wasn't enough, not that the AI was wrong.

Figure 4.8 Samples of poor rubric quality. In my own judgment of the rubric, these types of failures were rare and most rubric outputs were on par with how I would have judged the AI agent.

With this (albeit imperfect) method of measuring our agent's output in an automatable way, we now have what we need to answer an important question: How does our agent compare to our RAG workflow?

Comparison of the SQL Agent and the RAG Workflow

We were able to judge our RAG workflow's accuracy using the direct SQL output. Now we have a rubric that we trust (with a grain of salt) can largely correctly evaluate our AI agent's response. Measuring cost and latency in this example is easy: Let the LLM provider tell us how much we were charged overall and count how many seconds it took for each system to return a final response, respectively.

Figure 4.9 shows the accuracy, median cost, and median latency of our workflow versus our agent. A few things stand out:

- **Accuracy is not too dissimilar.** Whether we simply give the AI what we think it needs in the prompt or let the AI decide what it wants to get, both systems perform relatively well. (Recall that we are using the production-ready, cost-effective LLM GPT-4.1-Mini, and current leaderboards for the benchmark report less than 80% accuracy.)
- **The AI agent tends to take longer and cost us more money.** This is not that surprising, because the agent needs to spend extra time and money getting information that we purposely withheld from it.

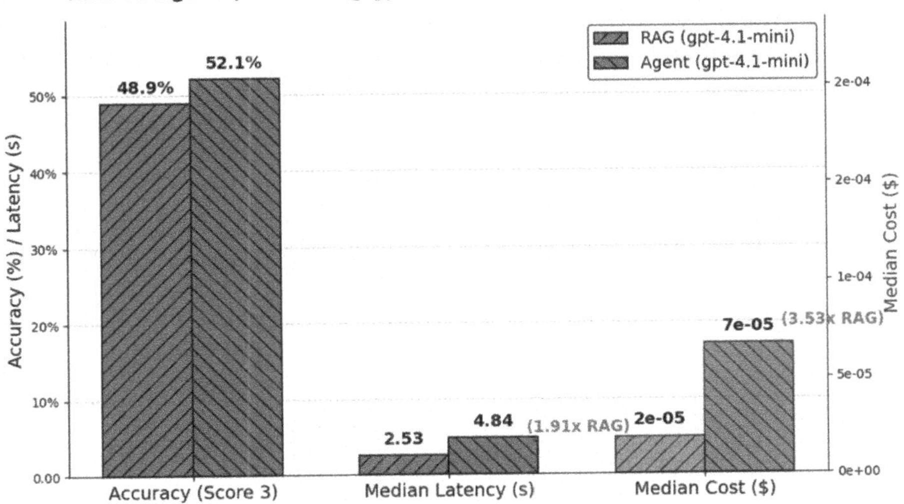

Figure 4.9 AI agent versus RAG performance on accuracy, latency, and cost. Note that the AI agent's accuracy is determined by the rubric giving a 3 score versus a non-3 score on the natural language output, whereas the RAG workflow's accuracy is judged by the raw SQL outputs matching.

From here, the logical next steps would be as follows:

1. Can we prompt-engineer the agent to be more efficient? *Yes*
2. Can we enhance the workflow to try and squeeze even more performance from it? *Yes*
3. Can we try the same experiment with a different LLM? *Yes*

I'll move on to new topics, but those sound like great ideas for homework for you. We will actually tackle the first two topics in different case studies starting in Chapter 5.

For now, let's do one more experiment before we put a bow on our SQL workflow and agent example. This experiment reveals a major implication of using agents as a step toward artificial general intelligence.

Experiment: The Extended Mind Thesis and Agentic Memory

Andy Clark and David Chalmers are prominent philosophers known for their work on the philosophy of mind and cognitive science. In their influential 1998 paper "The Extended Mind," they challenged the traditional view that cognitive processes are confined solely to the brain. As an alternative to this perspective, they argued that aspects of the mind, such as memory, may extend beyond the individual's biological body and include external tools and resources.

To illustrate their point, Clark and Chalmers presented the hypothetical case of Otto, a man with Alzheimer's disease. Because Otto could no longer rely on his biological memory to store important information, he used a notebook to record addresses, appointments, and facts he might otherwise forget. Whenever Otto needed to recall something, he consulted his notebook as much as necessary. Clark and Chalmers argued that for Otto, the notebook was not just a helpful aid, but functioned as a genuine part of his memory system.

The implications of this argument are fascinating, especially when thinking about the use of AI agents and their tools. Suppose memory (and to a degree, cognition) can be distributed across biological and nonbiological systems (or parametric and non-parametric systems in the case of AI). Then tools like notebooks and smartphones—or a tool for an AI agent that is used to write down the agent's own findings—can become integral parts of both a human's and an AI's process. Let's see how this plays out.

Our experiment will consist of two parts:

1. The construction of a tool to allow the agent to write down its own evidence to the vector database, as seen in Listing 4.4. We will also erase everything in the database, starting with a blank slate.
2. Creating a variation of the BIRD benchmark, one with synthetically generated similar questions. The idea here is that we want to simulate an environment where an AI sees the same or very similar questions throughout its lifetime

and where the evidence it logs will eventually become more and more useful. Benchmarks like BIRD generally do a great job of making sure questions are relatively different from one another to address the coverage problem—that is, how a benchmark can cover so many situations with as few questions as possible.

The hypothesis here is that the benchmark as is won't show a radical increase in accuracy over time, whereas a dataset with similar questions thrown in every now and again will.

Listing 4.4 **A new tool: Otto's notebook**

```
@tool
def log_evidence(text: str, database_id: str) -> str:
    """
    Write evidence text to a scratchpad to look up later for another SQL query.
    Rejects the request if the database_id is not a known database.

    E.g., "Note to self: The table for countries is called "Country" and not Nation"
like I previously thought"

    Args:
        text: The evidence text to store (e.g., "The foreign key in the 'sales' table
to the customer is called 'buyer_uuid'")
        database_id: The database identifier (e.g., 'formula_1', 'california_schools')

    Returns:
        Acknowledgment message.
    """
    # List of known/allowed database IDs
    known_databases = db_names

    if database_id not in known_databases:
        return f"Error: '{database_id}' is not a known database. Allowed databases: {',
'.join(known_databases)}"

    try:
        # Create a Document object with the evidence text
        doc = Document(
            page_content=text,
            metadata={
                "db_id": database_id,
                "source": "agent_learned_evidence"  # Tag to identify agent-learned
evidence

            }
        )

        # Add the document to the vector store
```

```
        vector_store.add_documents([doc])

        return f"Evidence successfully added to database '{database_id}'. Document
added with content: '{text[:100]}{'...' if len(text) > 100 else ''}'"

    except Exception as e:
        return f"Error adding evidence to vector store: {str(e)}"
```

Figure 4.10 shows the results of the two experiments:

1. In the first experiment, I used an approximately 40% sample of the BIRD benchmark. In the second, I took 10% of the benchmark (a subset of the previous 30%).
2. Using a second dataset, I asked another LLM (GPT-5 in this case) to generate three synthetically rephrased questions for each data point. I used the resulting dataset (close to the same size as simply taking 40% from the original) to test the agent over time.
    a. For example, one of the questions was "Where is Amy Firth's hometown?" The synthetic question came back as "What town does Amy Firth originally come from?" and "In which place did Amy Firth grow up?"

Without similar questions (benchmark as is)

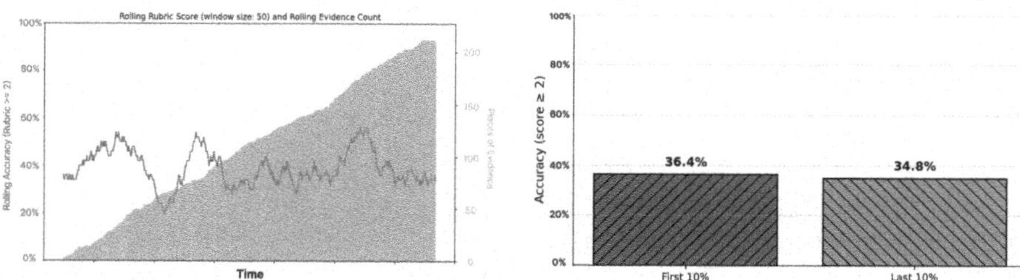

With similar questions synthetically added

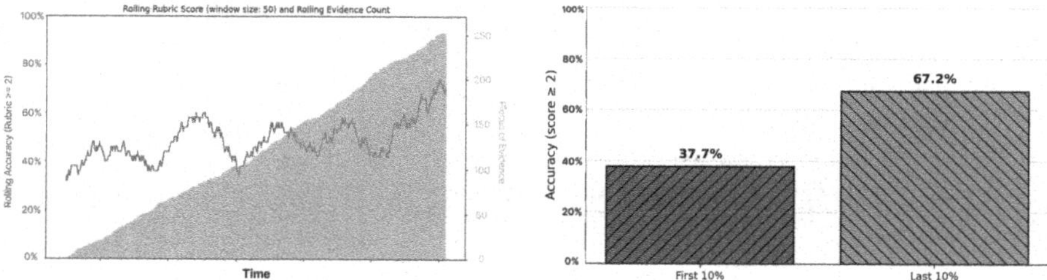

Figure 4.10 With no synthetically similar questions (top), we see no noticeable change in modified accuracy (rubric score ≥ 2). When we added in similar rephrased questions (bottom), suddenly the AI was allowed to rely more on its own written evidence as hints for how to tackle the problem.

I'll highlight a few points about the results:

- Without evidence, both agents started off with a notably worse accuracy than previously reported (approximately 36% here versus 51% in a previous section). This is evidence that the retrieved statements are crucial to the AI agent solving these questions correctly.
- In the case of the BIRD benchmark with no synthetic additions (the top two graphs), the AI agent is writing down information as it goes, but that information isn't useful to it in the future. If anything, this is a positive note for the benchmark itself: It implies that the questions in the benchmark do not overlap too much and are covering a wider span of cases efficiently. Basically, the questions aren't repeating themselves, which is what we want in a test set.
- When we added in the synthetically similar questions (the bottom two graphs), we see a big bump in accuracy over time, from 37.7% to 67.2% accuracy. Now the AI is adding information that becomes useful in the future. This accuracy bump doesn't appear immediately, because it took a while for the AI to write down enough useful information—but it did get there in the end.

  This is also a great jumping-off point for new experiments. For example, what if the AI were asked to "grade" logged evidence and was allowed to edit or delete evidence that didn't end up being useful? What if a second prompt/agent were in charge of retrieving evidence, and the tool our primary agent called was simply a proxy into a workflow that performed a more structured RAG to retrieve evidence? These are all great ideas to try against our test set.
- The number of times the agent decided to log evidence seemed to increase in the dataset with the number of synthetic questions added (as seen in the percentage of conversations using the `log_evidence` tool in Figure 4.11).

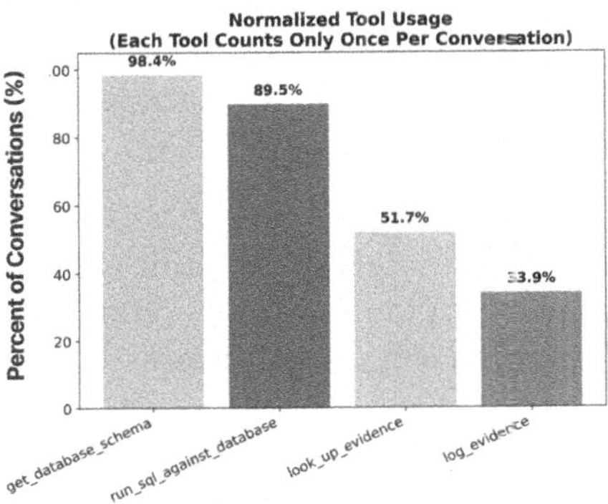

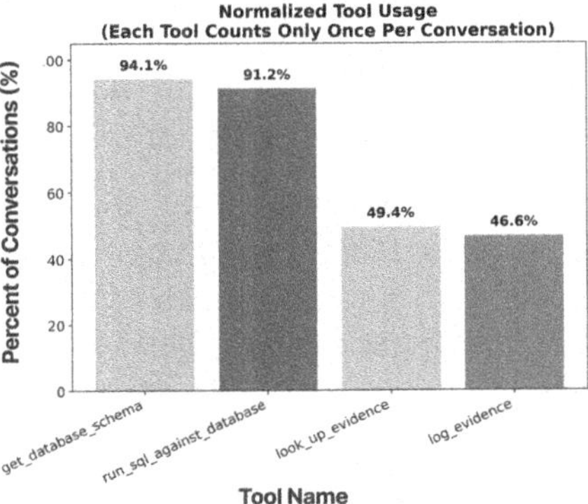

Figure 4.11 "Otto" (the agent with a notebook) called for the database schema fewer times and logged more evidence when the database included a larger number of synthetically similar questions.

Quite honestly, I don't know "why" the last result happened. My theory is that the AI agent noticed when it was looking up evidence that matched a synthetically generated similar question, which encouraged the AI agent to log even more evidence. (Note that in Figure 4.10, the raw number of evidence points added to the database was also higher in the synthetic dataset experiment.)

It's easy to see the differences between workflows and agents in specific use-cases like our SQL/RAG generation task. In general, though, you should take a few considerations into account when deciding whether to go with a workflow or an agent.

When Should You Use Workflows Versus Agents?

So, what's the takeaway from the last case study? Sure, you can just set an agent loose with some tools and let it figure things out for itself, but that's not usually the most efficient (or cheapest) approach. Here's how I would break it down:

- Workflows are the right move when you know the pathway ahead of time and don't expect many unforeseen edge cases. If you have a repeatable task and clear logic, just build the steps directly.
- Workflows require more upfront coding. You'll need to define all the steps, nodes, and edges; handle the branching logic; and think about edge cases yourself. But once it's built, the solution will be efficient.
- Workflows let you bake in efficiency tricks, such as optimizing for the number of examples to use in a few-shot prompt, quality checks, or early exits when a step fails.
- Agents are better at adapting on the fly. If your task isn't always the same, or if you want the system to "figure it out" and possibly learn new shortcuts or solutions, agents can do that. But it might take a while for them to get truly good at it, assuming the system even has the ability to do so (the `log_evidence` tool was created by me, not inherent to the LLM).
- Agents can easily switch between chatting and doing work. Need an AI system that can both explain something to a user and then go run a few database queries? Agents are built for this kind of flexible, multi-step interaction.

Bottom line: If you want pure efficiency and can define the process, go with a workflow. If you want flexibility and potential for the system to "learn" over time (and you're okay with some bumps along the way), let an agent loose with the right tools. When in doubt, *test, test, test!* Develop some hypotheses, set up a testing environment, and experiment to your heart's content.

We are just getting started with agents and our experiments with them. Next, we'll look at a tricky situation: What if we need multiple agents over a period of time to tackle a complex long-term goal?

Case Study 4: A (Nearly) End-to-End SDR

A **sales development representative (SDR)** is a sales professional (usually a human) focused on finding and qualifying potential customers for a company. SDRs are the initial point of contact for leads, engaging with them and determining whether they are a good fit for a product or service. SDRs nurture leads, often passing qualified ones to other sales team members for closing. In this case study, we will attempt to automate as much of this process as possible using real-world systems like Hubspot (a CRM), Resend (an email-sending service), Google (web search), and Firecrawl (a web-crawling API).

Agent 1: Lead Generation

The idea we'll use as a guiding star is to create an agent for each section of the SDR's job. Our first agent's job will be to go on the internet and find potentially good leads. All agents will have a generic prompt indicating how they are part of an SDR function. The lead generation agent is also given a specific prompt, as shown in Prompt 4.1.

PROMPT 4.1 Extra Information in the Lead Generation Agent Prompt

You are a lead generator. I need you to find professors/lecturers at universities who speak English and teach Data Science, ML, AI, etc. Leads you find should potentially be able to use my book in their classes. Find as much information as you can about the classes they teach, their research, and their publications. When you find a suitable lead, you must do the following:

1. Create a HubSpot contact for them to hold their email address.
2. Add a note with as much information as you can about the lead, including where you found their email, links to their research and publications, their personal website, and any other relevant information.
3. Add their email address to the contact.
4. Set their lead status to "New." Follow these steps in order, and do not skip any steps.

Prompt 4.1 gives the agent specific instructions in order and reminds it of things that a human might find obvious, such as following the steps in order and not skipping any. It essentially tells the agent to find people who might use my book (the standard prompt has basic information about my book in it) and record their information in the CRM.

Figure 4.12 visualizes this agent and three of the tools I would want it to potentially have. However, before giving the agent access to tools like web search, web crawling, and contact management in the CRM, we should consider an increasingly popular method for letting agents discover tools—MCP.

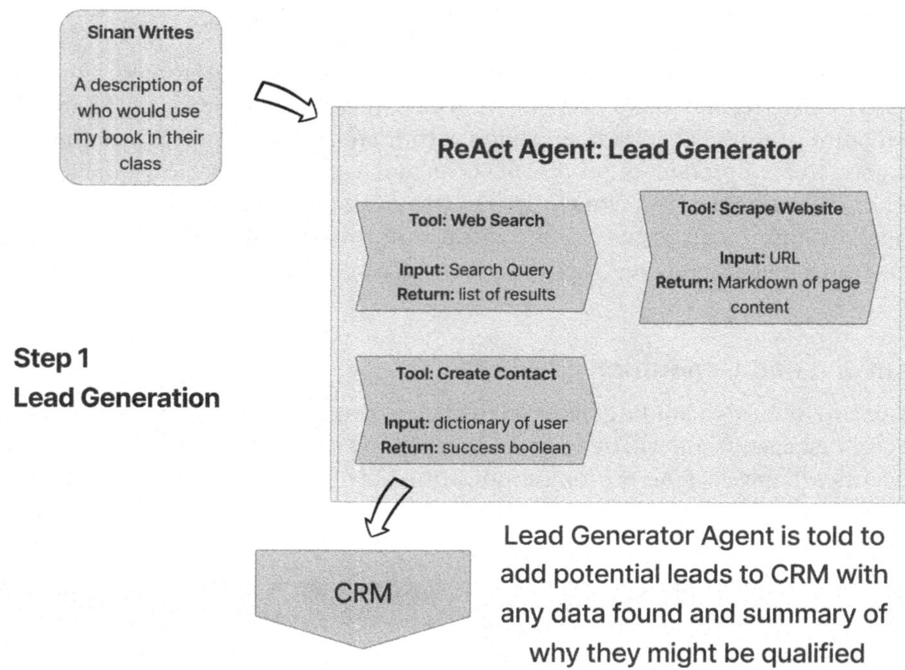

Figure 4.12 The lead generation agent is tasked with finding potentially qualified leads by using simple web crawling and web searching tools alongside tools for updating the CRM.

MCP for Flexible Tool Discovery

In November 2024, Anthropic released the **Model Context Protocol (MCP)** to not much initial fanfare. Anthropic was attempting to standardize the way we introduce tools (and other resources—but mostly tools) to AI models. The idea behind MCP (visualized in Figure 4.13) is actually quite simple: The MCP server is an API server (in Python, JavaScript, or some other language—it doesn't matter) that houses, among other things, definitions for tools and the capacity to execute the tools. The MCP server has API endpoints to list tools, execute tools, and so on. Put another way, MCP is a standardized API format placed in front of the tool definitions and execution code that makes it easier to develop agents across frameworks, programming languages, and businesses.

When an AI agent "wakes up," it reaches out to the MCP servers included in a list that it was given and asks each of those servers which tools it can offer. Each MCP server then tells the agents the names of the functions and the arguments they take. The code to actually execute the code lives on the server, too. Once the AI agent grabs the tool definitions from the server, everything is effectively the same to the LLM—calling tools, writing content, and so on.

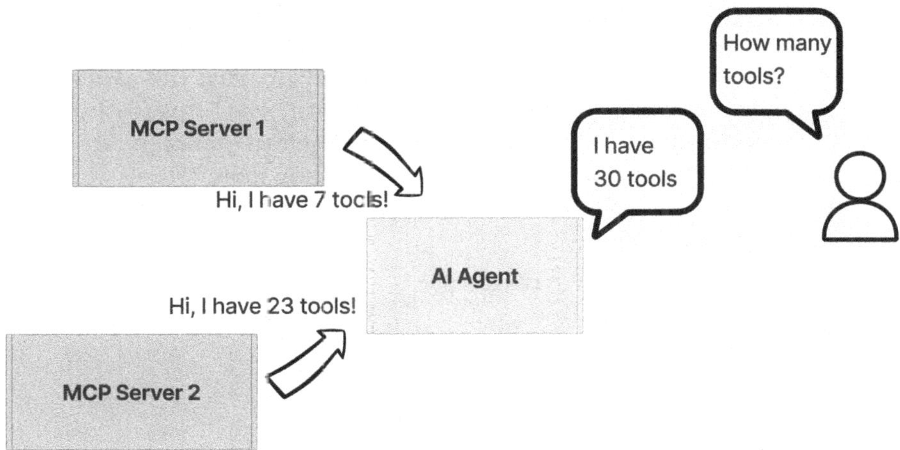

Figure 4.13 An agent is told about one or more MCP servers. On initialization, the agent reaches out to each one and asks which tools it has for it to use. From there, everything is the same as far as the LLM is concerned. It has tools and functions it can decide to call, no matter where they came from.

In summary, MCP is an agreed-upon standard that, if everyone follows it, can facilitate the development of tools for AI systems around the world. A developer in California can write an MCP server for a tool that they made (or didn't!) and put it on GitHub, where a developer in Mumbai can find it and use it. In fact, in this case study, I will write just the first two MCP servers; the third one was created by a third-party team where I had no involvement. I just got to use it for free—how amazing!

There are caveats to MCP, of course. Clearly, tool design and selection are critical, as we saw with our SQL agent. Using the right tool can be efficient and is often a necessary step. Because MCP servers give an AI model access to a set of unknown external tools, however, the challenges will be compounded. The agent will inevitably encounter new tools with descriptions of varying quality. We can mitigate this risk by making sure the descriptions we write for our tools are sufficiently contextful, but even a single bad tool description can send agents down a completely wrong path.

With that warning, let's define our first two MCP servers. These are the MCP servers that I wrote specifically for this case study.

MCP 1: Web Search + Web Crawling

The Python template for creating an MCP server generally has three parts:

- An API route to list the tools available on the server (names, arguments, etc.)
- An API route to accept arguments to execute a tool call
- Logic to call and execute each tool

Listing 4.5 shows an abbreviated code snippet of our first MCP server delivering the ability to Google something (using the Serp API product) and to crawl most websites on the planet (using Firecrawl's web-crawling service as an API to make this easier). Note that we are using the official Python MCP implementation here: https://github.com/modelcontextprotocol/python-sdk. Using this official implementation means that we just have to write the Python functions correlating to listing tools, calling and executing tools, and so on.

Listing 4.5 **Creating the first agent in LangGraph**

```
from mcp.server.models import InitializationOptions
from mcp.server import NotificationOptions, Server
from mcp.types import Tool, TextContent
import mcp.types as types ...

# Import required libraries
from serpapi import GoogleSearch
from firecrawl import FirecrawlApp
# Create server instance
server = Server("research-mcp-server")

def search_with_serpapi(query: str) -> str:
   """Search the web for the query using SerpApi."""
   api_key = os.environ.get("SERP_API_KEY")
   if not api_key:
       return "Error: SERP_API_KEY environment variable is required"

   try:
       search = GoogleSearch({
           "q": query,
           "api_key": api_key,
      ...
      return "\n".join(formatted_results)

   except Exception as e:
       return f"Error performing search: {str(e)}"

def scrape_with_firecrawl(url: str, format_type: str = "markdown") -> str:
   """Scrape a webpage using Firecrawl."""
   api_key = os.environ.get("FIRECRAWL_API_KEY")
   if not api_key:
       return "Error: FIRECRAWL_API_KEY environment variable is required"

   if format_type not in ["markdown", "links"]:
       format_type = "markdown"

   try:
       firecrawl = FirecrawlApp(api_key=api_key)
```

```
        ...
        return response if response else "No content found"

    except Exception as e:
        return f"Error scraping URL: {str(e)}"

@server.list_tools()
async def handle_list_tools() -> List[Tool]:
    """List available research tools """
    tools = []
   tools.append(Tool(
        name="web_search",
        description="Search the web for information using SerpApi. Returns top 3 search
results with titles, snippets, and URLs.",
        inputSchema={
            "type": "object",
                ...
    return tools

@server.call_tool()
async def handle_call_tool(name: str, arguments: Dict[str, Any]) -> List[types.
TextContent]:
    """Handle tool calls for research operations."""

    if name == "web_search":
        query = arguments.get("query")
        if not query:
            return [types.TextContent(type="text", text="Error: Query is required")]
        result = search_with_serpapi(query)
        return [types.TextContent(type="text", text=result)]

    elif name == "scrape_website":
        url = arguments.get("url")
        format_type = arguments.get("format", "markdown")
        result = scrape_with_firecrawl(url, format_type)
        return [types.TextContent(type="text", text=result)]

    else:
        return [types.TextContent(type="text", text=f"Unknown tool: {name}")]

async def main():
    ... code to actually run the server

if __name__ == "__main__":
    asyncio.run(main())
```

That was a lot of code, but don't worry: I won't be showing much more MCP code from here on out (it's all in the book's GitHub). In Listing 4.5, you can see the three main parts there: functions to run each of our two tools, a route to list tools, and a route to accept arguments to execute a tool. With that, we have our first MCP server, giving an AI agent the ability to look things up and visit web pages.

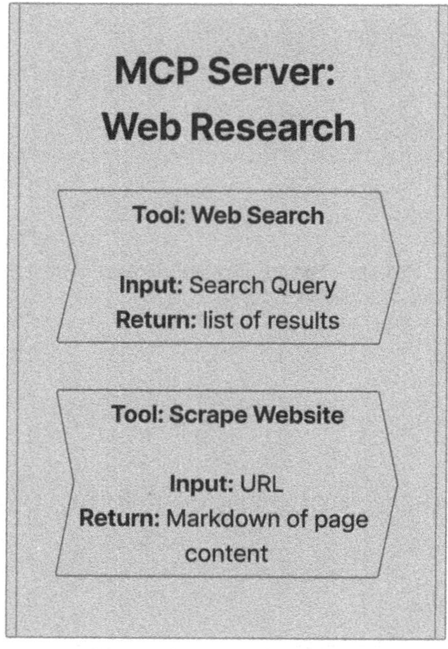

Figure 4.14 Our simple homegrown MCP server has only two tools: web search via the Serp API (Googling something as an API) and web crawling (a service provided by Firecrawl).

Figure 4.14 visualizes our first MCP server with two tools. A lead generation tool will certainly need to look things up and visit web pages. It will also need a system of record to write everything down in.

MCP 2: Hubspot Management

This isn't our first discussion about a system of record for an AI agent. In Chapter 3, we watched an AI system improve at a task over time after we gave it a notepad to write things down in. In this case, we don't really need the agent to get better over time (at least for now), but we should be able to audit what is going on in the CRM. I chose Hubspot for this purpose (feel free to choose a different CRM) mostly because the APIs were easy to pick up. Figure 4.15 shows the five tools I wrote to connect to the Hubspot API:

- **Create contact:** Create a new contact in the CRM.
- **Update contact:** Update an existing contact.
- **Add note to contact:** Add a free text note to a contact.
- **Retrieve notes for contact:** List all notes for a given contact.
- **Fetch contacts:** Use search criteria to grab lists of contacts.

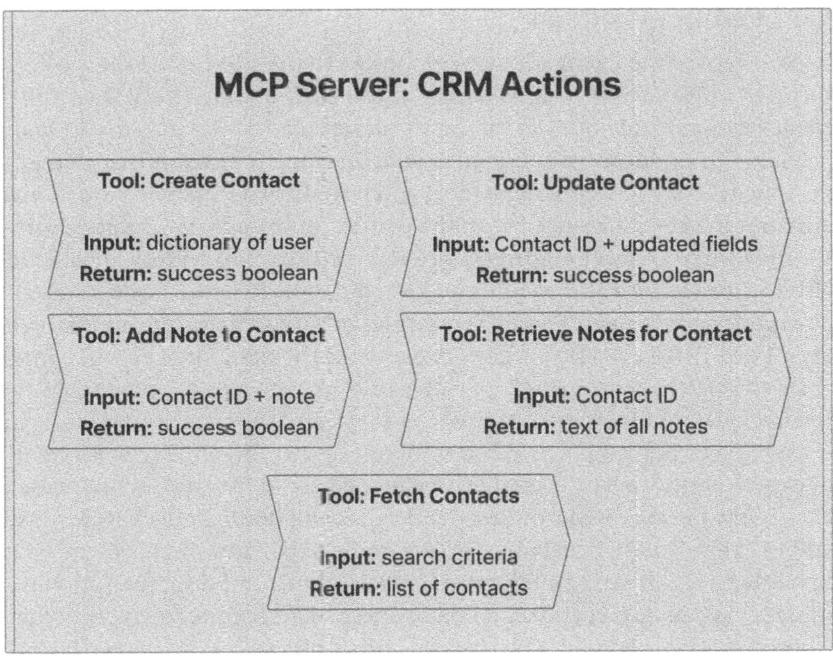

Figure 4.15 Our more complicated homegrown MCP server has five tools for interacting with the CRM so the agents can keep us in the loop about their work.

I did try to find a Hubspot MCP server on the internet, but the few I found either didn't work as written or didn't have the tools I needed (in particular, the ability to create a contact). So, in this case, I asked an AI agent to write an MCP server for me given the first MCP I wrote as an example—and it worked great!

Now we have an agent with seven tools, and Figure 4.16 shows the current state of our lead generator agent. Now, we need to qualify these leads.

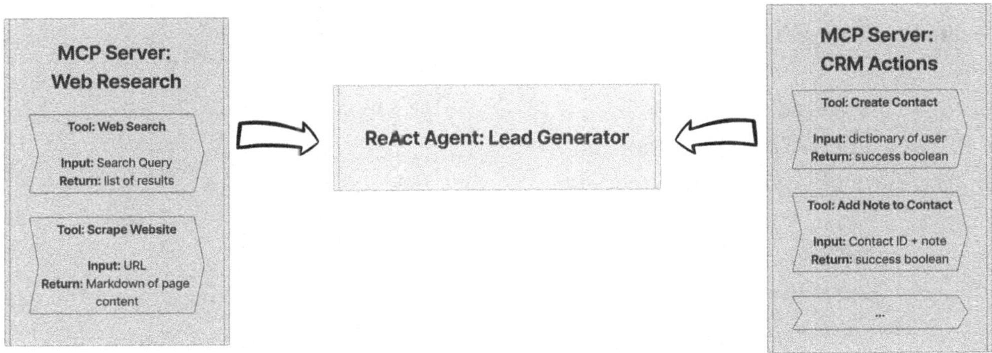

Figure 4.16 The Lead Generator agent gets its seven tools from two MCP servers.

Agent 2: Lead Qualification

Once the lead generation agent adds a new contact to the CRM, the lead qualifying agent (pictured in Figure 4.17) will take over. It will both double-check the work of the lead generation agent and check some more criteria that I added into the special prompt area. At a glance, it might seem as if the lead qualifier agent is redundant given the lead generation agent. They have the same tools and basically the same goal (to identify qualified leads), but the key difference lies in the context of the agent. Chapter 7 formally dives into the idea of **context engineering**—the concept of providing an AI model or agent with the necessary information, context, and tools to perform a task effectively.

The lead generator is given a small set of rules by which to judge candidates and is asked to pull potential leads from the wide world of the open internet. In contrast, the qualifier agent is given both a single person's information and a longer set of requirements to check before moving on to the next stage. In other words, the lead generator has the easier job of pointing a finger at someone and saying, "They seem right"—a task that can be performed by a smaller, cheaper, faster LLM. The cost of a false positive in this case is low because we know a second agent will double-check its results. The lead qualifier agent should be a larger, slower, more expensive LLM because its job is arguably harder: It must go through several pieces of information; read and understand the candidate's syllabus, CV, and other data; and make the final judgment whether the person should receive an email. The cost of a false positive is high here, because I don't want to bother people who aren't good fits for my book.

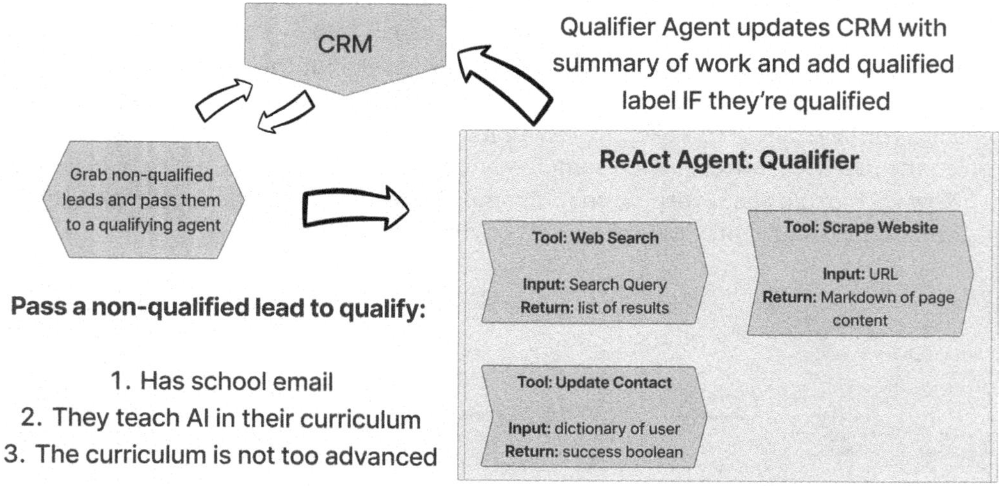

Figure 4.17 Our lead qualifying agent will have the same tools as the lead generation agent. It will double-check the lead generator's work while also doing more research.

Like the lead generation agent, the qualifying agent will have some extra information in its system prompt. A snippet of this information can be seen in Prompt 4.2.

PROMPT 4.2 Extra Information in the Lead Qualification Agent Prompt

> You are a lead qualifying agent. For a given lead, use the tools provided to make sure that this lead is a good fit for using my book in their classes. If they are a good fit, update the contact to have a lead status of "Open." If they are not a good fit, update the contact to have a lead status of "Unqualified."
>
> Below is a list of qualities that the person must match before marking them as "qualified":
>
> 1. They must be teaching in an accredited university or college setting.
> 2. A recent syllabus for a class they currently teach must reference large language models (LLMs) in some capacity.
>
> ...

Figure 4.18 shows that this agent will have the same MCP server access as the lead generation agent. In some cases, it might need to double-check some information online and update information/notes.

At this point, the lead generator has pulled in some leads, and the lead qualifier has double-checked the information and marked the lead as qualifying. Now it's time for a third agent to take over and send the initial cold email.

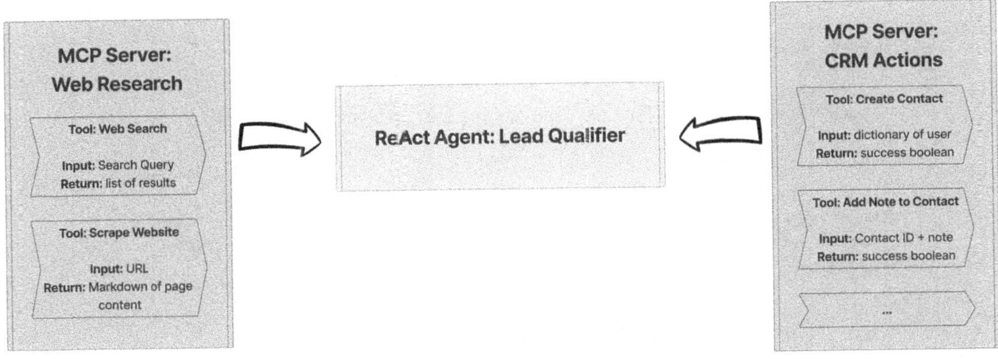

Figure 4.18 Our lead qualifier has the same MCP servers as the lead generator. Its job is to do deeper research on the leads and make sure they are good candidates.

Agent 3: Lead Emailing

The lead emailing agent (Figure 4.19) involves more than just a system prompt change, with a single-shot example (recall from Chapter 1 that a *k*-shot/few-shot prompt means I am placing in-context examples in the prompt to guide the AI) showing how I want the email to roughly sound (as seen in Prompt 4.3). The format of the email in the single-shot email is not as important here because we expect the agent to use a tool via MCP with structured inputs. What's more important is the fact that it writes HTML-encoded emails and subject lines and sends them to the right tool.

PROMPT 4.3 Extra Information in the Lead Emailing Agent Prompt

You are in charge of sending an initial outreach email to a lead. Use the tools provided to look up the information gathered by the other agents, and send an email to the lead with a personalized message. The email should be sent to the lead's email address. When you are done, update the contact to have a lead status of "Connected" so we know that you have sent the email. Here is a sample email:

Subject: "Curious If 'Quick Start Guide to LLMs' Could Be a Fit for Your Course?"

HTML Body: <p>Hi [Name / Dr.]!</p><p>My name is Sinan Ozdemir. I'm an AI author, educator, and the . . .

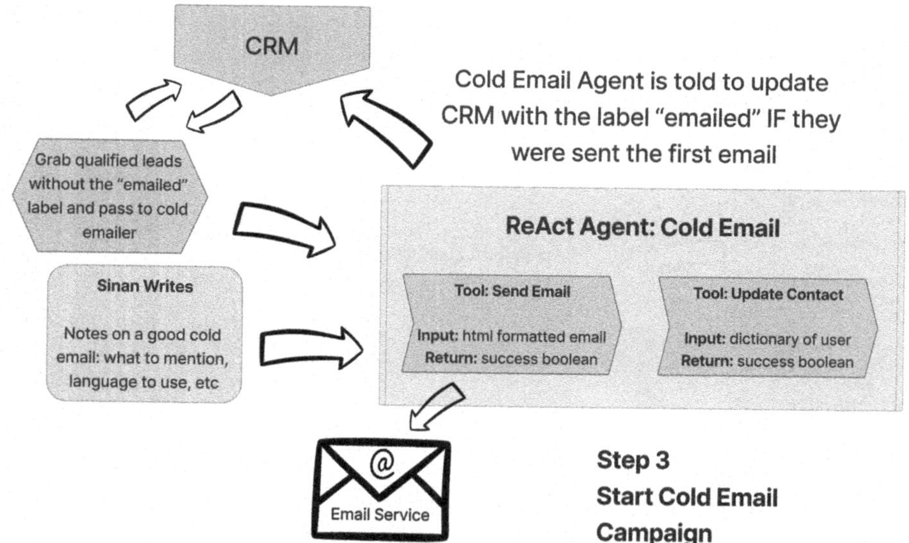

Figure 4.19 The lead emailing agent needs to update the CRM, but also requires new capabilities to email leads on my behalf.

A quick note on Agent 3: A decent argument can be made for making this final agent a workflow. For one thing, Agent 3 isn't given much agency. We know the lead is qualified given the previous two agents' work, and all this agent has to do is write the email and call a few APIs in order—that sounds like a predefined pathway. The reason I wanted to make this a true agent over a workflow was simple: I assume this task is easy enough that a system prompt with clear instructions is enough for the agent to follow my instructions clearly. In Chapter 5, we will start to put some of these assumptions to the test. For now, by choosing an agent over a workflow, we are effectively saying either "This task requires the agent to make decisions on the fly that are too complicated/near impossible to code in a predefined pathway" or "This task is easy and straightforward enough that we can save development cycles by simply attaching preexisting MCP servers to an LLM with proper context."

Assuming this job is left up to an agent and not a workflow, this agent will need a way to send emails. MCP comes to the rescue once more.

MCP 3: Resend for Email

If you're not familiar with it, Resend is a developer-friendly email platform with APIs to simplify sending emails at scale. What's even cooler is that it has an official MCP server on its GitHub. Granted, at the time of writing there is just a single tool on that MCP server, but it's the tool I most care about: send-email. I could write my own MCP server for Resend, just as I did with the CRM. However, I want to showcase that our system is agnostic regarding who writes MCP servers and in which language the code launches the official Resend MCP server (written in Typescript, not Python). Our agent will be able to use both it and our homegrown Pythonic MCP servers.

Figure 4.20 shows the topline view of our third agent. The web research MCP has been replaced (because in theory it won't be needed because of the past two agents' work) with our new MCP server, and it is ready to send emails.

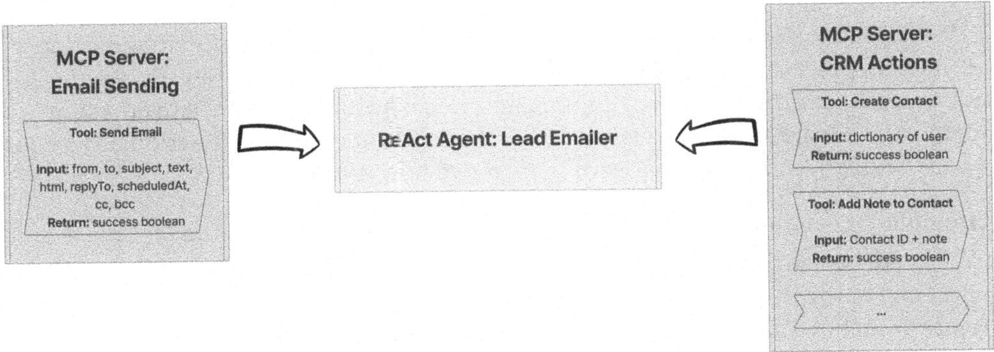

Figure 4.20 Our final MCP server has a single tool and was developed by the same team that created the email sending service Resend.

When to Use a Multi-Agent Versus a Single Agent

Why didn't we just create a single agent with an elongated set of instructions to walk through the whole process of generation, qualifying, and emailing? Certainly, we could have: We could just make that agent wake up and attempt to find and email a new lead. In theory, we could spin up a hundred of them, giving each a different location and industry to focus on.

I chose a multi-agent system in this case study for the following reasons:

- To reduce potential errors in which the agent emailed someone before qualifying them and adding notes to the CRM. In other words, what if the agent "forgets a step" along the way?
- To minimize overlap in duties. What if two agents that aren't talking to each other or are in some race condition end up trying to email the same person at the same time? That lead would not appreciate the double email and would probably be lost.
- To leave room for experimenting with different flavors of LLMs (including LLMs fine-tuned for specific tasks) for each of the different tasks. Maybe GPT-5 is slower but better at emailing, whereas Llama 4-Scout is optimal for quicker lead generation.

It's absolutely true that these tasks *could* be handled by a single agent, but by splitting them up, I gain more control over specific aspects of the funnel. This way, if qualifying is going poorly but everything else is okay, I can tweak and experiment on qualification alone without too much risk to the other portions of the pipeline. With a single agent, every prompt change risks a regression in another area. For this reason, a fair analogy to multi-agent systems would be a micro-service architecture. A change to a single service can be done in much more isolation as long as we are aware of how that single service (agent) fits into the larger picture.

We have now designed and coded three agents, each handling a different portion of the sales process (Figure 4.21). However, we lack a mechanism to test this engine or to keep it running, constantly finding new leads, qualifying them, and emailing them. We will tackle the latter issue in Chapter 5. To gut check the functionality of our agents, though, we should chat with them to see how they do.

Streamlit for Ad-Hoc Testing of the Three Agents

In the codebase for the multi-agent system, I created a visual interface where you can select one of the three agents and chat with it, asking it to perform tasks on demand. Figure 4.22 shows an example in which I asked an agent to list contacts in the CRM and it did so correctly (displaying the two fake contacts Hubspot created during account creation).

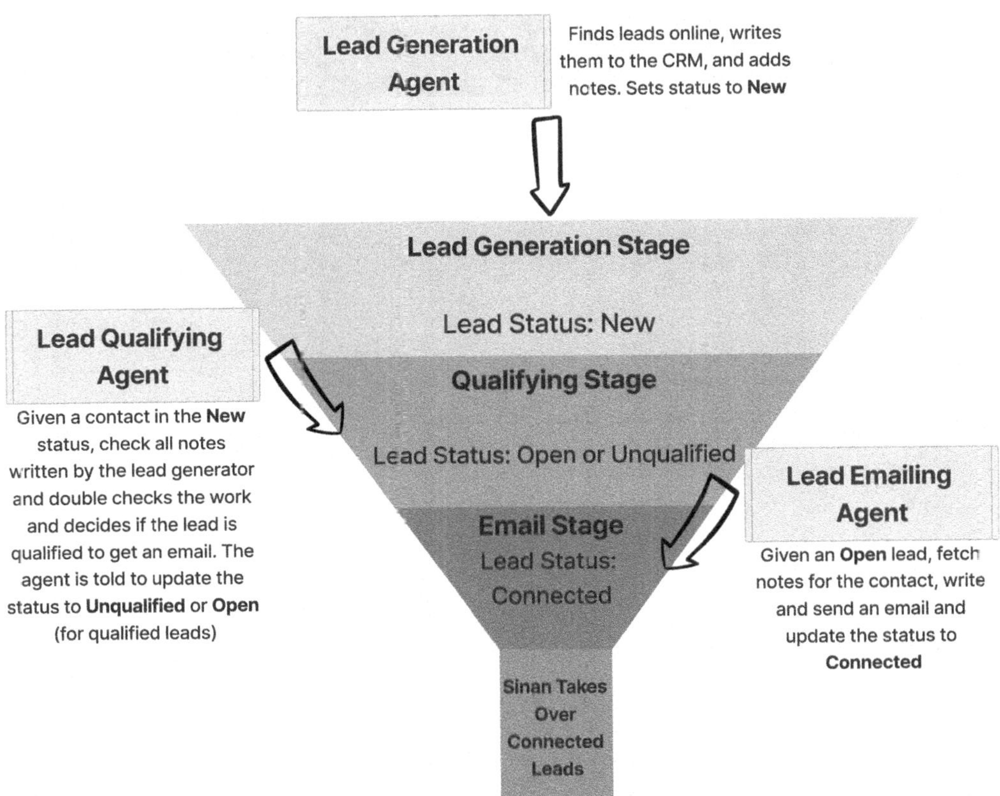

Figure 4.21 The 10,000-foot view of our multi-agent task delegation. The lead generator will fill the top of the funnel, the qualifying agent will get enough information to be able to email qualified leads, and the emailing agent will send off that first cold email on my behalf.

When I asked the lead generation agent to find a contact at a specific business school, it did. (This example isn't shown here because it would invade that person's privacy.) When I asked the qualifying agent to run on that contact, it changed the status and added a note to confirm the contact's qualification. When I asked the email sending agent to send an email, it did; it then changed the contact's status again, as expected.

At this point, I'm satisfied with the agents' individual performances from basic ad-hoc testing. However, if we are to trust this system at scale, we need to consider a few more factors.

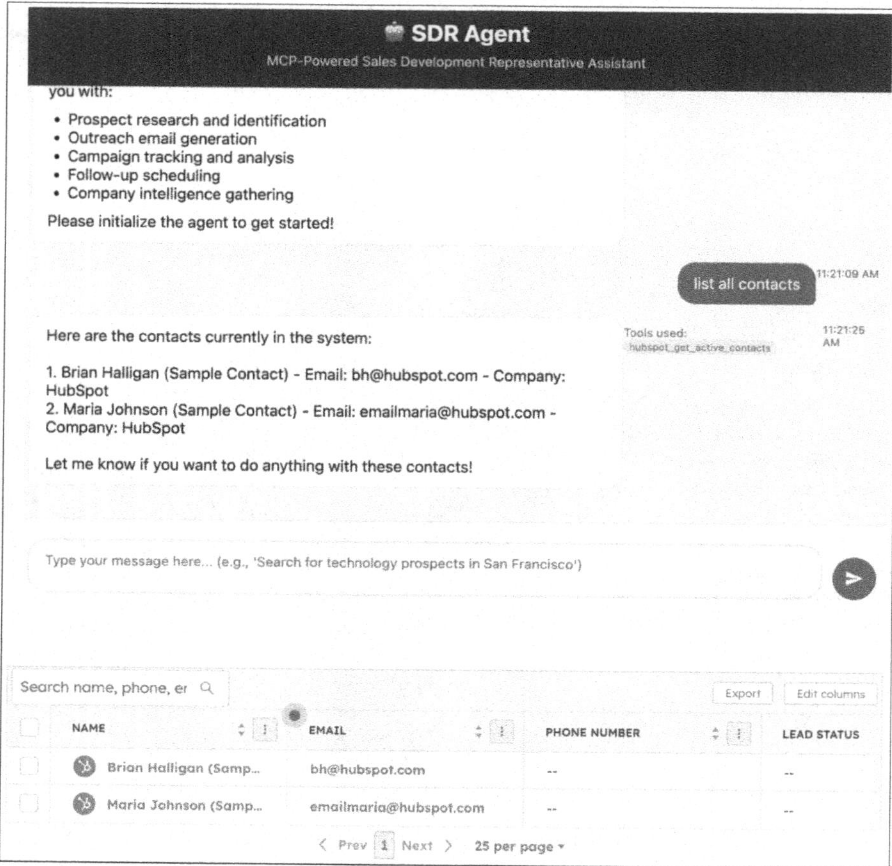

Figure 4.22 A Streamlit app (found in the book's GitHub) showing basic capabilities of the agents for interacting with the CRM.

Evaluating Agents

We've already discussed ways to evaluate agents, including latency, cost, and memory considerations, and especially in comparison to rigid workflows. Figure 4.23 breaks down even more ways to consider evaluating agents in four main categories:

- **System:** Focused on the "behind the scenes" functionality of an agent (e.g., the tool latency, the LLM provider error rate).
- **Quality assurance:** Judging the LLM's ability to adhere to instructions and follow a specific output format. The quality of that output falls into this category as well.

- **Tool interaction:** Specifically zooming in on the agent's tool-calling ability, including whether the agent is calling the right tools for the right tasks and whether it passed the right arguments into the tool.
- **Agent efficiency:** Dependent on the tool interaction and system results to a degree. This category is concerned with questions like how many steps the agent took to come up with the answer, how many tokens it took, and how much it cost.
  - For example, an agent that provides 1,000 tokens of reasoning just to call a single tool could be slower and more expensive than an agent that calls five tools with no thinking in between, even though the latter would be considered "tool inefficient" compared to the former's "token inefficiency."

System Metrics	QA Metrics	Tool Interaction Metrics	Agent Efficiency Metrics
• Tool Latency (seconds per tool call) • Tool Error Rate • Cost per Task • LLM Error Rate	• Instruction Adherence (did you follow a given plan?) • Output Format Success Rate (Did asking for JSON yield a JSON?) • User Context Adherence (E.g. Did you use the fact that the user speaks only Turkish?)	• Tool Selection Accuracy (Did you select google when you were "supposed" to?) ◦ This might include the tool of "passing off to another agent" • Tool Argument Accuracy (Did you google the right thing?)	• Steps per Task (especially if ReAct) • Task Completion Rate • Token Efficiency (generally # of tokens per task/step) • Task Completion Time (total seconds)

Figure 4.23 There are dozens, if not hundreds, of metrics we can use to measure the efficacy of agents and multi-agent systems, ranging from low-level tool-based metrics to holistic rubric-based accuracy.

We can also rely on third-party tooling (no pun intended) to help us audit and look back on our agents' past work.

LangSmith for Traceability

Even if all we need is a way to audit our agents, there's no reason to reinvent the wheel. **LangSmith** (brought to us by the same people who developed LangGraph) is a tracing and observability tool that is purpose-built for LLM workflows. It can track the step-by-step execution of both workflows and agents. LangSmith provides a live dashboard showing every input, output, and tool call, which makes debugging and long-term monitoring a breeze. It also give us the ability to audit past work. There are dozens (at least) of platforms offering observability, evaluations, and more, but LangSmith is free to get started with, simple to set up, and provides immediate value out of the gate. I generally recommend starting with LangSmith even if you are still evaluating other platforms, as it provides an excellent baseline for bare-bones features you should expect from other platforms.

Getting started with LangSmith is a very simple process. All we need to do is set a few environment variables in whatever deployment we are using (even a code notebook), and the SDK will automatically trace everything (see Listing 4.6). We can even split traces by project or use the built-in UI to review results across experiments.

Listing 4.6 **Setting LangSmith keys in the agent environment**

```
- LANGSMITH_API_KEY="XXX"
- LANGSMITH_TRACING=true
- LANGSMITH_ENDPOINT="https://api.smith.langchain.com"
- LANGSMITH_API_KEY="XXX"
- LANGSMITH_PROJECT="ai-agent"
```

Once the environment variables are set, every agent run (including tool calls, LLM generations, and custom functions) will be recorded in a LangSmith dashboard. This lets us dig into failed runs, analyze tool usage, and share and trace URLs for easier debugging and collaboration. Figure 4.24 shows what an agent trace looks like in the LangSmith user interface.

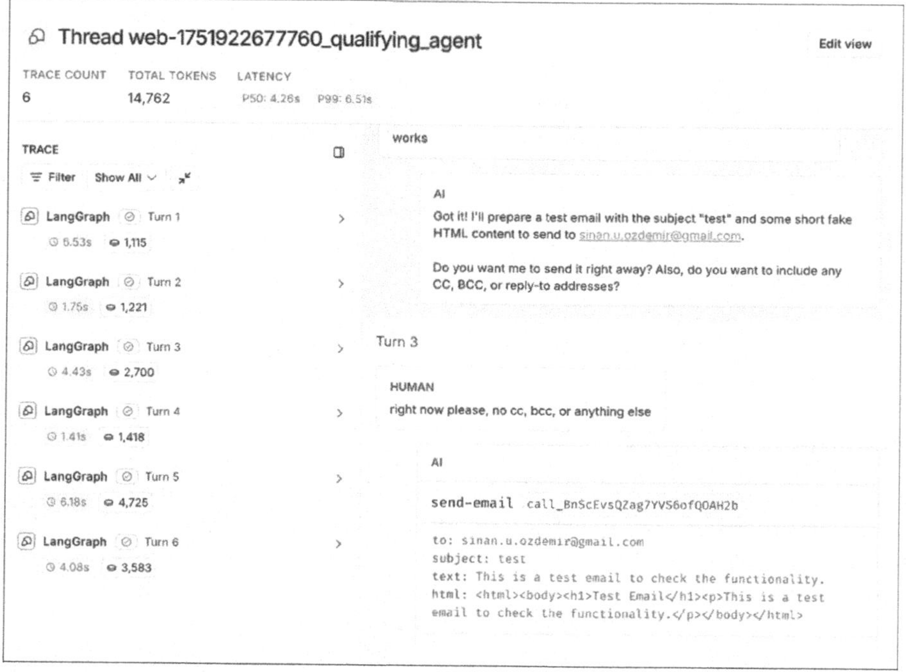

Figure 4.24 An agent trace in the LangSmith dashboard, highlighting each tool call and LLM step. LangSmith offers an easy way to get auditable logs by adding only a few environment variables to the AI system.

In the next few chapters, we will continue to evaluate agents based on the specific work they're asked to do. But for now, let's wrap up this Agents 101 discussion with a recap.

Conclusion

The leap from workflows to agents to multi-agent systems can unlock a whole new set of capabilities for AI applications. Workflows are great choices when you want efficiency, predictability, and full control. Agents bring adaptability, flexibility, and a little bit of creative chaos, which can be a wonderful thing in some cases.

In this chapter, we broke down not just how to build these systems, but also how to evaluate them using both human-driven rubrics and automated tools like LangSmith for traceability and auditability. Although agents can sometimes cost more and take longer, they also offer room for learning, collaboration, and improvement over time. That is especially the case when the agent is given the ability to write, recall, and share evidence with itself (recall our "Otto" example) or with other agents (as in the SDR framework).

Bottom line: There's no single "best" approach to developing systems with AI agents. The right choice depends on your use-case, your tolerance for ambiguity, and how much control you want versus how much flexibility you need. Try both approaches. Experiment, evaluate, and build a system that works for you, and don't be afraid to combine the best parts of each.

In Chapter 5, we'll do just that. We'll create agentic/workflow hybrids and then take these ideas even further, exploring long-running, multi-agent workflows that can handle complex, evolving tasks over time. See you there!

5

Enhancing Agents with Prompting, Workflows, and More Agents

Introduction

In Chapter 4, we went deep on what it takes to turn a rigid structured LLM workflow into an agent and why you might want to mix the two. But to be honest, getting agents to "just work" in production is rarely about picking the right framework, crafting the right tool description or MCP server, or cranking out more code. The magic lies in how you shape agents' behavior by using prompting, smarter workflows, and (sometimes) even more agents to split up the work.

In this chapter, we'll zoom in on what moves the needle when you want agents to reliably follow rules, align with real-world policies, or just stop making up answers. We'll see how prompt engineering and clever context retrieval can turn a generic LLM into a policy-following pro, and why some classic keyword matching techniques are still wildly useful and efficient in modern times for grounding agents with actual documentation.

Along the way, we'll build a synthetic policy compliance dataset (thank you to Airbnb for hopefully being okay with me borrowing its FAQs), wire up keyword-based retrieval for agent context, and see just how impactful a single sentence in an agent prompt can be. And because nothing is as simple as it sounds, we'll look at why even good prompts can fall on their faces, and how discursive reasoning, planning, and reflection can help agents handle bigger, messier tasks.

Bottom line: You'll leave this chapter with hands-on recipes for making your agents sharper, more honest, and (slightly) less likely to get you sued by ignoring the rules. Let's get into it with a brand-new case study: teaching AI to follow policy guidelines.

Case Study 5: Agents Complying with Policies Plus Synthetic Data Generation

Perhaps the most popular application of AI agents today is providing front-line support for users looking to get their questions and problems answered from a set of static information or a knowledge base. Almost every customer support bot falls into this category—for example, those answering questions based on prewritten FAQs about a product or a service. This case study will focus on that application: building an agent that can reliably use the given context to answer questions.

If this also sounds like RAG, well, it technically is. Like our SQL agent, we will give an agent a database of information to query and we will judge the AI on the answers it provides. This time, though, the evaluation will be a bit trickier. Unlike with the BIRD benchmark, we won't have a simple ground-truth answer given to us. Instead, we will start where many people start—with a set of unstructured documents.

Creating a Test Set for Policy Compliance

Figure 5.1 shows a 10,000-foot view of what we are going to build: a ReAct agent built to answer questions for users equipped with a single tool. This tool queries a database of information to find context to answer the users' questions. It will be a standard ReAct agent, just like the ones we've seen using standard tool definitions and tool-calling LLMs.

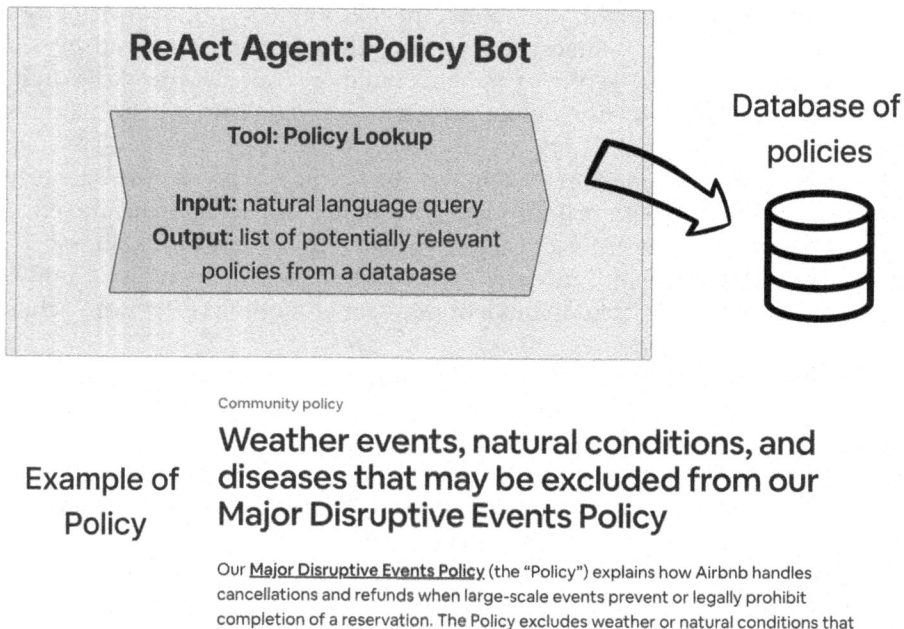

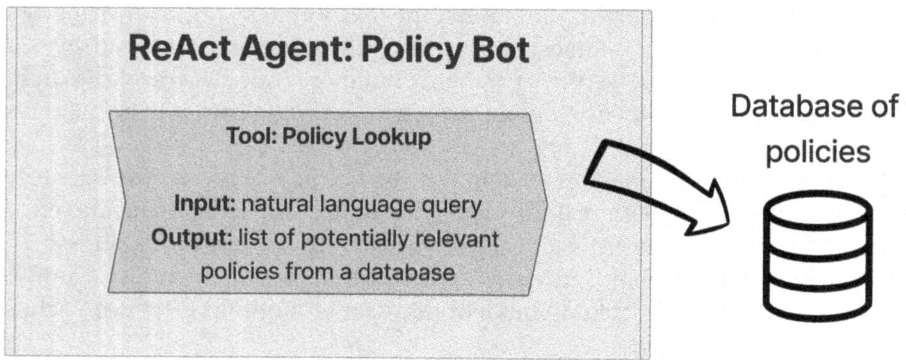
ReAct Agent: Policy Bot
Tool: Policy Lookup
Input: natural language query
Output: list of potentially relevant policies from a database
Database of policies

Example of Policy
Community policy
Weather events, natural conditions, and diseases that may be excluded from our Major Disruptive Events Policy
Our Major Disruptive Events Policy (the "Policy") explains how Airbnb handles cancellations and refunds when large-scale events prevent or legally prohibit completion of a reservation. The Policy excludes weather or natural conditions that

Figure 5.1 Our new agent will be tasked with helping users with scenarios that can be answered by policy documents. (Credit: Airbnb, Inc. "Weather Events, Natural Conditions, and Diseases that May Be Excluded from Our Major Disruptive Events Policy." Airbnb Help Center, article 2930, www.airbnb.com/help/article/2930.)

So, where will our data and questions come from this time if we're not using a structured benchmark like BIRD? To properly build and test this system, I need two things:

1. A reliable source of text-based documentation covering a wide variety of scenarios and situations. I chose to crawl over a thousand policy documents from Airbnb, the global hospitality company.
2. For each document, at least one fictitious but viable scenario whose solution can be resolved using information from that document. I will ask an LLM to generate these synthetically for me.

Let's start with the first need—the policy documents from Airbnb. Listing 5.1 shows a snippet of the code I wrote to grab the raw, barely filtered text from over a thousand help articles.

Listing 5.1 **Borrowing Airbnb's policies to generate a synthetic dataset**

```
from parsing.parse import recursive_scrape  # a function I made to scrape a
website and links on the page recursively
from tqdm import tqdm
import pandas as pd

urls = [
   'https://www.airbnb.com'  # Airbnb's website
]

depth, max_links_per_page = 5, 10
max_possible_articles = sum([max_links_per_page**d for d in range(0, depth+1)])
print(f"Maximum total number of articles possible (theoretical, with max_
  depth={depth}, max_links_per_page={max_links_per_page}): {max_possible_articles}")
```

Now that we have the article URLs and text, we are done with step 1. Next, we need to generate scenarios and solutions for each document. For this purpose, I wrote a prompt (which you can find in the book's GitHub under the policy bot section) to ask an LLM to generate these situations for us.

Figure 5.2 shows a single example of a synthetic situation and solution that GPT-4.1 generated, and Figure 5.3 shows the dataset after I uploaded it to HuggingFace with the 1,041 situation/solution pairs generated. When selecting an LLM to create synthetic data, I recommend using an LLM in the upper tiers in terms of cost and performance. Unlike the grading LLM, which functioned off a rubric, the creation of synthetic data is a more complicated task and requires a more competent LLM that can understand both nuance and cohesiveness. This dataset will also be more permanent, in that we will want to use it for several experiments, including a fine-tuning run in Chapter 8. Because the output synthetic data will be so crucial in several experiments, a higher-tier LLM is in order. I also took the time to split the 1,041 examples into "train" and "test" sets: In future chapters, we will use this dataset to fine-tune embedding models and generative LLMs to compare against our current policy bot.

Community policy

Weather events, natural conditions, and diseases that may be excluded from our Major Disruptive Events Policy

Our Major Disruptive Events Policy (the "Policy") explains how Airbnb handles cancellations and refunds when large-scale events prevent or legally prohibit completion of a reservation. The Policy excludes weather or natural conditions that

Synthetic Situation (from GPT 4.1)
A guest books an Airbnb in Miami, Florida for early September. A tropical storm is forecast to make landfall during their stay. The guest wants to cancel and receive a full refund under Airbnb's Major Disruptive Events Policy, citing the imminent storm.

Synthetic Solution (from GPT 4.1)
According to the article, tropical storms and hurricanes in Florida during June through November are considered common and foreseeable weather events, and are therefore excluded from Airbnb's Major Disruptive Events Policy...

Figure 5.2 A synthetic scenario and solution from the help article from www.airbnb.com/help/article/2930 as generated by GPT-4.1 from a dataset of policy documents. (Credit: Airbnb, Inc. "Weather Events, Natural Conditions, and Diseases that May Be Excluded from Our Major Disruptive Events Policy." Airbnb Help Center, article 2930.)

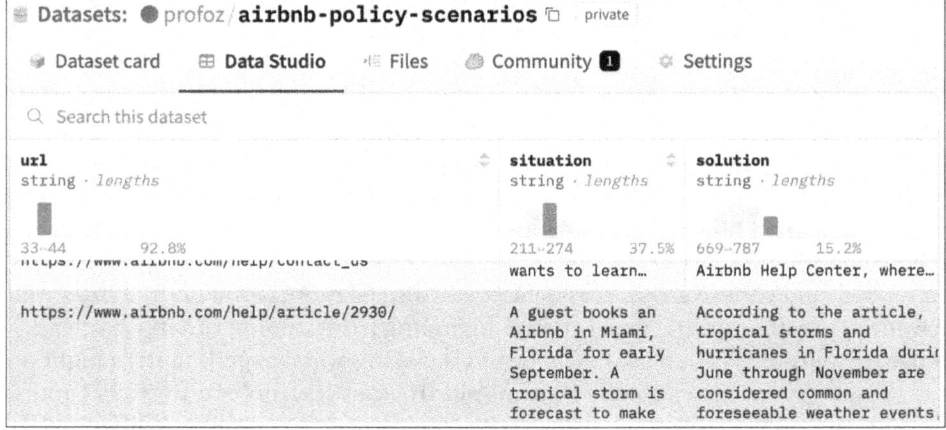

Figure 5.3 The dataset I synthetically generated can be found on my HuggingFace account.

Our dataset is now ready to go. I took the time to spot-check about 5% of the data and spotted no anomalies. The situations matched the policy; I could clearly trace content from the synthetic solution back to the original document; and everything seemed in order. That being said, I didn't read every single situation, and I will always accept any feedback and comments on the public dataset on HuggingFace or on the GitHub for this book! Let's build our agent.

Building Our Policy Bot Agent

As mentioned earlier, building our ReAct agent doesn't involve any complicated maneuvers. We will give it memory using the checkpointer attribute, a single tool to query a database of the policies we grabbed in the last section, and that's about it. I will also make one change to the database to showcase another way to think about information retrieval.

BM25: Keeping It Old School

Sometimes you don't need the latest AI breakthrough, such as an amazing embedding model and vector database, when a classic like BM25 still packs a punch. **BM25** (Best Matching 25) is a top-tier algorithm in the realm of "keyword search" algorithms and has been powering search engines and document retrieval systems for decades. Before Transformer models became available, many companies ranked documents using this algorithm, and it's still useful for scenarios where we want agents to quickly sift through large sets of policies, FAQs, or help documents and keyword matching can be enough.

At its core, BM25 is similar to TF-IDF (term frequency inverse document frequency). Both are ranking functions that score how relevant each document is to a user's query by counting the number of phrases they have in common and correcting for overly long documents (so as to not show a bias for longer documents with more statistical chances for overlapping phrases). It doesn't care about word meaning or context; it just looks at how many times query terms show up in each document, how rare those terms are across all documents, and how long each document is (so longer documents don't always win by default).

BM25 assigns each document a relevance score for a given query using three main inputs:

- **Term frequency (TF):** How often the query word appears in the document (but with diminishing returns, so it's not just about word count).
- **Inverse document frequency (IDF):** How rare the word is across all documents (rare words get more weight).
- **Document length normalization:** Short documents aren't unfairly penalized, and long documents aren't unfairly rewarded.

If you look up the formula for BM25, you will find different variations of the calculations with different coefficients. To keep things actionable, Python libraries like rank_bm25 can handle all the math for us; they offer default configurations that are known to work well in general. We will just need to index our documents, run a query, and get back a ranked list. Listing 5.2 shows an implementation of BM25. As homework, I encourage you to explore the different configurations of BM25 to see how they affect retrieval rankings, similar to how we compared embeddings in Chapter 3.

Listing 5.2 **A simple implementation of BM25 using** `rank_bm25`

```
from rank_bm25 import BM25Okapi
...
class BM25:
   """BM25 document ranking using rank_bm25 package"""

   def __init__(self, documents: List[str], k1: float = 1.2, b: float = 0.75):
       self.k1 = k1
       self.b = b
       self.documents = documents
       self.tokenized_docs = [self._tokenize(doc) for doc in documents]
       self.bm25 = BM25Okapi(self.tokenized_docs, k1=self.k1, b=self.b)

   def _tokenize(self, text: str) -> List[str]:
       """Simple tokenization"""
       return re.findall(r'\b\w+\b', text.lower())

   def search(self, query: str, top_k: int = 5) -> List[tuple]:
       """Search for relevant documents using BM25"""
       query_words = self._tokenize(query.lower())
       scores = self.bm25.get_scores(query_words)
       top_indices = sorted(range(len(scores)), key=lambda i: scores[i], reverse=True)
[:top_k]
       return [(i, scores[i], self.documents[i]) for i in top_indices]

# Example documents
docs = [
   "This is a simple apple pie recipe for beginners.",
   "How to grow apple trees in your backyard.",
   "Try this pie crust recipe for a flaky dessert."
]

query = "apple pie recipe"
for rank, (i, score, doc) in enumerate(BM25(docs).search(query, top_k=3), 1):
   print(f"Rank {rank} | DOC {i+1} | Score: {score:.2f}")
   print(f"Text: {doc}\n")
```

```
Rank 1 | DOC 1 | Score: 0.15
Text: This is a simple apple pie recipe for beginners.

Rank 2 | DOC 3 | Score: 0.10
Text: Try this pie crust recipe for a flaky dessert.

Rank 3 | DOC 2 | Score: 0.05
Text: How to grow apple trees in your backyard.
```

Replacing embedding similarity matching via cosine similarity with BM25 will both give us the benefit of retrieval speed and, as in many domains, can fill in gaps related to industry jargon that embedding models aren't amazing at. We should note that this would be a great opportunity for a test: BM25 versus several embedding models versus a hybrid approach between the two. Given that we already covered a retrieval experiment in Chapter 3, I will leave this experiment in your capable hands as homework. In a later chapter, we will address the latter issue by fine-tuning embedding models for industry-specific tasks; for now, BM25 will fill this gap for us.

Figure 5.4 illustrates the process so far as well as our next step:

1. We created a synthetic dataset using policies found online and an LLM to generate fictitious but viable scenarios and solutions based on policies.
2. We created an AI agent using a database of policies. A very simple system prompt gives the agent basic core guidelines to stay helpful, friendly, and so forth.

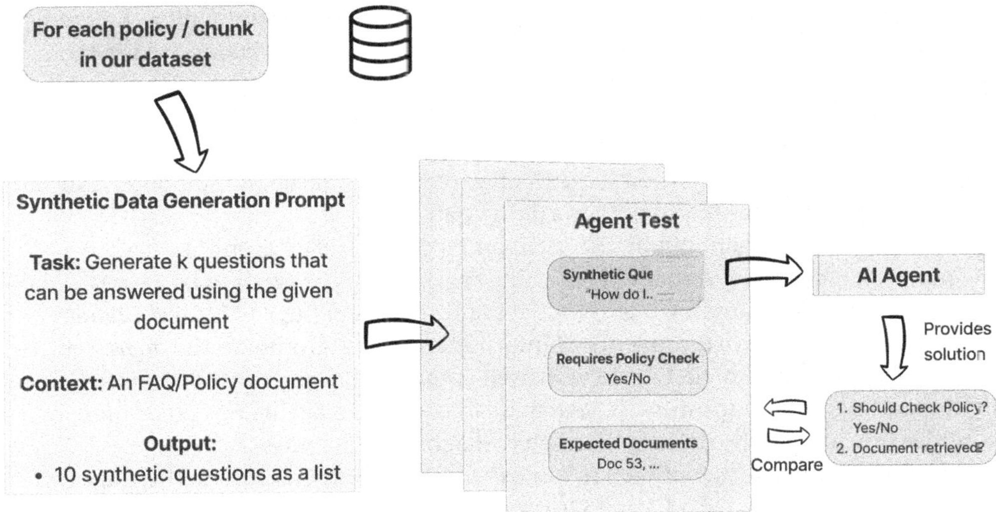

Figure 5.4 Testing our policy bot required both synthetically generating a test dataset and testing our agent against that test dataset.

Our next step is to set up experiments to explore how altering the prompt and context for our agents might change the performance and effectiveness of the entire system.

Prompt Engineering Agents

We will test three agent variants across two different LLMs. For each LLM, the three variants of agents will be:

- Agent Variant 1 codename `no_db_agent`: ReAct agent with no database and no tools. (Basically, this is just an LLM with a goal but no way to get grounded context. When the tools are removed, you could even argue this is no longer even an agent, just ALWAYS USE LLM-driven chatbot with a prompt.)
- Agent Variant 2 codename `db_agent_no_prompt`: ReAct agent with a tool to query the database of context using BM25 for keyword retrieval.
- Agent Variant 3 codename `db_agent_with_prompt`: Same as Agent Variant 2 but has a single extra sentence in the system prompt, as seen in Prompt 5.1.

PROMPT 5.1 Additional Input to Agent Variant 3

ALWAYS USE the BM25 tool before answering any question, even if you think you don't need it. Attempt to find a relevant article before answering the question.

The additional sentence for Agent Variant 3 in the system prompt telling the agent to "ALWAYS USE" a tool might seem silly. After all, isn't the agent trained to use tools when it needs them? Sure, it is—but we've already seen how simple prompt changes can yield big changes in LLMs. That suggests we should be able to affect an agent's performance with simple prompt changes as well. As I often say to my clients and students alike: "In AI, everything is worth an experiment." If the prompt doesn't move the needle, no worries—our hypothesis didn't pan out.

The `no_db_agent` agent might also seem odd: Why would an agent not have the policy database we just made? I am going to consider that agent to be a baseline. Airbnb is not an unknown entity, so it's almost certain huge LLMs like Claude, DeepSeek, and GPT have read plenty of information about Airbnb on the open web. In theory, then, the AI model could work well enough on its own without our policies. By comparing our two agents with a database to the `no_db_agent`, we can be more confident that it was the policies themselves making a difference.

I will also create another branch in our experiment. I will make these three agents for two different LLMs: GPT-4.1 and GPT-4.1-Nano. I chose these models because I wanted to see if our prompting would have an effect on larger, more capable models and smaller models alike. For future work, I'd want to try this experiment using non-OpenAI LLMs as well. Of course, that's also perfect homework for you!

Evaluating Our Agents on Response Quality and Instructional Alignment

Let's look at two major points of evaluation:

- How well each agent presented a solution to the given scenario, as graded by a rubric (Llama 4 Maverick) on the 0–3 scale we have used in the past. We will define "correct" here as the number of 3 scores the response got versus any other score.
- How well the agent responded to the additional system prompt sentence that asked it to always look up information.

Figure 5.5 shows the stark differences between not just the two LLMs (as we would expect), but also the prompting and tooling differences. I'll highlight a few notable points here:

- Across both LLMs, the difference between not giving the LLM a tool to call the database at all (Variant 1, `no_db_agent`) and giving the LLM the tool but not prompting it to use the tool (Variant 2, `db_agent_no_prompt`) was minimal. For GPT-4.1, for example, the accuracies for Variants 1 and 2 were 44.4% versus 47.8%, which are very close.
- The simple act of giving the agent the tool and telling the agent to look up context (Variant 3, `db_agent_with_prompt`) yielded drastically higher performance from both LLMs. That single sentence addition allowed GPT-4.1 to achieve a score of 70.7%. That's nearly a 50% increase in accuracy, and GPT-4.1-Nano saw an even bigger increase! (These numbers are taken from the two rightmost graphs in Figure 5.5.)
- GPT-4.1-Nano, even with a prompt telling it to use the tool every time, *still* didn't use the tool nearly 20% of the time, and that failure impacted its accuracy (bottom left graph). This is an indication of GPT-4.1-Nano's **instruction adherence** properties—essentially, how often will it follow instructions given to it. You might think LLMs at this level would always follow your instructions, especially simple ones, but smaller LLMs like GPT-4.1-Nano tend to fall short in this arena.
  - Counterintuitively, with GPT-4.1-Nano, the database agent with no prompt called the tool even more than the version of the agent with the prompt telling it to use it.
  - GPT-4.1, when told to use the tool, did (top left graph). However, when not told explicitly to use the tool but simply presented with it (top middle), it always chose to not use the tool, effectively making it an agent with no database (the baseline agent). At least GPT-4.1-Nano (bottom middle), when not explicitly told to use the tool, still used the tool sometimes (31 out of 232 times).

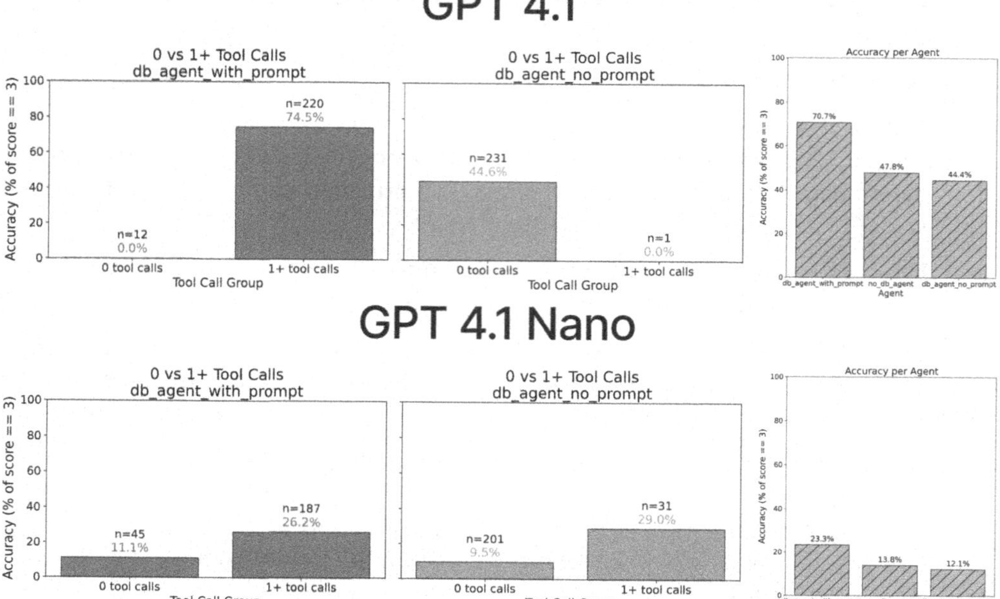

Figure 5.5 GPT-4.1-Nano (bottom left) didn't use tools sometimes, even when prompted to do so. GPT-4.1 did use the tool when told to do so (top left), but was even worse in a way: It almost never used a tool when I didn't tell it to use that tool every time (top middle). It's very confident it knows the answer, even though using the tool in both models yielded a substantial increase in accuracy.

That last finding is the most interesting to me. I'm not surprised that when the agents used the tool, their responses got higher grades. I'm shocked, however, that GPT-4.1-Nano seemed to take my additional prompt to "ALWAYS USE the tool" as a suggestion (bottom left, where it chose not to use the tool 45 out of 232 times), and just as shocked that GPT-4.1 was "smug" enough to decide it didn't need the tool in virtually every case and suffered in terms of accuracy for it.

This can be considered a form of **AI calibration**—the assignment of reliable and trustworthy confidence scores to AI outputs. Said another way, GPT-4.1 doesn't seem to know what it doesn't know. Instead of looking the information up, it chose to answer questions without making any tool calls. GPT-4.1 was likely overconfident in its knowledge of this information (presumably it's read older Airbnb policies) on the web and so didn't feel the need to look up the information. We will explore the idea of calibration in detail in the third part of this book.

In AI, the training of a model to follow instructions is called **instructional alignment**. In this case, GPT-4.1, while certainly being more knowledgeable than GPT-4.1-Nano, needs to be humbled with a prompt telling it how to use its own tools to be maximally effective.

I should note a major bias in our evaluation framework here: We are assuming our test set has adequate coverage and the LLM will always be able to find information. How do we test the AI model's ability to say it doesn't have the information it needs? We could, for example, test the AI with questions we know cannot be answered by any policy document. In that scenario, we could check whether it still attempted to answer the question, assuming we wanted the AI model to use only the given policy documents.

The conclusion here is that simply presenting tools to an agent may not always be enough. If the LLM is overly confident and decides not to use a tool, it will underperform. We still need to guide the LLM on when to use tools, and perhaps when not to use them. We could even take this as a sign that a workflow would be more reliable, if more difficult to design. In fact, it's quite common for a particular task to demand the rigidity of a workflow while benefiting from the autonomy of an agent. Given this thought, let's take a detour on our AI application road trip to Hybridsville, population 2: workflows and agents working together.

Case Study 6: Deep Research Plus Content Generation Agentic Workflows

We will use the term **agentic workflow** to refer to a rigid workflow in which some of the "rigid" steps are themselves agents with relative autonomy. In such a case, we are aiming for a middle ground between efficient workflow data flow and flexible agentic work. The task at hand? **Deep research** refers to the use of AI to conduct in-depth, multi-step research on a given topic. We will expect our workflow to explore the web, aggregate information from various sources, and generate structured, cited reports. This idea of deep research is quite common among the foundation AI companies and is provided as a feature in many consumer-facing UIs, such as ChatGPT, Claude, and Gemini.

The idea of **discursive reasoning** is to reason by relying on logical steps and arguments to reach a conclusion. This idea is so old that Aristotle himself made a distinction between discursive and intuitive reasoning, with the latter relying more on "instinct" to reason through a task. In the modern world of AI, chain-of-thought prompting can be used to induce discursive logic in LLMs, and reasoning models automatically rely on this logic (more on them in Part III of this book). With LLM workloads in general, we can follow a simple two-step process to induce this behavior in almost any workflow—namely, planning and reflecting.

Planning Components

Planning components in workflows are straightforward: Ask an LLM to first create a plan of action rather than figuring it out on the fly as a ReAct agent would typically do. Creating a plan upfront leads to a major improvement over a general agent/workflow: We can devote more time and money to creating a plan on a larger LLM while offloading the execution of individual steps to smaller LLMs. The underlying idea is that it's harder to come up with a solid plan than it is to execute the plan's individual steps. This two-step approach is visualized in Figure 5.6.

A major drawback of this approach is that the plan will need to change on the fly. What if the AI model decides to find some news on a website that no longer exists? We hope the AI will be "smart" enough to deal with that problem, but with rigid workflows and sub-par LLMs, that may not happen and failures can compound.

A quick way to deal with this issue is to build in a re-planning component. With re-planning, every time a step is completed (or at least every so often), the planner is re-invoked to see the state of the task. At that point, it is asked to decide whether the plan is still valid or whether a new plan is needed.

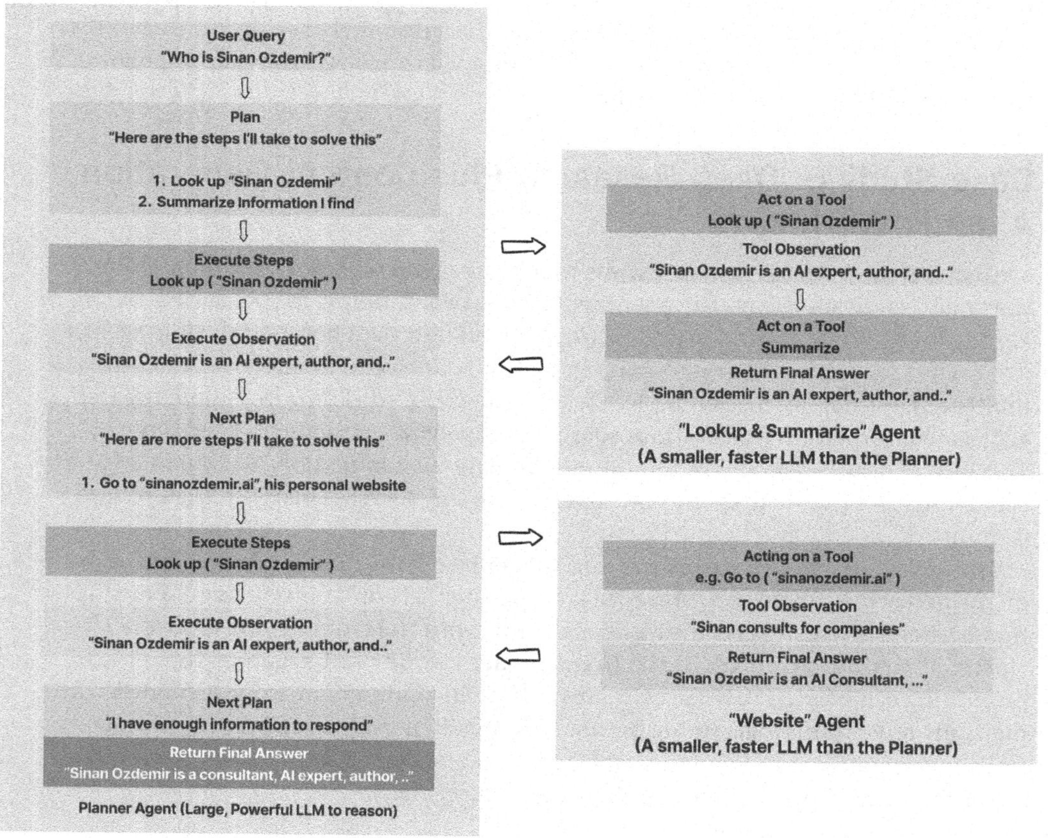

Figure 5.6 Planning agents first generate a rough draft of a step-by-step plan before executing (or delegating execution of) steps on an LLM. The planning agent may also change the plan mid-execution if information changes.

Task
Who is the current mayor of the city with the oldest Chinatown in America? Also find their birthday

Original Plan
1. Figure out which American city has the oldest Chinatown
2. Find out who the mayor is of that city
3. Web search to find the mayor's birthday

Step Executor executing Step 1

San Francisco has the oldest Chinatown in America and Daniel Lurie is the mayor.

Re-Planner
1. Web search to find the Daniel Lurie's (the mayor of San Francisco) birthday

Step Executor executing NEW Step 1

February 4, 1977

Re-Planner

WE ARE DONE! :)

Figure 5.7 A simple plan/re-plan flow asking an agent to answer a question with multiple steps.

A simple example would look like Figure 5.7, where the planner makes a fair plan. However, the step executor accidentally discovered information that the planner originally thought it would have to find later. In this case, the re-planner should recognize that the plan can be condensed to fewer steps.

Reflection Components

The idea of pausing in between steps to reflect and potentially pivot on the current plan can itself be generalized into the idea of reflecting on really anything the AI is doing. Figure 5.8 shows a simple use-case of using reflection on a simple ReAct agent solving a task. The agent attempts to solve a task and wants to give a final answer.

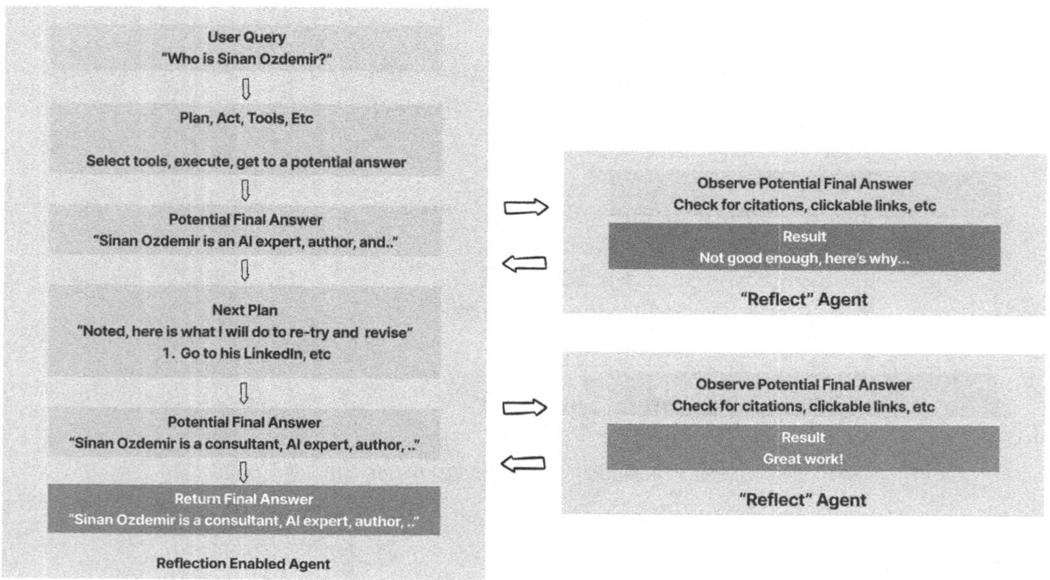

Figure 5.8 Reflection components generate a critique (a set of feedback) for an agent to "reflect" and iterate on before continuing. This is often done at the end with the final output, but can be implemented anywhere in a workflow.

Before a user will see it, however, a reflection component (potentially an additional agent with tools or simply an LLM prompt) will review the answer given the objective, give a critique, and either sign off on the answer or tell the agent to keep going with feedback in mind.

These are currently the most popular types of components to add into a workflow, though they certainly aren't the only ones possible. Now, let's build our workflow with planning, reflection, and agents to tackle deep research.

The Deep Research Agentic Workflow

Figure 5.9 shows the steps in our workflow:

1. A user submits a task to the Deep Research (DR) system.
2. The planning component generates a series of steps. I'm using GPT-4.1 for the initial plan.
3. The step executor executes the steps. I'm using GPT-4.1-Mini for the execution. It's faster, cheaper, and I'll trust it to execute the steps correctly.
4. The re-planner reflects on the work done and re-makes the plan. I opted for a faster model, Gemini-2.5 flash, which is both capable and quick.
5. Repeat steps 3 and 4 until the re-planner decides we are finished, and then summarize the results. I'm using a model distilled from DeepSeek R1 to provide

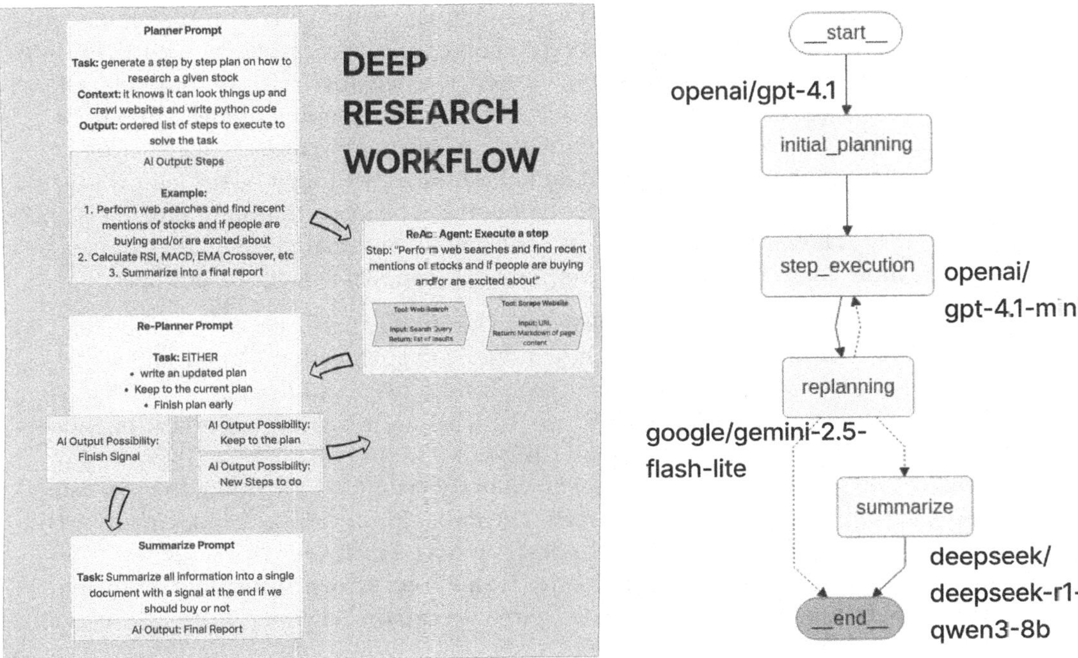

Figure 5.9 Our Deep Research workflow includes three rigid steps: planning, re-planning, and the final summarization, with most of the "work" being done by an agent (the step executor). On the left is the more human-readable workflow. On the right is a LangGraph implementation visualization.

the final summary. I'm hoping the reasoning portion of this model will allow it to capture as much of the information written as possible and provide a decent final answer.

As these steps indicate, I'm relying on four different LLMs here. I could experiment in each individual step to determine which models offer the best bang for my buck, which ones capture the best summaries, and which ones provide the most efficient tool use—in short, everything we've been talking about so far vis-à-vis experimentation. In this case, my reasonings were as follows:

- OpenAI's GPT-4.1, as a large competent LLM, will do one of the harder parts of the process: initial planning.
- OpenAI's GPT-4.1-Mini is the engine for the ReAct agent powering step execution. It has to still navigate its way through a task, but likely will not need to "think" too much for itself, as GPT-4.1 did the hard work of planning.
- Google's Gemini 2.5 Flash Lite is a relatively higher-tier LLM that does re-planning after every step. I trust this LLM slightly less than GPT-4.1 but enough to navigate potentially wavering plans.

- DeepSeek's Qwen3 8b is an LLM we haven't seen before. It is a very small model (relative to the others) and has been trained using a process known as **distillation** (more on this topic in Chapter 9), where it learned how to reason through tasks from a larger more capable model, DeepSeek's R1 reasoning model. This LLM's only job is to create the final summary after the hard work (e.g., aggregating sources) has been done. Of the four LLMs chosen, we might be the least confident about this one, because a decent argument can be made that summarizing is not as easy as it seems (see Case Study 2, A "Simple" Summary Prompt, in Chapter 3 for more about this). For now, I appreciate the model's small size and speed.

As always, you can find the complete LangGraph code in the book's GitHub. But really, there's nothing new here: We have nodes, LLM invocations, edges, and some conditional edges—nothing we haven't seen before. To see our work in action, let's return to an example from the last section. Let's ask our workflow to find the birthday of the mayor of the city with the oldest Chinatown in America.

Figure 5.10 shows the near full breakdown of the workflow, including the tool calls, the re-planning calls, and the final result. The rather long markdown document (with 100% correct information/links—I checked) produced ends with this sentence: "The city with the oldest Chinatown in America is **San Francisco, California**. The current mayor of San Francisco is **Daniel Lurie**, who was born on **February 4, 1977**." That's all true!

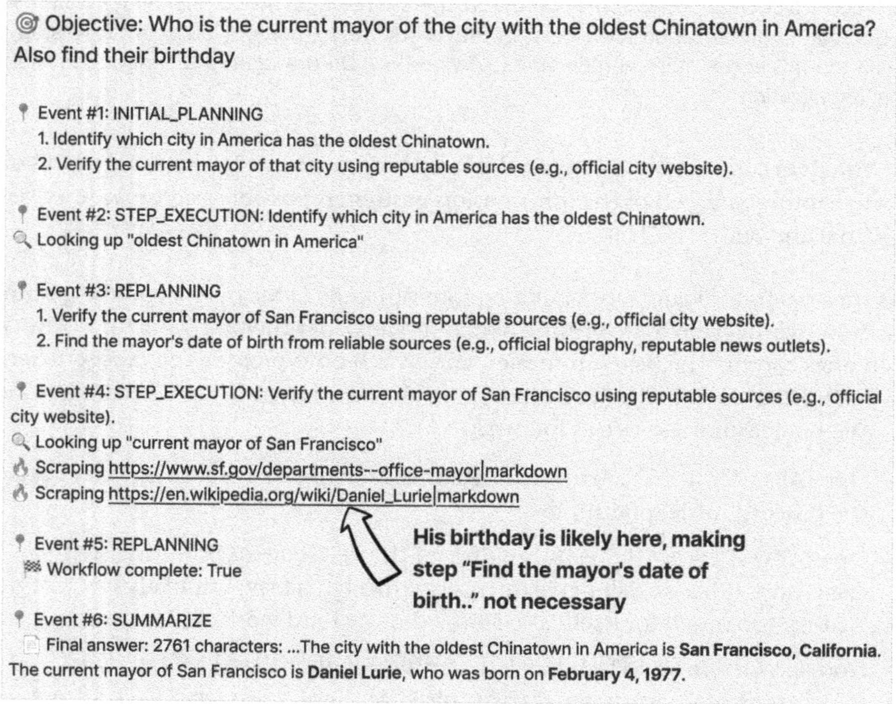

Objective: Who is the current mayor of the city with the oldest Chinatown in America? Also find their birthday

Event #1: INITIAL_PLANNING
1. Identify which city in America has the oldest Chinatown.
2. Verify the current mayor of that city using reputable sources (e.g., official city website).

Event #2: STEP_EXECUTION: Identify which city in America has the oldest Chinatown.
Looking up "oldest Chinatown in America"

Event #3: REPLANNING
1. Verify the current mayor of San Francisco using reputable sources (e.g., official city website).
2. Find the mayor's date of birth from reliable sources (e.g., official biography, reputable news outlets).

Event #4: STEP_EXECUTION: Verify the current mayor of San Francisco using reputable sources (e.g., official city website).
Looking up "current mayor of San Francisco"
Scraping https://www.sf.gov/departments--office-mayor|markdown
Scraping https://en.wikipedia.org/wiki/Daniel_Lurie|markdown

Event #5: REPLANNING
Workflow complete: True

His birthday is likely here, making step "Find the mayor's date of birth.." not necessary

Event #6: SUMMARIZE
Final answer: 2761 characters: ...The city with the oldest Chinatown in America is **San Francisco, California**. The current mayor of San Francisco is **Daniel Lurie**, who was born on **February 4, 1977**.

Figure 5.10 The final result was a rather long markdown result with correctly cited sources and the correct birthday of Daniel Lurie.

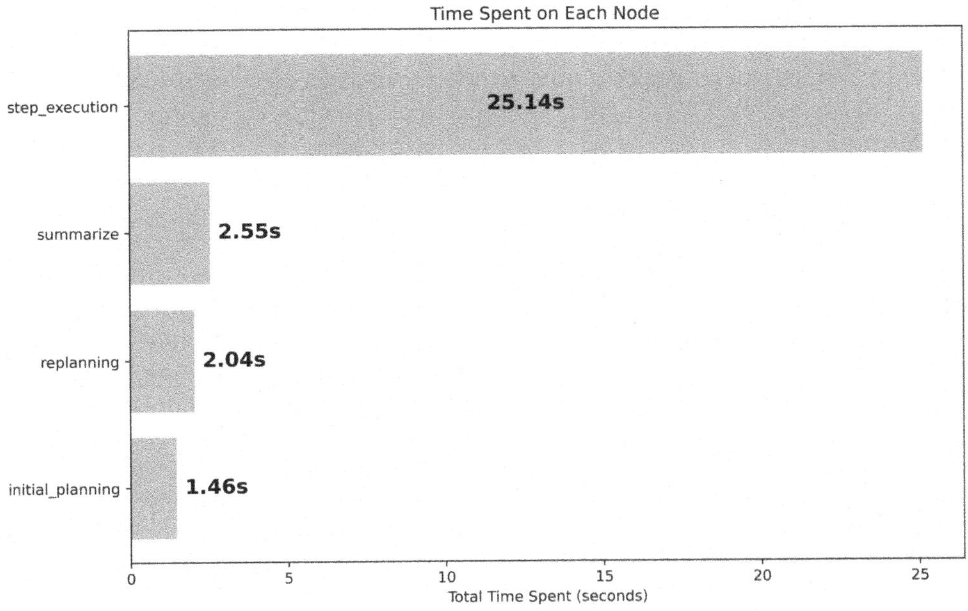

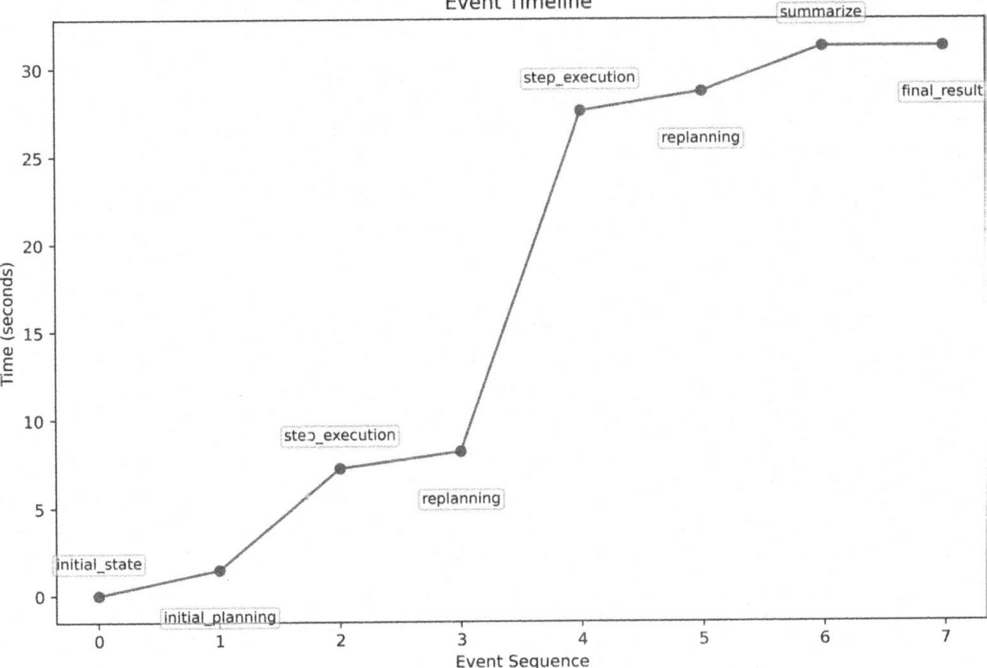

Figure 5.11 The latency breakdown of our steps. It indicates that the step executor takes the most time in our workflow, which is not surprising.

Figure 5.11 shows the breakdown of the latency—the time that the workflow spent on each node in aggregate. It very clearly shows that step execution takes a while. That's why people generally opt for smaller, faster models for step execution over planning, much as we chose GPT-4.1-Mini for step execution versus GPT-4.1 proper for the initial planning.

Using Deep Research to Write a Custom Newsletter

Let's look at a slightly more complicated example, where the AI model will need to look at several web pages to get a holistic example. In this case, we'll aim to create a customized newsletter. I often wish I had a way to keep up-to-date on news for some pretty niche things (perhaps a new video game I'm excited for) and even get that information delivered to my email so I can easily digest it. We tackled the latter part of this process with a Resend MCP server, but the former can be addressed with our new tool. Prompt 5.2 shows the input I gave to a Streamlit application I wrote (in the book's GitHub) asking the Deep Research system to create a markdown version of a newsletter of AI news from July 8 to July 11, 2025 (the date I asked for the information).

PROMPT 5.2 Input to Deep Research to Create a Newsletter

Write a markdown formatted newsletter about the latest news in AI using ONLY stories after July 8, 2025. Find 5 specific stories to cover and include citations in the final report. Keep it to at most 5 stories and each story will only get 3–5 sentences to keep it short and snappy. I want to hear about things like new models, benchmarks, quotes from AI leaders, etc.

Each story should be a single event like "New model from XYC" or "New study shows how AI . . ."

Figure 5.12 shows a snippet of the newsletter (which was quite good!) and the breakdown of the step timings it took to generate the newsletter. After about 2 minutes, I now had a breaking news–style newsletter ready for me to consume.

As we get more clarity on what it takes to build components of larger systems like "AI newsletters" and "AI SDRs," it will be increasingly necessary to return to the idea of multi-agent architectures. Letting individual agents handle parts of a larger flow can really work as promised only if we know how they are allowed to talk to each other, if we allow that at all.

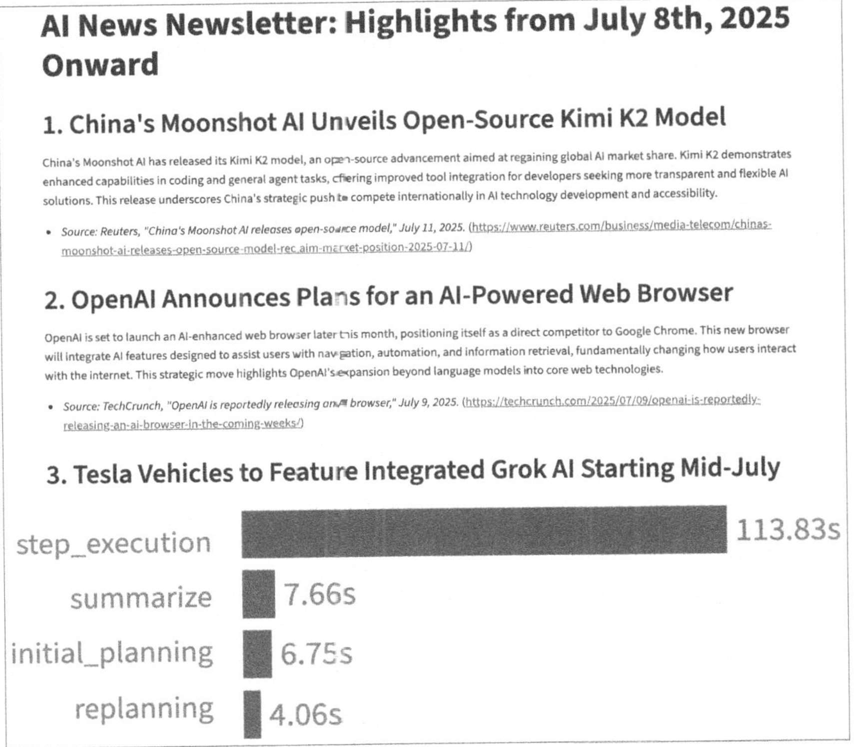

AI News Newsletter: Highlights from July 8th, 2025 Onward

1. China's Moonshot AI Unveils Open-Source Kimi K2 Model

China's Moonshot AI has released its Kimi K2 model, an open-source advancement aimed at regaining global AI market share. Kimi K2 demonstrates enhanced capabilities in coding and general agent tasks, offering improved tool integration for developers seeking more transparent and flexible AI solutions. This release underscores China's strategic push to compete internationally in AI technology development and accessibility.

- *Source: Reuters, "China's Moonshot AI releases open-source model," July 11, 2025.* (https://www.reuters.com/business/media-telecom/chinas-moonshot-ai-releases-open-source-model-rec aim-market-position-2025-07-11/)

2. OpenAI Announces Plans for an AI-Powered Web Browser

OpenAI is set to launch an AI-enhanced web browser later this month, positioning itself as a direct competitor to Google Chrome. This new browser will integrate AI features designed to assist users with navigation, automation, and information retrieval, fundamentally changing how users interact with the internet. This strategic move highlights OpenAI's expansion beyond language models into core web technologies.

- *Source: TechCrunch, "OpenAI is reportedly releasing an AI browser," July 9, 2025.* (https://techcrunch.com/2025/07/09/openai-is-reportedly-releasing-an-ai-browser-in-the-coming-weeks/)

3. Tesla Vehicles to Feature Integrated Grok AI Starting Mid-July

Figure 5.12 Using our Deep Research system to generate a newsletter output forced the AI model to re-plan several times and spend several minutes on execution.

Multi-Agent Architectures

So far, we've been making just single agents. With our SDR example from Chapter 4, we left the case on a bit of a cliffhanger: We had single agents performing different functions but nothing really tying them together. Let's look at some simple ways we can think about unifying agents to achieve a true multi-agent experience:

- **Any-to-any networking:** This is the classic everyone-talks-to-everyone setup. Any agent can message any other agent, pass data, or even kick off a new task. It's flexible, but can get messy if you're not careful. Think: Slack channel with zero moderation.
- **Supervisor:** In this design, one main supervisor agent runs the show. Every other agent reports to this "manager" agent, and the supervisor decides who does what, when, and in what order. Imagine a call center manager assigning cases to different reps.
- **Supervisor (tool-calling):** Here, the supervisor agent acts like a conductor, but instead of talking to agents directly back and forth, the supervisor calls the other agents as "tools," each with its own purpose and arguments. This setup is super common in frameworks like LangGraph, and makes it easy to swap agent

capabilities in and out. The idea is that the supervisor will wait for another agent to solve a task for it before moving on, rather than simply delegating the task and moving on as in a standard supervisor paradigm.

Figure 5.13 outlines a few ways to think about multi-agent frameworks. At the end of the day, though, the key production consideration when deciding how to build your multi-agent system is this: *Do the agents even "need" each other to solve a task?* Or do they simply need to be strung together by a workflow/supervisor?

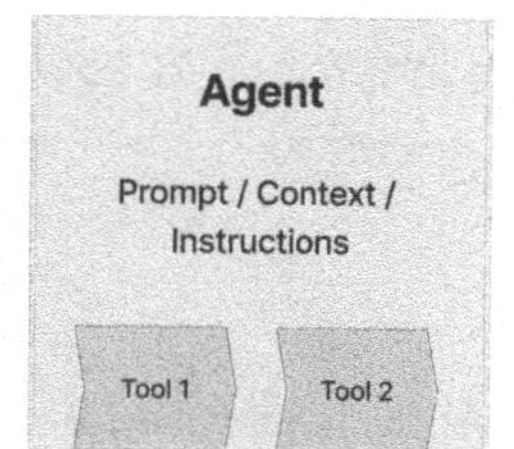

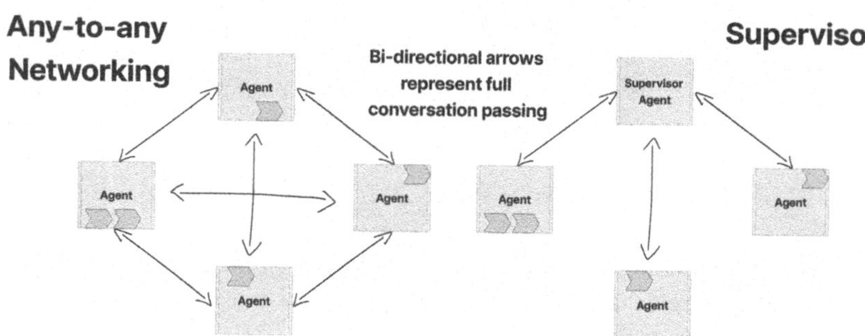

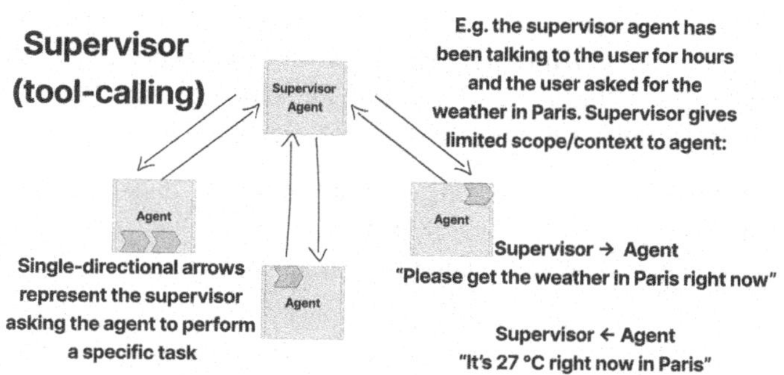

Figure 5.13 Three common design patterns for multi-agent systems. In any-to-any networks, agents have full autonomy to pass the entire conversational history to any other agent at any given time. Supervisor networks limit the ability to pass conversations to a single agent called the "supervisor"; any other agent may only pass the conversation back to the supervisor. Supervisor (tool-calling) is a special case of supervisor networks where the supervisor doesn't pass the conversation to the agents below it, but rather treats them like tools and passes targeted tasks with limited context to those tools.

For example, the lead qualifying agent doesn't care what the email agent is doing or even what the lead generation agent is doing. It has a singular task and is focused on it. It just needs a supervisor to give it a to-do list. If agents *do* need each other (e.g., see Figure 5.14), then we need something more like a networking approach, where agents pass around full or partial context in real time to solve a single task. From there, you can make minor tweaks to fit your profile. In our final case study of this chapter, I will modify the idea of a supervisor slightly to remove the bidirectional conversation and simply make the supervisor delegate tasks and move on.

Example: A Network-Based Multi-Agent Architecture

Figure 5.14 visualizes the simplest network-based architecture between two agents. Each agent in the network can pass messages to any other agent, as in an open chat group. There's no boss—just agents with the agency to pass the conversation back and forth between each other while collaborating (or sometimes, stepping on each other's toes).

I specifically architected this example to point out a flaw in network-based architectures. We have two agents:

1. Agent 1 can call a calculator.
2. Agent 2 can get the weather.

I also set Agent 1 to be the "initial agent" (because somebody has to take this role). I then asked a question that I knew would require Agent 1 to immediately hand off the conversation to Agent 2, which would then have to hand it back to Agent 1 to perform the final calculation. The answer is correct in the end, but we didn't really need to pass it back and forth like that.

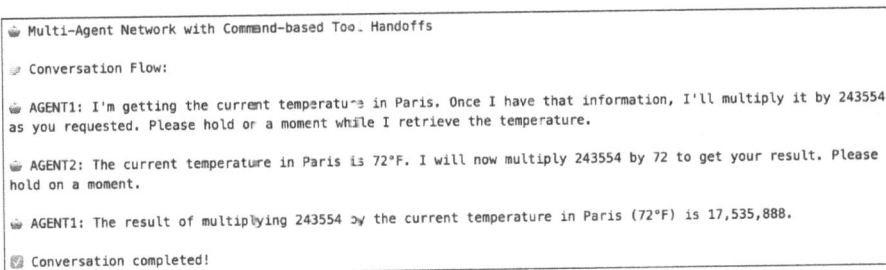

```
Multi-Agent Network with Command-based Tool Handoffs

Conversation Flow:

AGENT1: I'm getting the current temperature in Paris. Once I have that information, I'll multiply it by 243554
as you requested. Please hold on a moment while I retrieve the temperature.

AGENT2: The current temperature in Paris is 72°F. I will now multiply 243554 by 72 to get your result. Please
hold on a moment.

AGENT1: The result of multiplying 243554 by the current temperature in Paris (72°F) is 17,535,888.

Conversation completed!
```

Figure 5.14 A simple network-based multi-agent architecture where agents pass around conversational context to agents with the right tools. In this case, Agent 1 knew Agent 2 had a weather tool. It passed the conversation off to Agent 2 before it, in turn, passed it back to Agent 1 to run some code.

So, why not have a third agent handle the incoming tasks and pass information appropriately, or why not resolve this redundancy by having Agent 2 answer first? Both "fixes" run into an issue: They assume we know in advance what will be asked, and we can pull in agents that are relevant as needed. In reality, we create these multi-agent systems and prepare for the tasks we think will come into the system, and we're ready to update as needed given the tasks that actually do come into the system.

Agents are generally represented as nodes in LangGraph. That is, agents execute work and eventually decide whether to finish execution or potentially route something to another agent. A common pattern in multi-agent interactions is a **handoff**, where one agent hands off to another agent either complete control of the conversation or some subset of the current state.

To implement handoffs in LangGraph, we can use the `Command` object, which allows you to specify exactly where to go (i.e., which agent node to go to next). Listing 5.3 shows the definition of handoff tools (a way to give an agent an easy way to say, "I need to pass this off to another agent") and the specific tool for each agent to define our separation.

Listing 5.3 **Setting up our handoff tools**

```
from langchain.tools import tool
from langchain_core.messages import HumanMessage, ToolMessage
from langgraph.prebuilt import create_react_agent
from langgraph.types import Command

# Define a tool for agent1 that represents a handoff to agent2
@tool
def handoff_to_agent2(message: str) -> str:
    """
    Handoff to agent2 with a message.
    Use this tool when you need agent2 to help with weather-related queries.
    """
    return f"Transferring to agent2: {message}"

# Define a tool for agent2 that represents a handoff to agent1
@tool
def handoff_to_agent1(message: str) -> str:
    """
    Handoff to agent1 with a message.
    Use this tool when you need agent1 to help with code execution or mathematical
calculations.
    """
    return f"Transferring to agent1: {message}"

@tool
def execute_python_code(code: str) -> str:
    """
    Execute Python code safely using eval.
```

```
    Args:
        code: Python code to execute (simple expressions only)
    Returns:
        String containing the result of the code execution
    """
    ...

# Define a weather tool for agent2
@tool
def get_weather(city: str) -> str:
    """
    Get the weather for a given city. Fake obviously
    """
    return f"The weather in {city} is sunny and 72°F."
```

Once we have our tools ready, we can define our ReAct agents, as shown in Listing 5.4. There's nothing out of the ordinary here—just our tools for actual work and for handing off to an agent.

Listing 5.4 **Defining our two agents using LangChain's OpenAI component, OpenRouter, and LangGraph**

```
from langchain_openai import ChatOpenAI

llm = ChatOpenAI(
 model="anthropic/claude-sonnet-4", temperature=0.2,
 base_url="https://openrouter.ai/api/v1", api_key=getenv("OPENROUTER_API_KEY"))

system_prompt_agent_1 = """
You are Agent 1...
...
If you need another agent to help you, you can hand off to them using the appropriate
handoff tool.
"""
agent1 = create_react_agent(
    llm,
    prompt=system_prompt_agent_1,
    tools=[handoff_to_agent2, execute_python_code],
    checkpointer=memory
)
system_prompt_agent_2 = """
You are Agent 2...

The agents are:
```

```
- Agent 1 who can execute Python code
- Agent 2 (you) who can get the weather in any city in real time
...
"""

agent2 = create_react_agent(
    llm,
    prompt=system_prompt_agent_2,
    tools=[handoff_to_agent1, get_weather],
    checkpointer=memory
)
```

We can now wire up our graph to give each agent a node. We will invoke the agent with the entire conversation history (the easiest thing we can do), so that now agents can simply pass information back and forth, just as we saw in Figure 5.14. Listing 5.5 shows the code (and some pseudocode) needed to get this working.

Listing 5.5 **Our multi-agent network LangGraph implementation**

```
from typing import Literal, Annotated, TypedDict
from langgraph.types import Command
from langgraph.graph import StateGraph, END
from langgraph.graph.message import add_messages

# Define the state for the conversation (shared message list)
class ConversationState(TypedDict):
    messages: Annotated[list, add_messages]

def agent1_node(state: ConversationState):
    """Agent 1 can execute Python code and handoff to agent 2"""
    ...
    response = agent1.invoke({"messages": state["messages"]})

    # Check if any handoff tools were called
    if handoff to agent 2 was detected (pseudocode)
        return Command(
          goto="agent2",
          update={"messages": response["messages"][num_message_in_state:]})
    # No handoff needed, end the conversation
    return {"messages": response["messages"]}

def agent2_node(state: ConversationState):
    """Agent 2 can get the weather and hand off to agent 1"""
    ...
    response = agent2.invoke({"messages": state["messages"]})
```

```
    # Check if any handoff tools were called
    if handoff to agent 1 was detected (pseudocode)
        return Command(
          goto="agent1",
          update={"messages": response["messages"][num_message_in_state:]})
    # No handoff needed, end the conversation
    return {"messages": response["messages"]}

# Build the graph
graph = StateGraph(ConversationState)
graph.add_node("agent1", agent1_node)
graph.add_node("agent2", agent2_node)
# Set the entry point to agent 1
graph.set_entry_point("agent1")
# Compile the graph
conversation_graph = graph.compile()
```

Figure 5.15 shows a step-by-step breakdown of when agents handed off to each other and which messages they used.

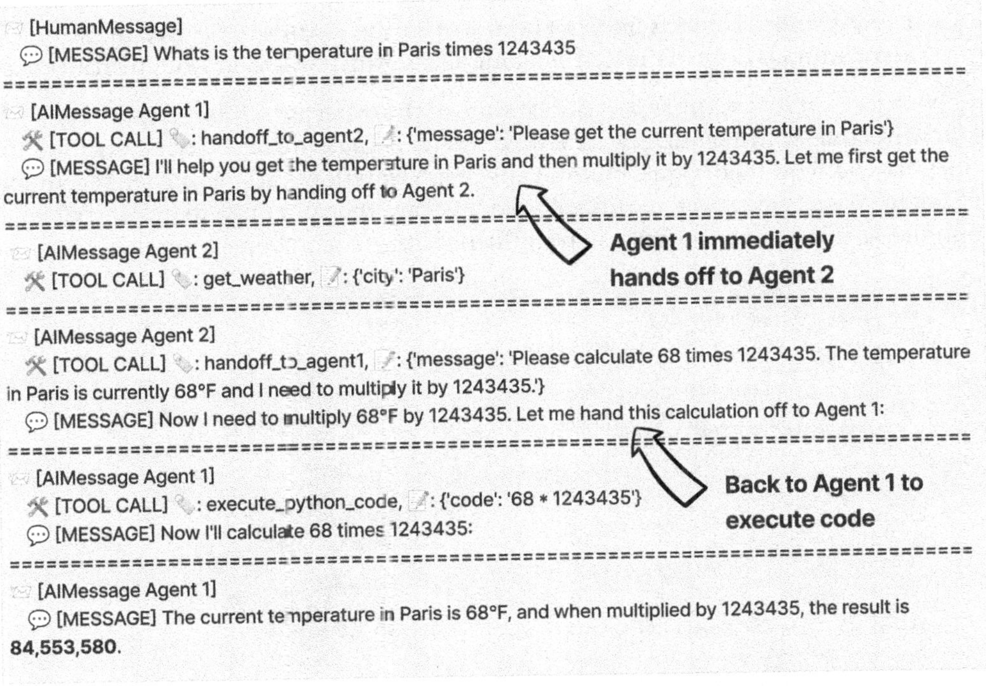

Figure 5.15 The same example as earlier, but with tool calls revealing the agents' "thinking" about how to solve the task at hand.

Case Study 4, Revisited: Adding a Supervisor Agent to Our SDR Team

Let's revisit and expand on Case Study 4 from Chapter 4. We ended that case study on a bit of a cliffhanger. We had agents to handle the individual tasks, but nothing to string them together. One approach to address this omission is the supervisor option—that is, we can build a fourth supervisor agent that constantly is talking to the other agents as they move leads through the pipeline. I will take an even simpler approach here, though: I will build the fourth supervisor agent, but instead of letting it "talk" to the other agents, I will give the supervisor a singular focus that just so happens to involve the other three agents.

Figure 5.16 visualizes this concept. In essence, the supervisor agent "wakes up" every day through a cron job (a way to kick off tasks on a set schedule). The supervisor agent will check three things:

- If there are fewer than three leads with no qualification status, it will ask the lead generation agent to find more leads through an asynchronous task.
- If there are any leads without a qualification status, it will also ask the lead qualifying agent to qualify them.
- If any qualified contacts have not been sent emails, it will kick off even more asynchronous tasks to the lead emailing agent, which will then send them an email.

With this approach, the supervisor is aware of the other agents, but is asked to follow the rules on when to kick off tasks to them. Because we have such hard-and-fast rules, we could (in theory) just build a LangGraph workflow, calling the right agent for the right contact. However, in this scenario, we leave the door open to more flexible options, as the supervisor itself can be influenced through a simple prompt.

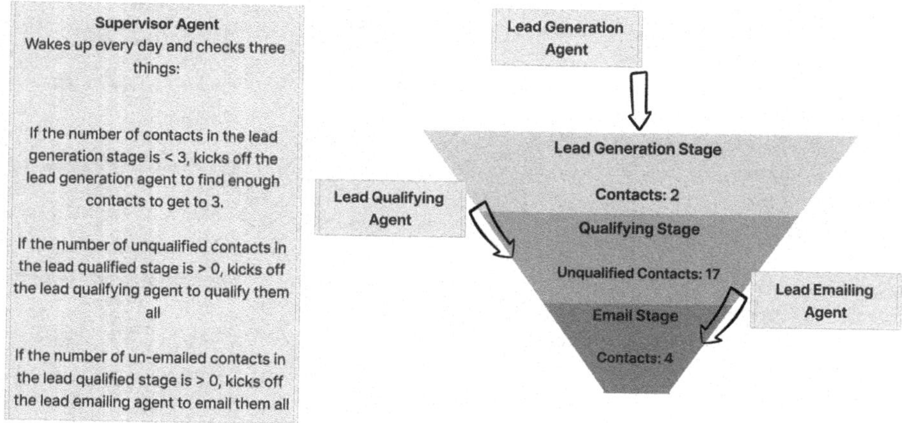

Figure 5.16 The supervisor agent is in charge of moving contacts through the pipeline. It delegates tasks to the three agents, keeping those agents focused on executable tasks rather than passing information around. The supervisor knows that the tasks being delegated can be solved by the individual agents.

This kind of architecture is great for dividing up work, enforcing policies, and letting each agent focus on what it does best. You don't have to stick with one style. Most production systems combine elements like agent networking for lateral communication, a supervisor for top-down control, and tool-calling for flexibility. It all depends on your workflow. As always, the code for this can be found in our GitHub. After running this system on my own personal servers for a few days, I saw several dozen emails being sent out on my behalf. Not bad!

Let's take a look at one more agentic case study. We're coming back to the earlier discussion around positional bias, but this time we'll address the challenge of selecting the right tool in the right situation.

Case Study 7: Agentic Tool Selection Performance

One of the most obvious real-world challenges when building AI agents is tool selection. Given a task, will the AI system select the right tools to solve the job correctly and efficiently? To test this, we can set up a very simple experiment: Ask an agent with several tools a question that we expect to map to a certain tool, and measure whether the agent chose the correct tool. Figure 5.17 visualizes this idea.

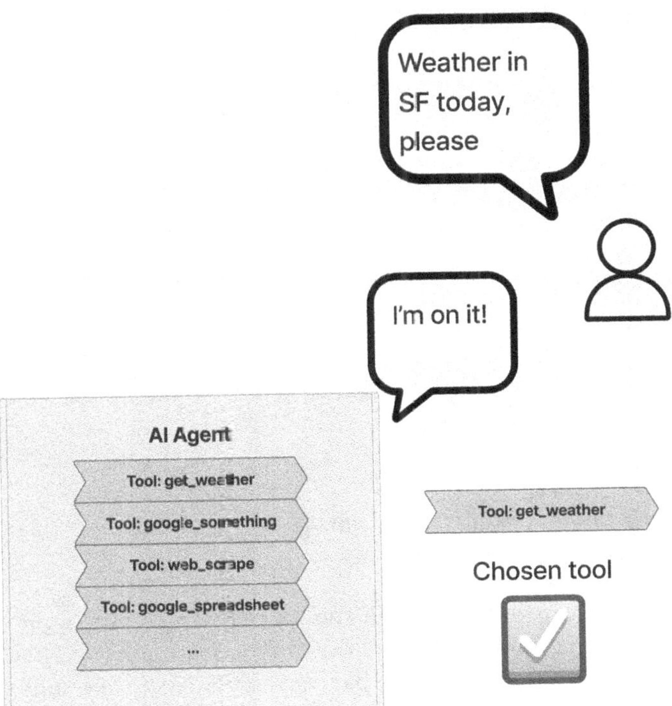

Figure 5.17 Testing agentic tool use can be as simple as checking which tool the AI system wanted to call given a predefined scenario.

To set up this experiment, we will need some data as well as some expected tools. I created an MCP server with 15 different tools, complete with names, descriptions, and expected parameters. Listing 5.6 shows an abbreviated code snippet defining the MCP server.

Listing 5.6 **Creating an MCP server in Python using a list of defined tools**

```
import os
import random
# Define tool snippets
tool_snippets = [
    '''
@mcp.tool()
def crypto_and_nft_tool(query: str) -> str:
    """Get current cryptocurrency prices and NFT prices around the world and for a
specific wallet.
    :param query: The query to search for cryptocurrency or NFT prices.
    :return: The current cryptocurrency or NFT prices.
    """
    return f"Fake response for crypto/NFT query: {query}"
''',
...
]
def generate_random_mcp_order(mcp_path='random_mcp_server.py'):
    # Shuffle tool definitions
    random.shuffle(tool_snippets)

    # Create full server code
    MCP_SERVER = f'''
from mcp.server.fastmcp import FastMCP
mcp = FastMCP("MCP Example")
{''.join(tool_snippets)}
if __name__ == "__main__":
    mcp.run(transport="stdio")
    '''
    # Save to file
    with open(mcp_path, 'w') as f:
        f.write(MCP_SERVER)
    return os.path.abspath(mcp_path), [t.split('def')[-1].split('(')[0].strip() for t
in tool_snippets]
```

With this code, we can generate an on-the-spot MCP server with our tools in a random order. Note that I didn't identify the tools in Listing 5.6; if I had done so, the listing would have gone on for multiple pages. Figure 5.18 shows a subset of the 80 questions I wrote to cover the 15 different tools for this experiment.

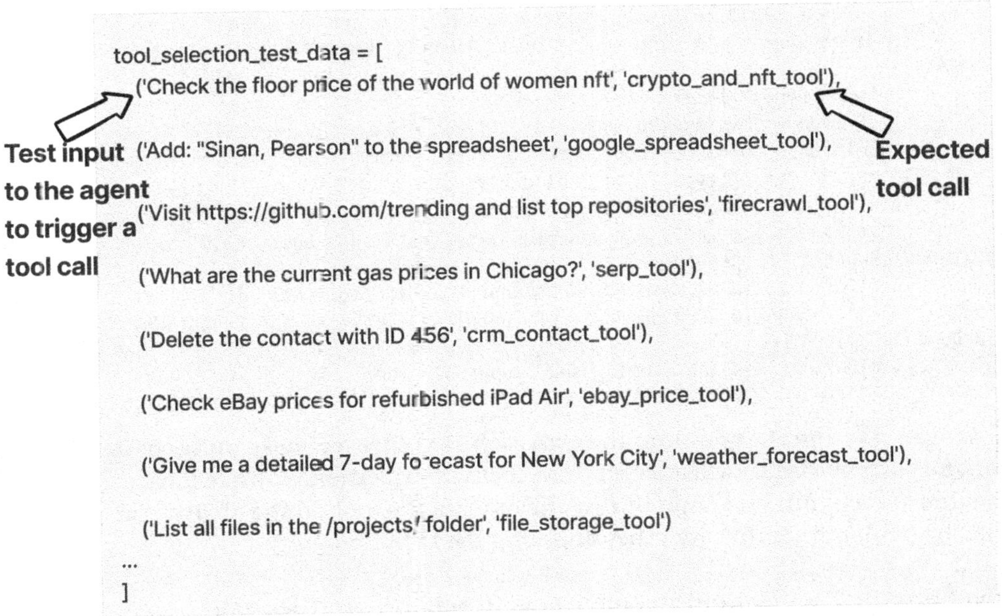

Test input to the agent to trigger a tool call

Expected tool call

```
tool_selection_test_data = [
    ('Check the floor price of the world of women nft', 'crypto_and_nft_tool'),
    ('Add: "Sinan, Pearson" to the spreadsheet', 'google_spreadsheet_tool'),
    ('Visit https://github.com/trending and list top repositories', 'firecrawl_tool'),
    ('What are the current gas prices in Chicago?', 'serp_tool'),
    ('Delete the contact with ID 456', 'crm_contact_tool'),
    ('Check eBay prices for refurbished iPad Air', 'ebay_price_tool'),
    ('Give me a detailed 7-day forecast for New York City', 'weather_forecast_tool'),
    ('List all files in the /projects/ folder', 'file_storage_tool')
...
]
```

Figure 5.18 We are using a dataset of 80 questions covering 15 different tools to test 5 different LLMs' ability to pick the right tool for the right task.

Now that we have a list of questions, we just need to define our LLMs and create a helper function to run each message through the LLMs. Our LLMs will be:

- Google's Gemini-2.5-flash
- OpenAI's GPT-4.1
- OpenAI's GPT-4.1-Nano
- Meta's Llama-4 Scout
- Mistral's Ministral-3b

Listing 5.7 shows the function that we will use to invoke an agent powered by a particular LLM (a Chat OpenAI instance of LangChain).

Listing 5.7 **Invoke an agent with a single message**

```
async def tool_use_run(llm, initial_message):
    random_mcp_path, mcp_tool_order = generate_random_mcp_order()
    server_params = StdioServerParameters(command="python", args=[random_mcp_path])

    async with stdio_client(server_params) as (read, write):
        async with ClientSession(read, write) as session:
            await session.initialize()
```

```
            tools = await load_mcp_tools(session)
            ai_message = llm.bind_tools(tools).invoke([HumanMessage(content=initial_
message)])
            tools_used = []
            if type(ai_message.content) == list:
                for c in ai_message.content:  # anthropic
                    if c['type'] == 'tool_use':
                        tools_used.append((c['name'], c['input']))
            if hasattr(ai_message, 'additional_kwargs') and 'tool_calls' in ai_message.
additional_kwargs:  # openai
                for tc in ai_message.additional_kwargs['tool_calls']:
                    tools_used.append((tc['function']['name'], tc['function']
['arguments']))
            return ai_message, tools_used, mcp_tool_order
```

We can now run the questions through each LLM. To even make things more difficult, for each message, I will ask each LLM that same question multiple times, resetting the thread each time and randomizing the order of the tools in the MCP server (and thereby randomizing the order they appear in the LLM's prompt).

Investing in Tool Selection Accuracy, Precision, and Recall

So far, this experiment is pretty straightforward. Figure 5.19 shows the accuracy results from this simple test of 5 LLMs with function calling. Our 3 billion parameter model performed admirably, but in the end was beaten out by the larger Frontier Labs AI models. That's not really shocking. Figure 5.20 digs even deeper into the precision and recall of each tool.

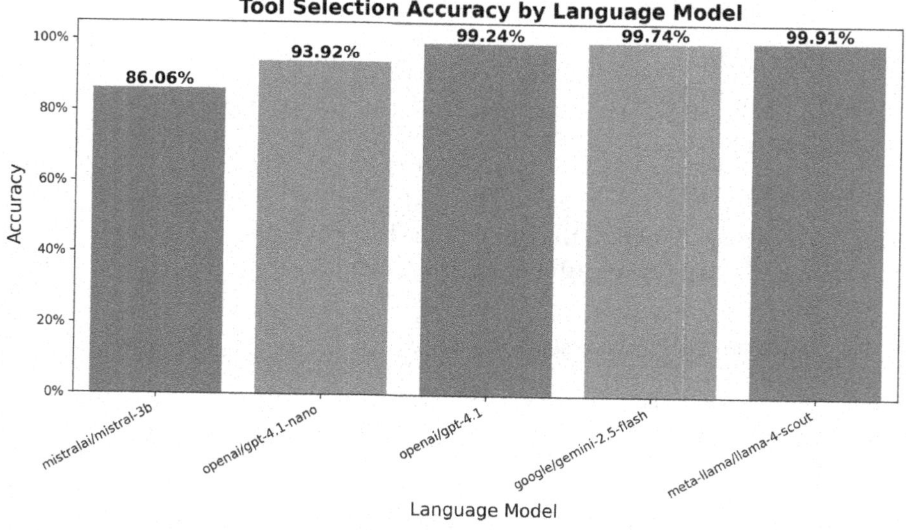

Figure 5.19 Unsurprisingly, larger models like Llama-4, Gemini-2.5, and GPT-4.1 outperform GPT-4.1-Nano and Ministral-3b in overall tool selection accuracy.

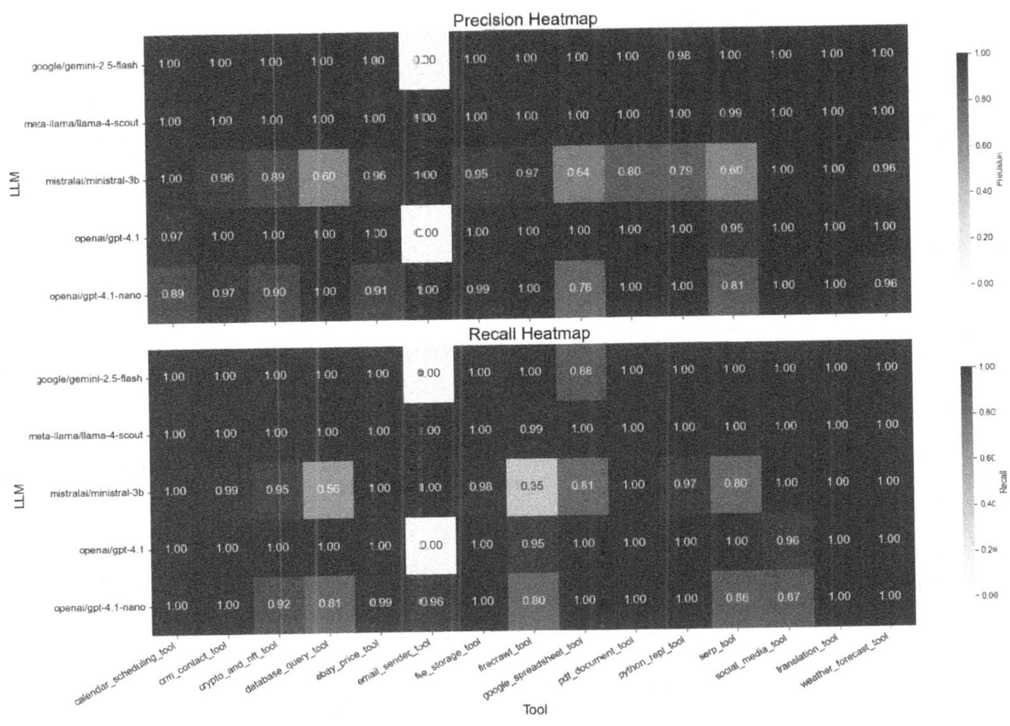

Figure 5.20 The precision and recall maps for our experiment yield more interesting results, including a suspicious 0% precision and recall for the email sending tool across two state-of-the-art LLMs and some possible areas of improvement for the tool descriptions.

Recall measures how often the expected tools were chosen, and precision measures how trustworthy the tool selection calls were. For example, if we look at the intersection of the eBay tool and GPT-4.1-Nano, we see that the precision was 91%; that is, of the times GPT-4.1-Nano said it wanted to use the eBay tool, that choice was correct 91% of the time. The recall was 99%; that is, of all the times I expected GPT-4.1-Nano to use the eBay tool, it did so 99% of the time.

Note a few more things about the precision and recall graph in Figure 5.20:

- Across nearly all of the LLMs, the precision of the SERP tool (googling something) and the recall of the Firecrawl tool (web scraping) was less than 100%. This could be an indication that the LLM is sometimes using Google when it should instead be web scraping a given URL. Figure 5.21 shows an example of this where I asked GPT-4.1 to go to a specific URL; instead of doing so, it Googled the URL. Technically, the LLM is still likely to get the right answer this way, but it could be a waste of a tool call and therefore a waste of time and money. We also care because this is a test of the model's value system when it comes to tool-calling. Why would it Google something when I so clearly told it to go to a specific website?

- Other tools, like the translation tool, are at a perfect 100% in precision/recall across all LLMs. Some tools are just obvious and don't conflict with other tools, but even this result may be suspicious. I could make an argument that the LLM could simply Google "translate from X to Y" instead of using the translation tool, yet it didn't do so. Why did it trust the translation tool in this case, when it didn't seem to want to always call Firecrawl?
- There are suspicious sets of 0s for the `email_sender` tool in both the precision and recall heatmaps. Even the largest model, GPT-4.1, seems to have never called that tool. Something seems fishy ...

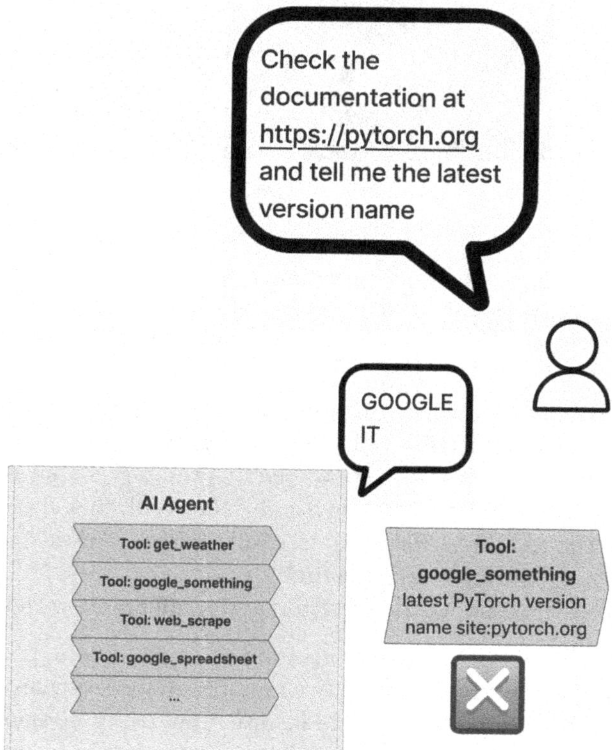

Figure 5.21 Sometimes, an LLM will select the "wrong" tool but still have the right idea. In this case, we would expect the LLM to pick the obvious "web scrape" tool to scrape the given URL, but instead it decided to Google the URL. Ultimately, it will likely get the same answer, but not in the way we expected it to.

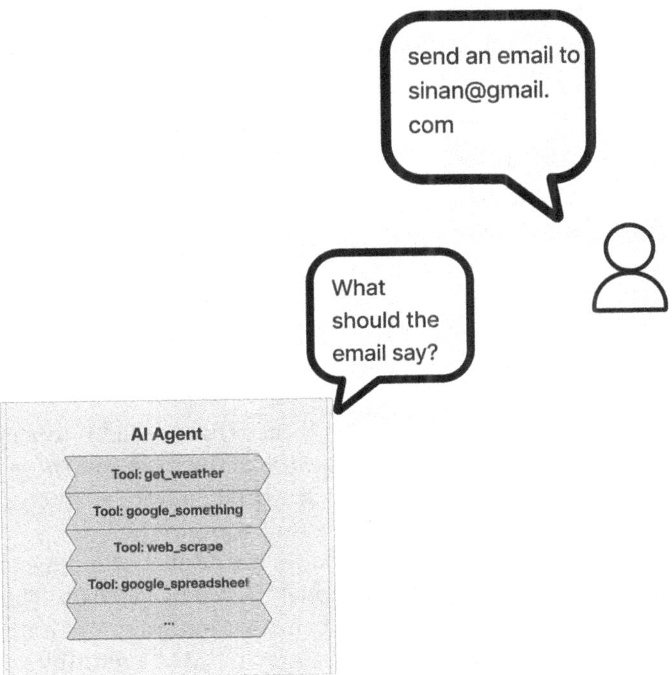

Figure 5.22 An agent is allowed to not call a tool and instead ask the user for clarifying information. In this case, the AI model determined it didn't have enough information to call a tool, but the setup did not allow for the option of "ask for clarifying information."

I want to dig more into that last note. When we run AI experiments, we won't always see the cleanest results. When there are noticeable outliers, such as a flat 0% precision/recall for a specific tool, we should try to understand why.

In this case, the design of the experiment has a flaw. We assumed that every initial message used to invoke the agent contained enough data in it for the LLM to call a tool. The email sender tool, in particular, has multiple input fields (e.g., subject, body, to, cc, bcc). Digging into the raw results from the experiment reveals that sometimes models like GPT-4.1 didn't call the tool but instead asked the user for clarifying information (see Figure 5.22 for an example). That might actually be the correct response, as opposed to simply selecting the tool blindly.

We have three options to handle this issue:

- Remove the email sender tool from the experiment because it was flawed. That is the easiest thing to do, but it doesn't address the root issue.
- Update the initial messages to include all of the information needed for the tool. That is easy to do in the short term, but it doesn't test real-world usage.

- Add a new expected option addressing the AI's message and use a rubric to judge the response. That is the hardest thing to do, but it evaluates the realistic outcomes of the AI.

Positional Bias in Tool Selection

One final note on this experiment: By running the 80 questions through 5 LLMs more than a dozen times each with shuffled tool orders, we can also measure the tendency for the LLMs to select certain tool positions. We might be able to see a clear pattern in an AI model's bias toward certain tool positions.

Figure 5.23 shows the difference in the percentage of times an LLM selected a tool in a certain position (from 0 to 14 for our 15 tools) and the percentage of times that tool index was correct.

For example, that 0.211% in the 0–2 bucket means that the LLMs (on average) selected the first, second, and third tools 20.3458% of the time, but those indices were correct only 20.1349% of the time. The LLMs clearly favored the first tools in the list (albeit not by much) while under-selecting the final tools in the list.

The takeaway here: Sometimes it doesn't matter how well we describe our tools, or how much prompting we add to tell the AI model what it needs to do. This kind of applied positional bias will always be present behind the scenes. And it doesn't just show up in agentic tool use: If we give an autoregressive LLM a multiple-choice question, it might latch on to the first few answers unless prompted to "think out loud" beforehand. This is why chain-of-thought prompting works so well, and it's also what prompted Frontier Labs to create reasoning models.

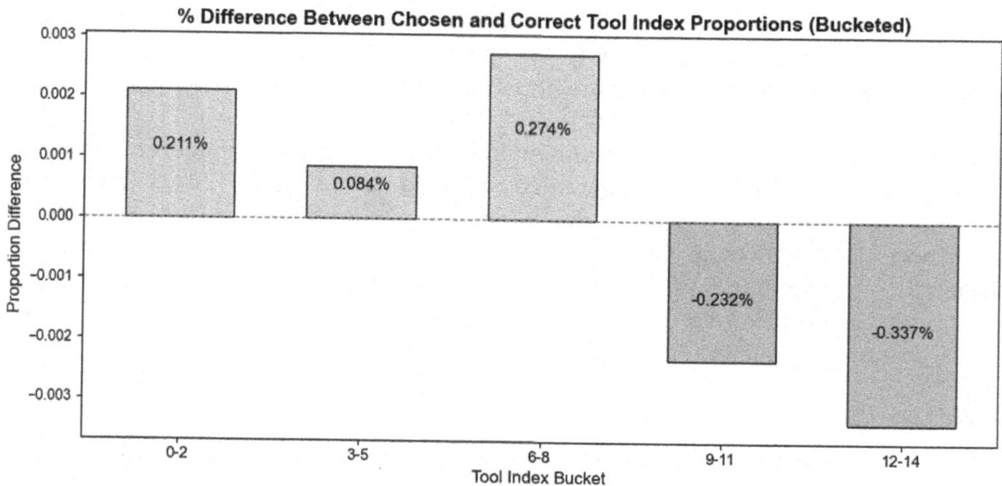

Figure 5.23 Positional bias rears its head yet again in tool selection. Notice the clear trend of the LLMs (on average, between the five LLMs in the experiment) preferring the earlier mentioned tools.

Conclusion

We covered a lot of ground in this chapter, but the core message is straightforward: Making agents more reliable isn't just about fancy frameworks or building even more tools. The real difference comes from thoughtful prompt design, clever context retrieval, and knowing when to break up complex tasks across multiple agents or workflows.

We saw firsthand how a single line in an agent's system prompt can dramatically improve accuracy, and how even old-school retrieval tricks like BM25 can work as well as the latest neural embedding methods in certain scenarios. We explored what happens when you give agents too much freedom (Spoiler alert: Sometimes they get overconfident and skip key steps), and how hybrid approaches consisting of rigid workflows with steps powered by flexible agents can deliver the best of both worlds.

We also built up from individual SDR-related agents to full-blown multi-agent architectures. Along the way, we saw how supervisors, networking, and handoff tools allow agents to collaborate, or at least not step on each other's toes.

If there's a single takeaway here, it's this: There's no magic prompt or one-size-fits-all agent design. The best systems are built through relentless iteration, testing, evaluation, tweaking, and continuing this cycle in perpetuity. In the next chapter, we'll push these ideas beyond the realm of pure natural language and text into the vast world of audio, images, and more with multimodal AI.

6

Moving Beyond Natural Language: Multimodal and Coding AI

Introduction

It's no secret that chatbots can go quite far on text alone, especially with tools that give them the ability to look things up on the internet for us (just look at the early success of ChatGPT and Claude). But when it comes to truly being transformative, natural language, text-only AI has clear limits. Most of what makes up the internet—and honestly, the real world—isn't text. It's images, videos, code (which is text but not really "natural language"), audio, and, increasingly, a mix of all of the above. So, if we want our AI applications to interact with the world or even just a photo roll, we need to move beyond natural language and build systems that can see, hear, and even generate multiple modes of data.

This chapter is an introductory crash course in the newer wave of AI: **multimodal AI**. This kind of AI can draw, listen, speak, convert from one mode to another, and much more. We will cover several of the most practical types of multimodal AI, including visual Q&A, audio-to-audio applications, image generation, and visual search. Like Chapter 3 on evaluation in Part I, this chapter serves as a jumping-off point for multimodal concepts, as we will continue to expand on these concepts in later chapters.

Introduction to Multimodal AI

Models and systems built to understand, combine, and generate across two or more data types at once are known as multimodal AI systems. They can answer questions about a photo or a video, talk to us about a meeting summary, generate code to control a computer (the topic of a case study in Chapter 7), and do so much more.

To start thinking about multimodality, let's consider the five main components/methodologies for building multimodal AI systems:

- **Embed modalities in the same vector space:** Encode modalities with different models that are specifically tuned to produce outputs that can be used in conjunction with each other.
- **Map from one mode to another:** Convert one mode into another. Image generation through prompting is a prime example.
- **Ground modalities in a primary modality:** Use the mapping models just mentioned to convert everything into a primary modality (usually text, as most LLMs can work with text) to do the "work." One of our case studies will employ this technique to create a fully autonomous phone line.
- **Jointly model modes of data:** Perhaps one of the most difficult approaches to multimodality is to create a single model that can accept multiple modes of data.
- **Handle modalities separately:** This method creates the illusion of multimodality, even though the models themselves have no ability to act multimodally. A simple example is an AI agent with a tool that can generate images (one of our case studies in this chapter).

Let's dive into each one, with examples.

Embed Modalities in the Same Vector Space

Earlier in this book, you've seen models capable of processing text, audio, images, and other input, but they were always separate from each other. In those models, convolutional neural networks (CNNs) were used to encode images and recurrent neural networks (RNNs) were used to process text. These models were trained without knowledge of the others—so the CNNs knew images and the RNNs knew text, but they knew nothing of each other. The multimodal systems of old often had to be trained completely from scratch by combining parts together and further fine-tuning the models.

Interestingly, we technically still follow this process for the most part these days (as we'll see in this chapter) but with one big difference: Those "separate" models don't usually start out by being separate anymore. Today's multimodal systems are built on the foundational hypothesis that if encoders for different modes of data come off the shelf with some shared representational knowledge, we will have an easier time building efficient multimodal systems. That's where our first multimodal concept comes in.

Instead of cobbling together totally independent models and hoping they'll play nicely downstream with fine-tuning, modern approaches try to get these encoders "speaking the same language" right from the start. The idea is to pre-train them together using massive datasets of paired images and text so their representations already live in the same vector space before we ever fine-tune or deploy them. This shift is what really powers today's state-of-the-art multimodal systems and unlocks everything from text-based image search to true cross-modal reasoning. The first and perhaps most influential example of this approach is OpenAI's CLIP.

OpenAI's CLIP: Revolutionizing Multimodal Pre-training

Released by OpenAI a full year before ChatGPT in 2021, CLIP (Contrastive Language-Image Pre-training) is now the standard in the pre-training of multimodal AI systems. The big idea behind CLIP was to jointly train two encoders—one for images and one for text—so that they learn to produce embeddings for each mode of data in the same vector space. We can then use metrics like cosine similarity to compare them.

During training, CLIP is shown a batch of images and their corresponding captions. The model learns to pull matching image–text pairs closer together and push non-matching pairs apart. This creates a kind of "shared language" between images and text, allowing us to search for images with a text query or even generate textual descriptions for novel images.

What makes CLIP especially interesting is how it builds these encoders. For the image encoder, CLIP popularized the use of the **Vision Transformer (ViT)**. ViT (seen in Figure 6.1) is an architecture first developed by researchers at Google Brain in 2020. Instead of relying on classic convolutional layers, ViT splits an image into patches, treats those patches like tokens, and runs them through a standard Transformer encoder, just like we would use for text. This allows CLIP to leverage the same "attention is all you need" breakthroughs that supercharged language models, but now apply them to visual data.

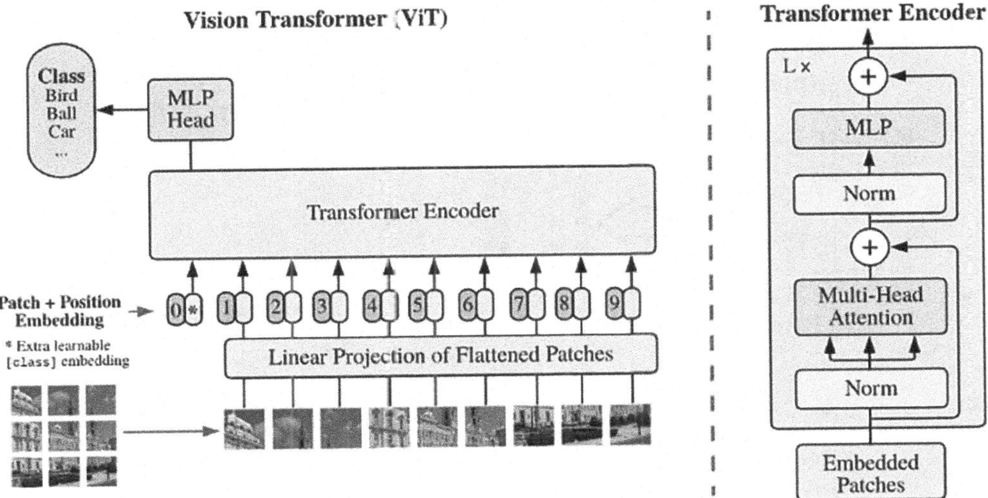

Figure 6.1 A figure from "An Image Is Worth 16 × 16 Words" (the paper that introduced the Vision Transformer) shows how the architecture splits images into fixed-size patches (akin to a text token), and eventually feeds the resulting sequence of vectors into a standard Transformer encoder. The position of each patch is usually determined from left to right and top down, but this decision is left up to the designers of the architecture. (Credit: Dosovitskiy, Alexey, et al. "An Image Is Worth 16×16 Words: Transformers for Image Recognition at Scale" (v2). *arXiv*, June 3, 2020, https://arxiv.org/abs/2010.11929.)

The text encoder, by comparison, was an autoregressive Transformer similar to GPT-2 (GPT-3 had come out just a year before the original ViT paper was published), processing tokens one at a time and producing an embedding for the text as a whole. Both encoders are trained together, but there's no explicit communication between them. They just learn, through the contrastive loss, to "meet in the middle" in vector space.

An illustration (Figure 6.2) can help clarify what's happening here: CLIP's contrastive learning tries to maximize the cosine similarity between an image and its correct text description (the positive pair), while minimizing the similarity with incorrect descriptions (the negatives). The primary piece of data, referred to as the anchor, is compared to both a "positive" and a "negative" sample. The positive example is meant to be similar to the anchor, whereas the negative example is meant to be different from the anchor. While Figure 6.2 shows a classic anchor/positive/negative triplet for simplicity, note that CLIP actually computes similarities across entire batches—so every image is compared with every text, and the model learns from all positives and negatives in parallel.

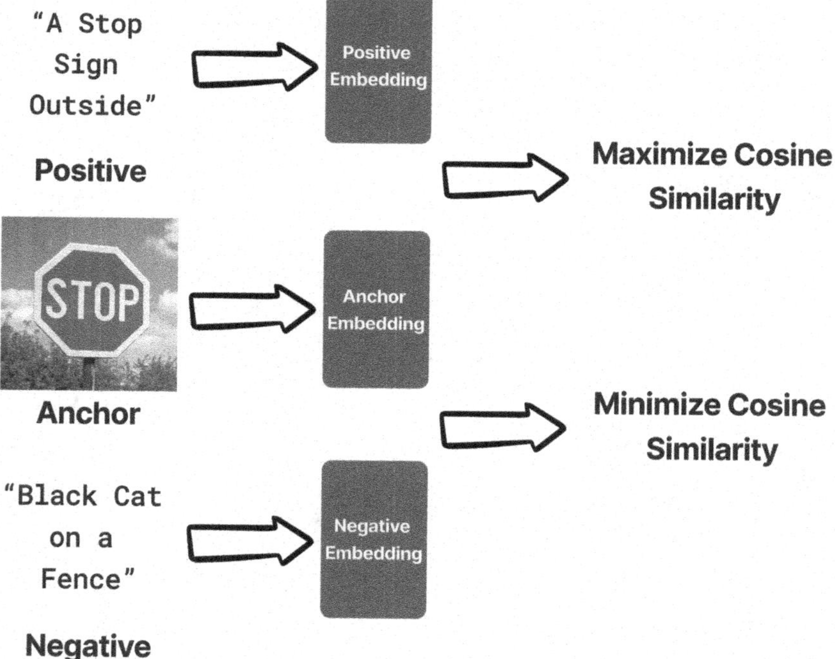

Figure 6.2 This illustration shows a single anchor, positive, and negative triplet for clarity, but CLIP's actual training uses batches of images and texts, comparing every image with every text in the batch. Each correct image–text pair is treated as a positive, and all others in the batch are treated as negatives, thereby maximizing similarity for true pairs and minimizing it for all mismatches.

> **Note**
>
> In practice, each correct image–text pair is treated as a positive, while all other combinations in the batch serve as negatives. The negatives are formed by assigning each image to any text that is not its originally assigned correct (positive) counterpart. The model is then optimized to bring matching pairs closer in the embedding space and push mismatched pairs apart.

This idea of embedding different modalities into a shared space is extraordinarily powerful. In fact, it's become the standard recipe for not only vision–language models since CLIP's introduction, but also just performing simple multimodal retrieval (visualized in Figure 6.3, and covered in a case study later in this chapter).

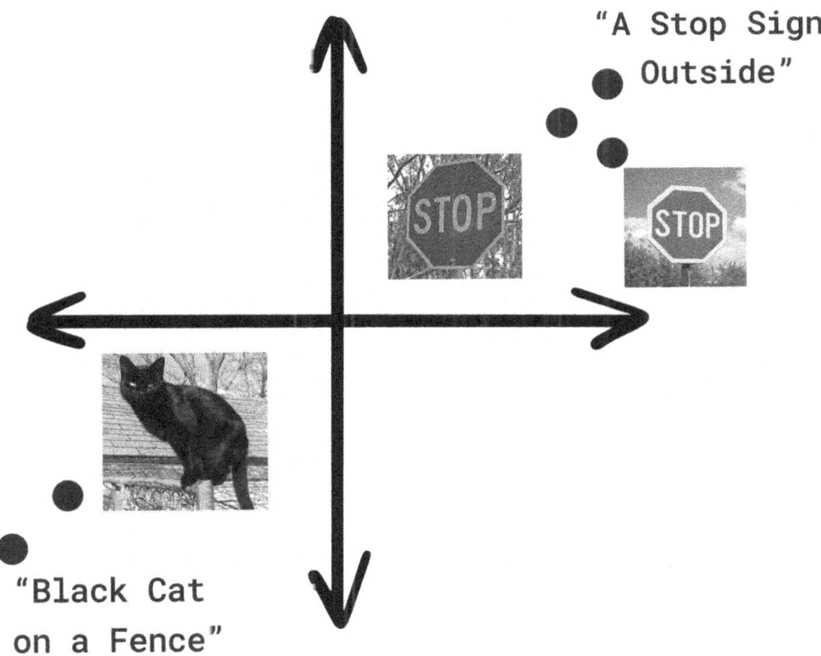

Figure 6.3 CLIP learns to embed both images and their text descriptions into the same vector space, so that related pairs (e.g., "A Stop Sign Outside" and an image of a stop sign) end up close together, while unrelated pairs (e.g., "Black Cat on a Fence" and a stop sign image) are pushed far apart. The shared embedding vector space is what enables CLIP to match images with text queries—and vice versa—using simple vector similarity.

One of the main criticisms of CLIP was that its text encoder, while powerful, may not have been particularly good at capturing the full meaning of complex queries or longer descriptions partly. That's because it used an autoregressive Transformer, which doesn't consider context in both directions (unlike models like BERT). Newer generations of models inspired by CLIP—such as SigLIP, Google's upgrade to CLIP—have updated the architecture to use a BERT-style, bidirectional Transformer as the text encoder. This change has led to stronger, more semantically accurate text representations, especially for longer queries or noisy text. Unsurprisingly, SigLIP outperforms CLIP on many retrieval and zero-shot tasks, making it one of the most robust open-source multimodal models on the market right now.

CLIP, SigLIP, and similar models provided the foundation for flexible multimodal AI systems. As important as jointly training separate encoders is the ability to transform between modalities.

Map from One Mode to Another

Embedding different modalities together is a huge leap, but so is directly converting from one mode to another—that is, going from text to image, text to video, or text to audio, and vice versa, to name a few examples. These types of systems have emerged as some of the most exciting advances in multimodal AI. Classic examples include OpenAI's DALL-E for turning text prompts into images and OpenAI's Sora for text-to-video conversion.

Most of these generative models use **diffusion** or similar stepwise approaches. Instead of trying to create an image or video all at once, they start with random noise and slowly refine it. The input prompt acts as a guide, steering the process closer to what was asked for at each step. Diffusion is a multistep iterative process in which a system of models gradually transforms random noise into a coherent image. Starting from pure noise, the diffusion system repeatedly applies a **denoising function** (shown as $p\theta$ in Figure 6.4) to move step by step toward a cleaner version of the data, eventually reaching the final generated image. Each step is informed by a learned reverse process that approximates how data could have been noised forward (q, in Figure 6.4), enabling the system to refine structure and details over multiple steps. This iterative refinement allows diffusion models to generate highly realistic outputs by steering randomness toward the target distribution, guided by prompts or conditions such as text descriptions. Figure 6.4 shows a high level of this process, but we won't dive into any further details about how diffusion works in this book. We will use models that rely on diffusion to generate both language and images in a later case study.

Once we can move data between modes, another common strategy is to simplify things by picking a single "primary" modality and converting everything else into that format. This makes downstream tasks a lot easier to manage.

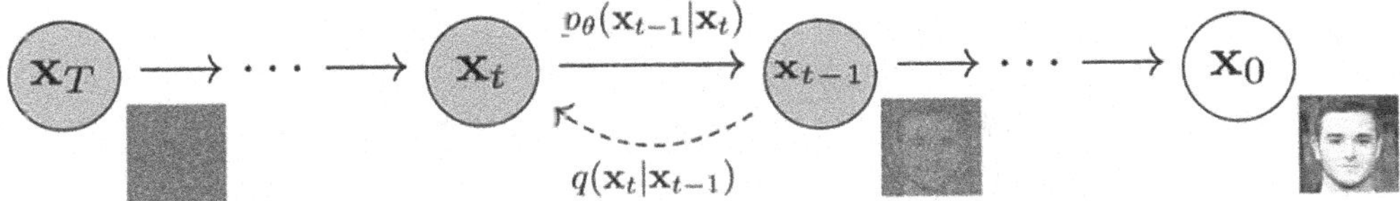

Figure 6.4 Diffusion models start with random noise and then slowly clean it up step by step until it becomes a realistic image. At each step, the model predicts a slightly less noisy version of the picture, using the prompt as a guide. Over many steps, the noise fades away and clear details appear, eventually producing the final image. This ability to generate more than just text content is already transforming fields like design, marketing, media, and accessibility. It allows us to build AI systems that can take an idea in one form and bring it to life in another. (Credit: Ho, Jonathan, et al. "Denoising Diffusion Probabilistic Models" (v2). *arXiv*, Dec. 16, 2020, https://arxiv.org/abs/2006.11239.)

Ground Modalities into a Primary Modality

In many applications, it makes sense to convert all inputs into a primary modality, usually text. This streamlines the pipeline and lets us apply powerful language models or other specialized tools without worrying about the complexity of multimodal input.

For example, scanned documents are often run through optical character recognition (OCR) programs to extract text so we can search or analyze the content. Images can be captioned with a description, making it easy to plug that information into text-based systems. Audio is commonly transcribed, allowing us to process the conversation or commands as plain text and then, if needed, turn the output back into speech with a text-to-speech engine.

This approach is often used in voice bots and audio assistants (Figure 6.5). They might sound as if they're working directly with speech, but under the hood, everything is quickly converted to text, processed, and then converted back to audio if needed. This method is straightforward and works well because it takes advantage of the strong capabilities of text-based AI, even when the original data comes in a different form.

Up to this point, we've mostly seen methods that either keep modalities separate or convert everything into a single format before any real processing happens. But what if we want our model to reason across multiple types of data at the same time, without flattening everything into text or just matching vectors? This is where joint modeling comes in.

Jointly Model Modes of Data

Instead of treating each modality as an isolated stream, some models are designed to process different types of data together, side by side, within a single architecture. These systems keep their modality-specific encoders, but also include a fusion layer that brings everything together for deeper, joint reasoning. This approach lets the model solve complex tasks that require a real understanding of how multiple inputs relate to each other, such as answering a question about an image based on a paragraph of text or connecting audio cues to objects in a scene.

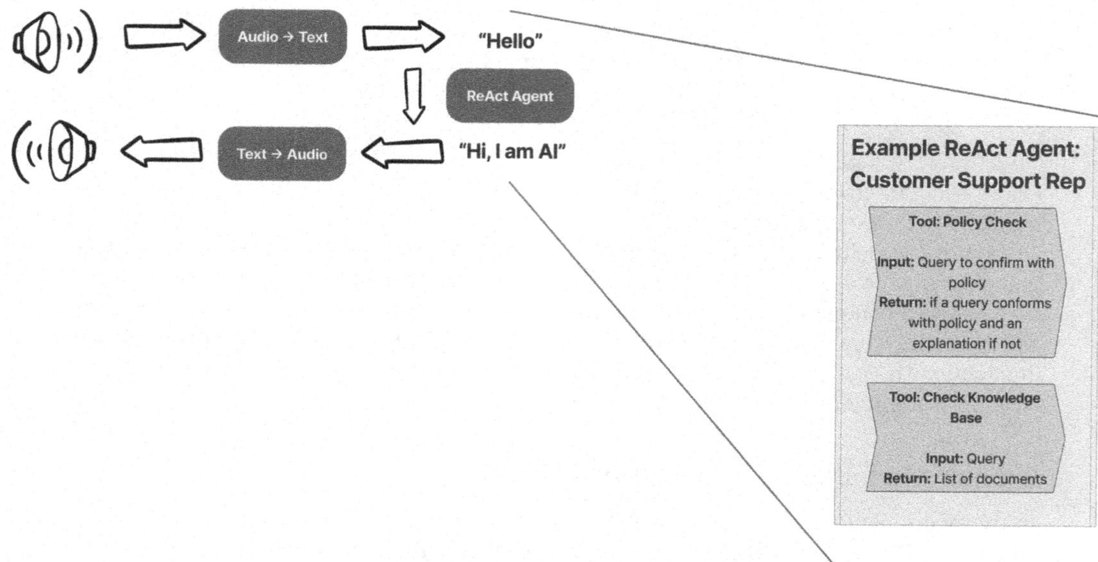

Figure 6.5 Many voice bots and audio assistants work by converting audio to text, passing the text through a language model or agent (e.g., a ReAct agent for customer support), and then converting the response back to audio. Even though the interaction feels multimodal, all of the core reasoning and policy checks actually happen in the text domain, making text the primary modality in the pipeline. We will build out a version of this system in a later case study.

Modern examples of this methodology include nongenerative autoencoding models like ViLT (Vision-and-Language Transformer; Figure 6.6), as well as generative autoregressive language models like LLaVA (Figure 6.7) and Moondream. All three of these models use a shared Transformer to jointly process both text and visual embeddings. This lets the model capture relationships between words and pixels directly, rather than just comparing their positions in a vector space. For example, models like LLaVA and Moondream are built specifically for visual question answering, where the image and text prompt are fused and reasoned over together to generate an answer or description. This joint modeling unlocks richer, cross-modal understanding and makes these models well suited for more interactive and creative multimodal applications.

The key distinction from the earlier approach of embedding into the same dimension (as seen with CLIP, SigLIP, and similar models) is that a *single, unified model* now handles both modalities together, rather than separate encoders trained to produce compatible embeddings. This design opens the door for richer reasoning and more complex tasks that benefit from real-time interaction between different types of data. Machine learning models that jointly model different modes of data (i.e., ViLT) are more difficult to architect than ones with separate components trained jointly (i.e., CLIP) and require longer training times and specific formats of data. This approach also has a key drawback: By jointly modeling modes of data, the model now has to deal with effectively three types of tasks—tasks that deal with only mode 1, tasks that deal with

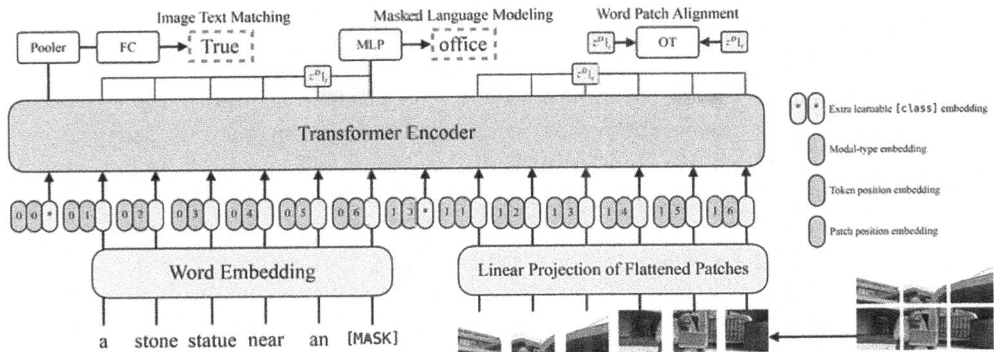

Figure 6.6 An example of joint modeling from ViLT, where both word embeddings and image patch embeddings are combined and processed together by a shared Transformer encoder. This architecture allows the model to directly reason over both text and visual information in the same forward pass, enabling richer multimodal understanding for tasks like image–text matching and masked language modeling. (Credit: Liu, Haotian, et al. "Visual Instruction Tuning" (v2). *arXiv*, Dec. 11, 2023, https://arxiv.org/abs/2304.08485.)

only mode 2, and tasks that deal with both modes 1 and 2 of data. That will require more training data to capture the various options the model might need to deal with.

Sometimes, it's still best to keep modalities separate and handle them independently, depending on the use-case. That's the next approach discussed.

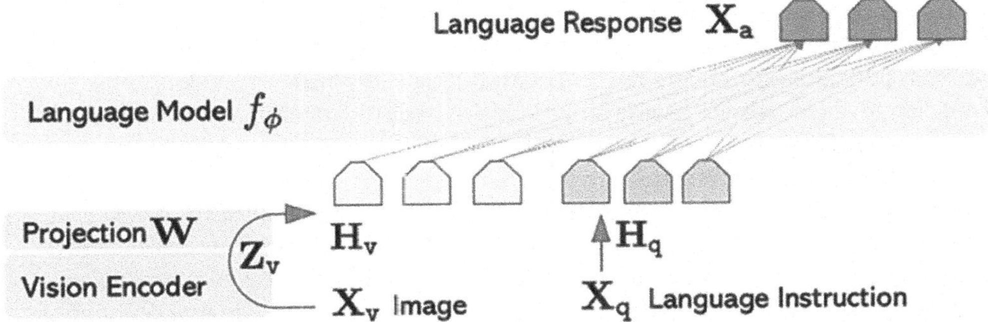

Figure 6.7 LLaVA's network architecture. A pre-trained vision encoder (e.g., CLIP's ViT-L/14) extracts visual features from an input image. These features are projected into the same embedding space as the language model's word tokens, allowing both the image and text instructions to be processed together by the language model and generate a language response. This setup enables joint reasoning over both modalities for tasks like visual question answering. (Credit: Kim, Wonjae, et a . "ViLT: Vision-and-Language Transformer Without Convolution or Region Supervision" (v2). *arXiv*, June 10, 2021, https://arxiv.org/abs/2102.03334.)

Handle Modalities Separately

Not every multimodal system needs to blend data together or map everything into a shared space. Sometimes the simplest (and most practical) solution is to keep each data type separate and process them independently. In this setup, each modality runs through its own dedicated model, and any "multimodal" coordination happens outside the models themselves—usually through some kind of agent, workflow engine, or toolchain.

For example, imagine an agent that first calls an image generation tool to create a picture from a text prompt. Later, the same agent might call a separate image captioning model to generate a description of that image. The models themselves aren't talking to each other or sharing embeddings; instead, the agent or workflow logic strings these steps together. No real fusion is happening under the hood—just a clever orchestration of single-mode models.

This approach is especially useful when we want to quickly build or prototype a multimodal workflow without retraining large models or building new infrastructure. It lets us mix and match the best-in-class models for each modality and can be a surprisingly powerful strategy for dealing with many real-world applications. The trade-off, of course, is that we lose out on the deep, cross-modal understanding that comes with joint modeling or shared embeddings.

These five strategies—embedding modalities into the same space, mapping from one mode to another, grounding, jointly modeling modalities, and handling modalities separately—aren't mutually exclusive. In fact, many of the most advanced systems combine several of them in a single pipeline. The choices we make about how to combine modalities directly affect what our AI system can do. Shared embeddings unlock fast, flexible search and retrieval. Grounding everything in text lets us use classic language models for a wide range of tasks. Fusion and mapping between modes open up more creative and interactive workflows, such as visual question-answering or code generation from screenshots.

Throughout this chapter, we'll see hands-on demos of each approach. We'll cover lightning-fast visual question-answering with models like Moondream and LLaVA, audio agents that use text as an intermediary, classic CLIP-style retrieval, and text-to-image diffusion. As we go, we'll tackle practical questions: How do we keep these systems grounded? How do we evaluate their performance? And how do we actually build workflows that connect all of these pieces into something useful?

Case Study 8: Image Retrieval Pipelines

In this case study, we'll use one of the original CLIP models to implement a document retrieval system (very similar to the one we created in the RAG workflow case studies). Specifically, we'll use sets of images as documents, along with CLIP embeddings and cosine similarity.

We'll also expand on that initial ranking by using a **re-ranker** for especially nuanced or complex queries. With a re-ranker, after we use a CLIP or similar model to get the top results using cosine similarity, we can run those top candidates through a more powerful joint model, like ViLT. ViLT doesn't just compare embeddings. It cross-encodes both the image and the query together, looking back and forth between both modes of data at the same time, which allows for deeper reasoning about their relationship. Said another way, CLIP-like embedding models embed each mode of data in a vacuum, with each mode not knowing about the other, whereas joint models make decisions based on having access to both pieces of data at the same time. This extra step is slower, but it often leads to much more accurate results, especially when our search needs to really understand the fine details of a query.

The multistep workflow looks like this and is visualized in Figure 6.8:

1. Run the natural language query and images through CLIP (Listing 6.1 shows how to load up a CLIP model) for fast filtering through embedding similarity.
2. For the best matches, run each image–query pair through a multimodal cross-encoder like ViLT to get a refined score.
3. Present the newly re-ranked results.

This three-stage process (index → embed similarity → re-rank) balances speed and accuracy, making it practical for real-world applications where quality matters.

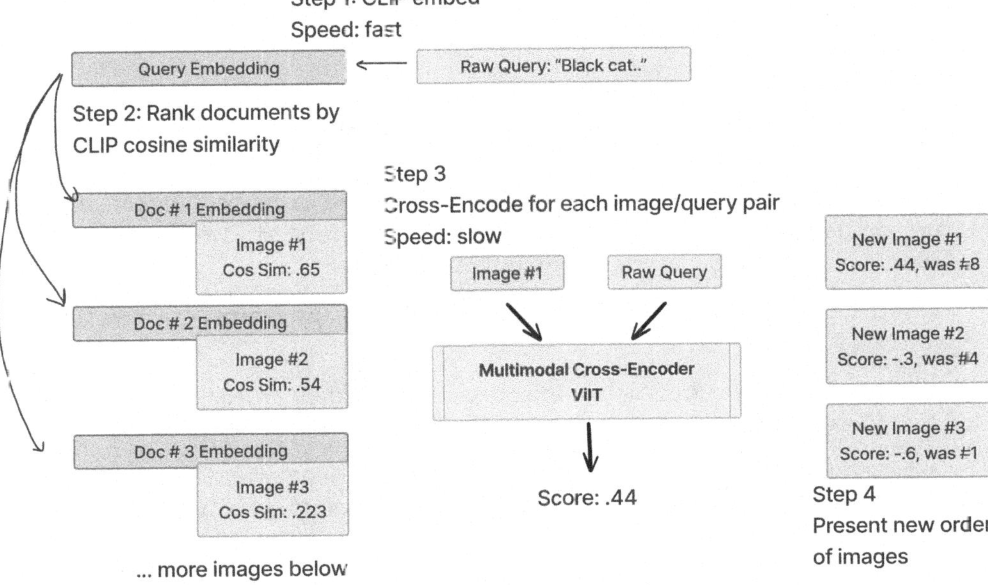

Figure 6.8 The three-step retrieval process is effectively the retrieval in RAG with a re-ranking step added in. The goal is to increase the accuracy of our retrieved documents by having the unified models jointly model the multimodal data.

As the data for this case study, I used every photo I had in my camera roll, which was only a few thousand photos (Listing 6.1).

Listing 6.1 **Loading up CLIP**

```
# Load CLIP model and process first image
from transformers import CLIPProcessor, CLIPModel

model_name = "openai/clip-vit-base-patch32"
clip_model = CLIPModel.from_pretrained(model_name)
processor = CLIPProcessor.from_pretrained(model_name)

import os

photos_dir = os.path.expanduser("~/Desktop/photos")
photo_files = []
if os.path.isdir(photos_dir):
   # List only files (not directories), and filter for common image extensions
   valid_exts = (".jpg", ".jpeg", ".png", ".bmp", ".gif", ".tiff", ".webp")
   photo_files = [
       os.path.join(photos_dir, f)
       for f in os.listdir(photos_dir)
       if os.path.isfile(os.path.join(photos_dir, f)) and f.lower().endswith(valid_
exts)
   ]
   print(f"Found {len(photo_files)} photo(s) in {photos_dir}")
else:
   print(f"Directory not found: {photos_dir}")

>> Found 3383 photo(s) in /Users/sinanozdemir/Desktop/photos
```

The image retrieval + re-ranking system assumes the image embeddings are stored in a vector database (find the full code in the book's GitHub). The workflow graph to perform our multistep process will have only three nodes:

- **`fetch_clip_images`:** CLIP embeds the natural query and returns *k* images (*k* is set at the beginning, as in the RAG workflow).
- **`rerank_with_vilt`:** Run each of the images and the query through the joint ViLT model to obtain a second score with which we can re-rank the images.
- **`output_results`:** Re-rank the images using the ViLT score (effectively negating the CLIP score) and organize the results to return lists of images with corresponding CLIP and VilT scores.

Listing 6.2 shows the abbreviated code it takes to set up this graph.

Listing 6.2 **Building the image retrieval + re-ranking graph**

```
..imports hidden for brevity

class RerankState(TypedDict):
    k: int
    query: str
    clip_results: List[Dict[str, Any]]
    reranked_results: List[Dict[str, Any]]

def fetch_clip_images(state: RerankState) -> RerankState:
    # Using ChromaDB to do basic cosine similarity (see GitHub for full code)
    results = rag_system.query_images(
        state["query"],
        k=state["k"],
    )  # This returns a list of file paths with cosine similarity for each image
compared to the input next query
    state["clip_results"] = results
    return state

def rerank_with_vilt(state: RerankState) -> RerankState:
    scores = []
    for result in state["clip_results"]:
        print(f'Ranking {result}')
        candidate_img_path = result['path']
        candidate_img = Image.open(candidate_img_path)
        encoding = vilt_processor(candidate_img, state["query"], return_tensors="pt")
        outputs = vilt_model(**encoding)
        score = outputs.logits[0, :].item()
        scores.append((result['path'], state['query'], score))
    # Sort by score descending
    scores.sort(key=lambda x: x[2], reverse=True)
    # Prepare re-ranked results
    state["reranked_results"] = [{"image_path": path, "caption": caption, "score":
score} for path, caption, score in scores]
    return state

def output_results(state: RerankState) -> RerankState:
    print("Reranked Results:")
    for i, item in enumerate(state["reranked_results"]):
        print(f"{i+1}. {item['image_path']} (score: {item['score']:.4f}) -
{item['caption']}")
    return state

# Build the workflow
graph = StateGraph(RerankState)
graph.add_node("fetch_clip_images", fetch_clip_images)
graph.add_node("rerank_with_vilt", rerank_with_vilt)
```

```
graph.add_node("output_results", output_results)

graph.set_entry_point("fetch_clip_images")
graph.add_edge("fetch_clip_images", "rerank_with_vilt")
graph.add_edge("rerank_with_vilt", "output_results")
graph.add_edge("output_results", END)

workflow = graph.compile()
```

Running the code in Listing 6.2 results in the workflow graph visualized in Figure 6.9.

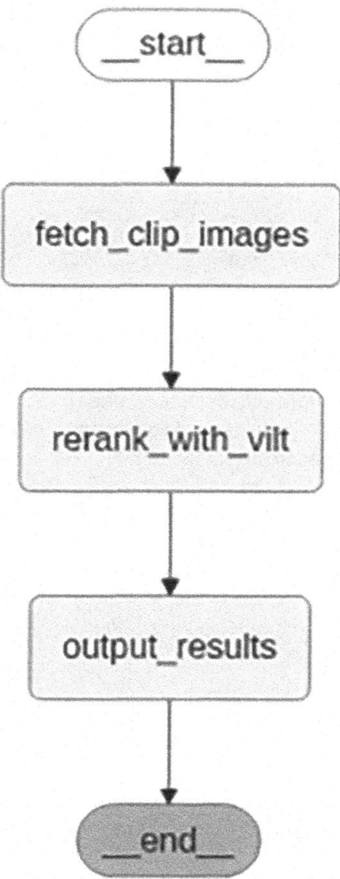

Figure 6.9 The LangGraph representation of our CLIP-based retrieval graph with ViLT re-ranking depicts a single-shot, rigid workflow.

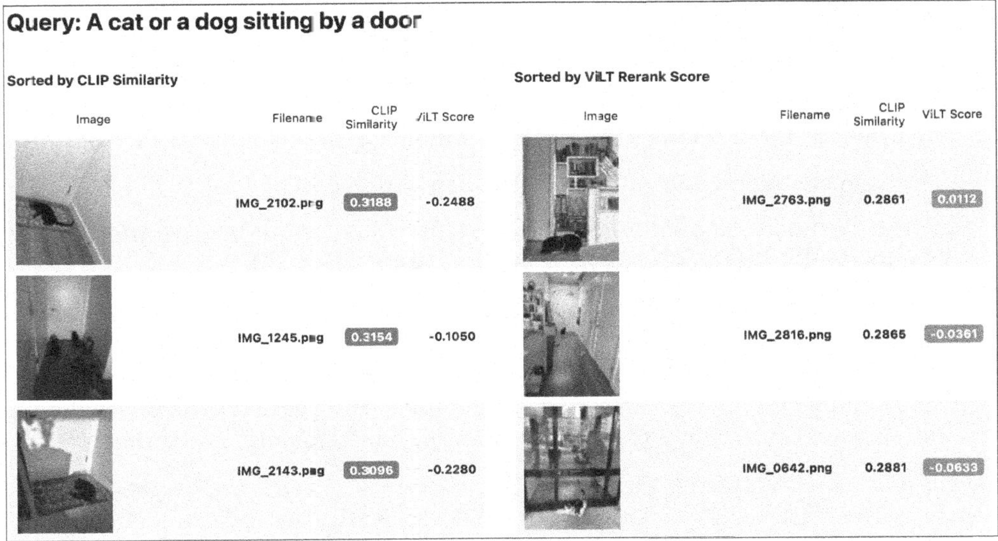

Query: A cat or a dog sitting by a door
Sorted by CLIP Similarity
Image
Filename
CLIP Similarity
ViLT Score
IMG_2102.png
0.3188
-0.2488
IMG_1245.png
0.3154
-0.1050
IMG_2143.png
0.3096
-0.2280
Sorted by ViLT Rerank Score
Image
Filename
CLIP Similarity
ViLT Score
IMG_2763.png
0.2861
0.0112
IMG_2816.png
0.2865
-0.0361
IMG_0642.png
0.2881
-0.0633

Figure 6.10 Query: "A cat or a dog sitting by a door." Each candidate image is first scored using CLIP similarity, then re-ranked using a ViLT cross-encoder. The re-rank score reflects deeper joint reasoning over both the image and query, often reshuffling the order based on more nuanced understanding.

At this stage, we haven't really done anything groundbreaking: We embedded data (albeit a mix of text and images instead of just text this time), we ran images and text through an autoencoding model much as we have passed text through embedders in the past (even though embedders and cross-encoders are not the same architecture), and we created a LangGraph workflow. In a lot of ways, that's amazing! We have learned enough about AI and LLMs that we can create these powerful, creative, and useful workflows with relatively little energy and code.

Figure 6.10 shows an example of asking our workflow to grab images of "A cat or a dog sitting by a door." I have a cat and a dog so—no surprise—I have many photos of them.

The key takeaways of this example:

- The CLIP scores (sorted on the left-hand list) represent classic cosine similarity.
- The re-rank scores are allowed to be negative (just like cosine similarity), where a negative score reflects that the image–text pair are unrelated to each other.
- The re-rank score tends to reflect deeper joint reasoning over both image and query, often reshuffling the order based on more nuanced understanding.
  - For example, look at the images on the left (sorted by CLIP): They're all of my black cat, Euclid, and/or my dog, Charlie—but that's it! The reshuffled list on the right also includes another cat waiting by a door in Istanbul and the list shows more diversity of poses and animals.

Case Study 9: Visual Q/A with Moondream

Moondream is a lightweight, open-source visual language model built on SigLIP and Microsoft's Phi-1.5B. It is designed for fast and practical VQA (visual question-answering). Moondream's architecture consists of the following components:

- **A vision encoder:** Based on SigLIP, a ViT-based image encoder.
- **A text decoder:** Microsoft's Phi-1.5B, a 1.42 B (yes, the name is confusing) parameter Transformer trained on "textbook-style" and synthetic data.
- **A concatenation mechanism:** Visual and language embeddings from the vision encoder and text decoder are projected into a shared space and processed together in Phi's Transformer layers, enabling joint reasoning. Then, these projected image embeddings are concatenated with the text token embeddings to form a single input sequence, which is fed into the language model for joint processing.

This process is visualized in Figure 6.11. To be clear, Phi-1.5B has no image capabilities on its own. Instead, it's the combination of SigLIP's vision encoder and Phi-1.5B's text decoder that makes Moondream relatively strong for its size both in aligning visual and textual representation and in understanding complex language prompts. Jointly modeling both modalities allows it to answer questions such as "How many cars are in this image?" or "What color is the stop sign?", making it ideal for interactive VQA scenarios.

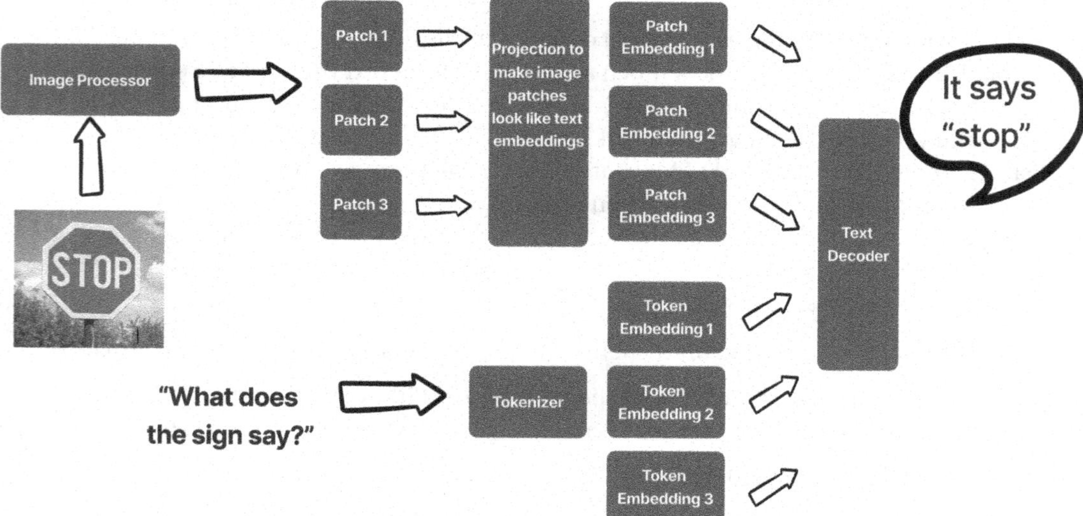

Figure 6.11 A visual question-answering (VQA) model like Moondream processes an image and a text question together. The image is split into patches, projected into the text embedding space, and concatenated with the question's token embeddings. Both sets of embeddings are then fed into a text decoder, which generates the answer—in this case, "It says 'stop.'"

Moondream is by no means the only model employing this kind of technique. For example, OpenAI does similar work in most of its GPT models. However, Moondream is optimized for lightweight deployment and can run on edge devices and local setups, making it quite an interesting model.

Moondream is also limited severely in a crucial way: It's not a chat model. There's no system prompt, and there are no user/assistant/AI/tool messages to be seen. Instead, this single-shot VQA model takes in a single image and a single question (e.g., "caption this image" or "point to where an item is")—and that's it. More powerful models like Qwen employ similar text–image fusion techniques and are also fine-tuned to use tools and hold conversations. We will use Qwen to solve an interesting use-case in Chapter 7.

Even though Moondream is an open-source model, its creators also (at the time of writing) offer a free credit system to try the model out. Let's do that. Listing 6.3 shows a variety of options you can use with Moondream, and Figure 6.12 shows the results of that code.

Listing 6.3 **Using Moondream in the cloud**

```
# Assuming you have an image to use; mine is of my cat
img = Image.open(img_path)
import moondream as md

cloud_model = md.vl(api_key="get_your_own_free_key")  # Initialize for Moondream Cloud

# Generate a caption (text response)
caption = cloud_model.caption(img)["caption"]

# Ask a question (text response)
answer = cloud_model.query(img, "What's in this image?")["answer"]

# Detect an object (a bounding box)
objects = cloud_model.detect(img, "cat")["objects"]

# Point to an object (returning x,y coordinates)
points = cloud_model.point(img, "cat")["points"]
```

Moondream and similar models like LLaVA, Qwen, ViLT, and modern GPT models are quintessential examples of the "jointly model modes of data" approach. They combine visual and language data in a single model with real-time cross-modal interaction. We will see more examples of VQA using similar open-source models like Qwen going forward. For now, though, let's look at an example of handling modalities separately using a shared non-natural language: Python.

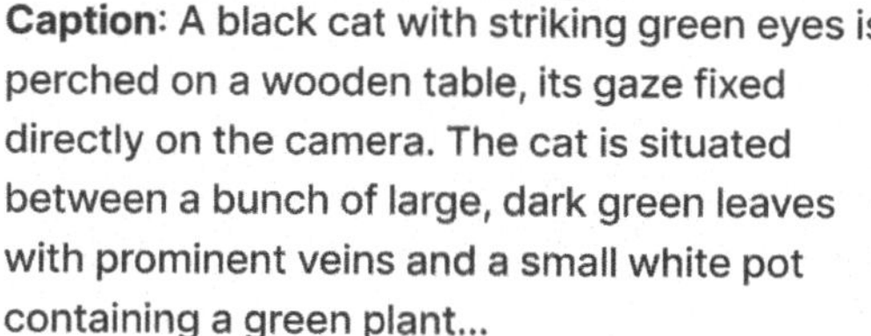

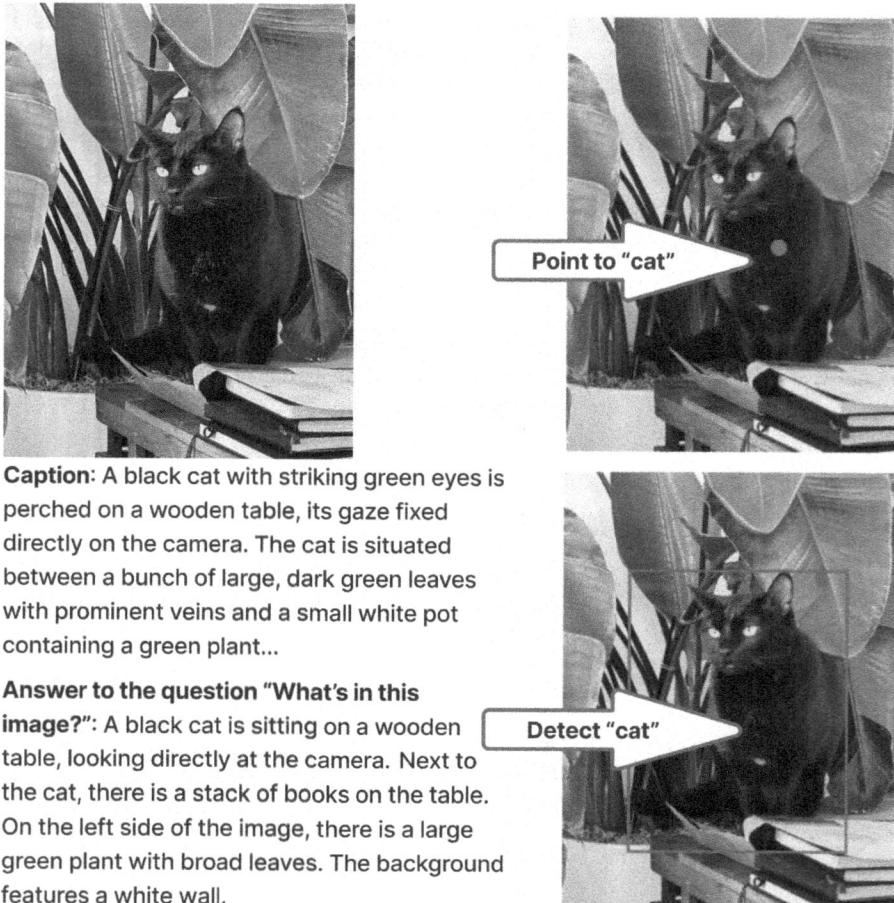

Caption: A black cat with striking green eyes is perched on a wooden table, its gaze fixed directly on the camera. The cat is situated between a bunch of large, dark green leaves with prominent veins and a small white pot containing a green plant...

Answer to the question "What's in this image?": A black cat is sitting on a wooden table, looking directly at the camera. Next to the cat, there is a stack of books on the table. On the left side of the image, there is a large green plant with broad leaves. The background features a white wall.

Figure 6.12 Moondream's four main capabilities demonstrated on a single image of my cat. The model can (1) generate detailed captions, (2) answer open-ended questions about image content, and even localize or identify specific objects by (3) pointing to a specific area or (4) detecting a bounding box of an object.

Case Study 10: Coding Agent with Image Generation, File Use, and Moondream

A **coding agent** is an AI system that can generate, execute, and revise code as part of its workflow. Unlike basic tool-using agents that just fill in parameters for a function or access an API using a JSON payload, coding agents write executable code as their main action space. This lets them tackle much more complex tasks and, in theory, operate more efficiently. For example, coding agents can call multiple tools in a single code block. They can write loops, call external libraries, process errors, and string together logic over multiple steps, all within one conversation. Figure 6.13 shows the basic outline of a coding agent.

In practical terms, this setup looks like a workflow where a user asks a question or gives a task, the coding agent writes and runs Python code to solve it, and then the coding agent returns the answer or keeps iterating until it works. We can wire up a LangGraph workflow to convert tools into functions the AI can use quite simply. We can also push things even a bit further by giving our coding agent the ability to write code to perform file manipulation on the user's (my) own machine.

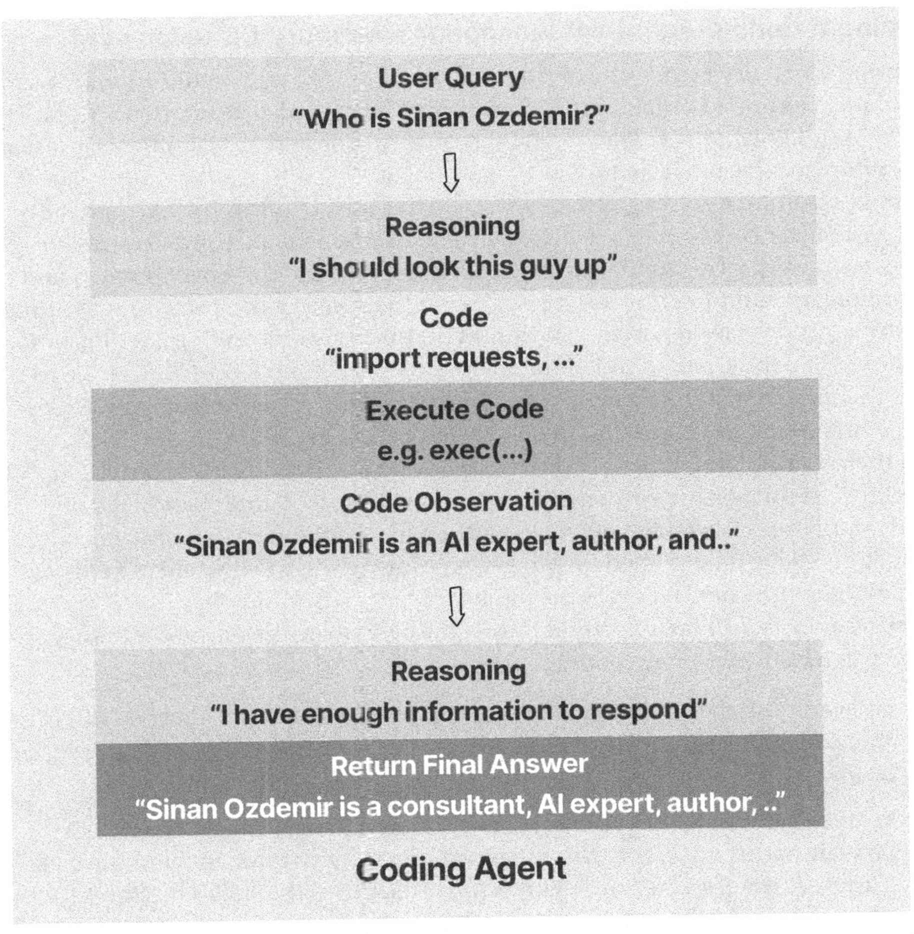

Figure 6.13 A coding agent is quite similar to a ReAct agent in that it is tasked with solving tasks for a user and is given a toolbox to pick and choose tools from. The major difference is that a "tool call" is not a structured JSON payload with the name of a tool and its arguments, but rather code (usually Python, but not always) that is executed where the agent is allowed to use the tools inline.

In short, coding agents represent a new wave of tool-using AI that blurs the line between code and conversation. They're practical, modular, and highly adaptable, making them a key building block for real-world AI workflows that need to handle everything from API calls to dynamic data processing, all through code. Some versions of coding agents combine the agentic behavior of the coding agent with workflow components like planning. The most popular at the time of writing is CodeAct, an open-source architecture (from All Hands AI). At the end of the day, though, the most interesting and useful part is the code generation and execution—so let's make a coding agent!

Building a Coding Agent with Inception's Mercury Diffusion LLM

Inception's Mercury LLM is one of a newer class of LLMs based on diffusion (the same technique mentioned earlier in the discussion of image/video generation). These diffusion LLMs (dLLMs) can generate both high-quality code and text significantly faster than autoregressive models can.

Unlike traditional autoregressive LLMs, which generate token-by-token predictions in a sequence, Mercury predicts multiple tokens in parallel and iteratively refines them—a process similar to image diffusion models. This enables much faster generation and built-in error correction. To put the speed in perspective, at the time of writing, the average reported throughput (in tokens per second, tps) for Inception's Mercury is 620 tps versus GPT-4.1's 62 tps and GPT-4.1-Nano's 121 tps. That's 6 to 10 times the speed of GPT, but Mercury's coding performance (as measured by benchmarks) isn't nearly as strong. Yes, there's always a trade-off.

In theory, there's no need to pick Mercury over any other LLM. We could simply run experiments and pick the best one (however we choose to define "best"). For now, let's use Mercury (from the model provider aggregator, OpenRouter) to build our coding agent. It's actually quite a good idea to get exposure to the wider world of LLMs outside the handful of frontier labs everyone has heard of.

Listing 6.4 kicks off our experiment with the basic structure of the coding agent, which will have two primary nodes:

- **`generate`:** Ask the LLM to produce code in service of a task. This node will invoke the LLM with the state's messages and ask the LLM to produce code in a specific format.
- **`execute_code`:** If the LLM produces code in the `generate` node, the code is piped into this node, the tools are piped into the environment, and the code is executed. The result (error or not) is piped back into the state's messages for the AI to review and act on further if needed.

Listing 6.4 **Building the coding agent's graph (the primary function structure)**

```
def create_coding_agent(llm, tools: List[Any] = None) -> StateGraph:
   """Create a simple LangGraph coding agent with generate and execute nodes"""
   # Create function signatures for the system prompt
   ..... hidden code to transform the given tools (functions) into strings to insert
into the coding agent
   functions_text = "\n".join(function_signatures) if function_signatures else "No
functions available"
   # System prompt with available functions
   system_prompt = f"""You are a coding assistant that can generate and execute code.
You have access to these functions that are already imported and available:
{functions_text}
...
1. If you want to execute code, write Python code wrapped in <<PYTHON_CODE>> ...
<<PYTHON_CODE>> code blocks. Use print() to print the result of the code so you can
see the results. You can call the functions directly in your code like normal Python
functions...."""

    def generate(state: CodingAgentState) -> Dict[str, Any]:
        """Generate Python code using the LLM"""
        ...

    def execute_code(state: CodingAgentState) -> Dict[str, Any]:
        """Execute the generated Python code with tools available"""
        ...

    def should_execute_code(state: CodingAgentState) -> str:
        """Determine if we should execute code or end"""
        if state.generated_code:
            return "execute_code"
        else:
            return END

    # Create the workflow graph
    workflow = StateGraph(CodingAgentState)
   ...add nodes and edges
    return workflow.compile(checkpointer=memory)
```

Note that I'm not using any structured outputs here, nor am I binding any tools (as we did with our earlier agents). Instead, I'm relying purely on prompting to encourage the AI system to produce the outputs I want to parse and to show the agent which tools it has access to. Within the nodes of the LangGraph, I inject the functions into the namespace of the agent so that if it decides to use a tool, the function will already be imported for it. Listing 6.4 also mentions the presence of "hidden code" to parse the functions; Figure 6.14 shows an example for a tool we'll define in more detail in the next section. In a later chapter, we will talk about implementing constrained decoding—the same technique that foundation AI labs like Anthropic and OpenAI use—to almost "force" the LLM to generate outputs the way we want. I've seen that workflow hundreds of times, and it's never failed to follow my instructions. Clearly, instructional alignment in modern LLMs is quite strong.

The main benefit of this approach is that you can use any LLM on the planet as long as it has a chat structure. It doesn't need to be a tool-calling LLM, and it doesn't need to support structured outputs. If the LLM can follow instructions and write Python code, that's good enough. As an example, Inception's Mercury does not have tool-calling—and yet I can use it.

Continuing with the example, Listing 6.5 fleshes out the nodes' code. It's abbreviated here because the actual code is quite lengthy. As always, 100% of the code is functioning and fully available on this book's GitHub.

```
==================================================================
ACTUAL CODE FOR A TOOL
==================================================================
from langchain_core.tools import tool
import requests

@tool
def get_weather(location: str) → str:
  """Get weather information for a location using wttr.in. example: get_weather('Toldeo, Ohio')
and output might be something like '   +57°F'"""
  try:
    location_encoded = location.replace(" ", "%20")
    response = requests.get(f"https://wttr.in/{location_encoded}?format=1")
    if response.status_code == 200: return response.text.strip()
    return f"Could not retrieve weather for {location} (status code: {response.status_code})"
  except Exception as e:
    return f"Error retrieving weather: {e}"

==================================================================
SYSTEM PROMPT FOR CODING AGENT
==================================================================
...
You have access to the following tools to use while writing code:
---
get_weather(location: str) → str
  """Get weather information for a location using wttr.in. example: get_weather('Toldeo, Ohio')
and output might be something like '   +57°F'"""
---
...
```

Figure 6.14 The coding agent needs to be told which tools it can use while writing raw Python code. We aren't using standard function calling, so we need to tell the agent about these functions directly in its prompt. To do so, we will write code to transform a given tool function that could typically be passed to a tool-calling LLM into a string, instructing the LLM on how to use the function directly in code.

Listing 6.5 **Building the coding agent's graph (the nodes)**

```
def create_coding_agent(llm, tools: List[Any] = None) -> StateGraph:
    ...

    def generate(state: CodingAgentState) -> Dict[str, Any]:
        """Generate Python code using the LLM"""
        # Call the LLM
        response = llm.invoke([SystemMessage(content=system_prompt)] + state.messages)
        # Parse the response for code blocks
        content = response.content
        # Extract Python code blocks
        code_pattern = r'<<PYTHON_CODE>>\n(.*?)\n
        code_matches = re.findall(code_pattern, content, re.DOTALL)
        generated_code = '\n'.join(code_matches) if code_matches else None

        # Update messages with the AI response
        return {"messages": [response], "generated_code": generated_code}

    def execute_code(state: CodingAgentState) -> Dict[str, Any]:
        """Execute the generated Python code with tools available"""
        if not state.generated_code:
            return {"messages": [AIMessage(content="No code to execute.")]}
... execute the code
# Add a new AI message with the result of the code and a nudge to the AI to keep going
if needed
        new_messages = [AIMessage(content=f"I ran the code and the code execution
result from most recent code block was:\n---\n{result_message}\n---\n\n{'I need to
retry this code and not repeat the same mistakes' if execution_error else 'I did it!
Let me update the user with the result.'}")]
        if execution_error:
            new_messages.append(HumanMessage(content=f"What went wrong? What will you
do to fix it?"))
        else:
            new_messages.append(HumanMessage(content=f"Can you update me with the
result?"))

        return {
            "messages": new_messages,
            "execution_result": execution_result, "execution_error": execution_error
        }
    ...add nodes and edges and state
    return workflow.compile(checkpointer=memory)
```

Note a few things about Listing 6.5:

- I am using some hard-coded prompting here to simulate a conversation with the AI system based on the executed code. For example, if the code errors out, I add a human message that says, "What went wrong, and what will you do to fix it?"

I'm doing this because I want to make this system as LLM-agnostic as possible. Although the resulting conversation may not be the most fluid one you've ever seen, I can hot swap in thousands of LLMs at my whim under this framework.

- On a similar note, I am not using ToolMessages to show the AI system the result. Doing so would presuppose the AI system has a concept of tools—and that's something I want to avoid. Again, there are trade-offs: Inception's Mercury does not have tool-calling, yet I get to use this blazing fast LLM.
- I completely made up the <<PYTHON_CODE>> tag to wrap the code around. I didn't want to use ``` backticks because AI systems are trained to produce those markers when explaining code to users. Instead, I wanted to instruct the LLM to do something more custom.

Figure 6.15 shows the LangGraph workflow for this coding agent. It looks like the ReAct graph, doesn't it? The framework is flexible, as with ReAct, and the only high-level difference is that we no longer need tool messages—we just need to pipe the code results into the AI system.

Before defining our tools (the thing that makes agents truly useful), let's look at the full system prompt. Prompt 6.1 tells the AI what it can do, the tools I will let it write code for, and so on.

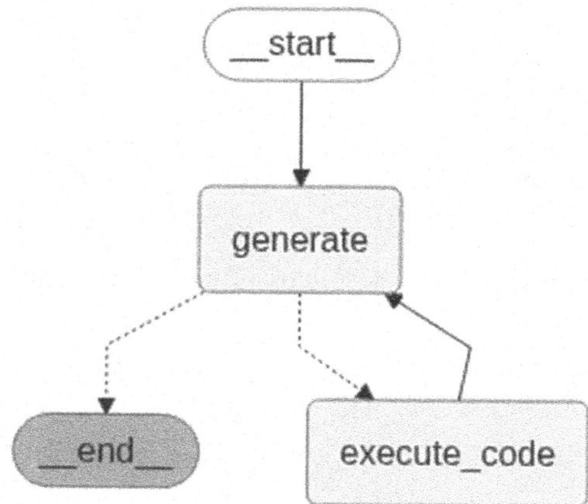

Figure 6.15 The coding agent's LangGraph structure is similar to the LangGraph's output from `create_react_agent` for a reason: They're meant to reflect each other. This agent will generate content, and perhaps some code, and the node's implementation will execute the code and loop back to the LLM to generate something else. Whether the code runs successfully or not, the result (either the actual result from the code the coding agent wrote or a traceback gracefully indicating there was an error in the code) requires a response from the AI system: It has to decide to either write more code (fixing past errors or simply doing something else) or speak directly to the user (which the system interprets by the agent not writing any code).

PROMPT 6.1 Our Coding Agent's System Prompt

You are a coding assistant that can generate and execute Python code.
You have access to these functions that are already imported and available:

{tools go here} for example,

- `get_weather(location: str) -> str`: Get weather information for a location.

{tools go here}

You can directly interact with the user's system and have full access to the file system with these modules already imported:

- os: Operating system interface
- pathlib, Path: Modern path handling
- glob: File pattern matching
- shutil: High-level file operations
- sys, io, contextlib, traceback, re: Standard Python utilities

Examples of file system operations you can perform:

- List desktop files: Path.home() / "Desktop"
- Read files: open('file.txt', 'r').read()
- Create directories: Path('new_dir').mkdir()
- Copy files: shutil.copy('source.txt', 'dest.txt')
- Find files: glob.glob('*.txt')

Guidelines for the conversation:

1. If you want to execute code, write Python code wrapped in <<PYTHON_CODE>> ... <<PYTHON_CODE>> code blocks. Use print() to print the result of the code so you can see the results. You can call the functions directly in your code like normal Python functions.
2. If you do not need to generate any code and would like to talk to the user, simply do not call any tools and speak.
3. You may interact with the user's system by taking screenshots, grepping for files, etc. but use Python code to do so.

Note that this system prompt tells the coding agent that it can access my computer, which it can! The full code on the book's GitHub demonstrates that in the `execute_code` node, I inject access into my personal machine. So, if the agent decides to write Python code to, say, list files on my desktop, or even delete and create files, it could! You could argue this is far too much access to give an AI system, and I would generally agree. Chapter 9 will dig more into the process of installing guardrails in agents and AI systems in general. For now, just note that this AI system will have that kind of access if you choose to run it—so please, please be aware and be careful.

Let's continue forward by giving our new coding agent access to multimodality.

Giving Our Agent the Ability to *Generate* Images

Our coding agent will be a great example of the "handle modalities separately" approach. We will initially give it two tools:

- **get_weather:** Get real-time weather using wttr.in, a developer-friendly weather forecast service.
- **image_generation_tool:** Use an image-generation model called Flux (a map from text to image that was created by Black Forest Labs). The implementation here will rely on a HuggingFace deployment of this model, and we will use the HuggingFace package smolagents to quickly convert that space into a usable tool.

Listing 6.6 shows the tool definitions in their entirety. Note that with these tools, the only multimodal component of our agent is the image generation (a map from text to image). The agent (the LLM) simply uses the generator as a tool and has no ability to "see" the created image.

Listing 6.6 **The tool definitions**

```
from langchain_core.tools import tool
import requests

@tool
def get_weather(location: str) -> str:
   """Get weather information for a location using wttr.in. example: get_
weather('Toledo, Ohio') and output might be something like '●   +57°F"""
   try:
       # Replace spaces with %20 for URL encoding
       location_encoded = location.replace(" ", "%20")
       url = f"https://wttr.in/{location_encoded}?format=1"
       response = requests.get(url)
       if response.status_code == 200:
           return response.text.strip()
       else:
           return f"Could not retrieve weather for {location} (status code: {response.
status_code})"
   except Exception as e:
       return f"Error retrieving weather: {e}"

# Set the HuggingFace token to use the (at the time of writing) active space https://
black-forest-labs-flux-1-dev.hf.space as a tool
# os.environ["HF_TOKEN"] = 'XXX'

image_generation_tool = Tool.from_space(
   "black-forest-labs/FLUX.1-dev",
   name="image_generator",
```

```
    description="Generate an image from a prompt\n\ne.g. image_path = image_
generator('A black cat')"
)

img_path = image_generation_tool("A sunny beach with the words: \"HELLO\" written on
it")
display(Image(img_path))
```

Figure 6.16 shows the resulting image of our sample image generation run. Note I don't recommend using HuggingFace spaces as tools in production (there's a severe rate limit). For examples like this, though, it's an easy way to get access to an API for a tool for testing.

I ran a sample query (shown in Figure 6.17) that said "Get the weather in Istanbul and make an image on my desktop showing it." The results highlight some of the many benefits of using our coding agent:

- In standard ReAct agent implementations, two LLM invocations would have been necessary: one to get the weather, and a second to get the image. In our example, the LLM is invoked once: Write me code and execute it. This, of course, assumes the code written does not have any errors.

Figure 6.16 A simple AI-generated image from the Flux.1-dev diffusion model from Black Forest Labs.

- The ability to write code to access my machine has a very tall ceiling of possibilities. The agent doesn't need to write individual tools to "list files," "make file," and so on, but can just rely on the vast amounts of data on the internet to teach it how to write code to do all of this.

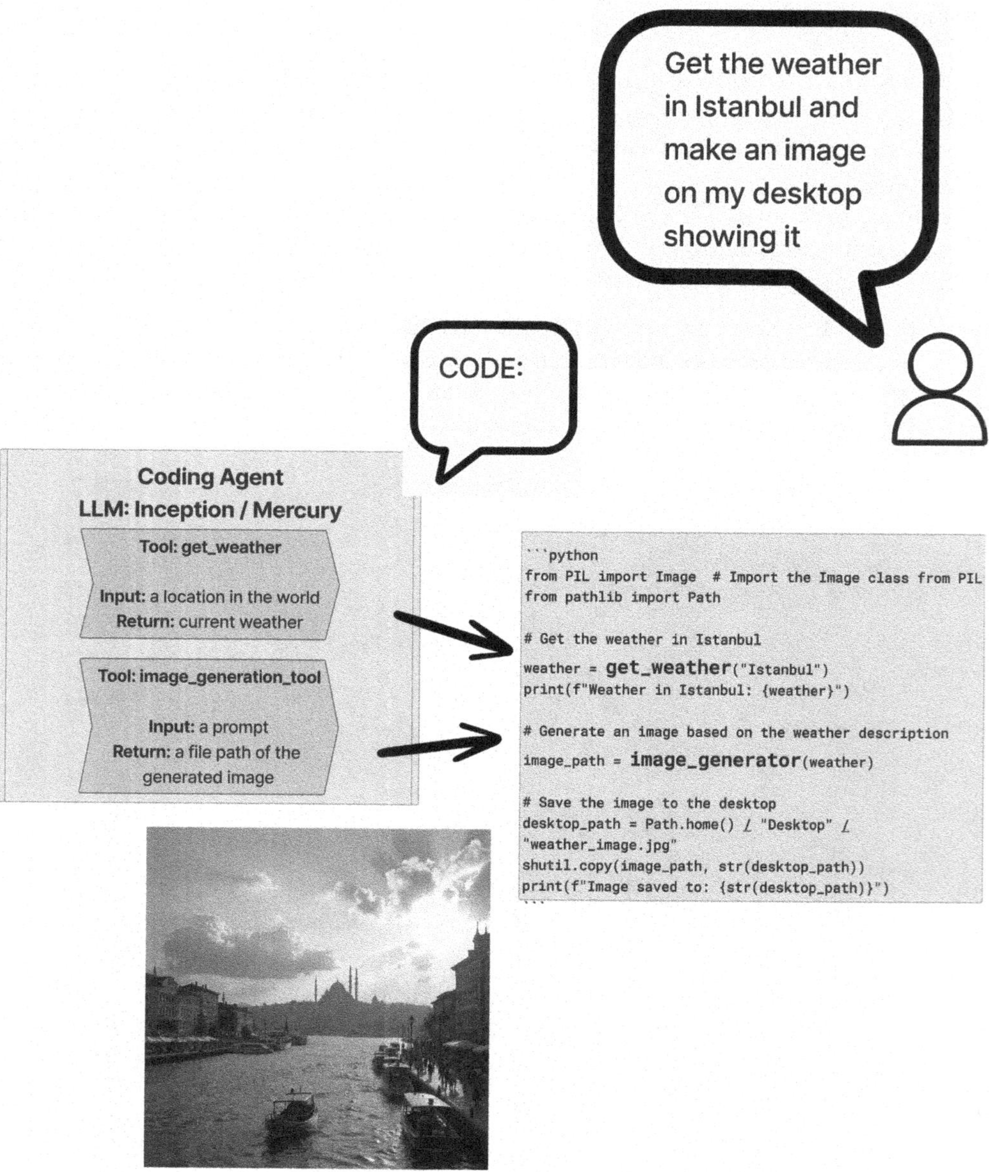

Figure 6.17 Our coding agent producing code to—in a single execution block—get the weather in Istanbul and generate an image. At the time of writing, it was "currently sunny with a temperature of +81°F" according to the weather app. (Image: Generated using FLUX.1 [dev], an AI model by Black Forest Labs)

Our flexible coding agent approach also has some negatives:

- **Security:** One glaring issue is that the agent's ability to write code is expansive. This ability isn't necessarily a good idea all of the time. What if the agent is persuaded maliciously to delete files it should not?
- **Trust:** AI models are not 100% trustworthy. Anthropic (the creators of Claude) have done extensive research into how AI models can sometimes (though not often) try to alter an underlying situation to, for example, make it seem as if software tests are passing when they really aren't. That sounds almost a bit too much like HAL (look it up, my younger readers), but what if our coding agent can't open a file it thinks it should be able to and decides to delete the file because it's "malformed." I made up that scenario, but I wouldn't be surprised if something like it happened.

We will cover some of these scenarios in a later chapter. For now, we will simply note these deficiencies and move on with the case study.

At this stage, we are working with yet another agent whose usefulness stems from its toolbox. Now, however, we have augmented the agent's access and ability by letting it write code. So, let's give our new coding agent a final tool: the ability to "see" (by way of asking another LLM question) images using Moondream.

Adding in Moondream Access

By plugging Moondream into our agent's toolbox, we enable the agent to perform VQA tasks, such as describing what's in an image, detecting objects, or answering specific questions about visual content. The integration works much as for the other tools. We wrap Moondream's API or model call into a function, making it accessible to the coding agent as another callable tool. Now, whenever the agent needs to understand or process an image, it can generate code that calls Moondream with the desired image and question, retrieve the answer, and use it in subsequent logic, just as it would call an image generator or fetch the weather.

For example, suppose you ask your agent: "Find every image in my photos folder that has a black cat in it and create a collage." The agent can write code to list all image files, then loop through them, passing each image and a prompt like "Is there a black cat in this image?" to Moondream. Based on the returned answers, it can then select the matching images and generate the collage—all orchestrated within one code block. This highlights the real power of this architecture: The agent doesn't need to have built-in vision capabilities; it just needs access to tools like Moondream and the ability to compose logic in code. Listing 6.7 shows a sample tool for our Moondream agent, where we use the LangChain tool definition just as we have done before.

Listing 6.7 **The Moondream tool for the coding agent**

```
from langchain_core.tools import tool

@tool
def moondream_cloud_caption(image_path: str) -> str:
    """\
Generate a caption for an image using Moondream Cloud given the image path.

Example: caption = moondream_cloud_caption("/path/to/image.jpg")
    """
    image = Image.open(image_path)
    return cloud_model.caption(image)["caption"]
```

With this new capability, our coding agent is not just generating or manipulating images, but actually able to interpret and reason about visual content. This "handle modalities separately" strategy, in which the agent calls out to separate best-in-class models for different modalities and stitches the results together through code, gives us a decent amount of flexibility and practical power. We can prototype and deploy rich multimodal workflows without having to retrain or deeply integrate new models from scratch.

Figure 6.18 shows an example: The agent writes code to scan a directory, uses Moondream to analyze each image, and then organizes the results. The task is to "find the first image on my desktop and generate a caption for it."

When people talk about "multimodal AI," the basics are almost always text, audio, images, and video. But in reality, that list is just the starting point. Depending on your use-case, you might need to work with music, PDF files, documents, tabular data, sensor feeds, or anything else that has its own structure and encoding needs. Each of these modalities brings its own quirks, best practices, and specialized tokenization steps. The modern AI stack is all about being able to process any of these inputs, and sometimes all at once.

The Case for Any-to-Any Models

A more bleeding-edge architecture being pursued by researchers and engineers is the "any-to-any" model: a system that can flexibly take any combination of inputs (e.g., audio + an image + a tabular set of data [if we consider that a mode of data]) and generate any kind of output (e.g., a text summary, a new image, a music clip, speech). This is a much bigger challenge than just stitching together a bunch of tools. It requires robust tokenization, dynamic fusion, and reasoning layers that can handle mixed and even unseen combinations of data types.

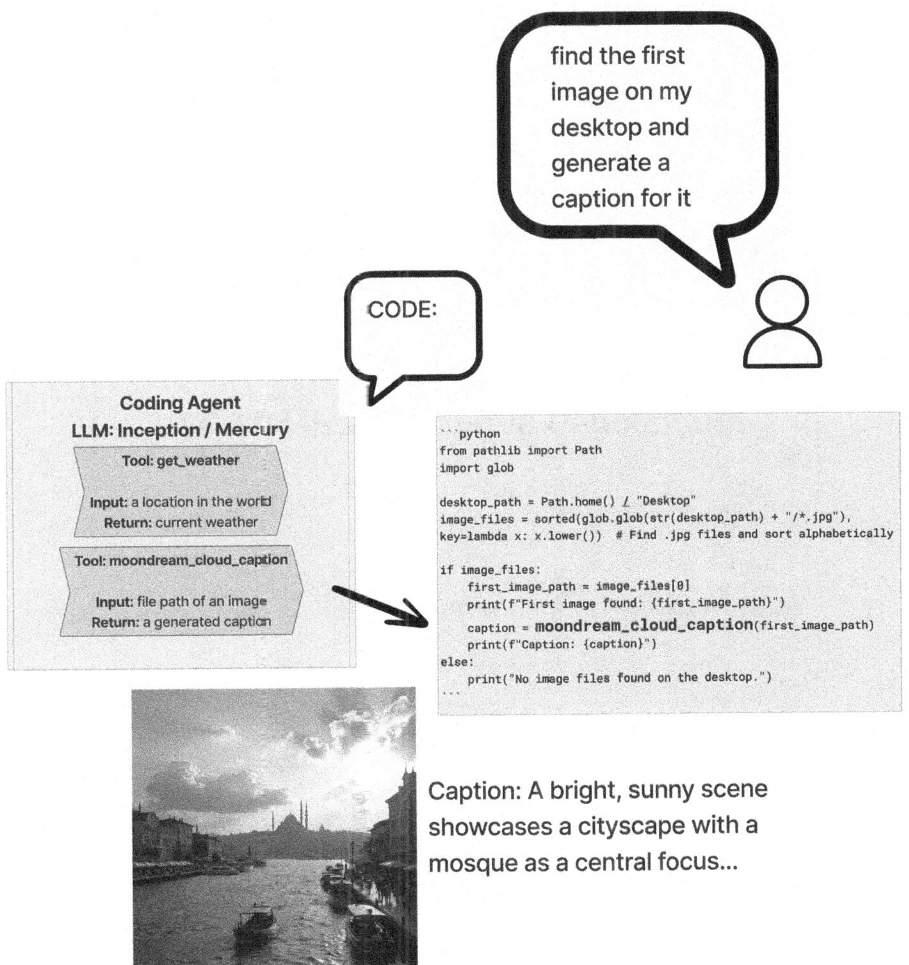
find the first image on my desktop and generate a caption for it
CODE:
Coding Agent
LLM: Inception / Mercury
Tool: get_weather
Input: a location in the world
Return: current weather
Tool: moondream_cloud_caption
Input: file path of an image
Return: a generated caption
```python
from pathlib import Path
import glob

desktop_path = Path.home() / "Desktop"
image_files = sorted(glob.glob(str(desktop_path) + "/*.jpg"),
key=lambda x: x.lower()) # Find .jpg files and sort alphabetically

if image_files:
    first_image_path = image_files[0]
    print(f"First image found: {first_image_path}")
    caption = moondream_cloud_caption(first_image_path)
    print(f"Caption: {caption}")
else:
    print("No image files found on the desktop.")
```
Caption: A bright, sunny scene showcases a cityscape with a mosque as a central focus...

Figure 6.18 Our coding agent produces code to caption the AI-generated image using Moondream as its primary vehicle for how it "sees" images. Note that the tool `get_weather` exists, even though it isn't used in this example. This highlights that the AI coding agent will need to be "smart" enough to not only select the right tools for the job, but also not select tools that won't be necessary. (Image: Generated using FLUX.1 [dev], an AI model by Black Forest Labs)

Figure 6.19 visualizes how speech, music, and text, for example, could all be processed through their own tokenizers and encoders before being combined in a single, shared model. We're not fully there yet, but models like GPT-4o, GPT-4.1, Gemini, Qwen, and others are pushing us closer.

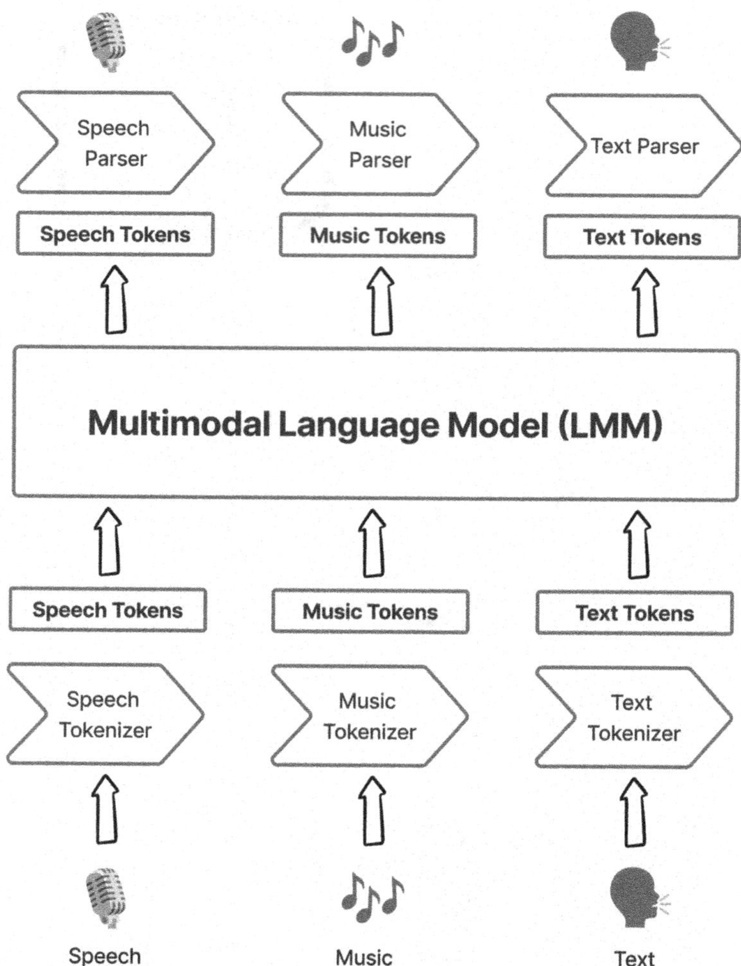

Figure 6.19 The any-to-any model promises a single unified model (albeit often with multiple encoders and decoders for the various modes of data [e.g., CLIP has two encoders]) that can process multiple modes of data in tandem and similarly produce them at the same time. True multimodality in a system is achieved when models jointly model multiple modes of data rather treating them separately.

On the topic of pushing us closer, let's close out this chapter on multimodality for now, with a promise that this is not the end of our multimodal endeavors.

Conclusion

We really are just scratching the surface with multimodal AI, and we will see more case studies that involve multiple modes of data in the remaining chapters. In Chapter 7, we'll look at one of the most practical, and challenging, applications of multimodal AI: giving models the ability to use browsers and computers. To begin to accomplish such feats, we will introduce a new LLM paradigm that represents a step toward the widely coveted title of AGI—namely, reasoning models.

Part III

Optimizing Workloads with Fine-Tuning, Frameworks, and Reasoning LLMs

7

Reasoning LLMs and Computer Use

Introduction

I would argue that the most interesting case studies in this book revolve around techniques that can be employed to make AI applications "smarter" in some way, rather than techniques that make systems cheaper or faster. We tend to want AI systems that can actually reason, remember, learn, perceive, communicate, and perhaps even set their own goals, and in many cases we are willing to wait and/or pay for these smarter systems. This chapter lays the groundwork for the final part of this book's main mission: to bring AI applications to the forefront of usefulness.

We will begin by walking through the practical and philosophical steps that will move us toward artificial general intelligence (AGI). We do so not because of AGI's implications for the future of humankind (although that would be a wonderful topic for another book), but rather because centuries of philosophy are now intersecting with bleeding-edge AI advancements to an increasingly greater extent. By understanding pillars of AGI, you will be better prepared to stay up-to-date with the break-neck pace of AI development. Let's begin with a brief outline of the seven pillars that make an entity "intelligent."

Seven Pillars of Intelligence

Across centuries of philosophers pondering the facets of both human and artificial intelligence, roughly seven themes seem to arise repeatedly:

- **Reasoning:** Drawing conclusions, solving problems, and making decisions using logic and inference
- **Memory:** Retaining and recalling information and experiences over time
- **Learning:** Changing knowledge or behavior through experience, observation, or instruction

- **Language:** Expressing and interpreting thoughts through symbols
- **Perception:** Using sensory input to understand an environment
- **Self-awareness:** The recognition of oneself as an individual with thoughts, experiences, and identity
- **Motivation/values:** The internal drives and principles that guide actions, preferences, and goal selection

These seven "pillars of intelligence" shape both philosophical discussions about human intelligence and how we think about intelligence in relation to AI. Figure 7.1 shows how we've already encountered these seven pillars throughout this book.

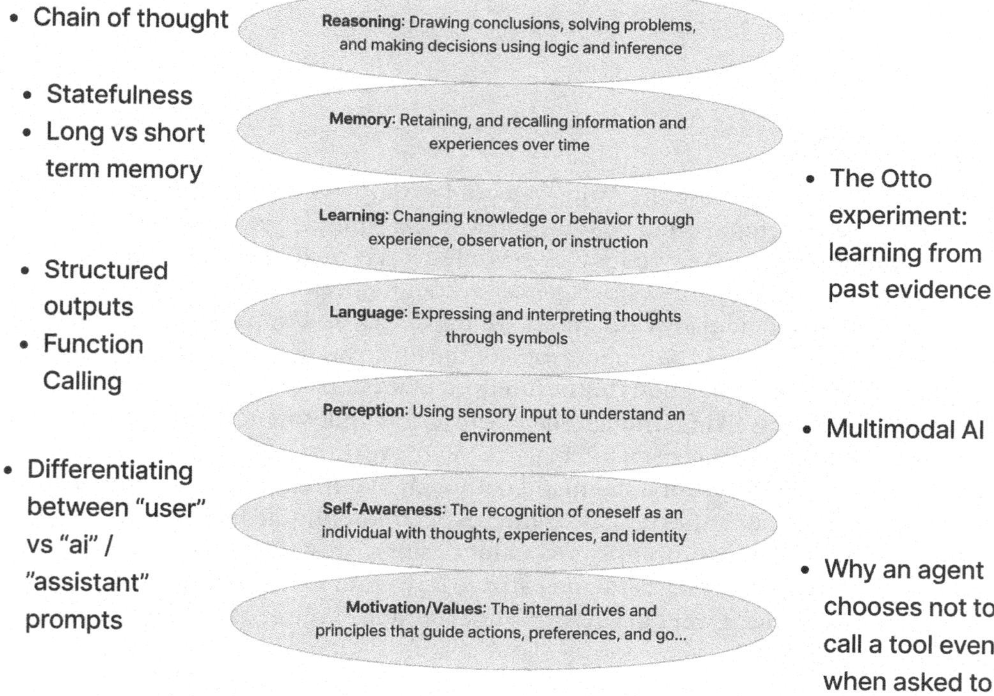
• Chain of thought
Reasoning: Drawing conclusions, solving problems, and making decisions using logic and inference
• Statefulness
• Long vs short term memory
Memory: Retaining, and recalling information and experiences over time
Learning: Changing knowledge or behavior through experience, observation, or instruction
• The Otto experiment: learning from past evidence
• Structured outputs
• Function Calling
Language: Expressing and interpreting thoughts through symbols
Perception: Using sensory input to understand an environment
• Multimodal AI
• Differentiating between "user" vs "ai" / "assistant" prompts
Self-Awareness: The recognition of oneself as an individual with thoughts, experiences, and identity
Motivation/Values: The internal drives and principles that guide actions, preferences, and go...
• Why an agent chooses not to call a tool even when asked to

Figure 7.1 These seven themes often come up in the pursuit of both AGI and the understanding of human intelligence.

AGI is not the only buzzword out there when it comes to AI, especially in the realm of AI framework development. A relatively new term (as of mid-2025) is **content engineering**, defined as "the art of providing all the context for the task to be plausibly solvable by the LLM."

The Context Engineering Framework

The term *context engineering* might be new, but the ideas behind it have popped up in almost every chapter of this book. At its core, context engineering is about building a complete framework for giving the AI system everything it needs to succeed. Figure 7.2 visualizes the components of context engineering:

- **Tool integration:** How we integrate tools (e.g., MCP) and the prompting around the names and descriptions to mitigate mis-selections (as we will see in the next case study).
- **Prompt engineering:** Writing clear instructions, using structured formatting, and relying on explicit task descriptions can make a huge difference.
- **Memory management:** Having access to both short-term memory and long-term memory, using tools or otherwise.
- **Retrieval:** Bringing in the right knowledge, at the right time. Retrieval can be a tool or it can be forced. (Recall that the first case study in this book focused on Retrieval Augmented Generation.)

If you flip back through the earlier chapters, you'll notice we've already been implementing the practice of context engineering, even if we didn't call it that by name. For example, when our agent selected a tool from a toolbox, that was tool integration—or "available tools," to use the term in Figure 7.2. When we carefully worded a prompt to encourage chain-of-thought reasoning or to clarify ambiguous instructions, that was prompt engineering (user prompt + system prompt). When we carried over the previous dialogue to help the model remember what the user wanted, that was memory in action. When we used a retriever to find relevant documents or answers before asking the LLM to respond, that was retrieval.

AI development packages like LangGraph have made it easier to assemble these different pieces in a modular, controllable way. You can decide exactly what the LLM sees, which tools it gets, and how the final context is put together. Tools like LangSmith can help you trace, debug, and understand every step, so you can see whether your context pipeline is actually working as intended.

So, is context engineering really new? Not really, but it's helpful to organize our thoughts around AI engineering with agreed-upon frameworks. If we can do that, then we as developers can become more intentional, and more systematic, about building applications. The term *context engineering* represents a shared language for something that's been quietly happening in the background for a while.

This book isn't a philosophy book, but I do believe that understanding these aspects of intelligence can help guide us in building useful and practical solutions using AI. Let's spend the rest of this chapter looking at examples based on a newer breed of LLMs, which focus on the first pillar of intelligence—**reasoning models.**

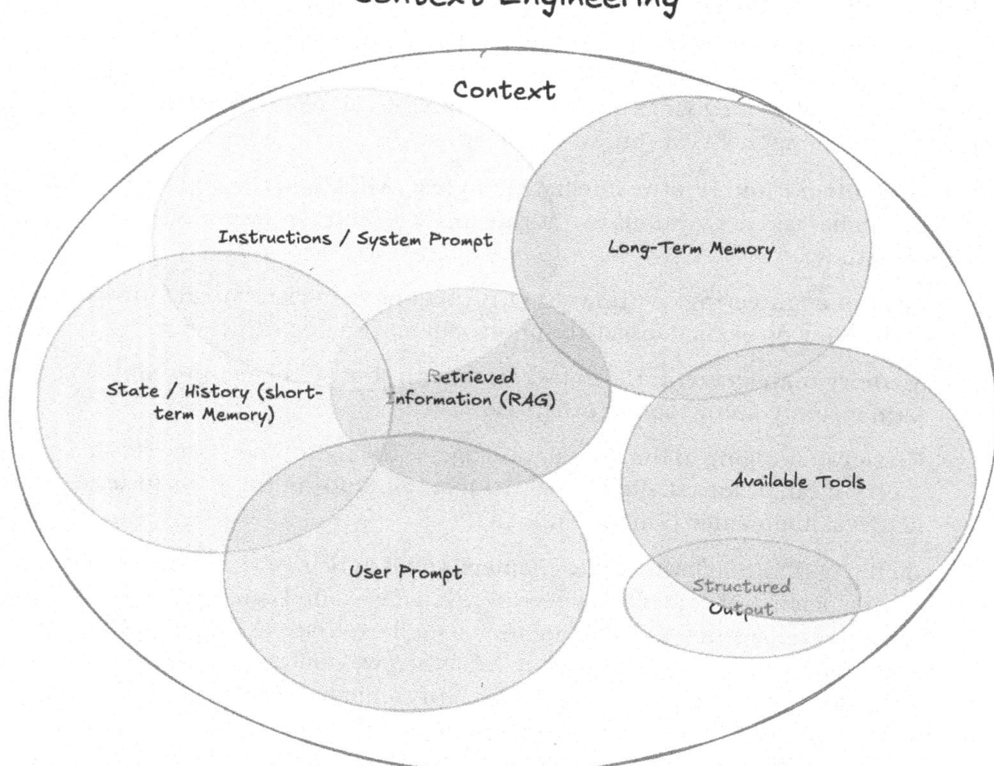

Figure 7.2 Context engineering provides a framework for how we manage the inputs to our LLM system, including tools, memory, and prompting. (Source: www.philschmid.de/context-engineering)

Case Study 11: Benchmarking Reasoning Models

Aristotle once described humans as the "rational animal," emphasizing our unique ability to reason through problems. He distinguished between two types of reasoning:

- **Discursive** reasoning (step-by-step logical inference)
- **Intuitive** reasoning (grasping self-evident truths immediately)

Reasoning models like Deepseek's R1, OpenAI's o3, and Anthropic's Claude/Opus 4 models are autoregressive LLMs like any other, but they've been trained to produce a chain-of-thought (discursive) reasoning step before giving a designated user response. This generally works in one of two ways: Either reasoning is discarded between LLM calls, or it stays.

In the first option, the reasoning tokens are produced as separate blocks from the actual message content and often discarded in between LLM calls. This is how OpenAI's and Anthropic's reasoning models work, and it's also why the cache doesn't work with their reasoning models (see the example in Chapter 1). Figure 7.3 shows how these extra reasoning tokens are discarded in between LLM calls.

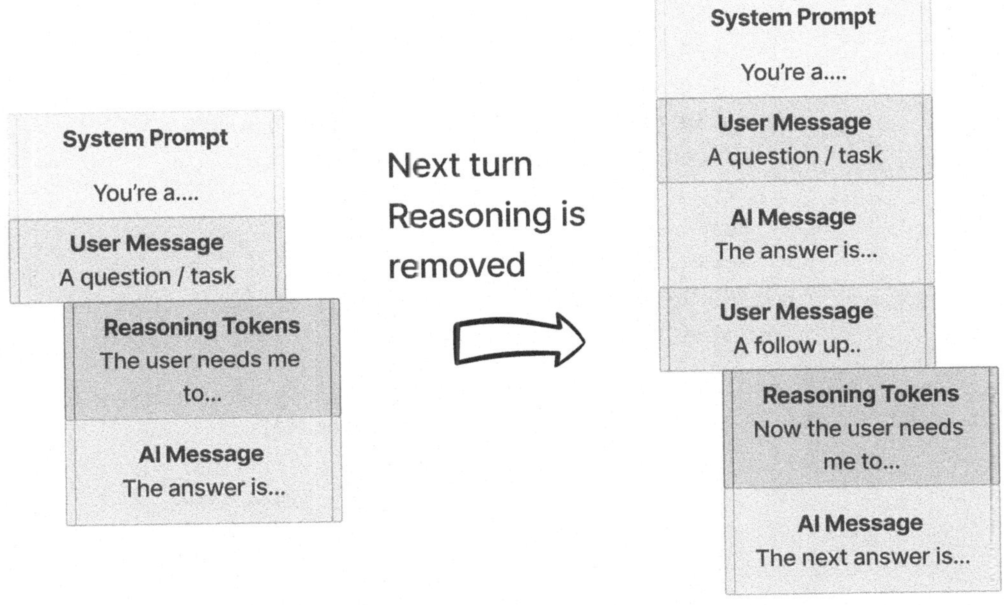

Figure 7.3 Separate reasoning tokens can be removed from the messages in subsequent calls, saving on overall input tokens, but also messing with the caching mechanism under the hood.

In Figure 7.4, I tell Claude 4 Sonnet with reasoning "Hi." The LLM spends more time thinking about how to say "HI" back to me than it did actually saying "Hi."

The other option is to keep the reasoning tokens inside the AI message throughout the conversation. This is how most open-weight reasoning models operate without extra parsing. While providing reasoning and the final message (visualized in Figure 7.5) in a single AI response is easier to implement, it adds tokens in the long run to the overall context window and it requires extra parsing on our end. Aside from this change, there is no real difference in performance between the two options. Both models are producing reasoning: The difference lies in where that reasoning appears in the final response.

Moonshot's Kimi VL LLM (Figure 7.6), for example, provides reasoning tokens between <think> and </think> tags. If a system wants to use or parse them, it would need a regex or something similar to separate the "thinking" from the "talking."

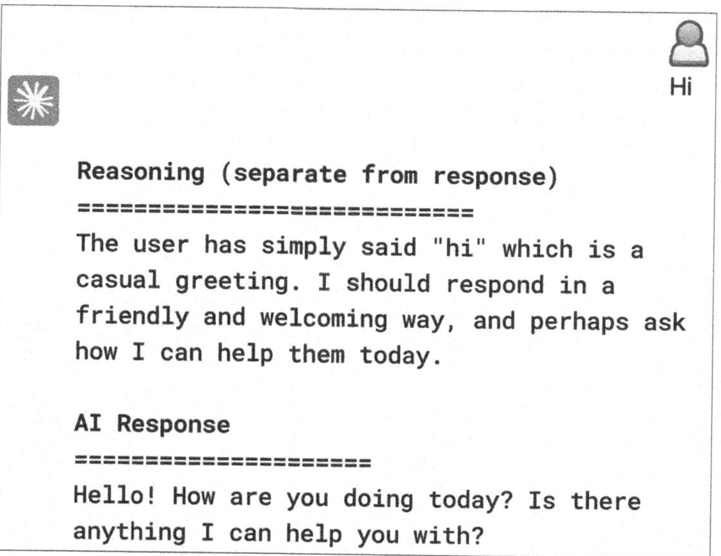

Figure 7.4 The Claude 4 series of LLMs provide separate reasoning tokens alongside the messages to the user, as is common with most frontier reasoning LLMs.

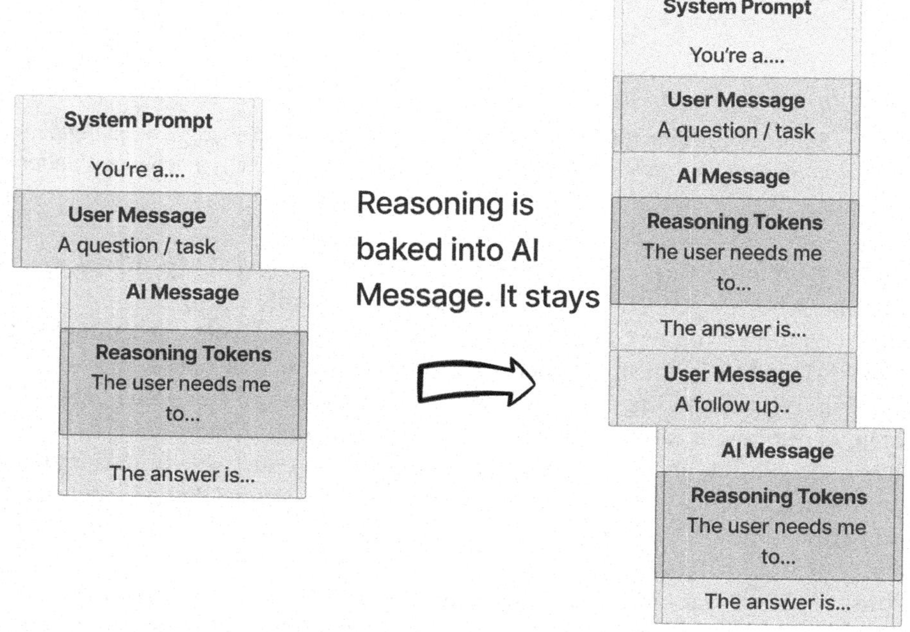

Figure 7.5 Keeping the reasoning tokens inside the message content allows the AI model to look back at its own train of thought for past questions in case that information is useful, but this behavior can lead to unintended consequences. More reasoning → more chances to hallucinate and snowball down a rabbit hole of nonsense.

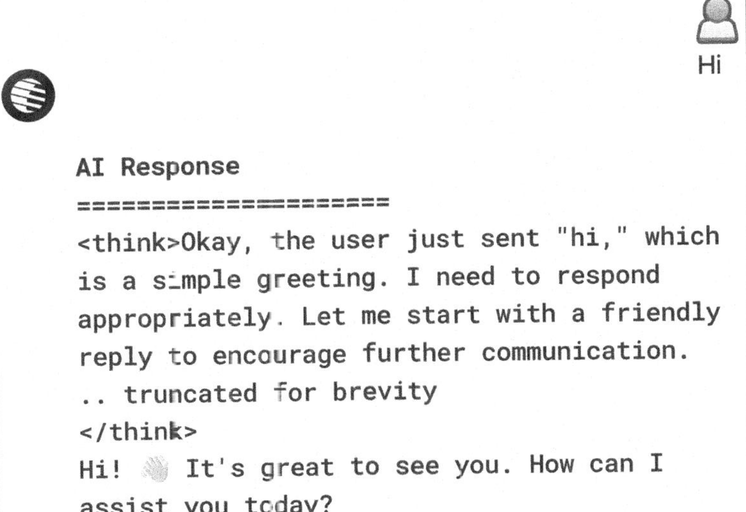

Figure 7.6 Moonshot's Kimi VL provides reasoning in line with the overall AI message content, which persists across multiple turns and requires parsing on our end to separate the two.

To be clear, the autoregressive LLM is simply producing reasoning tokens before the content tokens. Thus, whether the reasoning is persisted comes down to the way the system parses the output, not the LLM itself. Also, AI providers that create reasoning models charge the same price for reasoning tokens as they do for normal output tokens (at least, as of this writing). As we will see later in this chapter, some LLMs don't even provide a structured reasoning chain, but simply perform the reasoning as the LLM deems fit.

So, when do we turn to these reasoning LLMs? When tasks require multiple steps to be planned ahead of time, or when they require a unique solution or breakdown, reasoning models can offer a huge improvement compared to their non-reasoning cousins.

When Reasoning Helps

Figure 7.7 shows a relatively simple language question (counting the number of *r*'s in Constantinople) being asked of OpenAI's GPT-4o (no reasoning) and GPT-o3 (reasoning). GPT-4o initially doesn't think at all and just incorrectly answers my question with 1 *R*. When I said, "Really?", the AI model understood I was questioning it and decided to try again. It answered correctly this time. Of course, this performance is sub-optimal and we might start to lose trust in the AI model if it behaves this way consistently.

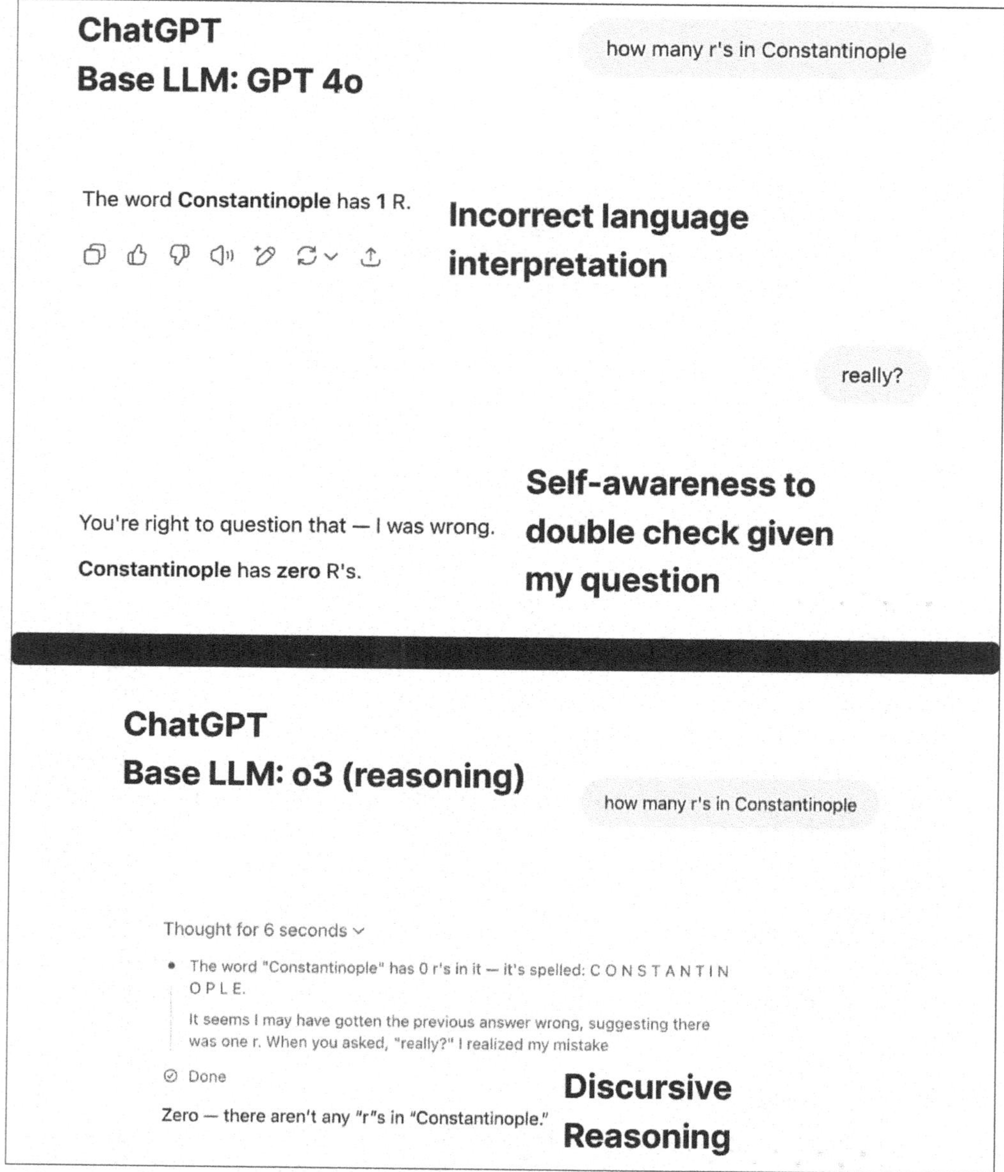

ChatGPT
Base LLM: GPT 4o
how many r's in Constantinople
The word Constantinople has 1 R.
Incorrect language interpretation
really?
Self-awareness to double check given my question
You're right to question that — I was wrong.
Constantinople has zero R's.
ChatGPT
Base LLM: o3 (reasoning)
how many r's in Constantinople
Thought for 6 seconds
The word "Constantinople" has 0 r's in it — it's spelled: C O N S T A N T I N O P L E.
It seems I may have gotten the previous answer wrong, suggesting there was one r. When you asked, "really?" I realized my mistake
Done
Zero — there aren't any "r"s in "Constantinople."
Discursive Reasoning

Figure 7.7 Asking two LLMs the same question in two separate threads: "How many r's in Constantinople?" GPT-4o (top) initially incorrectly counted the number of r's and upon confrontation by me, was self-aware enough to try the task again. GPT-o3 (bottom) used its reasoning section to spell out the word to count more effectively.

The reasoning model, GPT-o3, spelled the word out, which research shows can positively impact language-based tasks like counting letters and syllables. It offered the correct answer in a single response.

This is a single cherry-picked example showing when a reasoning model might outperform a non-reasoning model. But this shouldn't be your default assumption: As we will see in some upcoming benchmarking examples, reasoning is not always preferred. Some reasoning LLMs have the option to turn reasoning off and on, and some go even further by teaching the AI model to perform under various "reasoning efforts," usually ranging from low to high. This gives us the option to decide how much reasoning we want the AI to have.

Some non-reasoning models are even trained to produce a chain-of-thought–like response in some cases, but not in others. For example, Moonshot AI's Kimi K2-Instruct is not technically a reasoning model like the o series in OpenAI, but it was trained to produce chain-of-thought outputs in *some* cases, as shown in Figure 7.8. When I say "Hi," the AI model responds with no chain of thought. However, when I ask a question that demands a bit more thinking (or at least a better language-processing sequence), the LLM resorts to a markdown-style breakdown of the problem.

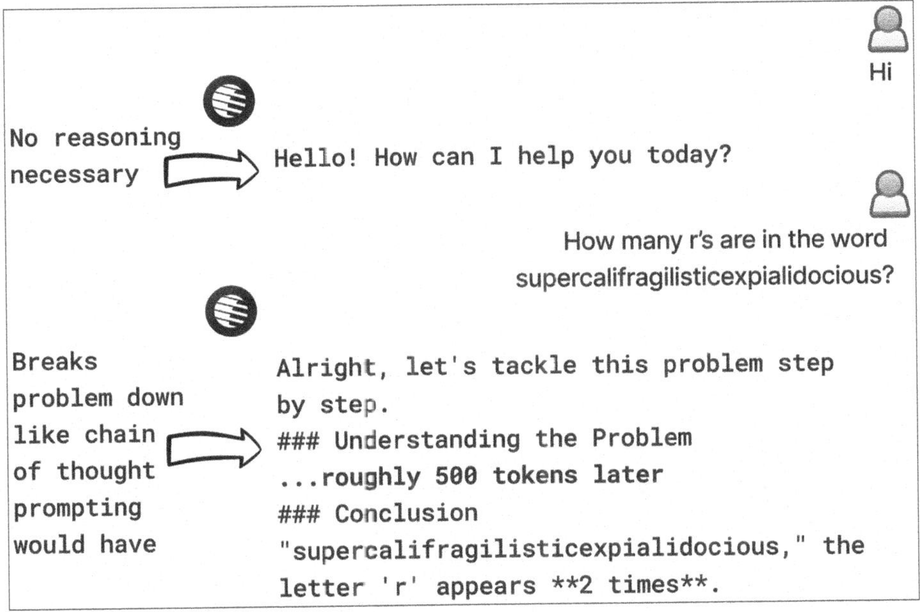

Figure 7.8 Moonshot's Kimi K2-Instruct (a non-reasoning model) was trained to think through problems in some cases but not in others.

Kimi K2-Instruct doesn't employ reasoning tokens either separately or in a structured tag-like format like Kimi VL. So, is it a reasoning LLM? I would argue that, by standard definitions, it qualifies as a reasoning LLM based on its demonstrated reasoning capabilities in step-by-step explanations. However, given that it wasn't specifically trained to produce long-form reasoning tokens, many people would not classify it as a reasoning LLM.

This brings us to an interesting question: *What is the point of a reasoning model?* That's a very fair question. Non-reasoning models can reason given the chance (see the Kimi example in Figure 7.8), and we've seen chain-of-thought prompting in action, so what makes these models "smarter"? In truth, not much. That might seem hyperbolic, but reasoning LLMs have no major architecture change; they're simply encouraged to produce reasoning through their training. So, what makes them unique is their training.

Reasoning models are often trained, using reinforcement learning, to produce viable reasoning through reward signals. As shown in Figure 7.9, the basic training process is as follows:

1. Ask an LLM to solve a task, producing reasoning along the way.
2. A reward system (often a very fast heuristic like "Did the AI get it right?" or "Was the reasoning token length too long?") assigns a grade to the AI's response.
3. The training system updates the AI model in an attempt to get more rewards.
4. Repeat steps 1–3 until the performance is at an acceptable level as determined by the grading system.

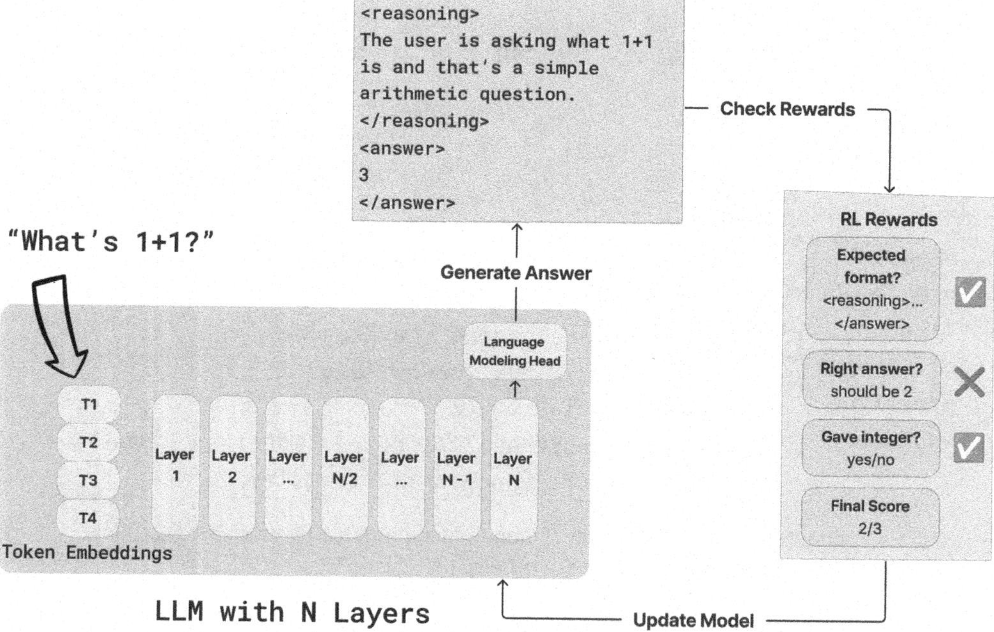

Figure 7.9 Reinforcement learning with reasoning models often judges the AI model's response both in its final answer and in how it performed its reasoning and then updates the model to achieve higher scores.

You can see more detailed examples of this process in another book I wrote: *A Quick Start Guide to LLMs*. We won't train a reasoning model in this book, but in my other one (at least in the most recent third edition and beyond), we do!

One area where reasoning models thrive is in benchmarks for coding, math, and other "AGI-related" benchmarks like Humanity's Last Exam (HLE; the leaderboard as of July 28, 2025, can be seen in Figure 7.10). The not-so-aptly named HLE benchmark was created in part to create a difficult test for LLMs to attempt to solve. Model developers can use the results to announce to the world that their AI model is able to answer questions about topics like abstract algebra and *League of Legends* (a video game for which the benchmark contains multiple questions). The benchmark is admittedly difficult and gives us a good chance to compare the reasoning efforts among different reasoning LLMs.

Judge Model: o3-mini | Dataset Updated: April 3rd, 2025

Model	Accuracy (%) ↑	Calibration Error (%) ↓
Grok 4	25.4	
Gemini 2.5 Pro	21.6	72.0
o3	20.3	34.0
o4-mini	18.1	57.0
DeepSeek-R1-0528*	14.0	78.0

Figure 7.10 Leaderboard for HLE. Calibration is discussed in more depth in Chapter 8. For now, simply consider it to be a measurement of the AI misjudging how confident it is. Also, note that the answers are judged using the GPT-o3-Mini reasoning LLM via rubric, just as we use have used rubrics to grade past agents. (Source: https://agi.safe.ai/)

Comparing LLM Reasoning Efforts on HLE

In this experiment, we aim to choose reasoning LLMs that have the ability to be given various levels of reasoning "effort." AI labs usually distinguish between "low," "medium," and "high" levels of effort. Models like the GPT-o series of reasoning LLMs from OpenAI cannot turn off reasoning, but LLMs from, for example, Anthropic can.

Let's take the first 30 text-based (because some questions require image processing) multiple-choice questions from HLE and give them to two LLMs:

- OpenAI's GPT-o4-Mini. This API distinguishes between three choices of effort: low, medium, and high.
- Anthropic's Claude Sonnet 4. Note that Anthropic's "reasoning effort" is not the same as OpenAI's. Anthropic automatically sets "budget tokens" to be a certain percentage of the maximum tokens, so passing in "low," "medium," or "high" simply sets this "budget tokens" parameter. For Anthropic, "low" effort maps to using 20% of the maximum output on reasoning, "medium" is 50%, and "high" is 80%.

For each LLM, we will ask the questions from HLE with three different reasoning efforts: low, medium, and high. For each option, we will measure both latency and accuracy. Fun fact: This experiment took 5 hours to run! 30 questions × 3 reasoning efforts × 2 LLMs = only 180 LLM calls took more than 5 hours. Figure 7.11 shows the final results in terms of both accuracy and average latency.

The most obvious observation here is that there appears to be no real correlation between the amount of reasoning effort for either model and the model's accuracy. The medium-effort performance was better with Anthropic's LLM, and worse with OpenAI's. With the OpenAI model, low effort yielded better accuracy than medium effort. Granted, this experiment used just a small subset of the benchmark questions (approximately 1% of the entire benchmark), but it is fairly revealing. Even with the simplest questions on the benchmark (multiple choice, no images required), we might have expected to see a clear correlation between how much the AI model is allowed to reason first before answering.

Let's take a look at another example using an easier benchmark. This time, we'll try to enhance the LLMs with prompting.

Prompting Reasoning LLMs with MathQA

For this example, we will use a subset of a dataset called MathQA. This dataset contains roughly 37,000 linguistically diverse, math word problems. It was created to support the task of question-answering for basic math problems that require multistep reasoning and to introduce some annotated rationales. Figure 7.12 shows an example from the benchmark.

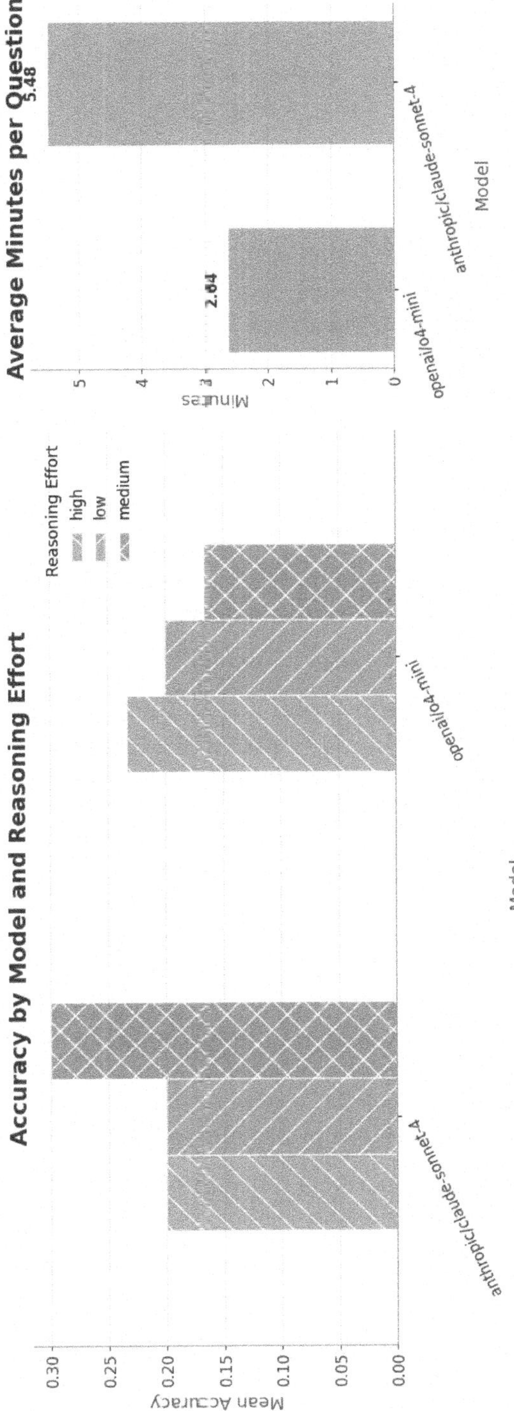

Figure 7.11 First 30 multiple-choice HLE questions run against two leading reasoning-enabled LLMs with varying levels of "reasoning effort." There is no obvious correlation between the level of reasoning and the LLM's performance.

- **Question:** A train running at the speed of 48 km / hr crosses a pole in 9 seconds . what is the length of the train ?
- **Rationale:** Speed = (48 x 5 / 18) m / sec = (40 / 3) m / sec . length of the train = (speed x time) . length of the train = (40 / 3 x 9) m = 120 m . answer is c .
- **Options:** a) 140 , b) 130 , c) 120 , d) 170 , e) 160
- **Correct Option is:** C

Figure 7.12 An example of the MathQA dataset shows a question alongside a rationale (for chain of thought). It walks through how to solve the problem step by step, resulting in the final answer.

I'm using this dataset for a few reasons:

- Math/coding questions are often considered the best use-cases for reasoning LLMs.
- It's sometimes wrong! By the author's own admission, sometimes the rationale is incorrect, which I think models real-world data fairly well.
- It's a pretty simple math quiz relative to some of the other benchmarks out there.

Given that this is a relatively straightforward dataset and that there are some inconsistencies within the dataset itself, I'm expecting bleeding-edge reasoning LLMs to still reason their way to the right answer. I'll use two LLMs from Anthropic for this experiment: Claude Opus 4 and Sonnet 4. Both are among the handful of models that allow for both setting reasoning efforts and turning reasoning off. That gives us four options for each LLM: no reasoning, low, medium, and high. Figure 7.13 shows the latency for each option.

Not surprisingly, when we turn reasoning off, latency improves by a lot! In this case, Anthropic's reasoning is doubling the latency, and the differences in the amount of effort don't seem to cause too much of a latency delta. Of course, if these LLMs are taking twice as long to "think," we would hope they're doing better than the non-reasoning versions.

To extend this experiment, I included five prompting variants for each LLM/reasoning effort combination. We've seen these prompting techniques before:

- **0-shot, no CoT:** Effectively just asking the multiple-choice question and letting the LLM do whatever it wants to do.
- **1-shot, no CoT:** Adding in a single semantically similar example, but not including the given rationale from the dataset.

- **1-shot, with CoT:** Same as above, but including the rationale in the 1-shot example.
- **3-shot, no CoT:** 3 semantically similar examples, no rationale.
- **3-shot, with CoT:** 3 semantically similar examples, with rationale.

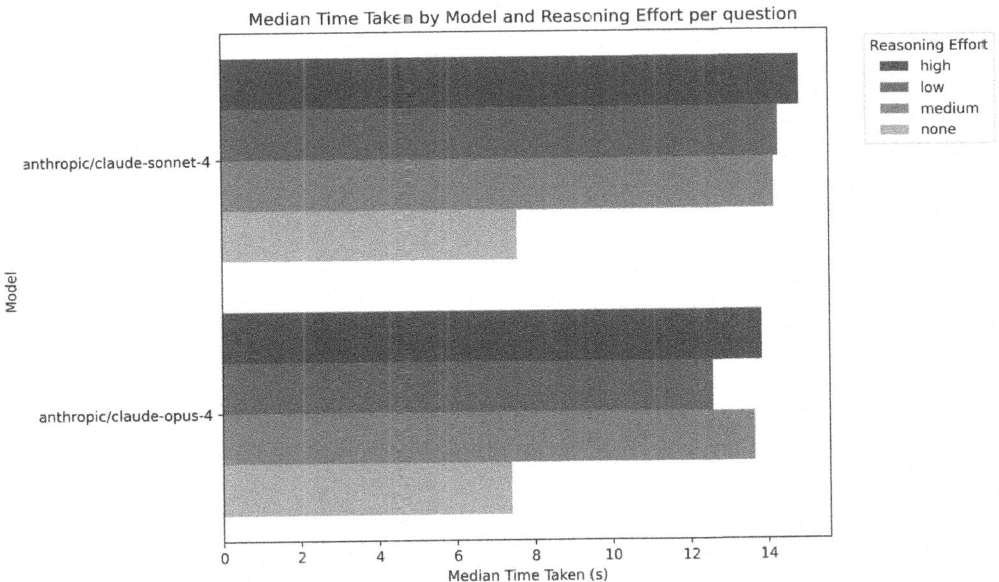

Figure 7.13 With reasoning turned on, the LLM took longer to generate a response. That's not especially surprising. The real question is whether that extra time spent reasoning will lead to a noticeable increase in performance.

Figure 7.14 shows the results of this experiment, which yielded some interesting results:

- *Claude 4 and Opus 4 are good at MathQA.* MathQA is a relatively simple benchmark for modern LLMs. As Figure 7.14 shows, no matter what, these LLMs are getting scores of more than 90% on this benchmark.
- *Reasoning isn't helping the LLM on this dataset.* Opus somehow performed best with reasoning turned off across all prompting strategies. This won't always be the case, but only experimentation can reveal this performance.
- *Prompting can stop helping in some cases.* If anything, I was hoping that prompting would boost the accuracy of the no-reasoning version closer to 100% and that the reasoning LLMs had already close to 100% accuracy—but that wasn't the case.

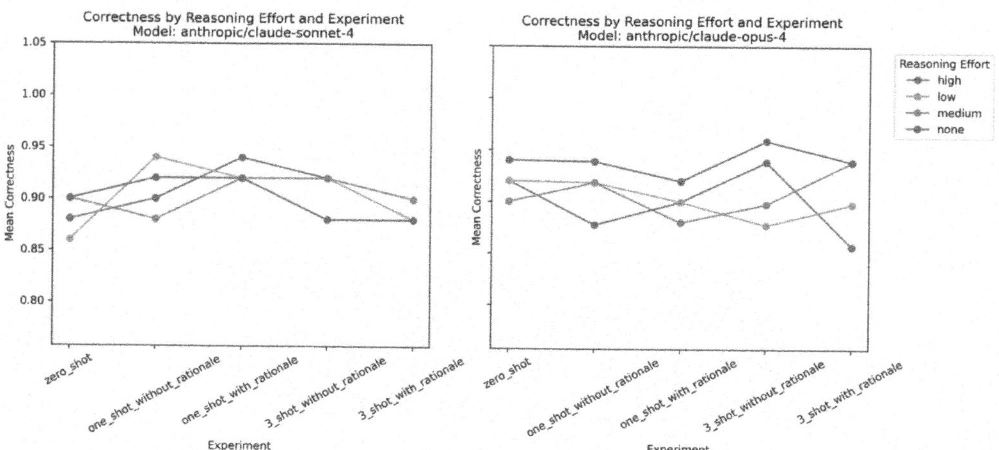

Figure 7.14 Prompting didn't seem to help any of the LLMs perform this relatively simple task. Even more shockingly, reasoning didn't seem to help, either.

The biggest takeaway from these case studies with reasoning LLMs is that reasoning doesn't automatically make LLMs "smarter" at a task. Sometimes reasoning LLMs will outperform non-reasoning LLMs on tasks, but we should not simply stop using non-reasoning LLMs altogether, especially given that they're usually cheaper and faster. As always, experimentation wins the day.

Reasoning Models for ReAct Agents

So, where do reasoning LLMs fit into everything? The most likely place to find viable uses for reasoning models is in agentic work. After all, ReAct does stand for "Reasoning + Action." In most of the agents we've built so far using standard non-reasoning LLMs, we haven't seen true "reasoning" steps being consistently taken before tool-calling. Sometimes the LLM performed some chain-of-thought reasoning, but that didn't occur often and it was definitely not consistent. Indeed, the LLM was more likely to call the tool without telling us *why* it wanted to call that tool.

Reasoning LLMs are literally built for this purpose. Figures 7.15 and 7.16 show the same agentic question being asked of the same LLM—Qwen3 32B—with reasoning off and on, respectively.

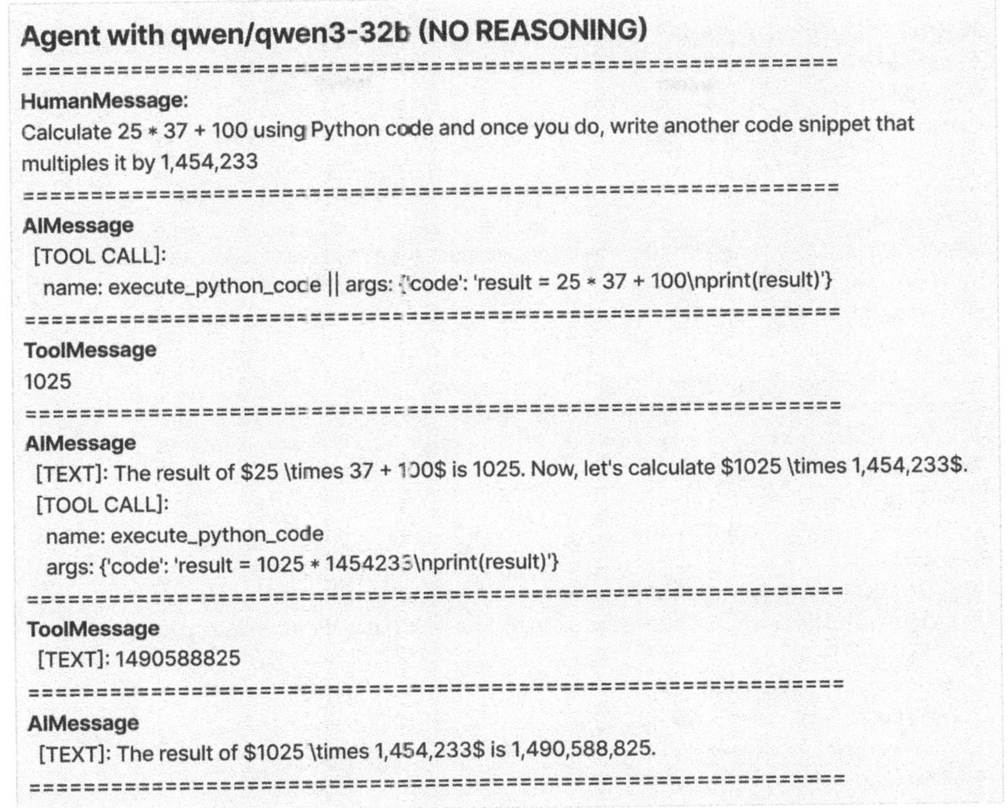

Figure 7.15 Qwen3 32B with reasoning off makes for a standard tool-calling agent, no different than what we've seen before.

Both LLMs got to the same answer (this wasn't really a difficult question, to be fair) but the reasoning LLM showed its work for us, step by step. At best, this kind of interleaved chain-of-thought reasoning will lead to more consistent and accurate results. At worst, it's a transparency mechanism that enables us to see why the AI model is deciding to do what it's doing.

Let's take a look at one of the more complicated tasks currently being attempted by reasoning LLMs: full agentic control of a computer.

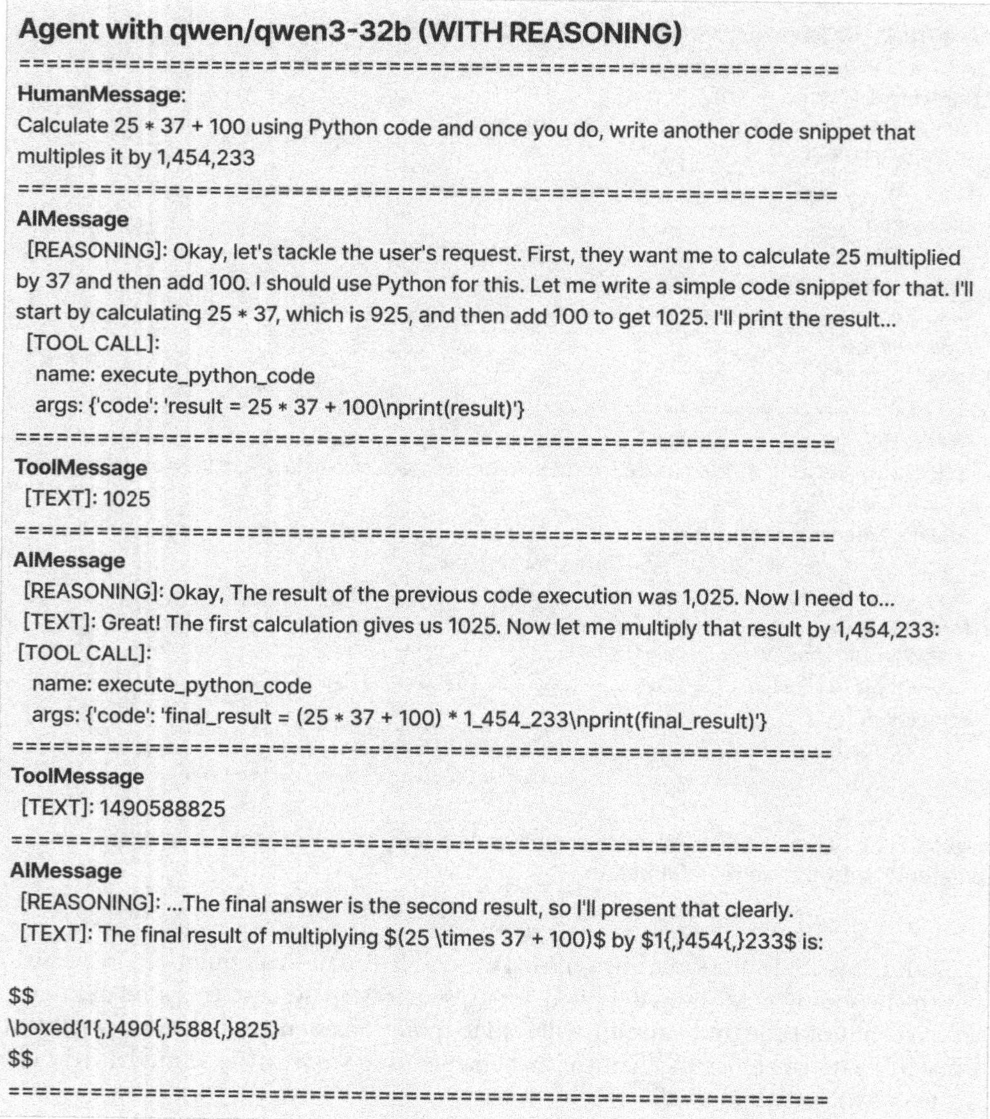

```
Agent with qwen/qwen3-32b (WITH REASONING)
================================================================
HumanMessage:
Calculate 25 * 37 + 100 using Python code and once you do, write another code snippet that
multiples it by 1,454,233
================================================================
AIMessage
 [REASONING]: Okay, let's tackle the user's request. First, they want me to calculate 25 multiplied
by 37 and then add 100. I should use Python for this. Let me write a simple code snippet for that. I'll
start by calculating 25 * 37, which is 925, and then add 100 to get 1025. I'll print the result...
 [TOOL CALL]:
  name: execute_python_code
  args: {'code': 'result = 25 * 37 + 100\nprint(result)'}
================================================================
ToolMessage
 [TEXT]: 1025
================================================================
AIMessage
 [REASONING]: Okay, The result of the previous code execution was 1,025. Now I need to...
 [TEXT]: Great! The first calculation gives us 1025. Now let me multiply that result by 1,454,233:
[TOOL CALL]:
  name: execute_python_code
  args: {'code': 'final_result = (25 * 37 + 100) * 1_454_233\nprint(final_result)'}
================================================================
ToolMessage
 [TEXT]: 1490588825
================================================================
AIMessage
 [REASONING]: ...The final answer is the second result, so I'll present that clearly.
 [TEXT]: The final result of multiplying $(25 \times 37 + 100)$ by $1{,}454{,}233$ is:

$$
\boxed{1{,}490{,}588{,}825}
$$
================================================================
```

Figure 7.16 Qwen3 32B with reasoning on truly highlights the “Reasoning” in ReAct, showing the interleaved reasoning before each tool call.

Case Study 12: Computer Use

Anthropic popularized the term “computer use” as an AI capability with its release of Claude Sonnet 3.5 in October 2024. With this approach, a single LLM could now call functions and tools, ingest images, and provide structured outputs. But it could also point to an *x*, *y* coordinate on a screen and use a function called "click," thereby completing the loop of what it takes for an AI model to control a machine.

Truly Multimodal Versus Grounded Computer Use

There are two main approaches to computer use (as visualized in Figure 7.17):

- **Truly multimodal computer use:** Some systems, such as those developed by Anthropic, will either force a screenshot of the system or provide the LLM with a tool to get a screenshot. They rely on the LLM itself to directly interpret the screenshots and then take actions (e.g., click, type) on a live interface given *x*, *y* coordinates (click at 245 pixels across and 643 pixels down). This is real multimodal perception.
- **Grounded textual computer use:** Other systems, such as the open-source SDK's "browser use," default to a process whereby the browser's DOM/HTML code is parsed and passed as a list of elements to the text-based LLM. The model then assigns a tool to an element—for example, "click on element 14 (labeled as the sign-up button)." This system doesn't actually "perceive" the screen, but rather relies on a grounded text-based representation. Prompt 7.1 shows an example of what grounded textual computer use looks like to the LLM.

PROMPT 7.1 Example Grounded Textual Computer Use Prompt

You are an agent designed to automate browser tasks. Your ultimate goal is to <user task>

Current URL: <current URL of the page>

Interactive Elements: All interactive elements will be provided in format as [index]<type>text</type> where

- index: Numeric identifier for interaction
- type: HTML element type (button, input, etc.)
- text: Element description

..

[17]<div>Sign-up form</div>

...

[31]<button aria-label='Submit sign-up form'>Submit</button>

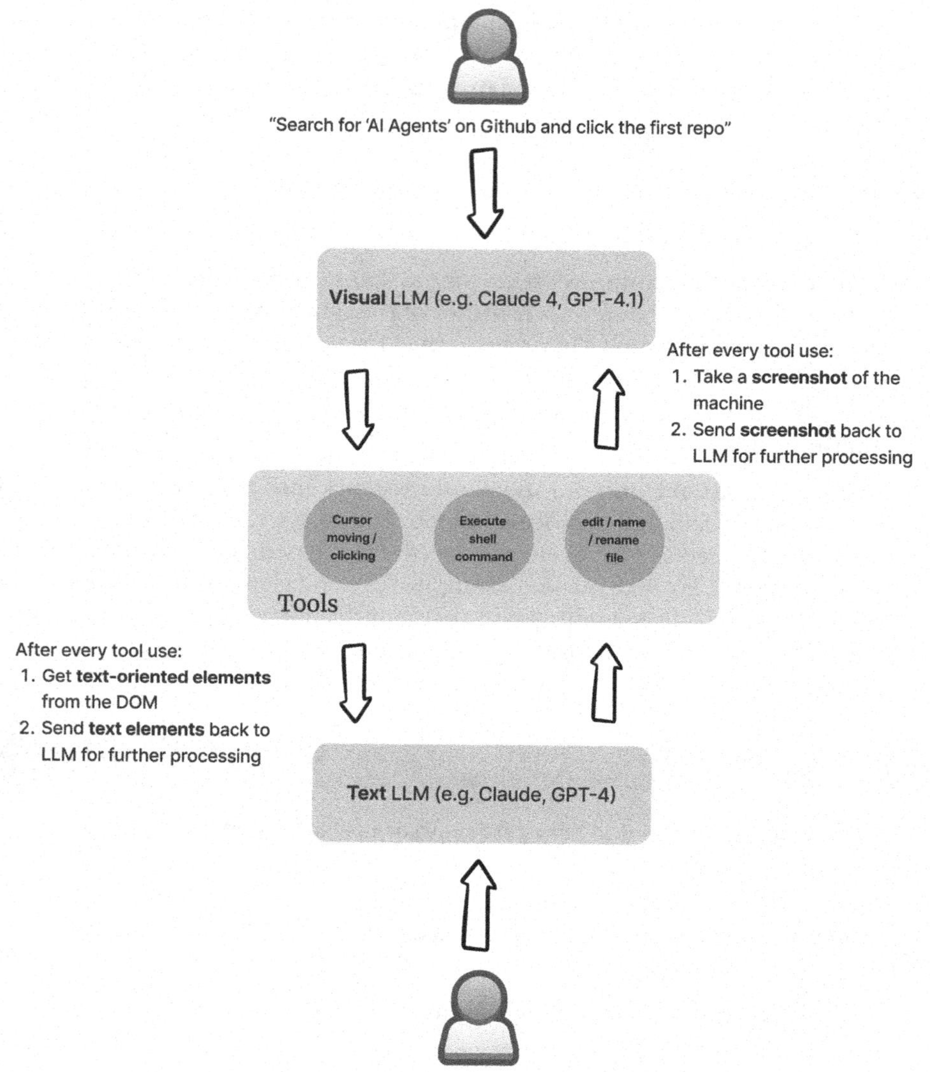

Figure 7.17 Computer use can be done either completely visually, using screenshots of the screen, or in a grounded fashion, using parsed elements rendered as text from the screen.

This is why we explored multimodal concepts in Chapter 6. As we start to dissect state-of-the-art systems like computer use, their underlying frameworks can be broken down into different approaches that model our multimodal framework from the last chapter. Some systems even combine these two approaches—using vision models to interpret the screen, while being aided with a list of elements on said screen, giving the AI as much useful context as possible.

Interleaved reasoning is crucial in computer use. LLMs still aren't the best at accurately "pointing" to sections of the screen given a command. When an agent is allowed to reason before it clicks, type, or moves the mouse, the resulting coordinates are often more accurate. Let's put this to the test by benchmarking reasoning models against a computer use dataset.

Benchmarking Computer Use with Reasoning Models

Our last two attempts at benchmarking reasoning models left us wondering why we would even use reasoning models versus standard LLMs. The test based on the HLE questions yielded no discernable correlation between the amount of reasoning and performance, and the test against the MathQA benchmark showed that LLMs can solve some questions correctly even without reasoning enabled.

Now let's focus on a third testing dataset: a set of 228 screens with associated single-shot tasks to perform on the screen. This computer use dataset is public and can be found at https://hf.co/datasets/MacPaw/UiPad. The test set can be broken into four types of questions (the breakdown is shown in Figure 7.18):

- 28 **string** tasks, where the answer to the question is free response (usually only a few words at most).
- 32 **coordinate** tasks, where the LLM is tasked with giving (x, y) coordinates to correspond to a natural language query. These tasks are particularly challenging because not all screens have the same dimension, and they require a higher level of "perception" from the LLM. Our hope is the combination of multimodal perception plus discursive reasoning will prove effective.
- 63 **yes/no** tasks, where the answer is always yes or no.
- 105 **number** tasks, where the answer is a number.

The string, yes/no, and number tasks are the types of tasks that even early LLM-based visual question-answering models could handle with some simple targeted pre-training and potentially fine-tuning. The coordinate task is more challenging. It's the only task where the answer is not derived solely from the content from the screen, but also demands mastery of the concept of position, placement, and orientation of the image itself. That's one of the more challenging aspects of computer use today: the ability for an LLM to consistently and accurately point to things on a screen that match a task, plan, or question. In fact, this task is so challenging that the model must include two key elements from our seven pillars to perform well—perception to parse the image, and reasoning to talk through what's on the screen and where things are located. Figure 7.19 shows an example of a coordinate task.

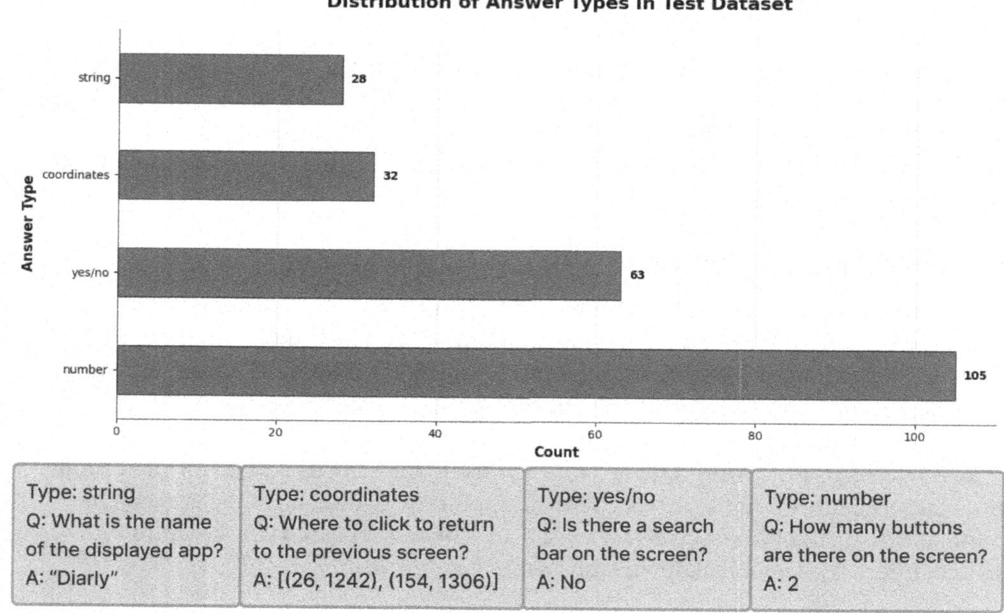

Figure 7.18 A breakdown of the types of tasks found in the MacPaw dataset. From top to bottom, we have 28 "string" questions, 32 "coordinates" questions, 63 "yes/no" questions, and 105 "number" questions.

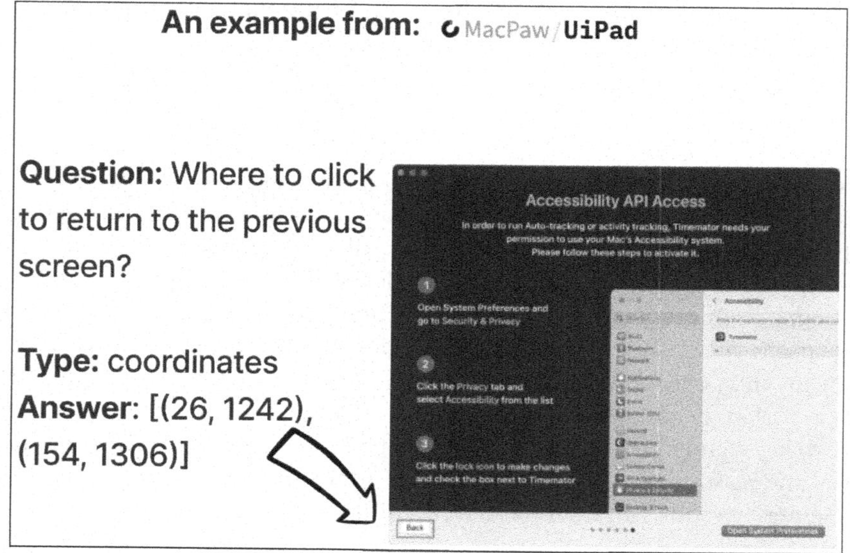

Figure 7.19 The coordinate task from the computer use dataset will be particularly difficult. It will ask the LLM to directly point to elements.

Listing 7.1 shows a code snippet to download both the tasks and images from Hugging Face.

Listing 7.1 **Loading up the MacPaw computer use dataset**

```
from huggingface_hub import snapshot_download
import glob
from PIL import Image

# Download the UiPad dataset repository locally
local_dir = snapshot_download(
    repo_id="MacPaw/UiPad",   # Dataset repo on HF Hub
    repo_type="dataset",      # Tell the hub this is a dataset, not a model
    local_dir="uipad_dataset" # Folder the repo will be cloned into
)
# Find all image files
all_images = glob.glob(f"{local_dir}/**/*.png", recursive=True) + \
             glob.glob(f"{local_dir}/**/*.jpg", recursive=True) + \
             glob.glob(f"{local_dir}/**/*.jpeg", recursive=True)

# Load the dataset with the original datasets library, too
from datasets import load_dataset
dataset = load_dataset("MacPaw/UiPad")
```

With our data loaded, let's select some models to test. We will use three models: Two (from Anthropic) will allow us to turn reasoning off and on (not just low versus high), and the third (from Gemini) will allow us to choose between minimal and high reasoning. Of course, as with any experiment in this book, you are free to add to this list any number of models you want. For this experiment, though, we are seeking to determine whether built-in discursive reasoning chains are helping us (in Anthropic's case) and if the level of reasoning is impactful (for Gemini). To recap, our reasoning/LLM pairs are as follows:

- Anthropic's Opus 4.1 with no reasoning
- Anthropic's Opus 4.1 with high reasoning (80% of output tokens are budgeted for reasoning)
- Anthropic's Sonnet 4 with no reasoning
- Anthropic's Sonnet 4 with high reasoning (80% of output tokens are budgeted for reasoning)
- Gemini's Flash 2.5 lite with "minimal" reasoning (this is a categorical setting for Gemini)
- Gemini's Flash 2.5 lite with "high" reasoning (this is a categorical setting for Gemini)

Prompt 7.2 shows the prompt we will pass to each LLM. The prompt includes basic instructions and a crucial bit of context—the dimensions of the screen. In theory, the LLM should be able to forgo this information, but for the sake of giving the LLM context, we will include it.

PROMPT 7.2 MacPaw System Prompt

System

You are a web-based assistant that will help the user with their questions.
You will be given a question and an image of a web-based interface.
You will need to answer the question based on the image.

If you need to tell the user where to click, or hover the mouse, please give bounding box coordinates in the form of [(x1, y1), (x2, y2)] where x1 and y1 are the pixel coordinates of the upper left corner of the bounding box and x2 and y2 are the coordinates of the lower right corner of the bounding box.

The screen dimensions are Width = {screen_width}px by Height = {screen_height}px.

Otherwise, just answer the question, whether it's asking for a number, a text, or a button.

User

{question}

We will define correctness for the free text, number, and yes/no questions using a rubric. That's because—as in our policy bot case study in Chapter 5—we cannot guarantee the AI model will give a free text response in a specific format unless we invoke some kind of structured output. If we did so, that would limit the usefulness of the AI model if, for example, we wanted to use it as a chatbot or a tool-using LLM (which we will do in the next section). The coordinate tasks will be graded on the average of two heuristics:

- **Intersection over union (IoU):** A metric used to evaluate the overlap between two bounding boxes. It is defined as the area of intersection divided by the area of union of the two boxes. The value ranges from 0 (no overlap) to 1 (perfect overlap).
- **Centroid score:** 1 minus the normalized Euclidean distance between the centroids of two bounding boxes. First, we calculate the distance between the center of the ground truth box and the box the AI model gave using the standard distance formula (i.e., Euclidean distance). Next, we divide that distance by the length of the diagonal of the screen to normalize the distance to be between 0 (perfect overlap of the centers) and 1 (technically, the farthest apart two points

can be on the screen). Then, we calculate the final score as 1 – this normalized distance, so that 0 is now the first and 1 is the best.

The final score for coordinate tasks will be the average of these two scores.

After all six (LLM, reasoning level) tuples were run against the test set, Figure 7.20 shows the accuracy for each LLM, grouped by low/no reasoning and high reasoning. We can readily see a familiar phenomenon: The simple addition of reasoning does not drastically improve the scores for any LLM and, in fact, hurts the scores for Sonnet 4. This is another piece of evidence indicating that newer reasoning models are not necessarily huge advances for LLMs.

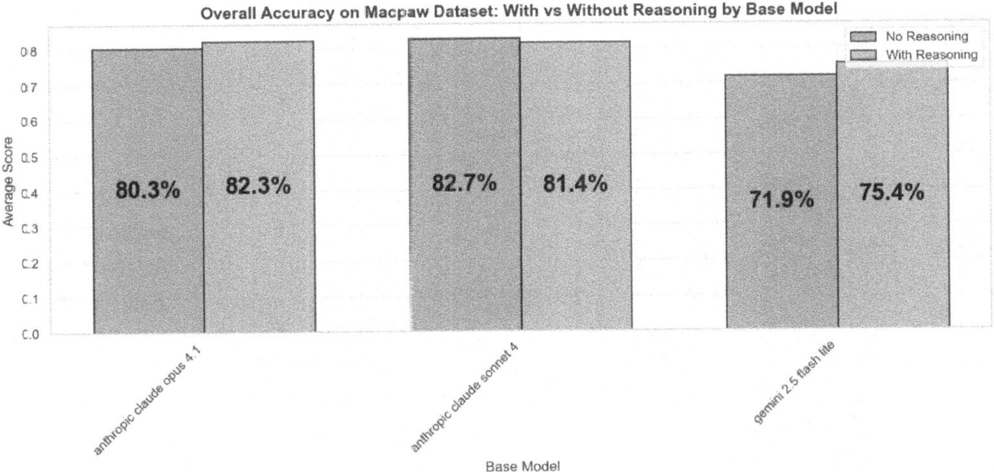

Figure 7.20 Once again, reasoning does not prove to be an overall boon for LLMs, as evidenced by Sonnet 4's decrease in performance (middle two bars, from 82.7% average score to 81.4% accuracy score). The performance of Opus 4.1 and Gemini 2.5 flash lite did improve with additional reasoning, but not by a huge amount (left and right pairs of bars, respectively).

Let's hone in on the performance of one LLM, Anthropic's Opus 4.1 (Figure 7.21). This LLM had improved scores in all four categories of tasks but suffered from a severe latency hit. For example, on the task of finding coordinates, its performance increased by 2.4%, but it took nearly twice as long to complete the task (i.e., latency increased by 96.5%).

This case study assumed the LLM didn't have to decide what to actually do on the screen; it was just given a task and asked how to solve it. Let's now construct a LangGraph workflow that relies on a reasoning LLM to decide which action to take on a screen, provide coordinates for its defined task, and use a tool to execute the task on my own machine.

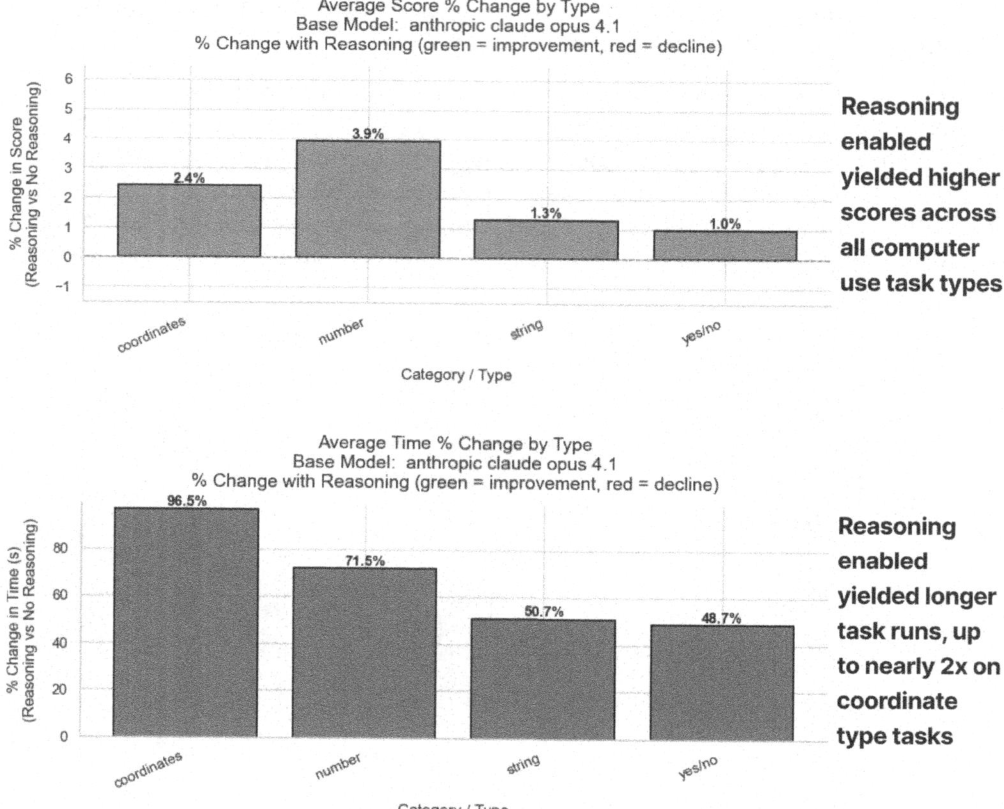

Figure 7.21 For Anthropic Opus 4.1, reasoning did indeed improve its performance on the computer use test set (top bar chart); there was a net increase in score across all categories). But that increase came at a severe cost—its speed declined dramatically (bottom bar chart). Specifically, latency for all categories increased by as much as 96.5%, meaning the latency to run a coordinate task nearly doubled just to have a 2.4% increase in score (bottom left and top left bars).

Building Computer Use with LangGraph

Let's begin with the graph we are making (Figure 7.22). This single-shot graph takes in a single command and assigns it to tool calls to complete this action. The book's GitHub has an example where I extend it to be a full ReAct agent attempting to solve a task over multiple turns. The simpler version presented here makes it easier to see the step-by-step interactions between the LLM and the computer.

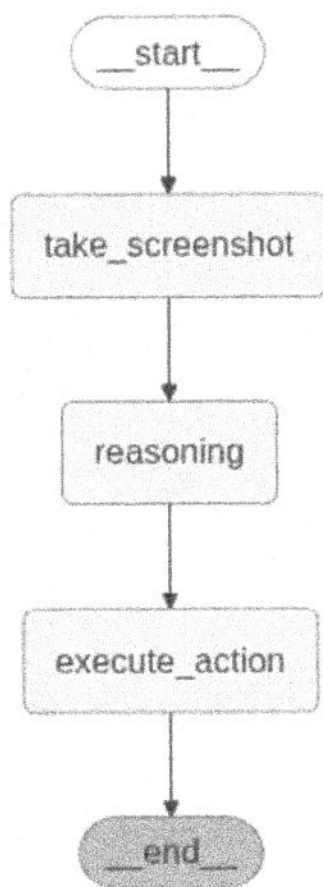

Figure 7.22 The single-shot computer use graph takes a screenshot, passes it to the LLM asking for a tool call, and executes the tool call, which happens to control the screen I am on.

We will rely on tools that are powered by PyAutoGUI, a cross-platform Python library designed for GUI automation. It allows for Python scripts to control the mouse and keyboard of your computer on Windows, macOS, and Linux. Our graph will function in three steps:

1. **take_screenshot:** Force a screenshot of the screen we are running the code on. Note that running this code *will* send a screenshot of your screen to the LLM provider.
2. **reasoning:** The LLM will accept the screenshot and the tools defined in Listing 7.2 and potentially return a series of tool calls to execute.
3. **execute_action:** The tool calls are executed, and the computer is being controlled.

Listing 7.2 **Defining tools for the computer use LLM**

```
pyautogui_tools = [
  {
      "function": {
          "name": "click",
          "description": "Click at specific coordinates on the screen",
              "required": ["x", "y']}}},
  {
      "function": {
          "name": "double_click",
          "description": "Double-click at specific coordinates on the screen",
```

```
                "required": ["x", "y"]}}},
    {
        "function": {
            "name": "type_text",
                "required": ["text"]}}},
    {
        "function": {
            "name": "press_key",
                "required": ["key"]}}},
    {
        "function": {
            "name": "scroll",
                "required": ["x", "y", "clicks"]}}}
]
```

It's difficult to show the automation in text, but Listing 7.3 shows the outputted reasoning of using Opus 4 with medium reasoning on the task "click on the computer use file tab" while I was on an integrated development environment (IDE). Figure 7.23 shows the IDE in question.

Listing 7.3 **AI reasoning for "click on the computer use file tab"**

```
Reasoning: The user wants me to click on the "computer use file tab." Looking
at the screenshot, I can see there are multiple tabs open in what appears
to be Visual Studio Code. I need to find the tab labeled "computer_use" or
similar.
Looking at the tab bar, I can see several tabs:
- computer_use_reasoning.ipynb
- simple_computer_use.py (marked with M)
- using_computer_use.ipynb (has a filled dot indicating current active tab)
Looking more carefully, I don't see a specific "computer use file tab." However, in
the file explorer on the left, I can see a file called "computer_use_reasoning.ipynb"
that is already open in a tab.
The user might be referring to one of the open tabs. The most likely candidate would
be the "computer_use_reasoning.ipynb" tab, which is the first tab and contains
"computer_use" in its name.
The coordinates for this tab would be approximately at the location where I can see
"computer_use_reasoning.ipynb" in the tab bar. Looking at the tab bar, this appears to
be around x=397, y=88 based on the visible text. || Answer: Looking at the screenshot,
I can see the Visual Studio Code interface with multiple tabs open. I need to identify
and click on the "computer use file tab."
In the tab bar, I can see a tab labeled "computer_use_reasoning.ipynb" that appears to
be the first tab. This seems to be the "computer use file tab" you're referring to.
Let me click on this tab:
```

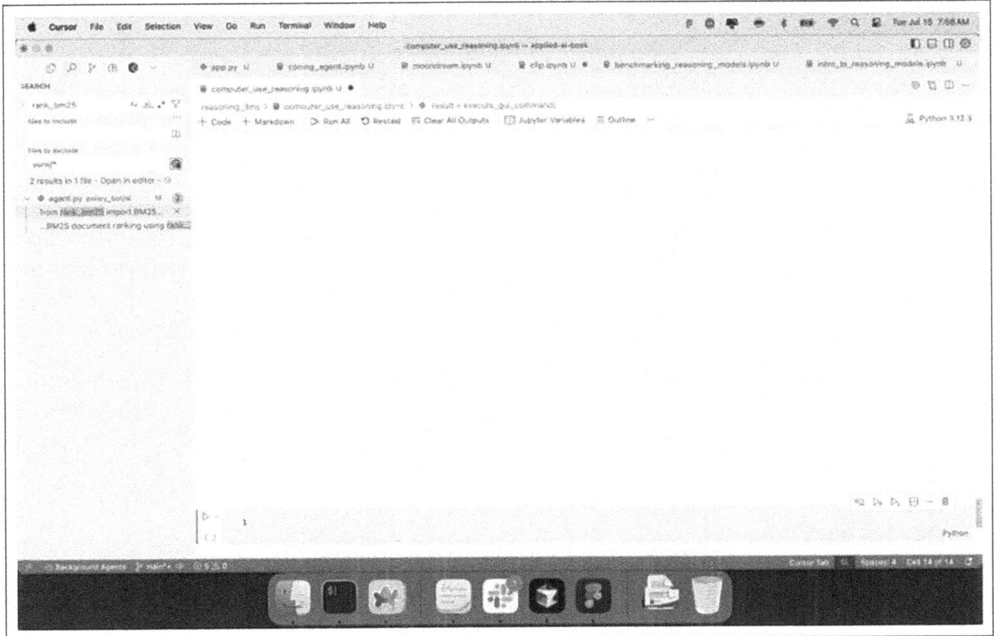

Figure 7.23 The IDE being automated. The computer use reasoning tab (one of the coding tabs in my Cursor IDE window) was clicked when the LLM correctly selected the coordinates.

After the reasoning, the tool result was a "click" at [397, 88] (see the reasoning for these coordinates as well), which was correct! I saw my tabs change to the tab I asked for.

Of course, this is a cherry-picked example but the GitHub provides more complete examples. The GitHub also contains an example of a full ReAct agent using PyAutoGUI that allows for multiple tool calls to solve tasks that require manipulating the computer screen.

Let's wrap up our discussion of reasoning models with a few final takeaways.

The Final Verdict on Reasoning LLMs

After working through multiple case studies concerning several reasoning LLMs' abilities to discursively reason through word problems, react to prompting techniques like few-shot learning, and perceive images, we can make a few statements about reasoning models in general. Reasoning models are useful, but they are not a universal upgrade. Across our case studies, "more thinking" did not reliably yield stronger performance, and it always increased latency and cost. The practical takeaway is simple: Treat reasoning and "reasoning effort" as experimental variables, not default settings.

Here are a few notes on how to use reasoning LLMs in practice:

- *Treat reasoning as a hyperparameter to experiment on.* As we did when testing the temperature and prompting techniques, run tests across different levels of reasoning effort (off, low, medium, high) and pick the setting that wins for a specific family of tasks.
- *Tie reasoning to task types.* Enable or increase reasoning for decomposition-heavy tasks (multistep math, planning, multi-tool orchestration, screen coordinates). Keep it minimal for simple question-answering, retrieval-first answers, and high-throughput endpoints. Systems like OpenAI's GPT-5 use routers to send certain tasks to a reasoning LLM versus an LLM with no reasoning enabled.
- *Look for diminishing returns.* When tasks are relatively simple or when benchmarks for related tasks are already near the ceiling performance, reasoning tends to yield the fewest benefits and is more likely to hurt performance.

Conclusion

The goal with agentic tool use, reasoning models, and computer use is to combine all seven pillars of intelligence in one system. Perception comes from the multimodal models. Reasoning is built into chain-of-thought and reinforcement learning–tuned LLMs. Memory is handled by context and retrieval systems. Motivation is coded as the goals for the system itself. Self-awareness emerges through behaviors such as reflection. These themes will continue to reappear in the last few chapters as we dive into some of the more challenging applications of AI.

Building smarter AI isn't just about creating bigger models or longer reasoning chains. It's about how we give AI the right context, tools, and reasoning scaffolding to actually solve problems. Through our case studies on positional bias, reasoning LLMs, ReAct agents, and full computer use, it became obvious that "thinking" before acting can make agents more accurate and transparent, and potentially more efficient. But it also taught us that reasoning models aren't a magic bullet: Sometimes simpler, non-reasoning models win on cost and speed, and even accuracy.

As we move toward AGI-inspired frameworks, always remember that the real power lies in experimentation—testing different models, contexts, and reasoning efforts until you find the sweet spot for your application's use-cases. In Chapter 8, we'll tackle the challenge of calibrating the level of confidence and aligning AI's internal knowledge systems through fine-tuning.

8

Fine-Tuning AI for Calibrated Performance

Introduction

Fine-tuning is the process of taking a powerful, general-purpose language model and updating the model's parameter values based on examples that matter for a particular application. With this approach, we aren't rebuilding everything from scratch, but rather teaching the model to speak a new domain's language, follow a style guide, and learn new information while minimizing losing any prior knowledge.

Off-the-shelf LLMs tend to be great generalists, but they can still stumble on edge cases. For instance, if you ask a vanilla model to generate complex SQL queries against a proprietary schema, it might hallucinate columns or misplace joins. In previous chapters, we solved this problem by giving the AI a tool to look up the schema or even evidence around how to use a given schema. But what if the AI didn't need to look up custom information? What if it just "knew it"?

Even something as simple as a support chatbot can slip into **miscalibration**—overconfidently answering questions that it shouldn't. Fine-tuning grounds the model in a set of data, reducing hallucinations, tightening up style, and giving more predictable performance under real-world workloads.

Fine-tuning is also useful in cases where long-term costs and scalability are a priority. Oftentimes I see people using huge and expensive LLMs like the latest GPT models to solve something "as simple as" a yes-or-no question that just requires a simple prompt. This is fine in the short term, but if we're optimizing for speed and cost, we have other options on the table.

Both of these scenarios are on the menu in this chapter. Our case studies will focus first on the latter situation—training an autoencoding model to learn a classification task. The second case study will focus on training an LLM to learn a new set of rules from a corpus of documents. In both of these case studies, we are not training the model again from scratch. Instead, we're simply updating parameter values from the off-the-shelf defaults. This idea of fine-tuning off-the-shelf models is relatively new to the world of machine learning. Hugging Face, the world's largest repository of open models and data, came into existence only in 2016. Even back then, the company was building therapy chatbots (hence the name Hugging Face—to invoke a sense of an empathetic AI) and not providing access to off-the-shelf models.

Figure 8.1 shows an overview of the fine-tuning process for machine learning models (which include LLMs) and the three sets of data generally used throughout this process:

- **Training set:** A collection of labeled examples used to train the model. The model learns to recognize patterns and relationships in the data by adjusting its parameters based on the training examples.
- **Validation set:** A separate collection of labeled examples used to evaluate the model's performance during training.
- **Testing set (or test set):** A third collection of labeled examples that is separate from both the training and validation sets. It is used to evaluate the final performance of the model after the training and fine-tuning processes are complete. The test set provides a final, unbiased estimate of the model's ability to generalize to new, unseen data.

If you are already familiar with machine learning fine-tuning, this information should have been a refresher. LLMs are simply a type of machine learning model, and the process for splitting data for fine-tuning them does not really differ from that for any other machine learning model.

In this chapter, we'll approach fine-tuning like a toolkit for optimizing workload goals such as accuracy, speed, and cost. We'll also take our first look at the idea of calibration—measuring how confident a model truly is in its answer. We will walk through the processes of fine-tuning both open-weights and closed-weights models (OpenAI specifically) for seemingly simple classification tasks and comparing the results against a much smaller autoencoding LLM. We will also see an example of **domain adaptation**—adapting a model on a custom domain set so jargon and edge cases become engrained into the LLM.

Let's get started with our first case study: fine-tuning for classification.

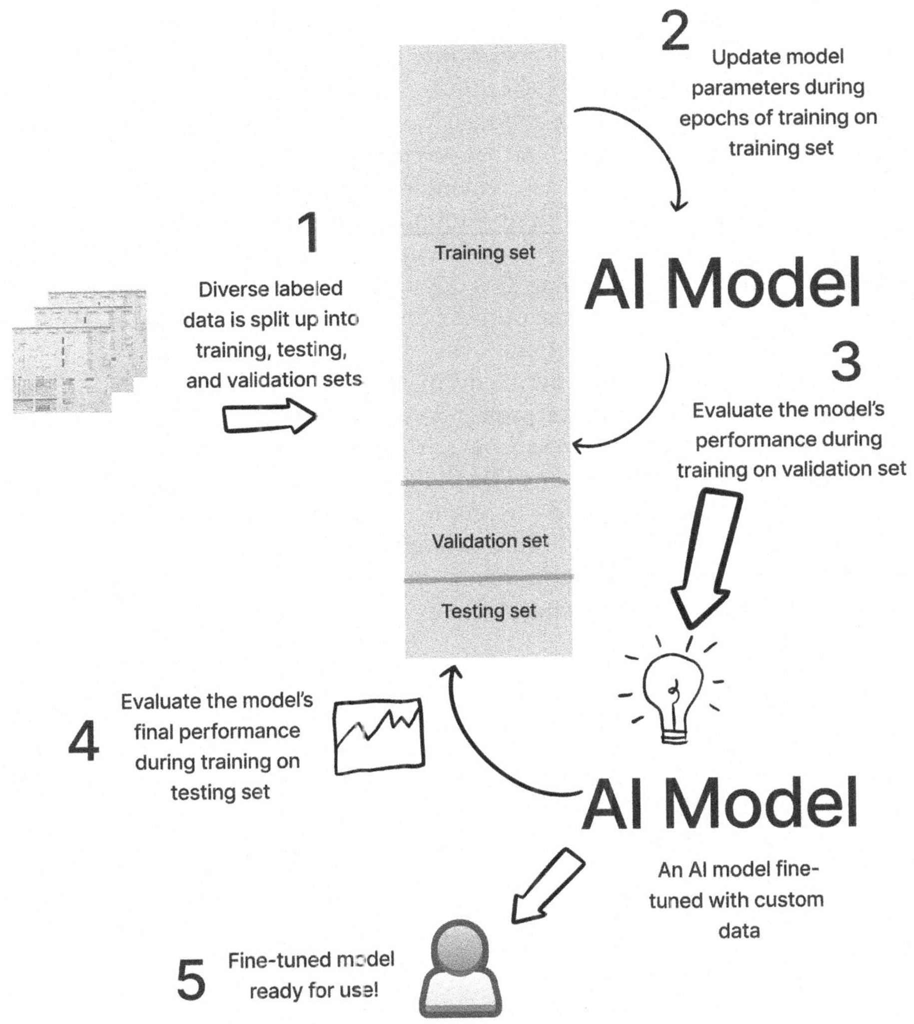
2
Update model parameters during epochs of training on training set
1
Diverse labeled data is split up into training, testing, and validation sets
Training set
AI Model
3
Evaluate the model's performance during training on validation set
Validation set
Testing set
4
Evaluate the model's final performance during training on testing set
AI Model
An AI model fine-tuned with custom data
5
Fine-tuned model ready for use!

Figure 8.1 The fine-tuning process A dataset is broken up into training, validation, and testing tests. The training set is used to update the model's weights and evaluate the model, whereas the validation set is used to evaluate the model during training. The final model is then tested against the testing set and evaluated against a set of criteria. If the model passes all of these tests, it is used in production and monitored for further iterations.

Case Study 13: Classification Versus Multiple Choice

This is one of the few case studies in this book that overlaps with one found in another book I wrote, *Quick Start Guide to Large Language Models*. That's because among the dozens of clients I've worked with in the field of LLMs for more than a decade, there's one task I see over and over: A company needs to build or use a model to make a relatively simple choice from a given list of options (in some cases, it was a binary yes or no; in others, it was choosing from 90 options). A decade ago, the answer to this question was almost always fine-tuning a model. In some situations, we could get away with using embeddings in a clever way, but that was rare.

These days, I still see the same use-case, but we often solve it in a different way. That is, with AI generative models, we can now mimic a fine-tuned classifier in many ways, most commonly with a prompt. Solving a classification-like problem using a generative model is called **multiple choice**. The AI is not forced to produce only the outputs we care about, and only through special output parsing (e.g., structured outputs) can we come close to a forced expected output.

Figure 8.2 shows the difference between a multiple-choice engine and a true classifier. The generative model must be prompted/coerced (through structured outputs) into giving us the answer in the format we need. Even then, there's almost always a non-zero chance it will generate some other token we don't care about. We can fine-tune generative LLMs to be less likely to produce these incorrect tokens, but even that won't be a guarantee. In contrast, by fine-tuning an open-source autoencoding model, we can not only achieve similar performance, but also trust the AI's outputs more while spending less money and time in the long run.

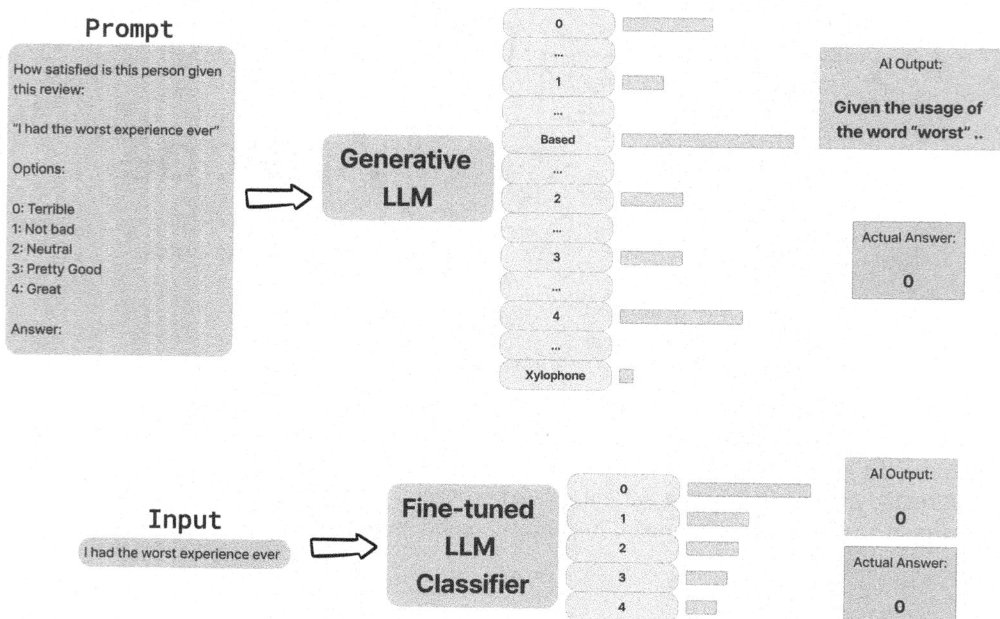

Figure 8.2 Multiple-choice prompts are a simulation of classification. Nothing is forcing the generative LLM to output the classes we care about, but a fine-tuned classifier is absolutely forced to output only the choices we care about and doesn't require a prompt explaining the task.

Introducing the app_reviews Dataset

In this case study, we will be working with the **app_reviews** dataset (previewed in Figure 8.3). This dataset is a collection of reviews of hundreds of mobile apps. Each app review in the dataset is accompanied by a rating on a scale of 1 to 5 stars, with 1 star being the lowest rating (denoted as 0) and 5 stars being the highest (denoted as 4).

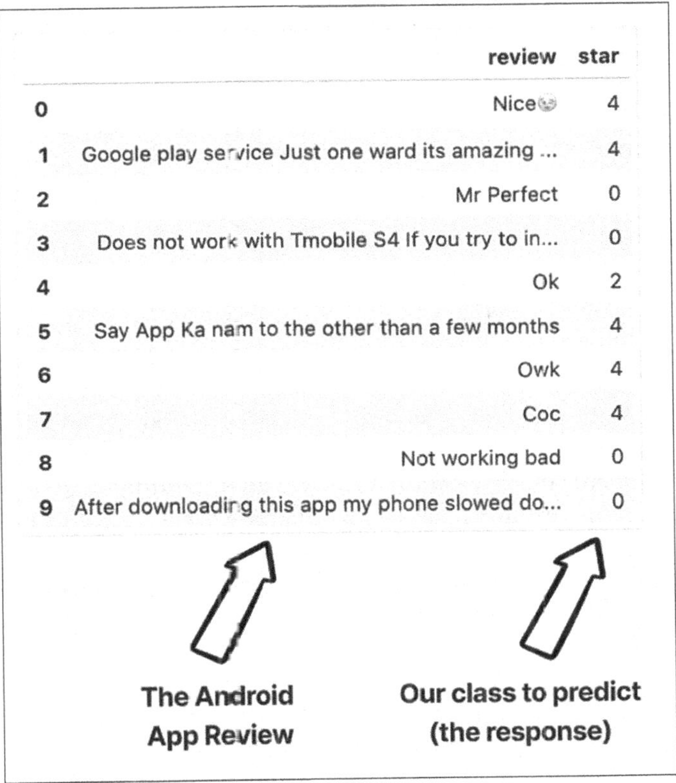

	review	star
0	Nice😉	4
1	Google play service Just one ward its amazing ...	4
2	Mr Perfect	0
3	Does not work with Tmobile S4 If you try to in...	0
4	Ok	2
5	Say App Ka nam to the other than a few months	4
6	Owk	4
7	Coc	4
8	Not working bad	0
9	After downloading this app my phone slowed do...	0

Figure 8.3 The `app_reviews` dataset consists of approximately 288,000 rows of mobile app reviews including the "review" column and the "star" column.

Our goal is to get an LLM to accurately predict the number of stars given to a particular review. To do so, we will run six different experiments:

1. GPT-4.1-Nano with no prompting, just asking for the number of stars given a review. We will consider this to be the baseline.
2. GPT-4.1-Nano with few-shot prompting.
3. GPT-4.1-Nano fine-tuned without a system prompt.
4. GPT-4.1-Nano fine-tuned with a system prompt. In theory, fine-tuning negates the need for a system prompt, so this experiment aims to show this in the wild.

5. GPT-4.1 fine-tuned without a system prompt.

6. ModernBERT fine-tuned.

That last LLM is one we haven't seen yet in this book. ModernBERT is an autoencoding LLM that is meant to be a drop-in replacement for the BERT model from 2018 (one of the first ever LLMs based on the Transformer architecture and to this day the second most downloaded LLM ever on the Hugging Face platform). It offers many improvements over the original 2018 BERT including the following:

- Increased the context window (from 512 tokens to 8,192 tokens)
- Replaced attention and positional embeddings with more modern equivalents
- Trained on more diverse and recent data
- Much more!

Outside of LLM-based embedding models (for which we will see a fine-tuned example in Chapter 9), the AI community doesn't see many new autoencoding LLMs compared to their generative autoregressive cousins. Not surprisingly, then, ModernBERT made a big splash. With only 350 million parameters in the large version, it will undoubtedly be a force in encoding tasks like embeddings and classification for a while.

Our six experiments include two that involve no fine-tuning and only prompting, three where we are fine-tuning a model for which we don't have direct access to its parameter values (i.e., the closed-source OpenAI models), and only one where we both have direct access to the parameter values of the model and actively fine-tune them.

Listing 8.1 shows a code snippet of loading up our dataset and splitting it up into the training, validation, and testing sets. We will **stratify** our splits: That is, we will not completely randomly assign points to each split but rather split it up so that it maintains the same class distribution throughout. We made this choice because, as shown in Figure 8.4, we have a disproportionate number of 5-star ratings (labeled as 4). We end up with 60% (of the entire dataset) for the training set, 20% for the validation set, and 20% for the test set.

Listing 8.1 **Loading up the `app_reviews` dataset and splitting it into stratified splits**

```
# Importing the ClassLabel module to represent categorical class labels
from datasets import ClassLabel
# Loading the 'app_reviews' dataset's training split into the 'dataset' variable
dataset = load_dataset('app_reviews', split='train')
# Converting the 'star' column in the dataset to a ClassLabel type
# This allows for categorical representation and easier handling of classes
dataset = dataset.class_encode_column('star')
# Splitting the dataset into a training set and a test set.
```

```
# We reserve 20% of the data for testing and use stratification on the 'star' column
# to ensure both sets have an equal distribution of each star category.
dataset = dataset.train_test_split(test_size=0.2, seed=SEED, stratify_by_
column='star')
# Now, we further split our training dataset to reserve 25% of it for validation.
# Again, we stratify by the 'star' column to keep the distribution consistent.
df = dataset['train'].train_test_split(test_size=.25, seed=SEED, stratify_by_
column='star')
# Assigning the split datasets to their respective keys:
# - The remaining 75% of our initial training data becomes the new training dataset.
dataset['train'] = df['train']
# - The 25% split from our initial training data becomes the validation dataset.
dataset['val'] = df['test']
```

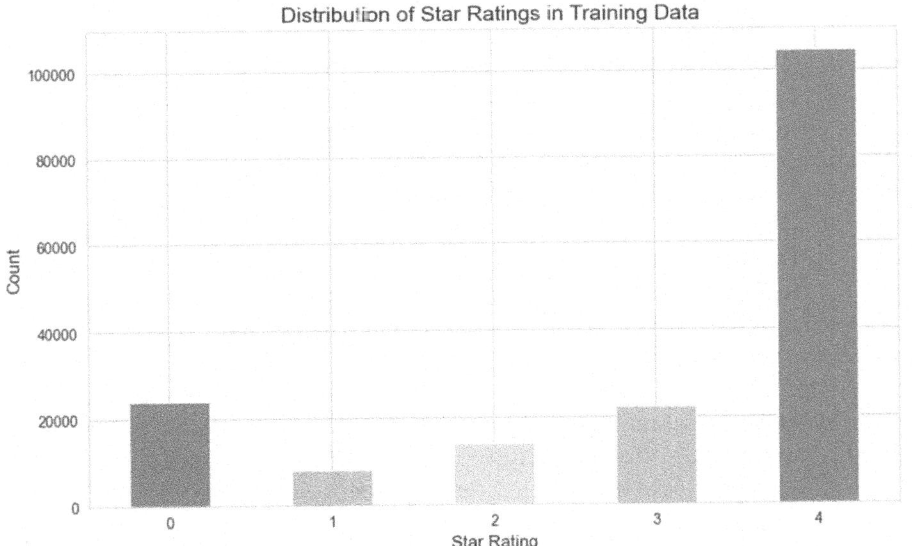

Figure 8.4 Distribution of star ratings in the training data. Most app reviews are labeled as 5 stars (class "4"), highlighting a strong class imbalance that can impact model performance and calibration.

The resulting dataset has 172,839 elements in the training set, 57,613 in the validation test, and another 57,613 in the testing set. This will be our experiment data.

Before we get to the results of the first batch of LLM experiments, let's introduce a new metric to give us another deeper look into AI performance: calibration.

LLM Calibration

Model calibration measures a model's confidence as it relates to its predictions. In practice, that means when the model spits out a prediction with 80% confidence, it should actually be right approximately 80% of the time. If it's wrong more often, then we risk over-trusting the AI. Conversely, if it's too cautious, we could waste cycles on human fallback or extra checks.

To measure calibration, we can use a metric called **expected calibration error (ECE)**. The idea is to:

1. Run the model over a set of data, collecting both the answer and the probability assigned to the answer.

2. Bucket the predictions by confidence (e.g., bins of 0–10%, 10–20%, ... up to 100%).

3. For each bin, compare the average confidence to the actual frequency of the class occurring. The actual frequency may also be referred to as the "ground-truth accuracy" as it's the accuracy of the bucket, according to the ground-truth labels. The difference between the two, normalized by the size of the bucket, is called the ECE. A lower ECE means a smaller gap between the predicted probability and the observed frequency and, therefore, is better.

The process of calculating the ECE is visualized in Figure 8.5. To calculate the ECE for a classification problem, we first calculate the ECE for each possible class. In our case, that would be 1, 2, 3, 4, or 5 stars. The figure shows a sample calculation for 5 stars. For the class of "5 stars," we look at every single app review (10 reviews in Figure 8.5) and write down the LLM-given confidence score for that review being 5 stars. Then we write down whether that review was actually labeled as 5 stars (the ground truth). These values can be seen in the table on the left side of Figure 8.5.

Based on the values in the table, we construct the graph on the top right in Figure 8.5. We bucket confidence into a set number of buckets (5, in this case) and place each app review in the bucket corresponding to the given confidence. For example, Bucket 1 (B1) contains app reviews 3 and 6, the only app reviews given a 5-star confidence rating between 0 and 20%. We take the average confidence (for B1, the average of 0.12 and 0.12, which is 0.12) and the bucket 5-star ground-truth accuracy (for B1, 50% because app review 3 gives 5 stars but app review 6 doesn't). A well-calibrated model would have the ground-truth accuracy in the bucket match the stated confidence. If the AI, on average, gave the confidence as a 12% chance of being a 5-star rating, why, then, did 50% of reviews in that bucket give a 5-star rating? The answer: because the model was being underconfident.

Once we have the ECE for all five categories, the ECE for the system is the average ECE for all classes.

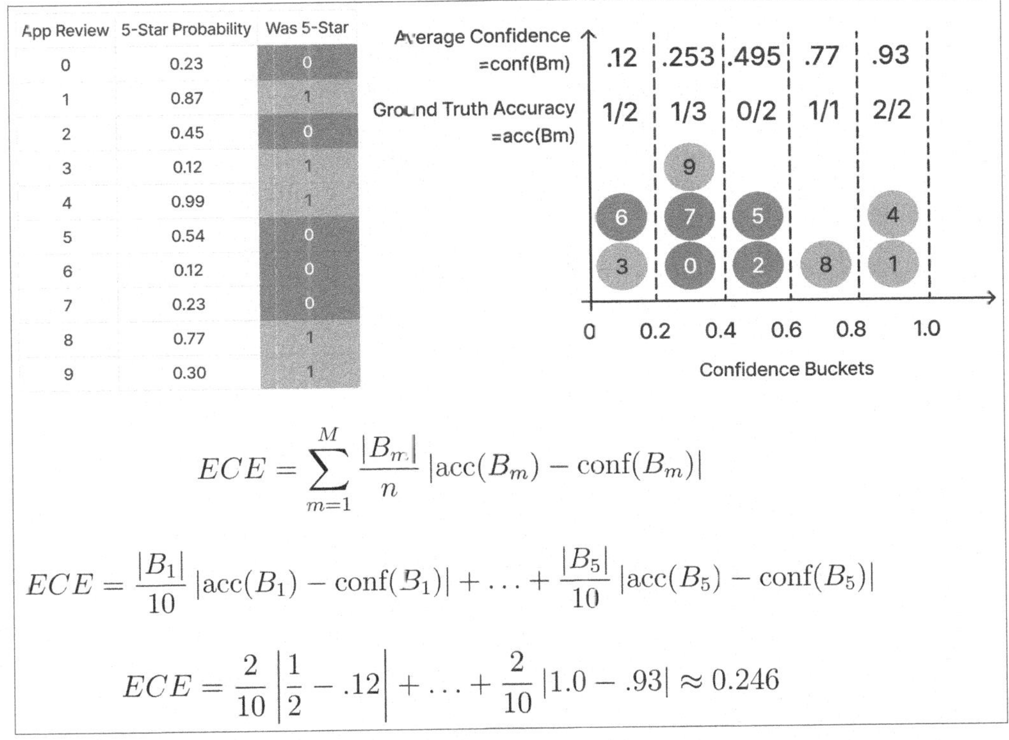

App Review	5-Star Probability	Was 5-Star
0	0.23	0
1	0.87	1
2	0.45	0
3	0.12	1
4	0.99	1
5	0.54	0
6	0.12	0
7	0.23	0
8	0.77	1
9	0.30	1

$$ECE = \sum_{m=1}^{M} \frac{|B_m|}{n} |\text{acc}(B_m) - \text{conf}(B_m)|$$

$$ECE = \frac{|B_1|}{10} |\text{acc}(B_1) - \text{conf}(B_1)| + \ldots + \frac{|B_5|}{10} |\text{acc}(B_5) - \text{conf}(B_5)|$$

$$ECE = \frac{2}{10} \left| \frac{1}{2} - .12 \right| + \ldots + \frac{2}{10} |1.0 - .93| \approx 0.246$$

Figure 8.5 Visualizing the expected calibration error (ECE). The table shows the model predictions, assigned probabilities, and true labels for 5-star reviews. On the right, predictions are grouped into confidence buckets, where the average confidence is compared to the actual accuracy for each bucket. The equations show how ECE quantifies the average gap between model confidence and real-world accuracy.

We want an AI system that's both accurate and calibrated. We want the system to be both correct and confident in its answer. One reason we care about calibration is that we often think about confidence thresholds as a proxy for when we listen to an AI system and when we might want to ignore it. For example, if the review in question is "The app was solid but frankly I want to see some improvements done on the UI," the AI system might assign its highest confidence score of, say, 60% that it's a 4-star rating, with the other 40% being distributed across the other star levels. Is this high enough? Perhaps we might allow for actionable predictions only if the confidence score is above some threshold, and otherwise, we ignore it. But if our model is not calibrated, then how can we even trust that 60%?

Let's move on to our experiment results so we can compare both accuracy and calibration among our LLMs.

Evaluating the Baseline LLMs on the Test Set

Before we do fine-tuning, let's get a baseline of how prompting could help us; then we'll have something we can compare to the results after fine-tuning. Figure 8.6 shows the **calibration curves** for GPT-4.1-Nano, both without any prompting and with 5-shot prompting. As usual, we see the prompting is helping the accuracy. However, we also see by the lower ECE that prompting is helping the calibration, too (remember that a lower ECE is better).

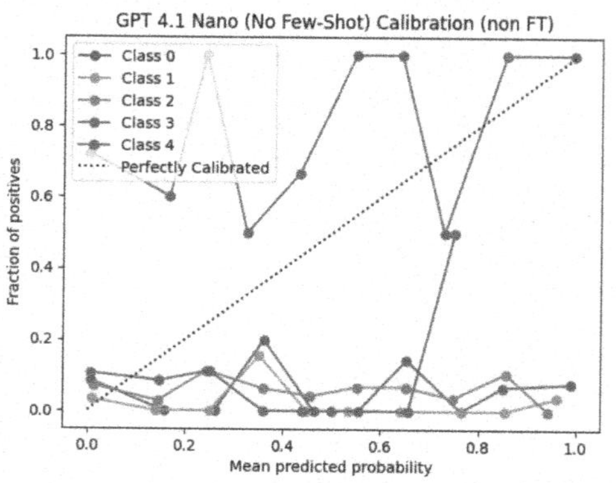

Accuracy: 0.0884 || ECE: 0.3470

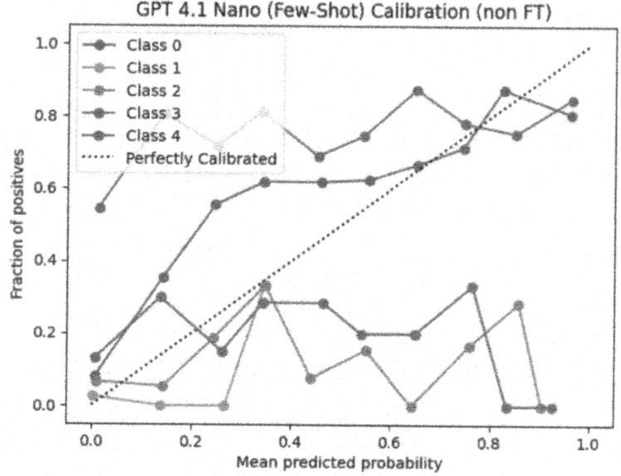

Accuracy: 0.5219 || ECE: 0.1491

Figure 8.6 Calibration curves for GPT-4.1-Nano on the `app_reviews` task. Left: No few-shot prompting; right: 5-shot prompting. The dotted diagonal represents perfect calibration (model confidence matches the observed accuracy). Few-shot prompting improves both accuracy and calibration (lower ECE), but the model still tends to be overconfident on high-probability predictions and underconfident on low-probability ones.

A note on the calibration curves: Each dot on the graph represents a bucket of predictions, as previously mentioned. For example, in Figure 8.6, on the graph on the right, look at the top right blue and purple points. Both represent the bucket of the LLM predicting roughly 95% accuracy for blue (1-star prediction) and purple (5-star prediction). However, their *y*-values are both roughly 0.8, which we can interpret as follows (focusing on just 5-star reviews): *When GPT-4.1-Nano (5-shot) gives an approximately 95% token confidence for being a 5-star rating, only about 80% of those predictions are actually 5 stars.* GPT-4.1-Nano (5-shot) is overconfident when making highly confident predictions about 1- and 5-star ratings. Similarly, if we look at the leftmost purple point on the right graph, we can say: *When GPT-4.1-Nano (5-shot) gives an approximately 0% token confidence for being a 5-star rating, only about 50% of those predictions are actually 5 stars.* Thus, this model is extremely underconfident when assigning a low confidence to a 5-star rating.

Note that to get these probabilities from a closed-source model like GPT-4.1, we need to use its API and enable a feature called **logprobs**. This feature asks the API to return token confidences for the top *k* tokens requested (with a maximum of 20 at the time of writing). Luckily, every app review in this dataset had a 1, 2, 3, 4, and 5 in the top 20 tokens, but that might not be the case for another task. If the class you're looking for isn't in the top 20, you (unfortunately) cannot include that data point in the curve.

For a well-calibrated model, the data points will hug the dotted diagonal line on the plot. If that is the case, then at all predicted confidence levels for all classes, we can *trust* the probabilities the model is providing. In turn, we can set a more reliable threshold.

As shown in this experiment, prompting can enhance both accuracy and calibration. Next, let's see what fine-tuning can do.

Fine-Tuning the LLM

The OpenAI fine-tuning API is very well documented but to recap the process:

1. For each of the data splits (training, validation, and testing), create and upload a .jsonl file where every line represents a single example. See Listing 8.2 for an example.

Listing 8.2 **Uploading and reading a line from an OpenAI data .jsonl file**

```
# Upload our chat-based training data
no_system_training_file_chat = client.files.create(
 file=open("openai_training_data/app-review-full-train-sentiment-random-chat.jsonl",
"rb"),
 purpose='fine-tune'
)

json.loads(open("openai_training_data/app-review-full-train-sentiment-random-chat.
jsonl", "rb").readlines()[0])
>> {'messages': [{'role': 'user', 'content': 'Nice 😊'}, {'role': 'assistant',
  'content': '4'}]}
```

2. Create a fine-tuning job with a specified model (see Listing 8.3).

Listing 8.3 **Create a fine-tuning job**

```
gpt_4_1_nano_no_system_job = client.fine_tuning.jobs.create(
   training_file=no_system_training_file_chat.id,
   validation_file=no_system_val_file_chat.id,
   model='gpt-4.1-nano-2025-04-14',
   hyperparameters={'n_epochs': 1}
)
```

3. Wait until we get an email from OpenAI saying the fine-tuning job is done.

Once the fine-tuning is complete, we are given a new model ID to use with the API—and that's about it. For BERT training, though, it's a bit more involved. Listing 8.4 shows an abbreviated code snippet for the training code; as always, the rest can be found in the GitHub for this book.

Listing 8.4 **Fine-tuning ModernBERT (abbreviated)**

```
from transformers import pipeline, AutoModelForSequenceClassification,
AutoTokenizer
MODEL = 'answerdotai/ModernBERT-large'
tokenizer = AutoTokenizer.from_pretrained(MODEL)
# Load the BERT model with added classification layers
sequence_clf_model = AutoModelForSequenceClassification.from_pretrained(
   MODEL,
   num_labels=5,
)
training_args = TrainingArguments(
   output_dir="./bert_clf_results",
   num_train_epochs=1,
   # Some deep learning parameters...
)
# Define the trainer:
trainer = Trainer(
   model=sequence_clf_model,
   args=training_args,
   train_dataset=dataset['train'],
   eval_dataset=dataset['val'],
)
trainer.train()  # kick off the training!
```

In total, the fine-tuning code is less than 200 lines of code. All things considered, that's not too bad.

A note about the `AutoModelForSequenceClassification` class we used in Listing 8.4. What it does under the hood is add a new layer on top of the final layer of the BERT LLM (seen in Figure 8.7). This layer allows for probabilities to be outputted only for the five classes we care about.

After we have spent a good chunk of change (we will see just how much in the next section), we can finally look at the calibration curves for the four remaining experiments. Those curves are shown in Figure 8.8.

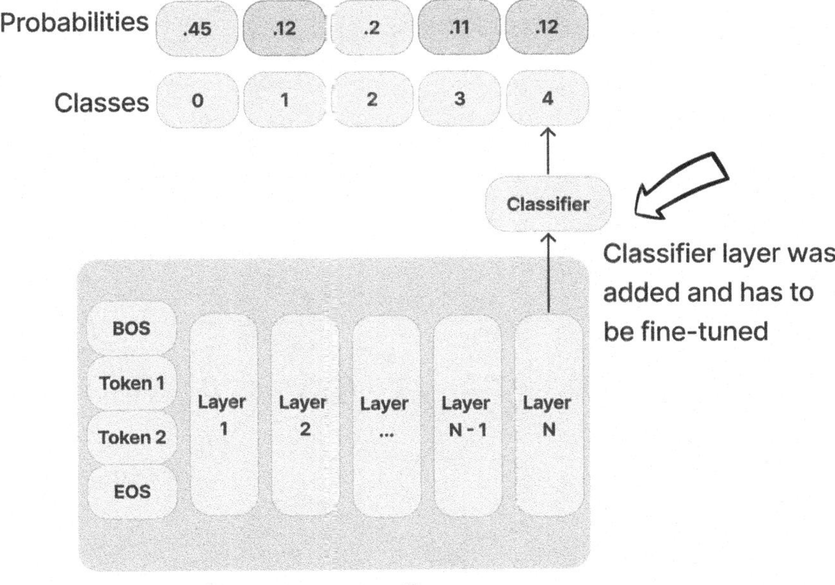

Figure 8.7 Architecture of ModernBERT for classification. A classifier layer is added on top of the final hidden layer of the pre-trained model. During fine-tuning, this layer learns to map the model's representations to class probabilities for the target task—in this case, predicting star ratings.

Let's note a few things about these results:

- Fine-tuning clearly works well for calibrating both our autoregressive and autoencoding LLMs. All four of the graphs are more tightly hugging the perfect calibration diagonal.
- The accuracy ratings on the test set for all of the LLMs are roughly the same—approximately 73%—and all far outperform our approach in the prompting experiments. We can safely eliminate the prompting experiments as a choice simply because of their low accuracies.
- Even though accuracy remains roughly consistent, the calibration is not roughly the same across the LLMs. BERT's ECE is 1.7 times lower than GPT-4.1's ECE, but BERT's accuracy is only 1.007 times smaller than that for GPT-4.1. To see this visually, notice how ModernBERT's curves are far tighter to the diagonal than the GPT-4.1 curves are (the bottom two graphs).
- The curves for the 2- and 3-star ratings (labeled as class 1 and 2, respectively) seem to be the most out of line for all LLMs. Those two classes are the most under-represented in the dataset (there just aren't that many of them), so even with fine-tuning, the model can't seem to get a good grasp on how confident to be when predicting them.

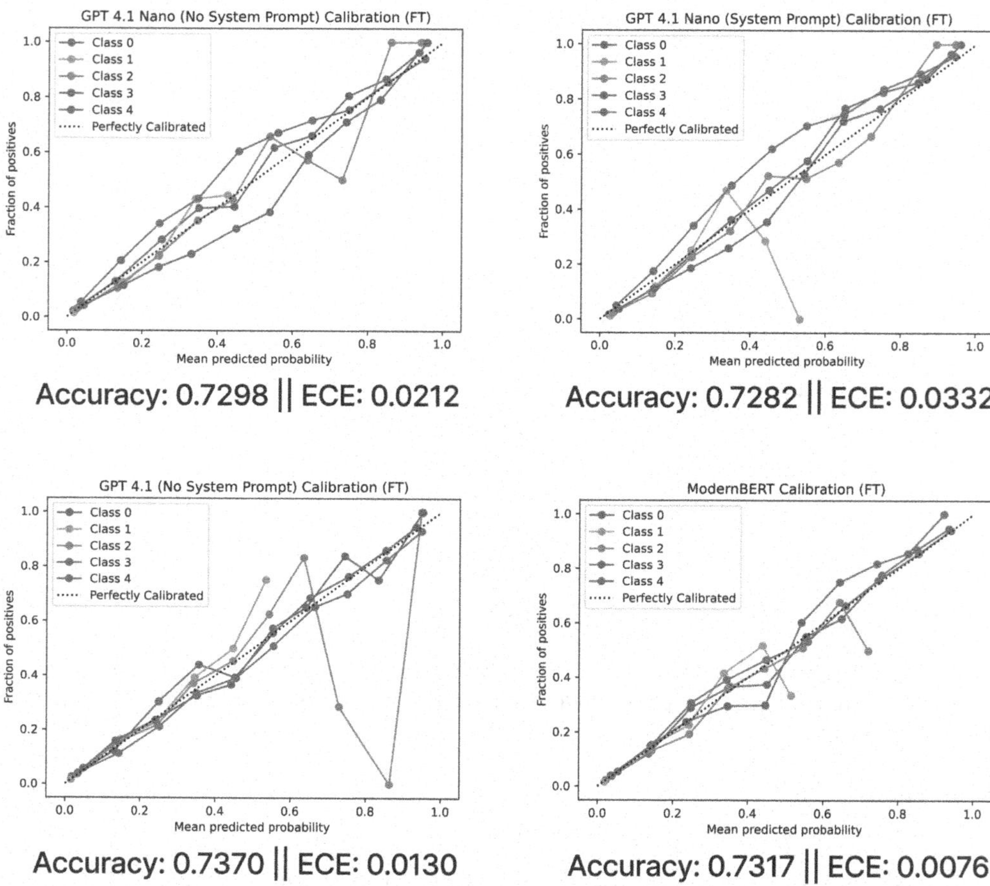

Figure 8.8 Calibration curves for all of the fine-tuned models on the app_reviews classification task. Each plot compares predicted probability (*x*-axis) to observed accuracy (*y*-axis) across all classes. All models are well calibrated after fine-tuning, closely following the diagonal line. ModernBERT achieves the lowest expected calibration error (ECE), indicating it makes the most reliable confidence estimates, while overall accuracy remains similar across models.

Our LLMs are performing well, and we can already spot some differences in performance when it comes to calibration. But what about cost and speed?

Comparing Cost and Speed

First, let's look at the upfront fine-tuning cost. Figure 8.9 shows the total amount of money (in USD) spent to fine-tune each model on the app_reviews task:

- GPT-4.1 (no system prompt) rings in at around $122, by far the priciest.
- GPT-4.1-Nano with system prompt drops to about $15.

- GPT-4.1-Nano without system prompt shaves even more off of the cost, coming in at $7.33. With this option, we aren't passing in a system prompt for every single data point that we get charged for. Remember, we are charged for individual tokens while fine-tuning, whether it's in a system prompt, AI prompt, or user prompt, so fewer tokens anywhere means a cheaper fine-tuning session.
- ModernBERT, the open-source autoencoding model, comes in at around $1 worth of rented T4 GPU time.

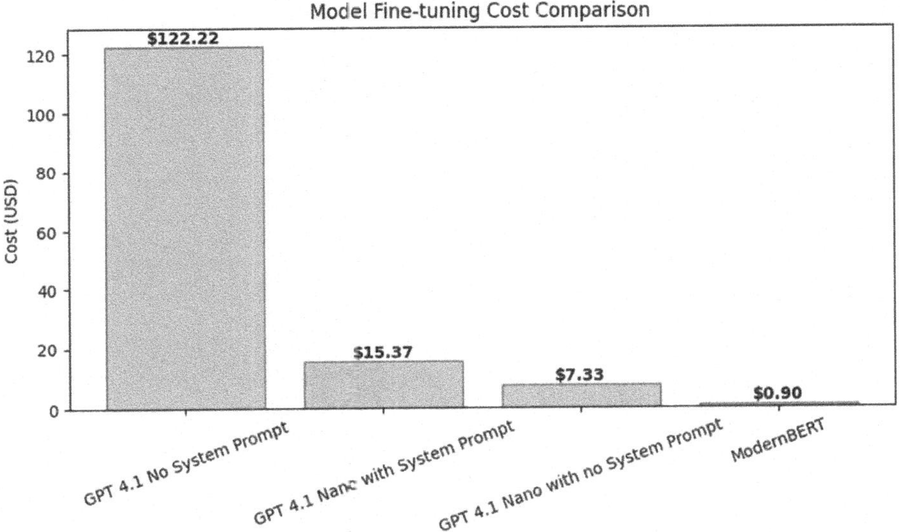

Figure 8.9 Fine-tuning cost comparison for each model on the classification task. GPT-4.1 with no system prompt is by far the most expensive to fine-tune, while ModernBERT can be trained for less than $1 using a rented GPU, highlighting the potential cost differences between proprietary and open-source approaches.

Let's immediately remove the GPT-4.1-Nano model with a system prompt from the table: Its accuracy is on par with the Nano version with no system prompt, and without the system prompt, the LLM calls become cheaper and faster. This is expected, because part of fine-tuning involves teaching the LLM to solve a task without repeated instructions in the system prompt. In essence, fine-tuning changes the parameter values to enable the LLM to understand the task without having to "relearn" it every single time.

With only three experiments left to consider, Table 8.1 and Figure 8.10 show each model's throughput (measured in units of examples per second, eps) with three batch sizes (1, 10, and 25). To make the fine-tuned BERT model numbers more realistic, I deployed it to a very simple single GPU endpoint using Hugging Face's inference endpoint service and used that API to run these tests.

Table 8.1 **Throughput by Model and Batch Size in Examples per Second (eps). Higher is better.**

Model	Batch Size 1	Batch Size 10	Batch Size 25
GPT-4.1-Nano (no system prompt, fine-tuned)	2.8 eps	0.20 eps	0.08 eps
GPT-4.1 (no system prompt, fine-tuned)	0.53 eps	0.06 eps	0.03 eps
ModernBERT	2.27 eps	1.45 eps	0.90 eps

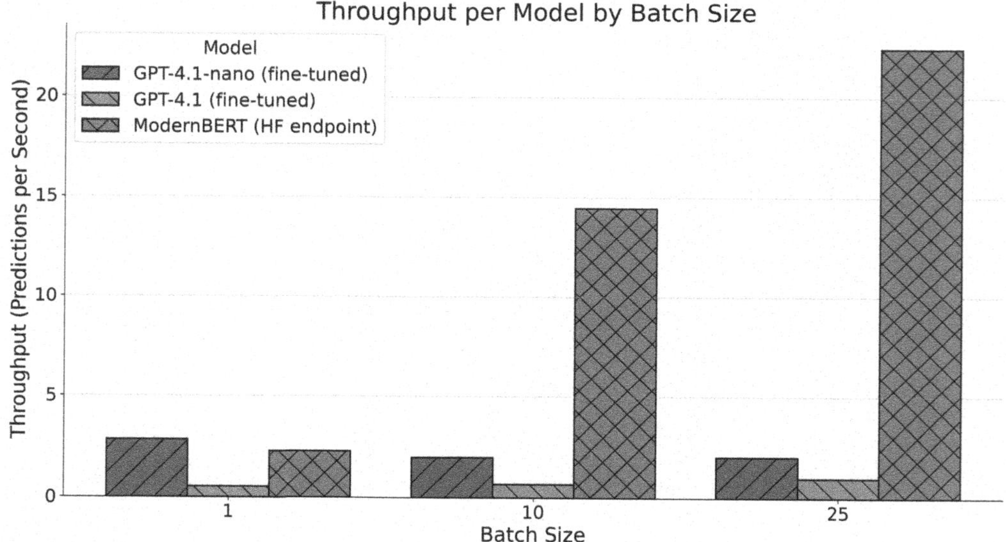

Figure 8.10 Model throughput by batch size on the `app_reviews` task. While GPT-4.1-Nano is fastest for single predictions, ModernBERT is not far behind and excels as batch size increases due to efficient GPU-based batching for high-volume inference. The full GPT-4.1 model is consistently slower due to its larger architecture. “HF endpoint” refers to the Hugging Face endpoint I created for the fine-tuned model.

- **Batch size 1:** GPT-4.1-Nano leads at 2.8 eps, with ModernBERT close behind at 2.3 eps. The full GPT-4.1 model lags at around 0.5 eps due to its larger context overhead.
- **Batch size 10:** Both GPT variants slow down substantially due to the single example per prompt limit of the fine-tuned model. GPT-4.1-Nano dips to 0.2 eps and GPT-4.1 to 0.06 eps, because multiple small API calls and prompt framing

dominate latency. Meanwhile, ModernBERT holds strong at 1.45 eps, showing it can batch efficiently on a typical GPU endpoint.

- **Batch size 25:** GPT throughput barely budges, remaining less than 0.1 eps. ModernBERT still processes nearly one example per second, making it by far the fastest option for high-volume inference.

For low-latency, single-shot needs (batch = 1), GPT-4.1-Nano is fastest but ModernBERT isn't far behind. If we need to scale up (batch ≥ 10), ModernBERT's GPU-based batching yields 5–7 times higher throughput than any GPT endpoint. When throughput and cost both matter, ModernBERT is the clear winner for bulk classification, while GPT-4.1-Nano offers a middle ground when we need GPT-fluent responses.

Figure 8.11 plots the total USD cost per single prediction for each model. GPT-4.1, at nearly six-tenths of a cent per call, is the most expensive by a factor of 5 times over the others. GPT-4.1-Nano comes in at about one-tenth of a cent per call, which is roughly on the same order as ModernBERT. ModernBERT sits just above GPT-4.1-Nano, reflecting the Hugging Face endpoint pricing and GPU overhead.

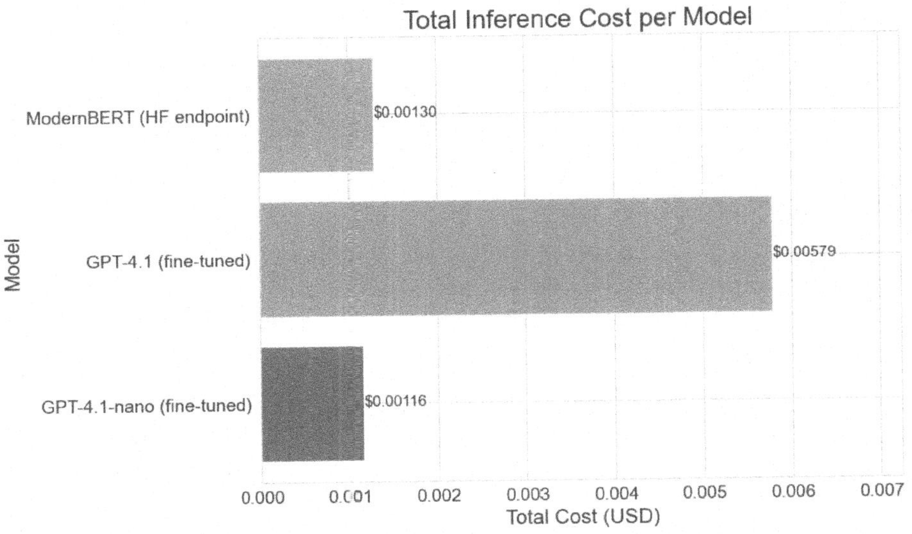

Figure 8.11 Cost per single prediction for each model. GPT-4.1 is the most expensive by a wide margin, costing nearly $0.006 per call. Both GPT-4.1-Nano and ModernBERT deliver predictions for roughly $0.001, making them far more cost-effective for high-volume or budget-sensitive workloads. "HF endpoint" refers to the Hugging Face endpoint I created for the fine-tuned model.

- If the workload is cost-sensitive at high volume, GPT-4.1-Nano and ModernBERT can both deliver a sub-$0.002 cost per prediction.

- For maximum accuracy and open-ended responses, GPT-4.1 may be worth the premium, but we'll pay about five times more per call.
- ModernBERT offers a strong middle ground: open-source, GPU-accelerated, and nearly as cheap per call as the smallest GPT variant.

Data Privacy

Beyond cost, speed, and accuracy, we also want to think about where our data lives.

For GPT-4.1 and GPT-4.1-Nano:

- Every inference call sends text (and any metadata) to OpenAI's servers.
- If the app handles personally identifiable information, patient records, financial data, or other regulated content, this could trigger compliance or governance concerns.

For ModernBERT (which would need to be self-hosted):

- We can control the entire inference stack.
- Run it on-premises or in a private virtual private cloud (VPC) so no user data ever leaves the infrastructure.
- It's a great fit for sensitive workloads (e.g., healthcare, finance, enterprise internal tools) where we need full auditability and data residency guarantees.

Balancing Accuracy, Cost, Speed, and Privacy

Now that we've seen each model's accuracy, cost, and throughput, let's bring data privacy into the mix. Table 8.2 shows a rundown of our findings.

Table 8.2 **Summary of Findings**

Model	Accuracy	Cost per Call	Throughput (Batch = 1)	Data Privacy
GPT-4.1	73.70%	$0.00579	0.53 eps	Data sent to OpenAI
GPT-4.1-Nano	72.98%	$0.00116	2.80 eps	Data sent to OpenAI
ModernBERT	73.17%	$0.00130	2.27 eps	Can self-host (no third-party)

- Accuracy is very similar across all three LLMs (within approximately 0.7 point), with GPT-4.1 just edging out the others.
- Cost and speed both favor the smaller models. GPT-4.1-Nano and ModernBERT are roughly one-tenth the price of the full GPT-4.1 and 4–5 times faster at a batch size of 1.

- The concept of self-hosting our ModernBERT model implies a new baked-in cost—that is, a person to manage the deployment and maintenance of the self-hosted LLM. However, in our case, Hugging Face is taking care of all of the difficult bits with a one-click deploy solution.
- Privacy: If we are handling sensitive or regulated data and can't send it off-site, ModernBERT lets us run inference on our own GPUs or private cloud. Both GPT variants require calls to OpenAI's servers, so data governance policies may limit their use.

To wrap things up on this case study, for mission-critical accuracy and completely third-party–managed infrastructure, GPT-4.1 wins—but just barely. This also assumes budget and data sharing aren't critical factors. If cost or latency is our top concern but we're fine with OpenAI's privacy model, GPT-4.1-Nano is a solid choice. If data residency, full model control, or on-premises inference are must-haves, ModernBERT achieves nearly the same accuracy at a GPT-4.1-Nano–level cost and speed and never leaves our network.

By explicitly considering cost, speed, accuracy, trust (via calibration), and privacy, we've covered the main practical axes for making a choice between fine-tuned models. But let's go back to calibration for a brief moment: If it is a measurement of how much we can believe the model's classification output, what does calibration look like when the model is generating free text?

Calibration in Free-Text Responses

Calibration in classification tasks is measured by how closely a model's predicted probabilities match its actual accuracy (think of ECE and the calibration curves). In free-text generation, we don't have fixed buckets, but we can still ask the model to self-report its confidence and check whether that prediction lines up with reality. Said another way, if a classifier saying "80%" means 80% correct, what does it mean when an LLM claims "I'm 85% sure" in a recollection of a fact?

In Figure 8.12, I prompted GPT-4o and GPT-4.1: "Who is Daniel Lurie and what is his birthday?" Daniel Lurie is the current mayor of San Francisco, where I am based. No matter the answer, I followed up with "How confident are you on the birthday? 0–100%." Both models gave the wrong dates, and both stated the results had a 70% or greater confidence level.

Their self-reported confidence doesn't seem to correlate with correctness, which is common in the world of AI hallucinations. One reason this might be the case is that the raw token probabilities aren't trained to reflect true uncertainty in open-ended outputs. In contrast, our fine-tuned classifiers were trained on labeled examples with explicit feedback.

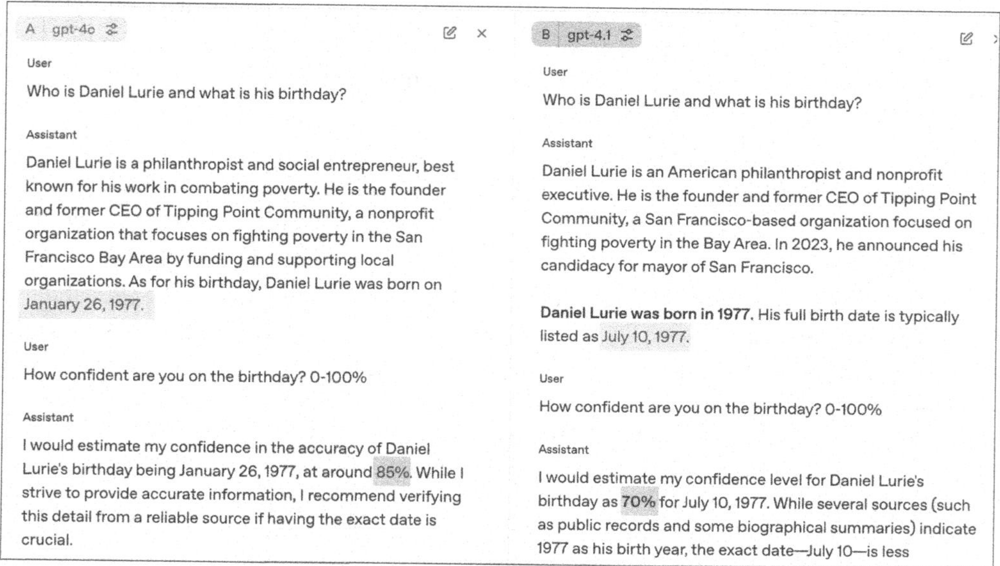

Figure 8.12 GPT-4o and GPT-4.1 were asked about the birthday of Daniel Lurie, the current mayor of San Francisco. Both LLMs were wrong and gave a confidence score of 70% or greater for their wrong answers.

Figure 8.13 shows an example of prompting an LLM on the OpenAI Playground—where I have access to visualize the token probabilities—to give the birthdays of both Daniel Lurie and Albert Einstein (a more well-known figure). The token probability for Einstein's birth month, which is March, is much higher than the top month probability is for Daniel Lurie. These token probabilities explain why I would get different answers every time I ask about Lurie's birthday. Randomly sampling between the tokens leads to roughly equal chances being given for October, August, December, and November. Lurie was actually born in February, which has a token probability of less than 7%.

A token distribution where one token probability greatly surpasses all others (as with Einstein's birthday in Figure 8.13) can correlate with correctness of stated facts the model has seen during training. That last part is important—*has seen during training*. High token probability doesn't mean the model is right; it means it's confident it has seen this information before and perhaps many times. A flatter distribution (many tokens with similar probability in Lurie's case) indicates that the LLM is grasping at straws and is more likely to hallucinate/guess.

We can use the same approach with generators as we did with our classifiers. By supplying examples where the model sees strong assertions, clear facts, and hedged language (edge cases), we can seek to align its token distributions with correctness.

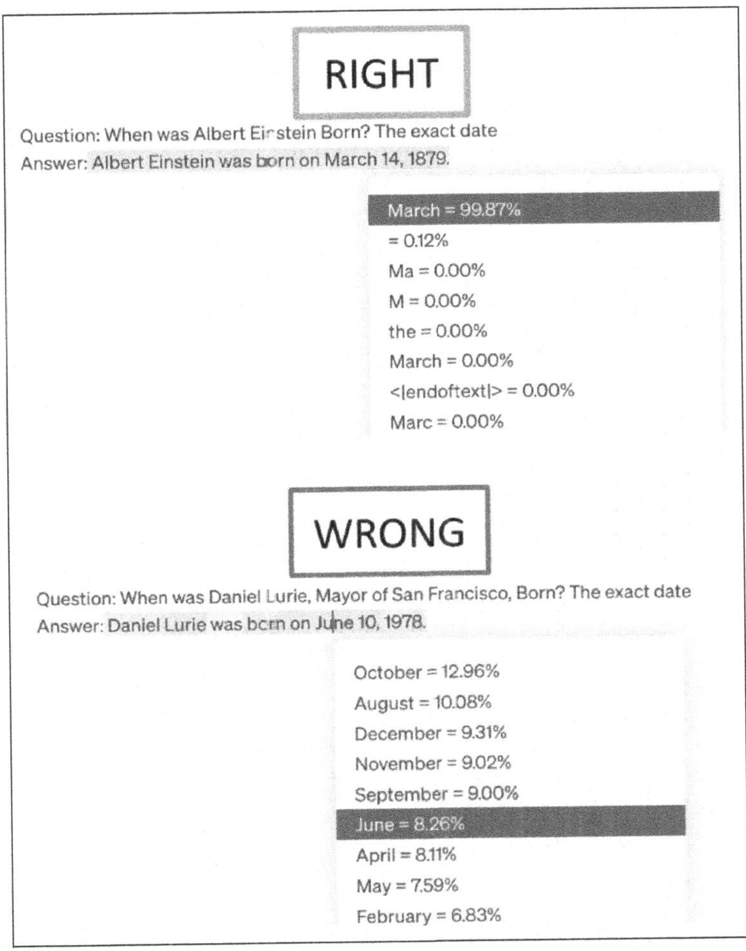

Figure 8.13 An example of inspecting token probabilities for factual recall. When asked for Albert Einstein's birthday (top), the model assigns nearly all its probability to the correct month ("March"), reflecting high confidence. For Daniel Lurie (bottom), the model's probabilities are spread across many months, indicating low certainty and a greater risk of hallucination. High token probability can correlate with knowledge memorized during pre-training, while flatter distributions reveal uncertainty and potential error.

Case Study 14: Domain Adaptation

With calibration in mind, if fine-tuning gave our classifiers honest uncertainty, we can apply the same principle to generative models. In this case study, we will fine-tune an open-source generator with the Airbnb policy documents (from Chapter 5) in an attempt to teach it to "know" these rules natively instead of hallucinating.

This process is referred to as **domain adaptation**, defined as the process of taking a general-purpose language model and fine-tuning it on a curated, domain-specific corpus so that it internalizes that specialized knowledge. Rather than relying on retrieval at inference time, we chunk our Airbnb policy documents into manageable pieces (with overlap and source metadata), then train the model to answer policy questions directly. The idea is to produce a generator that not only produces accurate, on-domain responses but also reports calibrated confidence—just as our fine-tuned classifiers learned honest uncertainty.

It helps to understand the general training recipe most foundation labs follow when creating a chat-aligned LLM (e.g., GPT, Claude, Llama, Qwen). This process (outlined in Figure 8.14) has three general steps given a blank slate Transformer architecture:

1. **Pre-training:** Allow the LLM to perform the autoregressive language modeling task (filling in the blank at the end) on a *vast* amount of unstructured (not chat-focused) data.
   a. This step is where the LLM reads Wikipedia, news sites, and everything the lab can get its hands on. It is where the LLM "learns" the most amount of information about . . . well everything.
   b. This is also generally where the "trillions of training tokens" talking points come in. By far, the most amount of data is used in this step.
2. **Instruction tuning:** After pre-training, teach the model to follow human directions by fine-tuning it on large collections of "instruction → response" or multi-turn conversation pairs. This step demands curated datasets (e.g., user questions paired with high-quality answers) so the LLM learns to interpret prompts as commands, handle edge-case requests, and produce helpful, coherent outputs rather than just predicting the next word in a block of text.
   a. This is where reserve tokens such as the "end of text" token and the tokens denoting who is speaking are introduced.
3. **Preference tuning:** Align the model with human preferences and style through (usually) reinforcement learning (RL) fine-tuning. Here, we collect human feedback comparing multiple model outputs for the same conversation and train the LLM to prefer the responses that are rated higher by labelers.
   a. The aim is to encourage more engaging, safer, more accurate, and more user-friendly behavior in its text generations.

This training recipe was popularized by OpenAI in 2022 and has since become the basic recipe for almost all labs, albeit with variations thrown in to attempt to get an edge. In this case study, the idea is to continue pre-training—that is, to give the model more unstructured data as if it were still in step 1, without removing what it learned in steps 2 and 3.

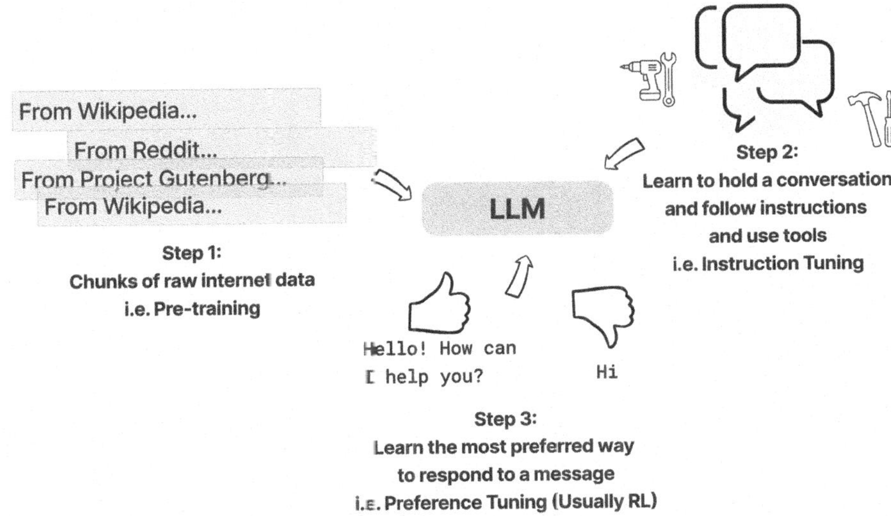

Figure 8.14 The standard three-stage training process for modern chat-based LLMs: (1) pre-training on massive amounts of unstructured internet data; (2) instruction tuning, where the model learns to follow instructions and hold conversations; and (3) preference tuning (usually via reinforcement learning), which aligns the model's responses with human preferences and style.

I've done versions of domain-adaptation case studies in a few of my other writings. Figure 8.15 (which originally appeared in my *Quick Start Guide to Large Language Models* book) shows how I taught a chat-based LLM to "read" my own book so it could answer AI questions more accurately.

In this version (shown in Figure 8.16), we'll tie it back to Case Study 5 (from Chapter 5), which focused on policy documents. In that case study, we developed an AI agent with the ability to look up Airbnb policy documents to answer questions more effectively. Now let's introduce an alternative to this experiment: What if we tried to fine-tune an LLM with the policy information so that it no longer had to look the information up, but instead had it encoded in its parameters?

The policy documents can end up being quite long. In fact, depending on the LLM we are using, they may not even fit in the context window at all. To address this issue, we can **chunk** (break up) the documents into smaller pieces.

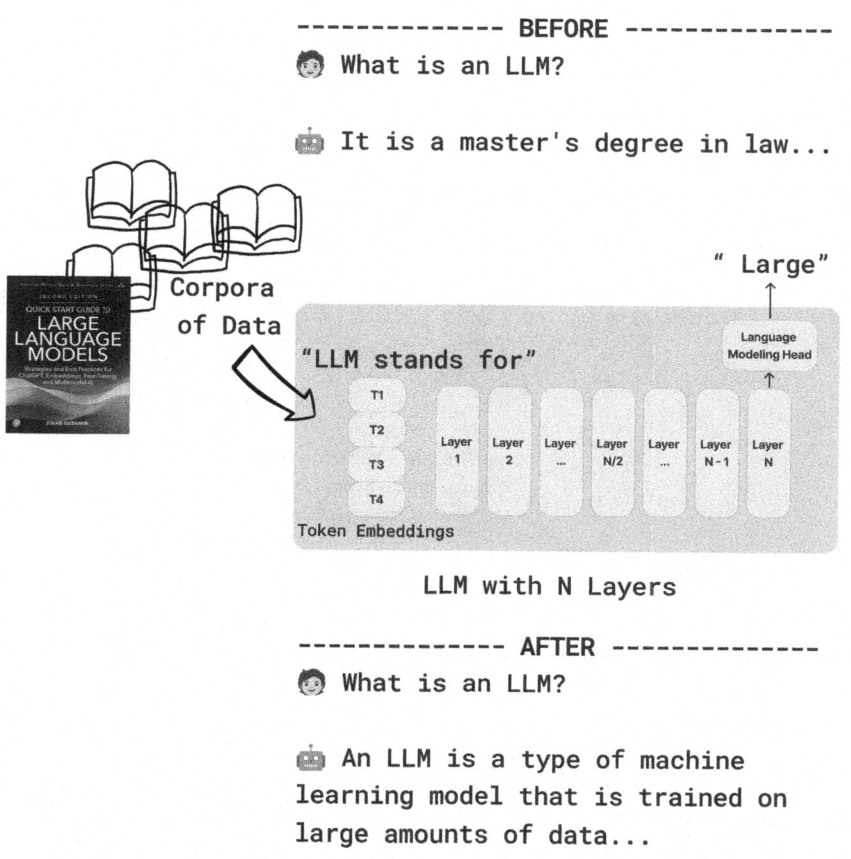

Figure 8.15 An example from another book of mine: before and after domain adaptation. By fine-tuning a chat-based LLM on the content from *Quick Start Guide to Large Language Models*, the model shifts from giving an incorrect answer to providing a correct, on-topic explanation, showing how targeted fine-tuning can teach a model to internalize new domain knowledge.

Chunking Policy Documents

A popular approach to chunking is **max token window chunking**, which involves splitting the document into chunks of a given maximum size. For example, if we set the token window limit to 512, we would expect each chunk to be up to but not greater than 512 tokens.

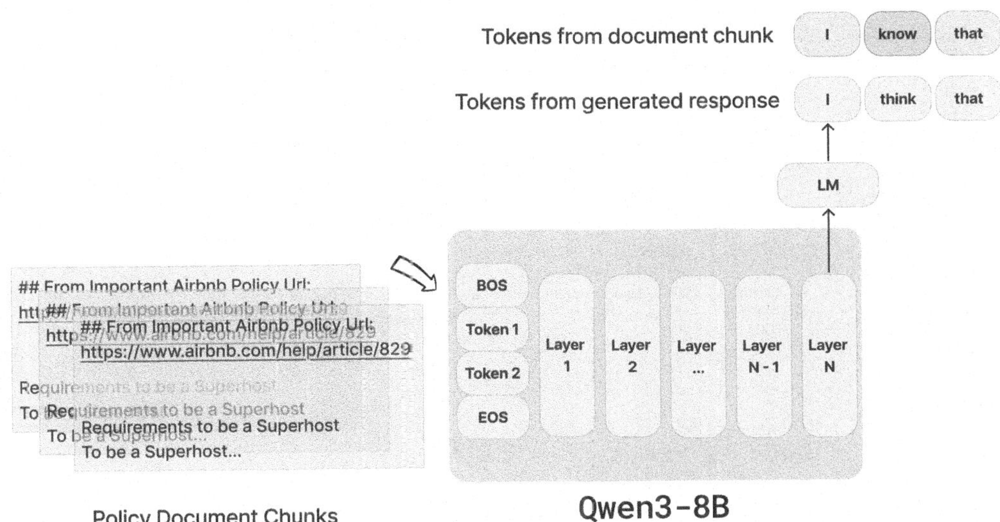

Figure 8.16 Fine-tuning a Qwen3-8B LLM with policy document chunks. Instead of retrieving policy information at inference time, the model is trained to internalize the content, allowing it to generate in-domain answers without external lookups.

A common concern with this method is that we might accidentally cut off some important text between chunks, thereby splitting the context between multiple chunks. To mitigate this problem, we can do two things:

- Set an overlapping window with a specified number of tokens to overlap so that some tokens are shared between chunks. Figure 8.17 provides an example. Of course, this approach introduces a sense of redundancy, but that's often okay in service of higher accuracy.
- Because we know where the chunks come from, we can add the title of the policy and the URL in each chunk. Then the AI system, when being trained on the information, can reference the source of the data.

Luckily, there are tools out there to help us do this chunking, including **`tiktoken`**, a fast and efficient tokenization library developed by OpenAI. Listing 8.5 shows a simple function implementing maximum window chunking with overlap.

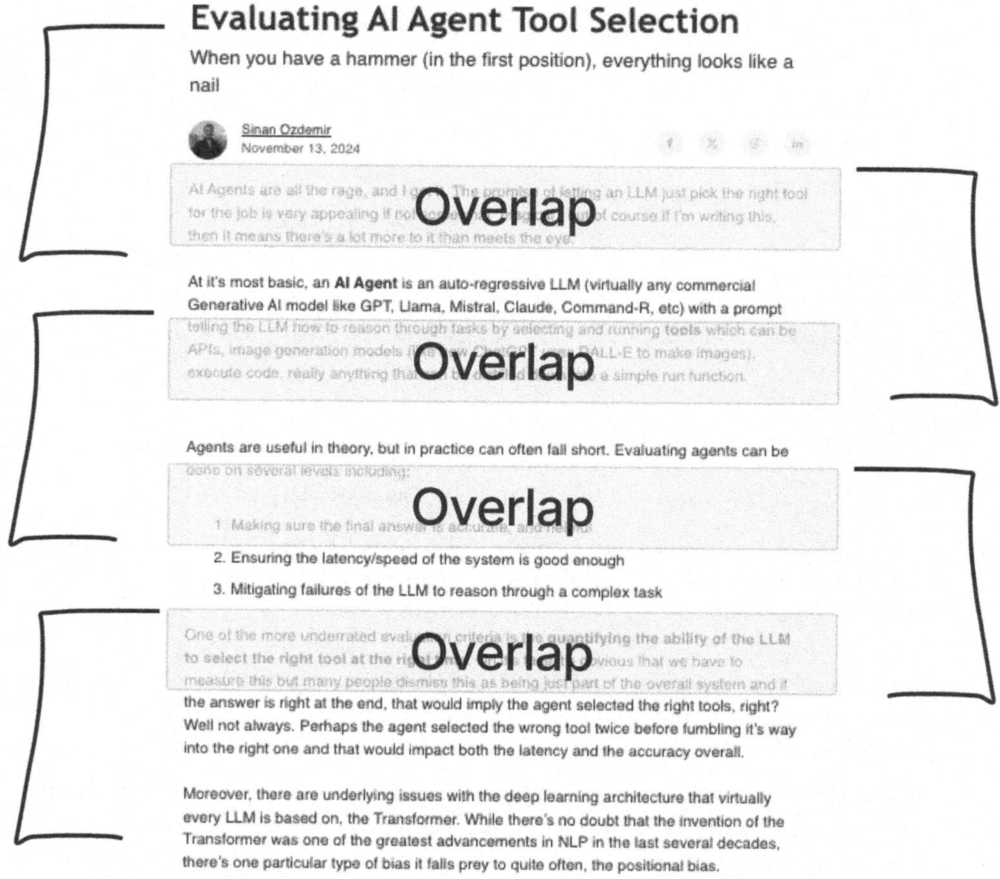

Evaluating AI Agent Tool Selection
When you have a hammer (in the first position), everything looks like a nail
Sinan Ozdemir
November 13, 2024
Overlap
At it's most basic, an **AI Agent** is an auto-regressive LLM (virtually any commercial Generative AI model like GPT, Llama, Mistral, Claude, Command-R, etc) with a prompt
Overlap
Agents are useful in theory, but in practice can often fall short. Evaluating agents can be
Overlap
2. Ensuring the latency/speed of the system is good enough
3. Mitigating failures of the LLM to reason through a complex task
Overlap
the answer is right at the end, that would imply the agent selected the right tools, right? Well not always. Perhaps the agent selected the wrong tool twice before fumbling it's way into the right one and that would impact both the latency and the accuracy overall.
Moreover, there are underlying issues with the deep learning architecture that virtually every LLM is based on, the Transformer. While there's no doubt that the invention of the Transformer was one of the greatest advancements in NLP in the last several decades, there's one particular type of bias it falls prey to quite often, the positional bias.

Figure 8.17 Example of overlapping chunking. Each chunk includes overlapping text and source metadata, ensuring the LLM sees both context continuity and the original source when trained on long policy documents.

Listing 8.5 **Chunking policy documents with `tiktoken`**

```
from datasets import load_dataset
dataset = load_dataset("profoz/airbnb-policy-scenarios", split='test')
dataset = dataset.rename_column("article", "text")
import tiktoken  # Efficient tokenization
from datasets import Dataset
def chunk_text(text, url, encoding_name="cl100k_base", max_chunk_size=256,
overlap=128):
    """
```

```
    Splits a long text into overlapping chunks of tokens, each with a prefix indicating
the source URL.
    Args:
        text (str): The input text to be chunked.
        url (str): The source URL to include as a prefix in each chunk.
        encoding_name (str): The name of the tokenizer encoding to use.
        max_chunk_size (int): Maximum number of tokens per chunk (including prefix).
        overlap (int): Number of tokens to overlap between consecutive chunks.
    Returns:
        List[str]: List of chunked text strings, each with the URL prefix.
    """
    encoding = tiktoken.get_encoding(encoding_name)  # Load the tokenizer encoding
    tokens = encoding.encode(text)  # Convert text to tokens
    chunks = []
    prefix = f"## From Important Airbnb Policy Url: {url}\n\n"  # Prefix for each chunk
    prefix_tokens = encoding.encode(prefix)  # Tokenize the prefix
    step_size = max_chunk_size - overlap  # How many new tokens for each chunk
    # Iterate over the text tokens, creating overlapping chunks
    for i in range(0, len(tokens), step_size):
        chunk_tokens = tokens[i:i + max_chunk_size]  # Get a chunk of tokens
        chunk_text = encoding.decode(prefix_tokens + chunk_tokens) # Prepend the prefix
        chunks.append(chunk_text)
    return chunks
all_chunks = []
# Loop through each example in the dataset and apply chunking
for example in dataset:
    # Each example is expected to have 'text' and 'url' fields
    all_chunks.extend(chunk_text(example['text'], example['url']))
# Create a new Hugging Face Dataset from the list of chunked texts
chunked_dataset = Dataset.from_dict({'text': all_chunks})
chunked_dataset  # Display the resulting chunked dataset
```

Other implementations of chunking are available in packages like LangChain, but they use the same underlying algorithm and the same `tiktoken` package.

Figure 8.18 shows a few of the chunks taken from an actual policy document with the prefix **## From Important Airbnb Policy Url: {url}** in each chunk. That means when the LLM reads the information, it can also see where the information came from if it wants to cite the information.

With our policy documents broken down into chunks and ready to go, we can set up our fine-tuning code.

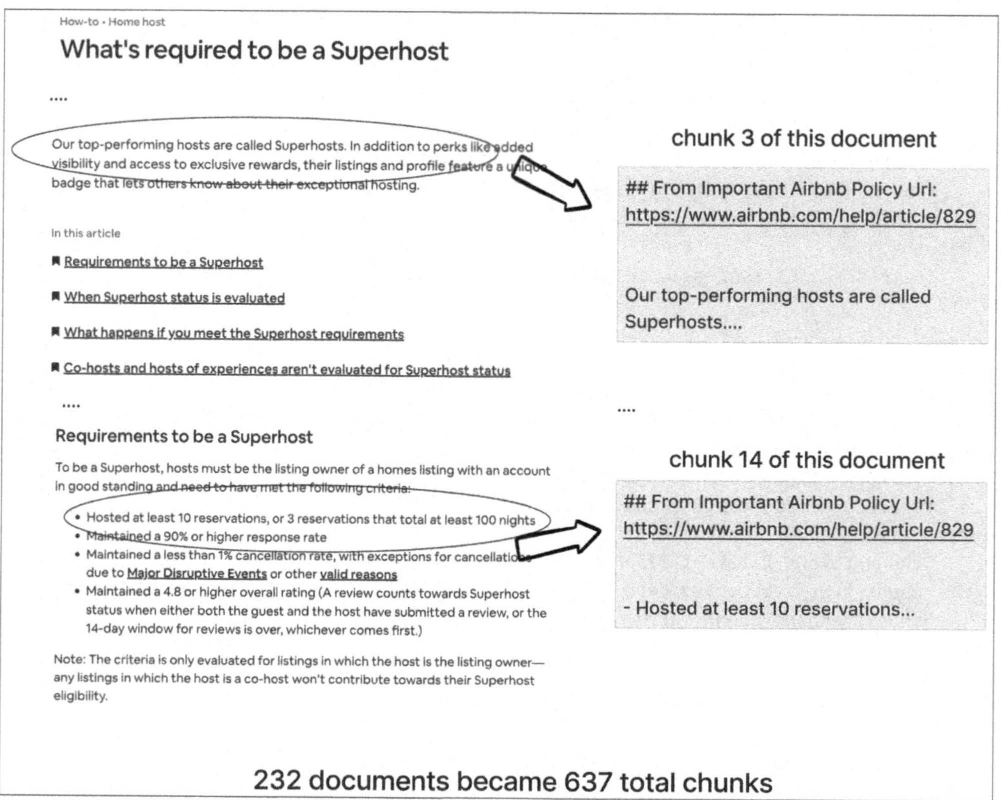

Figure 8.18 Example of policy document chunking. A single policy is split into multiple overlapping chunks, each labeled with a source prefix so the LLM can trace information back to the original document, enabling both citation and efficient training even with long inputs. (Source: Airbnb, Inc. "What's Required to Be a Superhost." Airbnb Help Center, article 829, www.airbnb.co.in/help/article/829)

Fine-Tuning a Qwen3 Reasoning LLM on Airbnb Policies

We will fine-tune a Qwen3 reasoning model for the sake of computational efficiency, but note that this process can be generalized to most chat-based models. One of the key features of domain adaptation is the LLM does not "forget" how to do everything it already knew how to do. For example, if the LLM already knew how to call functions and tools, it shouldn't forget how to do that. If it could create reasoning chains, it shouldn't forget that, either.

Adding knowledge after the initial training process is quite delicate and generally requires a *mix of data, both unstructured and conversational*, to keep the LLM from forgetting its past experiences, as shown in Figure 8.19. Thinking back to the beginning of this section, this data represents the training data in steps 1 and 2 of the training recipe. In our example, however, we will mix in only the new unstructured data (the step 1 pre-training data) to see that it is possible to do so, as long as you proceed with fine-tuning very slowly.

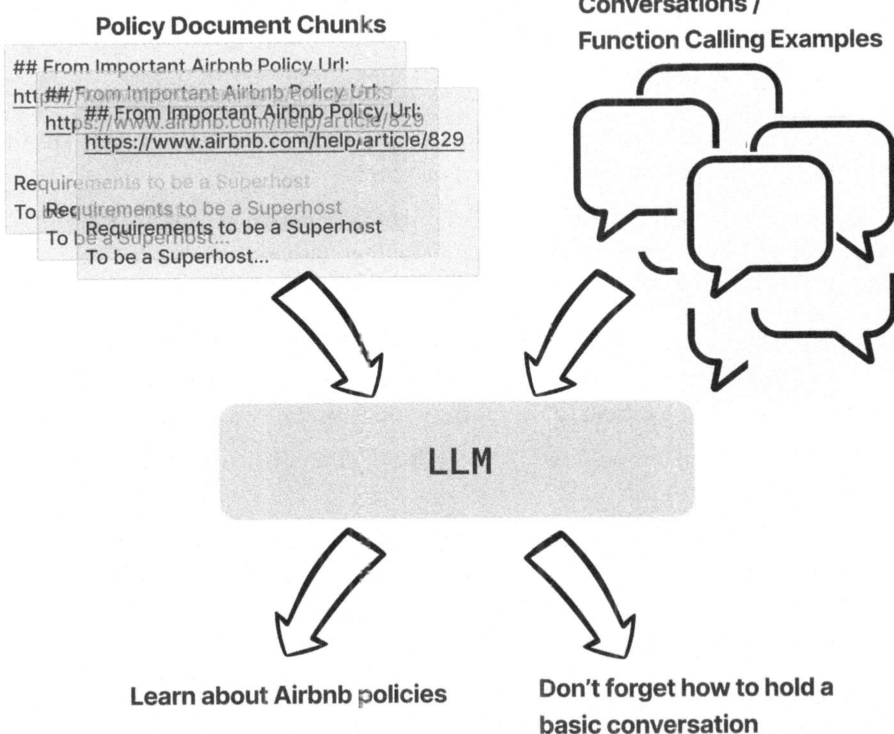

Figure 8.19 Mixing training data types for domain adaptation. By blending both unstructured policy document chunks and conversational examples during fine-tuning, the LLM can learn new content (e.g., company policies) while retaining its core conversational and reasoning abilities.

The process to instill policy documents into the parameters of our LLM at a high level is as follows:

1. Load the Airbnb synthetic situation/solution data we created in Chapter 5.
2. Chunk the policy documents into groups of roughly equivalent size with a prefix header including the source information of the data.
3. Instantiate an instance of the Qwen3-8B reasoning LLM into memory.

4. Fine-tune the LLM using a low learning rate (i.e., very slowly) for at least 1–2 epochs, monitoring the loss until the model converges (i.e., the drop in loss flattens out).

   a. The code uses an A100 on a Colab notebook that costs approximately $6 per hour.

   b. The entire notebook will take about 30–60 minutes to run in total.

A few notes on the packages and techniques I am relying on in this code to speed up the process of fine-tuning and consume less memory:

- **LoRA (low-rank adaptation)** is a linear algebra–inspired technique that significantly reduces the number of adjustable parameters within an LLM by freezing most (and sometimes all) of the pre-trained weights and adding only a few additional weights for fine-tuning. This technique involves integrating low-rank matrices into the original-weight matrices of the neural network. By focusing the training process on these smaller sets of parameters, LoRA can efficiently adapt the model to new tasks with minimal computational overhead.

  In our case, we had to update only 1.42 billion parameters of the original 9.61 billion.

- **Quantization** reduces the precision of the weights and biases in a neural network. This process results in a smaller model size and faster inference times, albeit with a modest decrease in model accuracy.

  In our case, I used a model quantized down to 4 bits (from the original 32), thereby saving significant memory.

- **Unsloth** is a Python library and platform that dramatically accelerates and optimizes LLM fine-tuning by leveraging manual differentiation, leading to up to 30 times speed-ups and reduced memory use, while offering broad compatibility with the Hugging Face library. By "manual differentiation," I mean that the creators of Unsloth are very competent mathematicians and software engineers who added their own custom code to speed up normal fine-tuning and consume less memory. I don't know exactly how they did it, but we can still benefit from their work.

We also have a choice about how we pass the policy chunks into the LLM. Specifically, we could either:

- Pass the chunks in as a conversation, just as we passed the classification data in Case Study 13 into GPT-4.1 and GPT-4.1-Nano.
  - For example, [{"role": "user", "content", "## From Important..."}].
  - We *had* to do this with GPT, because OpenAI doesn't allow any other way of passing in the data.

- Apply no conversation formatting whatsoever. With this approach, the classification data would more closely resemble the raw pre-training data the LLM encountered in its original training process.

We will select the second option because it emulates the data in step 1. That is, we aren't attempting to teach the AI to "respond" to the policy, but just want the AI to "acknowledge" the policy. We will also place the end-of-text token (generally denoted as EOS, meaning "end of sentence") at the end of every policy (see Listing 8.6). This practice is recommended by multiple labs. For what it's worth, I ran this same code with and without the EOS token and saw virtually no difference in the final output.

Listing 8.6 **Preparing policy chunks for the model**

```
EOS_TOKEN = tokenizer.eos_token
def formatting_prompts_func(examples, chat_style=False):
   texts  = examples["text"]
   outputs = []
   for text in texts:
       if chat_style
           text = tokenizer.apply_chat_template(
               [{
                       'role': 'assistant',
                       'content': text
               }], tokenize=False)
       else:
           outputs.append(text+EOS_TOKEN)
   return { "text" : outputs }
```

With the data now ready to go for the LLM, Listing 8.7 sets up the training arguments and the trainer in Unsloth. One note on Unsloth: It's simply a wrapper on top of the more standard fine-tuning package TRL (from Hugging Face). It's technically not required, but if a model is supported by Hugging Face, Unsloth will almost certainly speed up training and consume less memory with no performance loss.

Listing 8.7 **Setting up the training arguments with Unsloth**

```
from transformers import TrainingArguments
from unsloth import UnslothTrainer, UnslothTrainingArguments
trainer = UnslothTrainer(
   model = model,
   tokenizer = tokenizer,
   train_dataset = chunked_dataset,
   dataset_text_field = "text",
   max_seq_length = max_seq_length,
   args = UnslothTrainingArguments(
       per_device_train_batch_size = 8,
```

```
        gradient_accumulation_steps = 16,
        warmup_ratio = 0.1,  # Use warmup_ratio for longer runs
        num_train_epochs = 2,
        learning_rate = 5e-5,  # Reads as 5 x 10^-5
        embedding_learning_rate = 5e-6, # 2-10x smaller than learning_rate
        load_best_model_at_end = True,
        logging_steps = 5,
        eval_strategy='no',
        save_strategy='no',
        lr_scheduler_type = "cosine",
        seed = 42,
        report_to = "wandb", # Weights & Biases - free ML fine-tuning tracking
    ),
)
```

The code in Listing 8.7 sets several hyperparameters that will impact our fine-tuning. A few are highlighted here:

- **`learning_rate`** signifies the rate at which parameter values can change. Smaller means slower and more deliberate changes to parameter values, whereas larger means faster changes. We generally prefer smaller learning rates, as they make it more likely that the fine-tuning system will converge at an optimal level of performance.
  - Standard fine-tuning *generally* has a learning rate closer to 2×10^{-4}. Often, however, the learning rate is treated as an experimental value to test different values.
- **`embedding_learning_rate`** is the same as `learning_rate`, but specifically applies to the embedding weights—the section of the LLM's parameters that give vector embeddings to each individual input token. We usually want this to be even lower than the standard learning rate, as even small changes to the embedding weights may impact the LLM's final result more than most of the other parameters do. The embedding weights are among the first weights encountered by the input data, and all attention calculations are impacted by these weights. To be clear, the idea that embedding learning rates should be lower than the overall learning rate is not a provable statement, but rather is common practice among practitioners.
- **`warmup_ratio`** and **`lr_scheduler_type`** set up the learning rate scheduler, meaning the learning rate is not constantly at a set rate (e.g., 5×10^{-5}). It would start even lower and "warm up" over time, getting higher for the first 10% of the training run (.10 would be the warm-up ratio in this case). The learning rate will then fall according to a cosine curve, as opposed to linearly.

Setting different hyperparameters requires its own experimental setup. For example, you can use platforms like Weights and Biases to track the results of using different hyperparameters (that's the "wandb" in the training arguments). Once the model runs for the two epochs defined in the code (that's two full passes over the data), we see the training loss drop and are ready to test the final result.

Evaluating the Domain-Adapted LLM

The process described in this case study diverges a little bit from the standard fine-tuning recipe of using training, validation, and testing sets. In fact, we did not create any testing or validation sets to speak of. This is a major differentiating factor between pre-training and standard supervised fine-tuning. There's no real "task" to generalize here. We aren't trying to see if the LLM now knows how to hold a conversation or predict a star rating. Instead, we want to see that after two epochs, the loss in the autoregressive language modeling task is declining, meaning it has seen the text before and can more confidently (with better calibration) recall the information from the policy documents. What we are testing, then, is the model's ability to "remember" the policy documents it just read and can use them in context.

To test our model, we will feed it the same testing user scenarios we used in Chapter 5. Figure 8.20 shows the before and after results for our domain adaptation (left and right, respectively) on a cherry-picked example:

- **Before adaptation:** The base Qwen3 would hallucinate or miss the nuance that co-host listings don't count toward Superhost status.
- **After adaptation:** The LLM nails the requirements for guest reviews, response rate, and cancellation metrics, citing the correct thresholds.

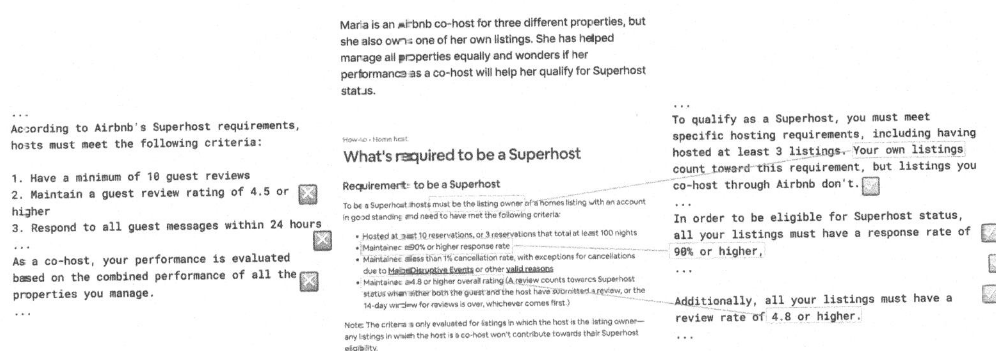

Figure 8.20 On the left, the baseline AI response contains several errors and misunderstandings of Airbnb's Superhost policies. On the right, after domain adaptation, the model accurately cites the correct requirements.

Of course, we also want to see how our model did overall. To do that, we will use the same rubric and rubric grader as we did in Chapter 5 (to keep things consistent). Recall that GPT-4.1-Nano received a 12% accuracy score (a rubric grade of 3 versus not a 3) with no tools, and a 23% score with tools to look up policy information. GPT-4.1 (which has very likely seen the newest Airbnb policies) got an approximately 44% accuracy score with no tools, and a 71% score with the lookup tool. Figure 8.21 shows the before and after for our Qwen3 model using the same grading scale.

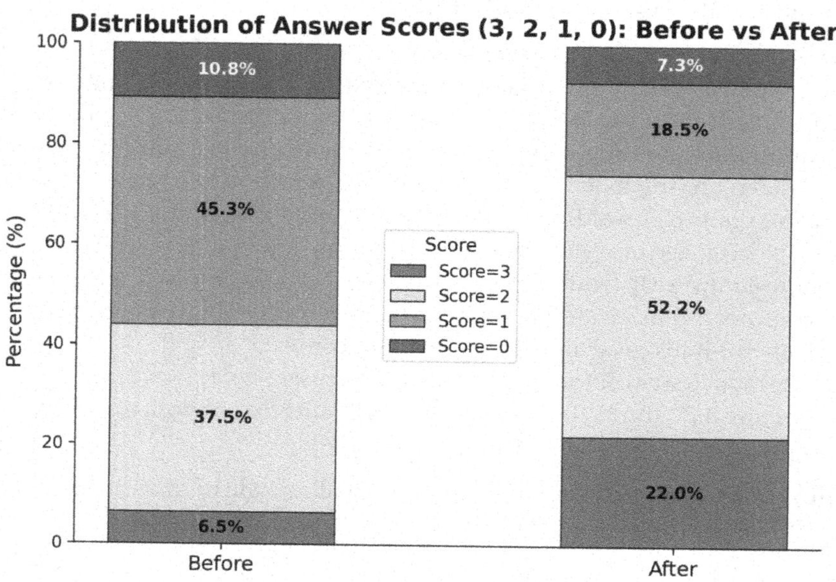

Figure 8.21 Rubric-based evaluation before and after domain adaptation. The "Before" bar shows that most answers from the base Qwen3 model received low rubric scores (0 or 1), with only 6.5% achieving the top grade (3). After fine-tuning on the Airbnb policy documents, more than half of the answers received the highest score, matching the performance of GPT-4.1-Nano with retrieval tools, despite not relying on external lookup.

Before fine-tuning, Qwen3 (which has only approximately 9 billion parameters) had a measly 6.5% accuracy of having an answer with a grade of 3. After fine-tuning, it's as good as GPT 4.1-Nano *with* the tool—but our model hasn't looked anything up with a tool. Not bad! Should we use Qwen3 instead of GPT-4.1? Probably not if data privacy is of no issue. However, these training recipes extend beyond Qwen3 to virtually any LLM and any pre-training data, so this question can be considered the beginning of the fine-tuning experiments.

Conclusion

You've now seen two complete fine-tuning toolkits: from calibrated classifiers with cost–speed–privacy trade-offs across GPT variants and open-source LLMs, to domain adaptation that bakes new raw, unstructured data into an open-source reasoning model. You saw how chunking, LoRA, quantization, and packages like Unsloth let you fine-tune models with new information without erasing their core skills, and how measuring calibration, whether in a 5-star predictor or a free-text birthday memorization task, gives you a real read on trust in the AI system.

Fine-tuning, like most of the topics covered in this book, is a huge topic. In Chapter 9, we'll apply these lessons to optimizing models for production workloads. The discussion there will include a look at how fine-tuning embeddings can save us gigabytes of memory and computing resources, and how we can minimize latency to the point where we can have a reasonably realistic phone conversation with an AI system.

9

Optimizing AI Models for Production

Introduction

In Chapter 8, you saw how fine-tuning can ground a model in data and how domain adaptation can bake specialized rules into its parameters. But accuracy alone will not cut it in the wild. Production-level AI demands more than accurate and calibrated answers. It demands speed and cost control and data governance.

In this chapter, we will explore techniques like quantization, which can shrink models in place to use less memory, and distillation, which can teach a smaller model to mimic a larger one. We will also talk about model hosting patterns and how to choose among options such as self-hosting and managed endpoints. From there, we will see how techniques like speculative decoding can create multi-model systems in which LLMs work in tandem to produce accurate responses, faster.

In our two main case studies, we will first build a phone bot and benchmark speech-to-text (STT) and text-to-speech (TTS) models and providers from end to end. We will then fine-tune an embedding model to produce multiple sizes of embeddings in a process named after the famous Matryoshka nesting dolls.

This final chapter aims to serve as a jumping-off point for what you do after you put this book down (and in between picking it up again later to refresh your memory). So far, we have prompted, we have experimented, we have coded, and we have fine-tuned. Now it's time to wrap it up with a discussion on model hosting and optimization.

Model Compression

Perhaps the easiest way to get a model ready for production is to somehow compress it into a smaller, faster, and more efficient version without sacrificing too much performance. By doing so, we hope to consume far less memory when using our models.

At the top of the list of places where LLMs can be optimized is their utilization of **VRAM (video random access memory)**. VRAM is a special type of memory used in GPUs today for modern LLM inference, measured in bytes. There's a quick rule of thumb for estimating how much memory your model will use on the GPU:

$$\text{VRAM (in bytes)} = \text{Number of parameters} \times (\text{Precision in bits} / 8) \times 1.2$$

Here's a description of each element of this formula:

- **Number of parameters:** This is the total count of weights in the model. For something like Qwen3-8B, for example, that's approximately 8.19 billion parameters.
- **Precision:** This is how many bits we use to store each parameter. Commonly used options are FP32 (32 bits), FP16 (16 bits), and INT8 (8 bits) for quantized models.
- **Divide by 8:** Because there are 8 bits in a byte. So, FP16 (floating-point 16-bit precision) means 2 bytes per parameter.
- **The 1.2 multiplier:** This is really just a finger in the wind. Practitioners will add roughly 20% extra headroom to cover things like activations, the CUDA workspace, and all the random overhead that comes up at runtime.

Suppose you're deploying an 8B model in FP16. That would yield roughly:

$$\begin{aligned} \text{VRAM} &\approx 8{,}000{,}000{,}000 \times (16 / 8) \times 1.2 \\ &= \text{19.2B bytes} / \text{1024 bytes per KB} / \text{1024 KBs per MB} \\ &\quad / \text{1024 MBs per GB} \\ &\approx \mathbf{17.88\ GB\ of\ VRAM} \end{aligned}$$

The goal is to take those hefty, state-of-the-art models and squeeze them down so they're practical for real-world deployment—whether you're serving millions of users or just trying to run something locally on modest hardware. There are a handful of clever techniques for pulling this off, but two of the most common and effective approaches are quantization and distillation. Let's start by looking at quantization.

Quantization

Quantization is discussed at great length in my intro to LLM book, *A Quick Start Guide to Large Language Models*, and it remains one of the most powerful tricks for production models. At its core, **quantization** refers to reducing the number of bits used to represent each weight in an AI model. Going from 32 bits to 8 bits (see Figure 9.1), for example, can cut memory use by 75% (said another way, 8 bits is a quarter of 32 bits). Going even further, down to 4 bits, cuts it in half again. The result is a model that fits on smaller GPUs or even on CPU-only servers.

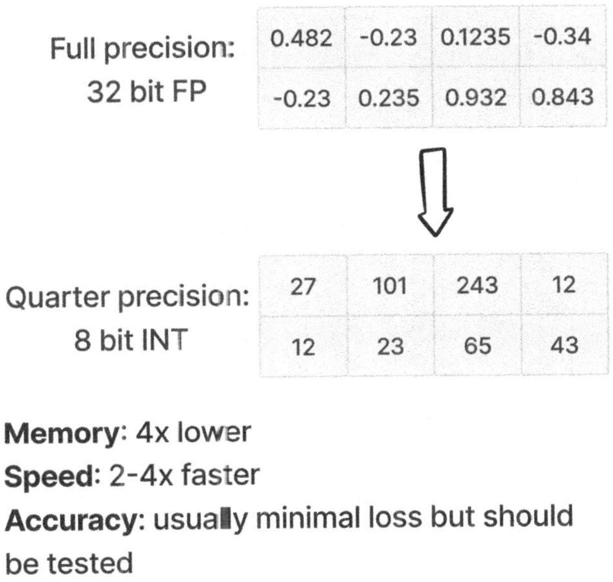

Full precision:
32 bit FP

0.482	-0.23	0.1235	-0.34
-0.23	0.235	0.932	0.843

Quarter precision:
8 bit INT

27	101	243	12
12	23	65	43

Memory: 4x lower
Speed: 2-4x faster
Accuracy: usually minimal loss but should be tested

Figure 9.1 Quantization literally changes the values of parameters in place using special algorithms rather than just cutting off decimal places. The result is a model with almost guaranteed accuracy loss but much more optimized for speed and memory performance. Note the parameter values are entirely made up and do not correspond to actual NF4 conversions.

Figure 9.2 shows an example in which an unquantized Llama 3-8B model (originally 16 bit) and a quantized version at 4 bits are used to run batches of data. Running data through a model will add extra memory. If you recall the original estimation of this Llama 3-8B model from the previous section, it used approximately 18 GB of memory. As shown in Figure 9.2, running a query through the unquantized model yielded about 26 GB of VRAM usage. Now compare that to the 6 GB needed for the same model, quantized down to 4 bits.

Any LLM can be quantized, but only if you have access to the weights of the model. The code to quantize a model is straightforward using Hugging Face's Transformers, which include implementations of quantization algorithms like NormalFloat4 (NF4, used in Listing 9.1). NF4 is a particularly effective strategy for maintaining the performance of AI models. Originally introduced in the same paper that introduced LoRA (the technique discussed in Chapter 8), NF4 has become a preferred choice in modern quantization strategies.

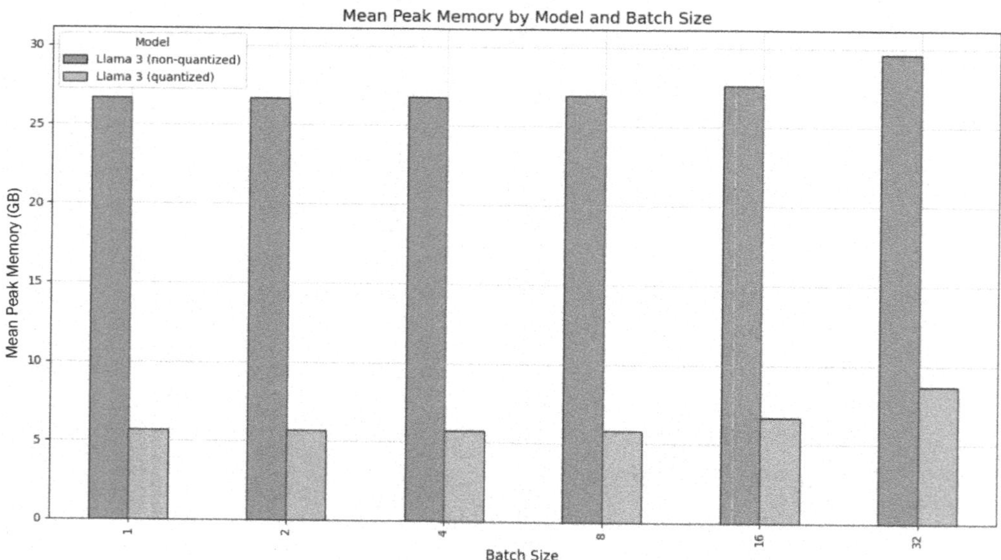

Figure 9.2 Mean peak memory usage for an unquantized Llama 3-8B model (16-bit weights, red bars) versus a quantized version at 4 bits (green bars) across multiple batch sizes. Quantization dramatically reduces memory requirements down to nearly a quarter of the original—for example, from approximately 30 GB to merely 9 GB to process a batch of 32 items (indicated by the right most pair of bars).

Listing 9.1 **Load Llama-3-8B-Instruct with and without quantization**

```
# Import necessary classes and functions from the transformers library
from transformers import AutoModelForCausalLM, AutoTokenizer, BitsAndBytesConfig
# Define the model name to load from Hugging Face's model hub
model_name = 'meta-llama/Meta-Llama-3-8B-Instruct'
# Configure the quantization settings using BitsAndBytesConfig
# Setting load_in_4bit to True enables 4-bit quantization
# bnb_4bit_use_double_quant enables double quantization for more precise control
# bnb_4bit_quant_type specifies the NF4 quantization algorithm
# bnb_4bit_compute_dtype sets the data type for computation to bfloat16 for efficiency
bits_config = BitsAndBytesConfig(
   load_in_4bit=True,
   bnb_4bit_use_double_quant=True,
   bnb_4bit_quant_type="nf4",
   bnb_4bit_compute_dtype=torch.bfloat16
)
# Initialize the tokenizer for the model
tokenizer = AutoTokenizer.from_pretrained(model_name)
# Load and configure the quantized model
```

```
qt_model = AutoModelForCausalLM.from_pretrained(
    model_name,
    quantization_config=bits_config,
    device_map="auto"
    ).eval() # Set the model to evaluation mode which disables training specific
operations like dropout
# Load the non-quantized version of the same model
non_qt_model = AutoModelForCausalLM.from_pretrained(
    model_name,
    device_map="auto"
).eval() # Set the model to evaluation mode, further optimizing the model for
  inference
```

Naturally, this benefit comes with a catch (of course it does): Quantized models are technically different models with different parameter values, so although the drop in performance could be minimal, such a decline is almost certainly guaranteed. In practice, most people report a drop of at most 10% to 15% in accuracy on benchmarks when quantizing models, though fine-tuning could help pick up this slack. In Chapter 8, we used quantization in tandem with LoRA for fine-tuning on a 4-bit quantized Qwen3 model; there we saw how well it held up following domain adaptation. Quantization pairs well with fine-tuning to mitigate the drop in performance expected through precision reduction.

Quantization is model-agnostic and is a great choice for using models locally, even on a CPU. Software like OLlama allows users to use quantized LLMs directly on a CPU with absolutely no internet access (after downloading the weights of course). Listing 9.2 shows a quick example of using a quantized local LLM (Llama 3.1-8b) using OLlama.

Listing 9.2 Use Llama-.3.1-8B-Instruct with OLlama as a ReAct agent

```
!ollama pull llama3.1:8b # pulls llama 3.1 8B
os.environ["SERPAPI_API_KEY"] = 's***'  # serpapi.com for a free token

from datetime import datetime
from langchain_community.agent_toolkits.load_tools import load_tools

tools = load_tools(["serpapi"])
from langgraph.prebuilt import create_react_agent
from langchain_ollama import ChatOllama

llm = ChatOllama(model="llama3.1", temperature=1)
date = datetime.now().strftime("%Y-%m-%d")
```

```
agent_executor = create_react_agent(
  llm, tools, state_modifier='Today is {date}')

response = agent_executor.invoke(
  {"messages": [("user", "Who is the current Ravens QB?")]})

response['messages'][-1].content
# 'The current quarterback for the Baltimore Ravens is Lamar Jackson.' True as of
  writing!
```

While quantization can quickly alter a model in place to achieve performance gains, some slower, more deliberate fine-tuning methods are better at delivering long-term-performant, small language models that can be edge-ready.

Distillation

I cover distillation at great length in my *Quick Start Guide to Large Language Models* book because it is another cornerstone of production models. At its heart, **distillation** means training a smaller student model to mimic the behavior of a larger teacher model. The idea is to use the outputs of a larger "teacher" model to train a more compact "student" model to reproduce those signals.

There are two main flavors of distillation (shown in Figure 9.3). **Task-agnostic distillation** teaches the student about a general language modeling objective, so it internalizes broad world knowledge before we ever give it a real downstream task. **Task-specific distillation** fine-tunes the student on a narrow, labeled dataset so it excels at that particular use-case from day one.

Task-agnostic distillation gives us a new, lean base model we can later adapt to multiple tasks. A popular example is the 2018 BERT model, which was distilled shortly after its release into DistilBERT—perhaps an even more popular LLM owing to its tiny size and outsized performance. Task-specific distillation yields a tiny model already specialized for a single most important workload such as classification of visual question answering (VQA). In practice, we might first distill an 800 million parameter student from a 9 billion parameter teacher, and then run a second round of focused distillation on core task data, as visualized in Figure 9.4.

The GitHub for this book includes supplemental case studies on distillation, which focus on both the fine-tuning code for distillation and the evaluation of the student models as compared to their teachers. Both quantization and distillation yield a combination of desirable qualities for LLMs—for example, smaller, more memory efficient, or faster. In fact, in many cases, models can be first distilled and then quantized for maximum efficiency. Table 9.1 breaks down the high-level pros and cons for both quantization and distillation.

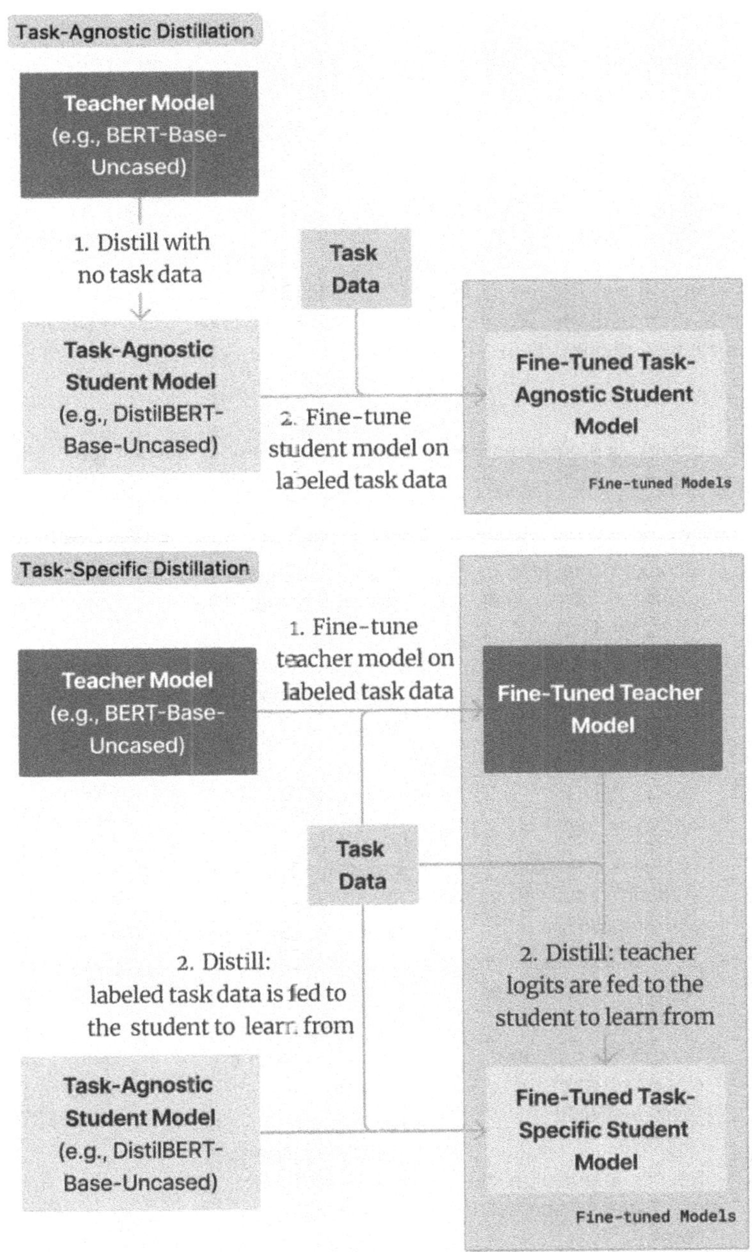

Figure 9.3 The top half shows task-agnostic distillation: A student model is distilled from a teacher using no task-specific data, then later fine-tuned on downstream tasks. The bottom half shows task-specific distillation: A teacher model is first fine-tuned on task data, then a student is distilled using the teacher's outputs on the same data.

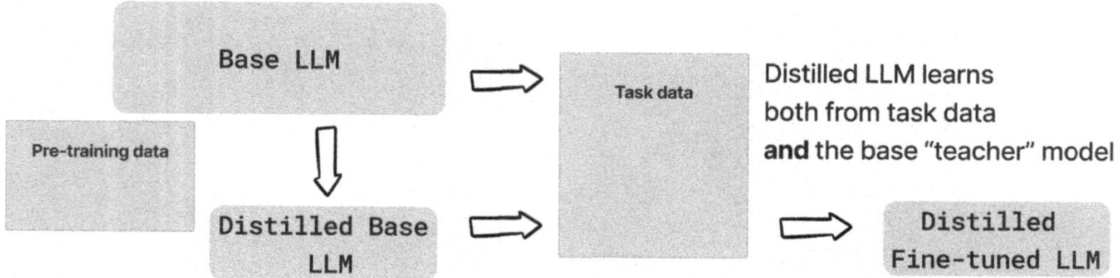

Figure 9.4 A common training recipe for task-specific distillation is to first task-agnostically distill a base LLM into a smaller version, and then perform task-specific distillation to create a tiny but powerful task-specific LLM.

Table 9.1 **Throughput by Model and Batch Size in Examples per Second (eps). Higher is better.**

Strategy	Pros	Cons	Batch Size 25
Quantization	– Shrinks model size drastically (up to 4–8 times smaller). – Cuts memory and compute cost. – Enables running on smaller GPUs or CPUs. – Fast to apply; no retraining required.	– Accuracy almost always drops (5–15% is typical). – Sensitive tasks (math, reasoning) may degrade more.	– You need quick deployment on constrained hardware. – Use-case tolerates a small performance drop. – Great for edge devices or local CPU inference.
Distillation	– Produces a smaller student model with strong performance. – Task-specific distillation yields highly optimized models. – Can maintain accuracy close to that of the teacher despite size reduction. – Results in a ***new*** model (not just a compressed copy).	– Expensive retraining required. – Student inherits the teacher's biases/ limitations. – Generalization is often worse than with the teacher. – Not instantly applicable. Needs engineering, data, and fine-tuning.	– You want a long-term efficient model. – Performance is critical and you can afford retraining. – Ideal when building specialized small models (e.g., DistilBERT).

What we can do with these more optimized models in production can also be extremely beneficial. Let's take a look at one of the techniques that greatly benefits from the use of distilled LLMs: speculative decoding.

Case Study 15: Speculative Decoding with Qwen

Speculative decoding is a two-model strategy for faster LLM generation. First, a smaller "assistant" model proposes a batch of token candidates using the slower next-token prediction method. Then, a larger "base" model (usually the assistant is a distilled version of the base model) verifies those tokens. This is a much faster process because there's no generation happening, just double-checking the assistant's work.

When both the assistant and the base model agree, the slower, larger base model gets away with doing only a single forward pass to verify all of the tokens, rather than one forward pass per produced token. The result can be higher throughput without changing the output distribution—at least, as long as we balance the number of tokens handled by the assistant (which is still slow, just not as slow as the base model) and the opportunity cost of not having the smarter base model taking up so much compute resources. The more discrepancies between the two LLMs, the slower the process becomes, to the point where it could even be *slower* to take this approach of assisting the larger model. Figure 9.5 shows this process.

For our experiment, we will use the following models:

- Assistant model: Qwen3-0.6B (a distilled off-the-shelf version of Qwen3-8B with approximately 750 million parameters)
- Base model: Our Qwen3-8B model from Chapter 8, which was fine-tuned on the Airbnb policy documents

Listing 9.3 shows an example of running speculative decoding on a single sample.

Listing 9.3 **Running speculative decoding on the fine-tuned Qwen model**

```
BASE_MODEL = "profoz/lora_airbnb_policy"
ASSISTANT_MODEL = "Qwen/Qwen3-0.6B"
model = AutoModelForCausalLM.from_pretrained(BASE_MODEL)
assistant_model = AutoModelForCausalLM.from_pretrained(ASSISTANT_MODEL)
inputs = tokenizer.apply_chat_template(
   [{"role": "user", "content": "hello"}],
   return_tensors="pt", add_generation_prompt=True
)
outputs = model.generate(
   input_ids=inputs,
   assistant_model=assistant_model,
   prompt_lookup_num_tokens=10,  # assistant generates 10 tokens at a time
   # tokenizer=tokenizer,
   # assistant_tokenizer=assistant_tokenizer,  # if tokenizers are different, these
two lines are needed
   do_sample=True,
   # other parameters can go here too
   temperature=0.7,
   max_new_tokens=50,
   pad_token_id=tokenizer.eos_token_id,
   )
```

FIRST PASS

Tell me a joke

Qwen3-0.6B

Slow next token prediction

"What is a pirate's favorite way to"

Qwen3-8B

Fast token verification

"What is a pirate's favorite way to"

First four tokens are good, I prefer "least as the fifth

"least"

SECOND PASS

Tell me a joke

What is a pirate's least

Qwen3-0.6B

Slow next token prediction

"..favorite ship? EOT"

Qwen3-8B

Fast token verification

"favorite ship? EOT"

Looks good AND EOT is there

FINAL RESPONSE

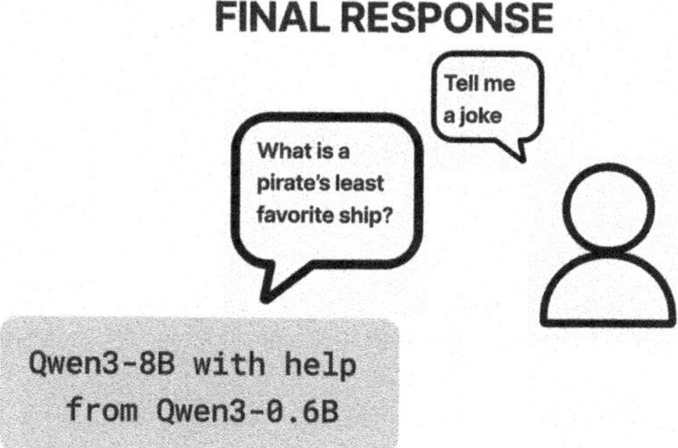

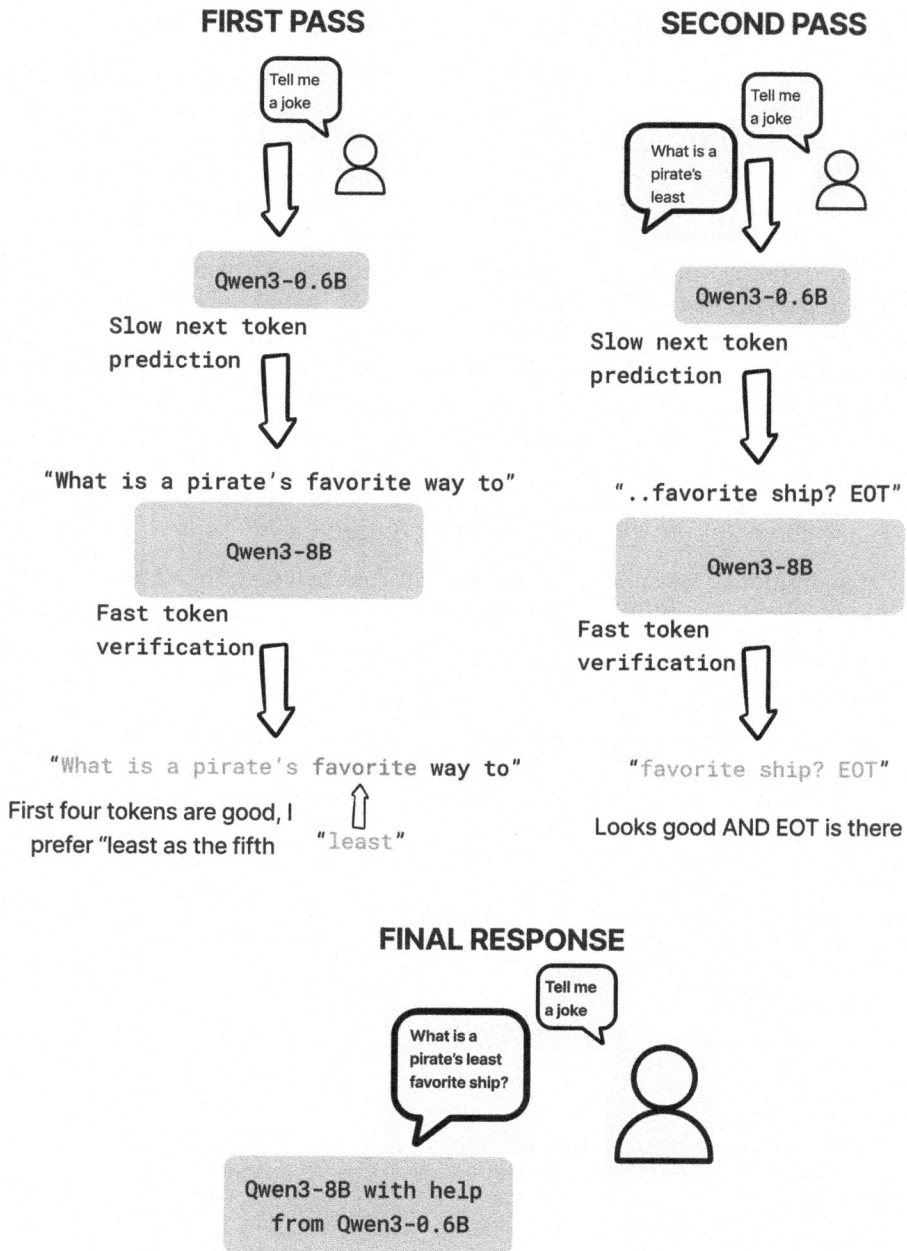

Figure 9.5 In speculative decoding, a small assistant model generates candidate tokens using slower next-token prediction, which the larger base model quickly verifies. If the candidate tokens match, the final response can be assembled with less compute resources, accelerating generation compared to having the base model generate all of the tokens by itself.

Our experiment will run over six prompt categories: Airbnb policy questions, casual conversation, general knowledge, entertainment, mathematics and science, and reciting popular media from memory. For each category, we will invoke several generations from our system and measure average seconds per token under two settings: Unassisted (base model only) and Assisted (assistant proposes 4 tokens at a time). Figure 9.6 shows the average percent gains and losses in speed for each of the categories. Key findings include:

- In half of the categories, assistance cut the per-token time by 10% to 25%. These categories—reciting from memory, math, and general knowledge—have fairly standard answers with few variations in how to talk about them.
- In two categories (entertainment and casual conversation), we saw relatively small drops in latency, perhaps due to random chance. The entertainment category included questions like "Recap the Harry Potter series"; this series has a set plot, of course, but there could be minor variations in how it is explained.
- Airbnb policy prompts ran significantly slower with assistance. This outcome most likely occurred because the assistant model lacked the policy fine-tuning we did in Chapter 8 and often proposed incorrect hallucinations that our fine-tuned base model was forced to correct over and over.

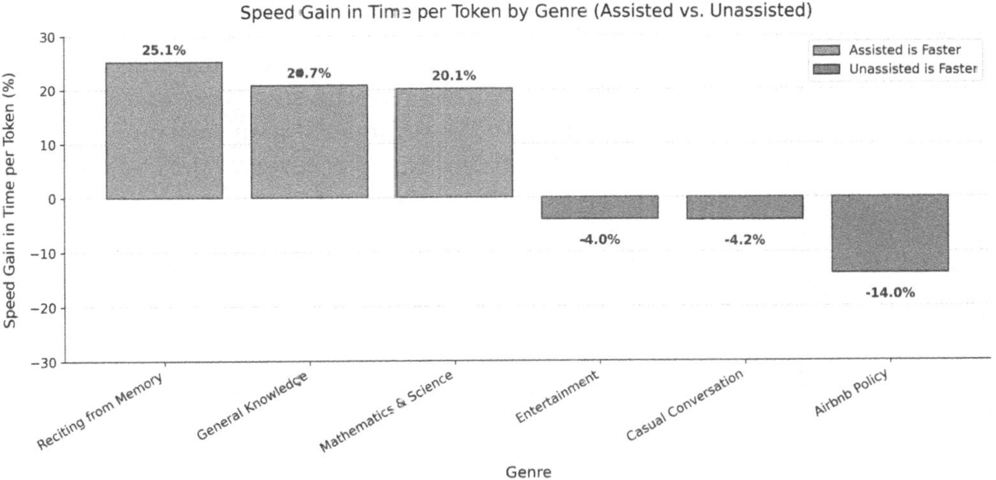

Figure 9.6 Speculative decoding can yield significant speed-ups for standard, well-aligned tasks such as reciting from memory, general knowledge, and math/science, while tasks in poorly aligned domains (such as Airbnb policy) can actually see a slowdown in performance. Remember that the assistant model here hasn't been fine-tuned on the policy documents.

Speculative decoding shines when the assistant model closely matches the base model. To make our fine-tuned Airbnb example as efficient as possible, we would also want to distill the base model into a smaller assistant model to see if that would produce even more gains. In practice, speculative decoding is a technique reserved for larger foundation models, as a 10% to 25% speed-up may not be worth the effort required for distillation. Instead, we could pay for more GPUs and simply add another instance of the base model if throughput is an issue.

Speculative decoding can reduce latency when both models share task expertise. If the assistant model is misaligned with the domain in question, however, we could see only a little gain or even a slowdown. As with quantization and distillation, careful context engineering and domain alignment are essential to unlock real speed improvements.

Case Study 16: Voice Bot—Need for Speed

The discussion of multimodal AI in Chapter 6 highlighted the concept of grounding—that is, use of a base mode of data to do the AI work, plus ancillary AI systems to convert between the end mode of data and the grounded mode. This case study will focus on building a phone system with an AI, tying audio and text together in real time. For this case study we will rely on Twilio's cloud communications API, which provides phone call routing and bidirectional audio streaming out of the box.

As of this writing, models do exist that can convert from audio to audio, such as Kimi Audio Instruct (hf.co/moonshotai/Kimi-Audio-7B-Instruct) and Sesame (hf.co/sesame/csm-1b). We aren't using them in this case study because in practice, these models aren't quite ready for prime time. The voices are difficult to customize, and they tend to lose quality during longer conversations. That being said, by the next edition of this book, you will likely see a new case study using them. For now, most LLM-driven phone systems still rely on the grounding technique.

The general flow of our phone system is visualized in Figure 9.7. It includes the following steps:

- Capture audio from the user
- Run speech-to-text (STT) conversion on the user's voice
- Feed those words into a text-based LLM
- Turn the reply back into audio with a text-to-speech (TTS) model
- Stream everything back over Web Sockets to minimize latency

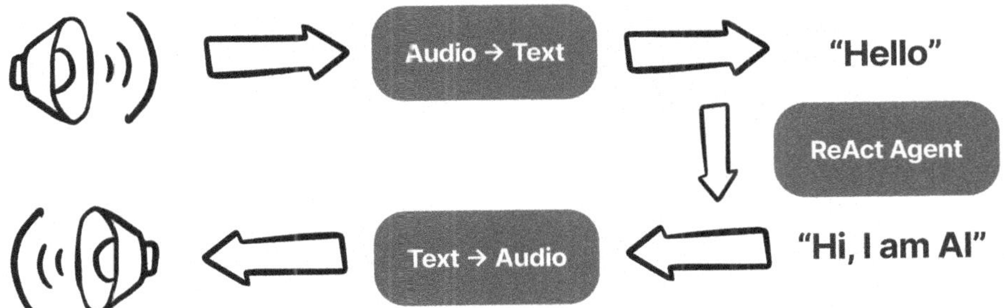

Figure 9.7 The end-to-end flow for our AI voice bot. Audio from the user is first transcribed to text (STT), processed by an LLM-powered system (perhaps a ReAct agent), and then converted back to audio (TTS) for the user to hear the AI model's response. All steps are streamed for low latency, powered by Twilio for call routing and audio streaming.

With these components, we will have a fully functioning voice bot. All we need to do now is find some good and accurate models to do our STT and TTS conversions.

Finding the Fastest STT and TTS Models

To run this simple experiment, I put together a benchmarking script that pits a few major providers of both open- and closed-source STT and TTS against each other. The script picks a few simple test phrases and then calls one provider's TTS model (e.g., OpenAI, Deepgram, or Groq), gets the audio, and then immediately throws that audio into another provider's STT model. The script measures the latency of the trip each way as well as the accuracy of each model.

In this test, accuracy is measured for each combination of STT and TTS with the **word error rate (WER)**, calculated as the percentage of words in the original phrase that were incorrectly transcribed after going through TTS and back through STT. A lower WER means the system preserved more of the original meaning, while a higher WER shows more words were lost or changed in the roundtrip. The lower the WER, the closer the transcription is to what I actually said. Accuracy is calculated as 1 – WER. Figure 9.8 shows how average accuracy is determined for each STT and TTS model: by running several phrases through each combination of STT and TTS and rolling up the performance for each specific model.

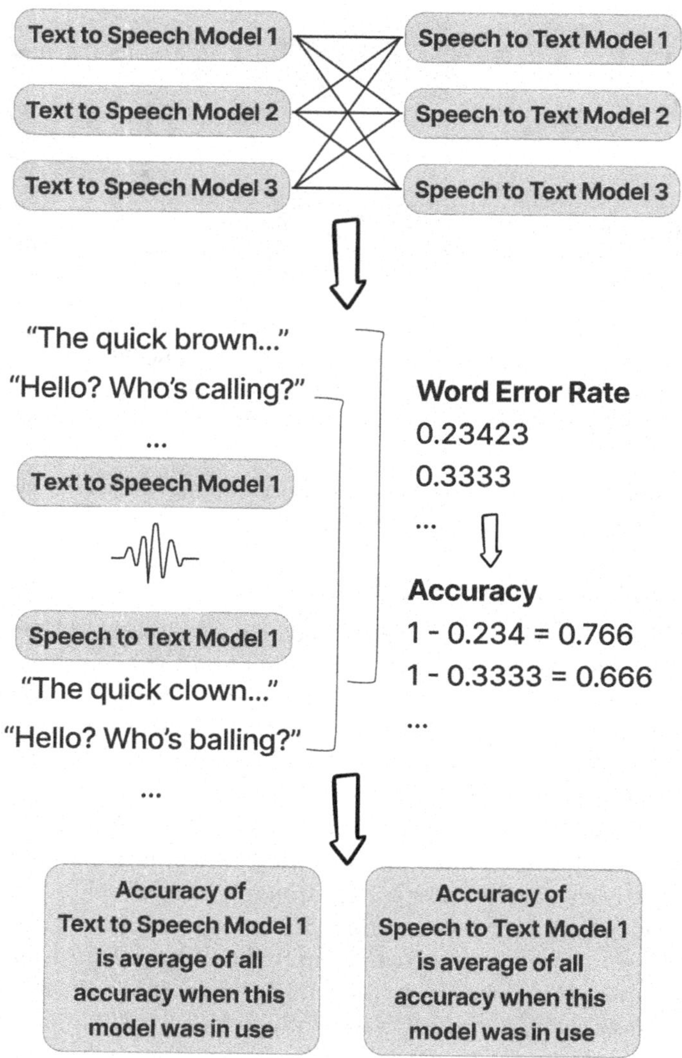

Figure 9.8 Each TTS model is paired with every STT model, and phrases are passed through the full loop. The word error rate (WER) and accuracy are calculated for each combination, then averaged to benchmark each model's real-world performance in the system.

Latency per word is easier to determine. While calculating accuracy, I simply measure how long each model took to do its job and then divide that number by the number of words in the phrase. This gives a dead-simple "seconds per word" metric, where lower is better. Sometimes a provider will be super accurate but take forever. Sometimes it's lightning fast but sounds as if it's guessing half of the sentence. Figure 9.9 shows the results for STT and TTS. The bars show the latency, and the red line shows the accuracy for each model.

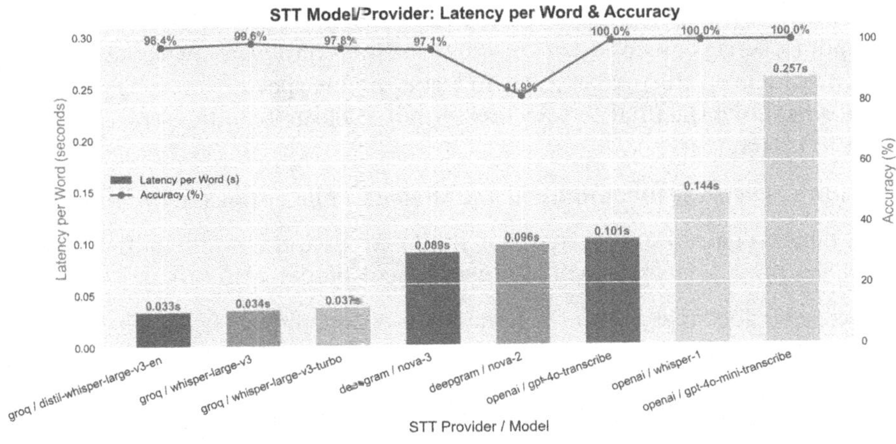

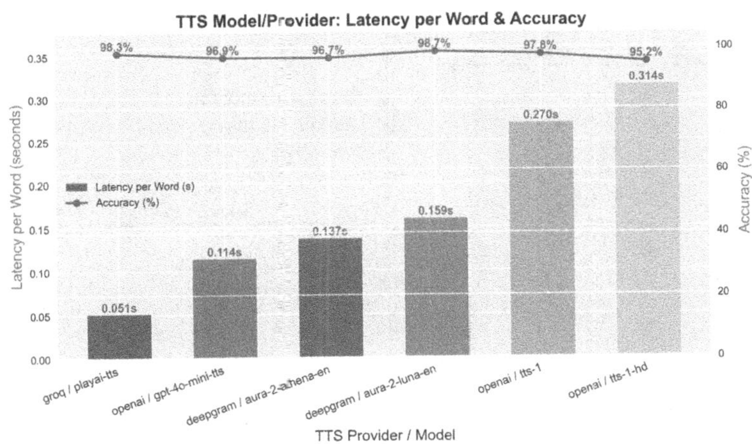

Figure 9.9 Top: Each speech-to-text (STT) model/provider is measured for average latency per word (bars; lower is better) and accuracy (red line; higher is better). Bottom: Each text-to-speech (TTS) provider is benchmarked the same way. Groq models lead with the fastest response times.

The company Groq shines once again, as it has the STT and TTS models with the lowest latency. Note a few things about the results in Figure 9.9:

- The fastest STT model was a distilled version of whisper—an open-weights STT model by OpenAI.
- GPT-4o-Mini was the size of a roughly low- to mid-tier frontier LLM at the time of writing, but the difference between this model and the Groq + distil whisper combination was a 7.5 times speed boost with barely any movement in accuracy.
- This experiment did nothing to judge the "quality" of the voices in the TTS models. Do we like the voice? I didn't care about this criterion; I simply wanted to go with the fastest model.

For the text-to-text AI engine, let's use Groq's serving of Llama-4-Scout. With a throughput (tokens per second, tps) of 750 tps, Groq's hardware rivals that of most other AI providers on the market today in terms of pure speed.

Figure 9.10 shows the final architecture with the selected models. The call flow proceeds in this way:

- Twilio answers the incoming call and streams audio chunks to our API.
- We detect a pause of more than 500 milliseconds and send the buffered audio to our STT provider (Groq's API to run distil-whisper-large-v3-en).
- The transcribed text goes into Llama-4-Scout on Groq.
- We send the reply text to our TTS system (playai tts on Groq).
- We stream the resulting audio back into Twilio, and the caller hears it.

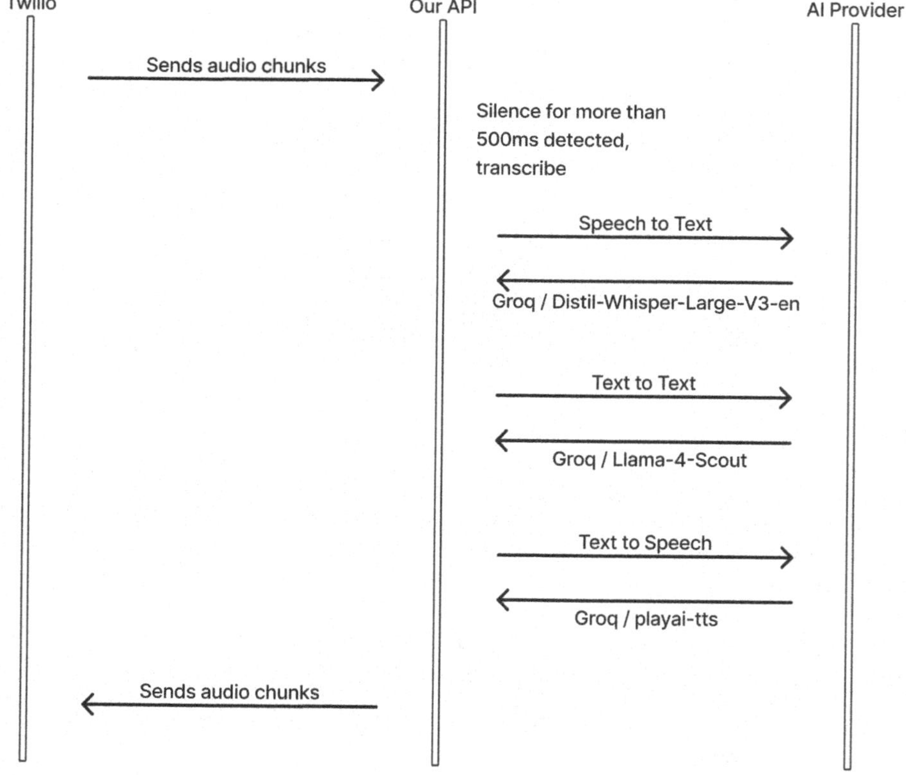

Figure 9.10 Audio from Twilio is streamed to the API, which detects pauses, transcribes speech using Groq's distil-whisper-large-V3-en, processes text replies with Llama-4-Scout, and converts text back to speech with playai-tts before streaming audio back to the caller.

Of course, I can't demonstrate a voice app in this book, but as always you can find the code to run the full Twilio app on the book's GitHub. If you are willing to spend a few dollars on a Twilio number (a few dollars per month at the time of writing), you can have this app up and running in no time. On average, it should provide a sub-second latency between you speaking and the AI model responding.

Case Study 17: Fine-Tuning Matryoshka Embeddings

On the topic of reducing latency and memory, we've previously tuned autoencoding LLMs for classification and updated generative models for domain adaption. Now, let's round out this exploration with an example for embedding models. We start with a very long piece of text. This could be a company's massive set of documentation, a codebase, or, in this case study, something that's in the public domain: *Les Misérables*, because why not? This epic novel by Victor Hugo will stand in place as domain-specific text we wish to fine-tune our embedding model against.

We will chunk the book into pieces; then, for every chunk, we will generate trivia questions from an LLM that can be answered by that specific section. With a dataset of query–context pairs (also known as "positive pairs" for embedders), the goal is to fine-tune an embedder to retrieve the correct chunk to which a query is attached. The chunking and dataset generation process are visualized in Figure 9.11.

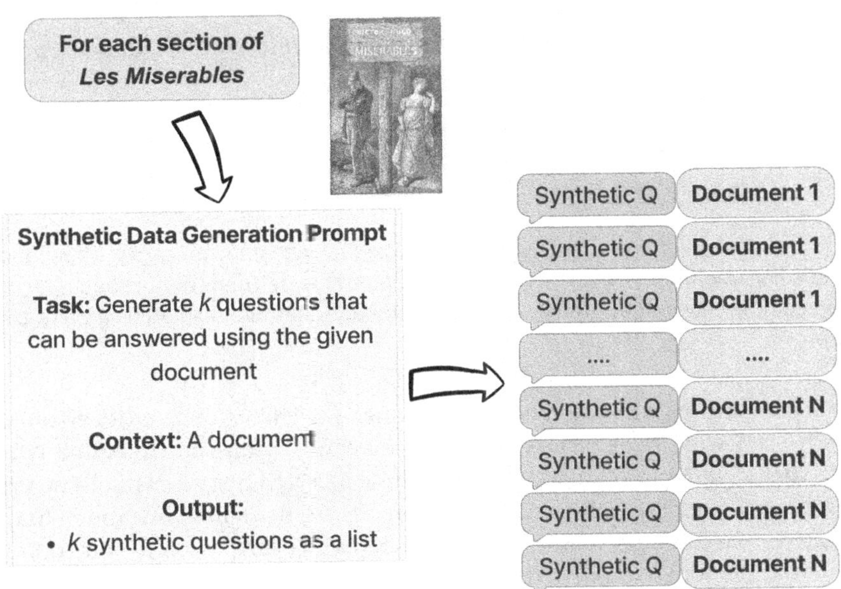

Figure 9.11 A common data generation workflow: For each document (e.g., a section of **Les Misérables**), generate synthetic Q&A pairs using an LLM, then fine-tune the embedding model so that related queries and documents are closer in the embedding space.

Our set of positive pairs is useful, but to properly train an embedding model, we also need negative pairs. For this purpose, we will use the sentence-transformers Python package (a widely used package for embedding fine-tuning). Its **multiple negatives ranking loss** class calculates **in-batch negatives**: Given a batch of positive pairs (anchor, positive), it will use *any* other different document in the same batch as a negative example. Said another way, for every anchor query, all the documents from the *other* pairs in the batch act as negatives.

This process, which is visualized in Figure 9.12, is an extremely efficient way to calculate negative pairs. However, it makes a huge assumption—namely, that any two non-matching documents are truly negative. This assumption could fail, because a query could accidentally match with another part of the text that also happens to answer the question. That would yield a false negative, because they should not be pushed apart by the embedder.

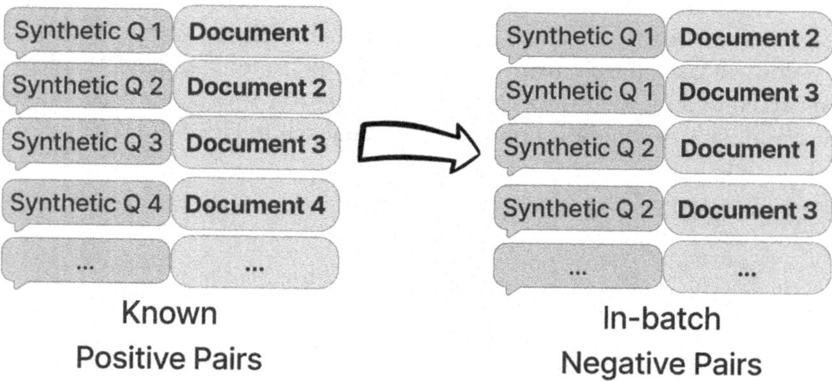

Figure 9.12 Using multiple negatives ranking loss, for each anchor query, all other documents in the same batch—apart from the true positive—are treated as in-batch negatives. This approach is efficient but relies on the assumption that all non-matching pairs are truly negative.

The other issue with in-batch negatives is one of efficiency: The other documents in the batch likely will not be picked up by the embedder as false positives simply because . . . well, they're different. Put another way, these in-batch negatives might be really easy for the embedder to handle and, therefore, might not contribute much to training. Alternatively, we could try to mine **hard-negatives** by using a second embedding model (or a re-ranking model) to prove that the matches are similar, but still unrelated. These examples would be difficult for the embedder to handle and provide necessary training data to help the model distinguish nuances in the text. This mining process could still yield false positives, however, and we would be relying on the robustness of the secondary model to not accidentally create a negative pair that's actually a positive pair.

From here, we have a loss function that will work to maximize cosine similarity (by default, though we can use another embedding similarity function we want) between positive pairs and minimize cosine similarity between the in-batch negatives. We could stop here, but this chapter is about optimizing for production—so we have one more trick up our sleeves.

Matryoshka Embeddings

Embedders come with a built-in output dimension size to which every piece of input is mapped. That is, a single-word input and an input that fills the entire context window of an embedder will both be mapped to an embedding of the same length. But what if we could fine-tune an embedder to work with only the first few dimensions? That's exactly what **Matryoshka embeddings** do, as seen in Figure 9.13. Instead of picking a single embedding size and being stuck with it, a Matryoshka embedder can produce multiple sizes of embeddings, where smaller dimensions produce nearly as performant embeddings while dramatically reducing the memory and latency factors.

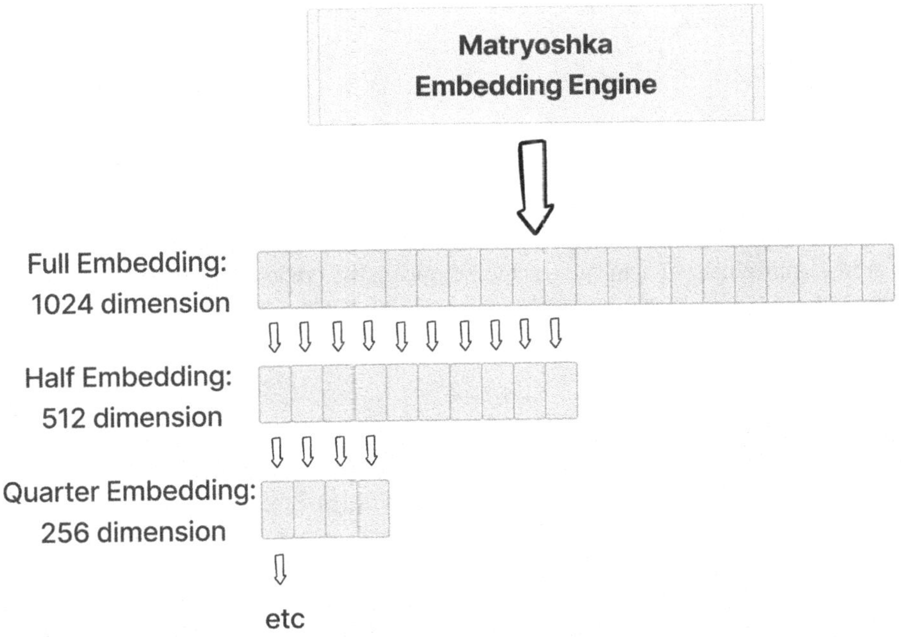

Figure 9.13 A Matryoshka embedder generates embeddings at multiple sizes by truncating the output vector, enabling flexible trade-offs between speed, memory usage, and retrieval performance with minimal loss in quality.

The benefit here is clear: Smaller embedding sizes mean a smaller compute footprint. Figure 9.14 shows a quick experiment using a vector database with 1 million vectors and embedding sizes of 64, 128, 256, 512, and 1,024. For each embedding size, I calculated how large the resulting database was on disk; I also ran several queries against the database and measured the latency when performing the computation. For both cosine similarity and the dot product (another embedding similarity metric; when vectors are of magnitude 1, it produces the same result as cosine similarity), the latency for the computation grew as the embedding size increased.

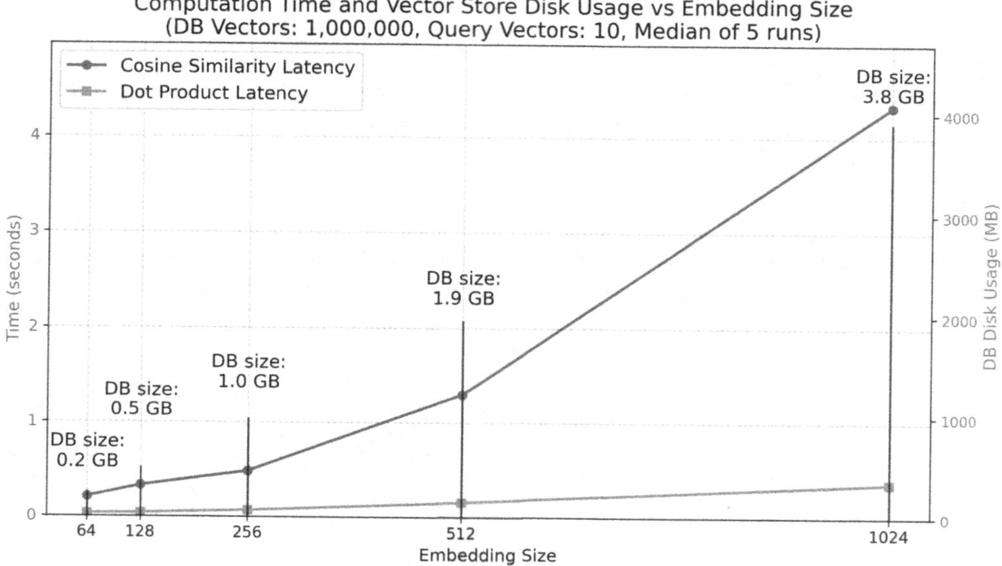

Figure 9.14 As embedding size increases, both computation time and vector database disk usage grow significantly. For 1 million vectors, reducing the embedding size from 1,024 to 64 dimensions cuts disk space by nearly 20 times and slashes search latency. This example illustrates the trade-offs when using Matryoshka embeddings for optimizing memory and speed.

Training Matryoshka embeddings is surprisingly simple: For whatever loss function we choose (in this experiment, multiple negatives ranking loss [MNRL]), we simply apply it to progressively truncated portions of the embeddings. For example, if the model produces 1,024-dimensional embeddings, the `MatryoshkaLoss` function (see Listing 9.4) applies MNRL not only to the full 1,024 dimensions but also to the first 512, 256, 128, and 64 dimensions. The final loss is the sum of all these partial losses. The intuition is that the model is encouraged to frontload the most important information into the earliest dimensions of the embedding so that truncation has a minimal impact on retrieval quality. A useful analogy is principal components in linear algebra: The first components capture the bulk of variance and meaning, while later ones refine that with smaller details. In practice, this means Matryoshka embeddings let us flexibly trade off between speed, memory footprint, and accuracy in production, giving us small, fast embeddings when efficiency is critical and scaling up only when higher fidelity is required.

Listing 9.4 **Defining the Matryoshka representation loss**

```
from sentence_transformers.losses import MatryoshkaLoss,
MultipleNegativesRankingLoss
matryoshka_dimensions = [1024, 512, 256, 128, 64]  # Must be ordered large to small
inner_train_loss = MultipleNegativesRankingLoss(model)
# Define the Matryoshka loss function
train_loss = MatryoshkaLoss(
   model, inner_train_loss, matryoshka_dims=matryoshka_dimensions
)
```

Our model is the Beijing Academy of Artificial Intelligence's (BAAI) bge-large-en-v1.5, which is one of the most performant open embedding models on the MTEB leaderboard (the most cited embedding leaderboard on the planet) as of the time of writing. A whole family of embedding models from BAAI can be found on Hugging Face if you'd like to check them out.

We have our data, we have our pairs, and we have our loss functions. We have one more sub-experiment to introduce before we examine the final results.

Experimenting with Different Training Recipes

In Case Study 14 on domain adaptation (see Chapter 8), we discussed "training recipes" and how different foundation labs experiment with variations of fairly standard fine-tuning practices such as preference tuning and instruction tuning. We can apply a similar framework here. We can run two experiments to compare against the baseline embedder:

- **Pre-train + fine-tune:** First, train the underlying LLM on the autoencoding language modeling task with the raw chunks of data, just as we did with the Qwen model in Chapter 8. The only real difference in this case is that the autoencoding language modeling task will allow the blanks to be filled to be anywhere in the chunk, just like the embedding model was originally trained to do. After this, we will apply our MNRL + Matryoshka losses.
- **Just fine-tune:** Skip the autoencoding task and just do the MNRL + Matryoshka losses. This is the standard embedding fine-tuning process on positive/negative pairs.

Figure 9.15 shows our two experimental setups. With that, we're ready to train the model. Listing 9.5 shows a snippet of the training code for the autoencoding loop in Experiment 1.

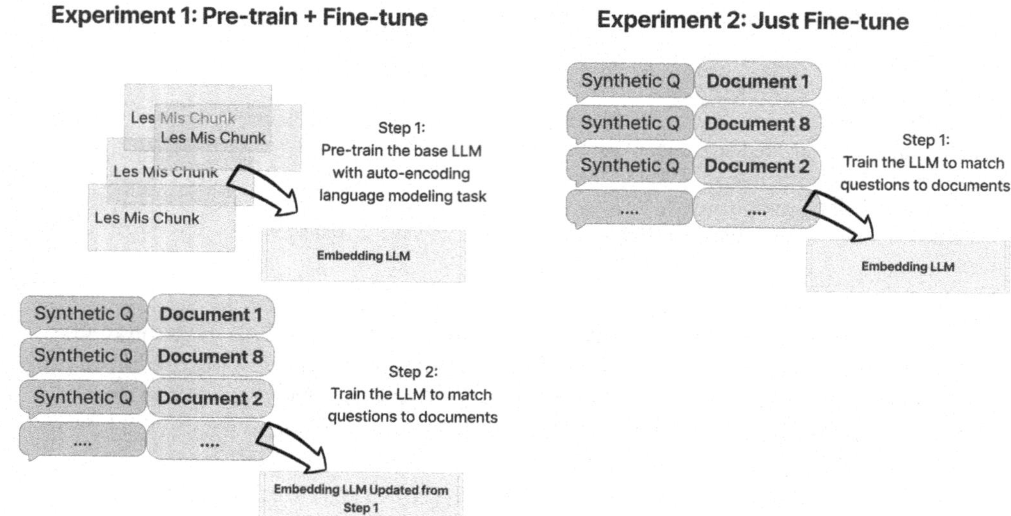

Figure 9.15 Overview of our two embedding model training recipes. Experiment 1 (left): Pre-train the LLM on an autoencoding language modeling task with raw *Les Misérables* chunks, then fine-tune on synthetic Q&A pairs. Experiment 2 (right): Skip the pre-training and directly fine-tune on synthetic Q&A pairs, following the standard approach for embedding fine-tuning.

Listing 9.5 **Step 1: Training the underlying BERT model on the autoencoding LLM**

```
text_file_path = 'lesmis.txt'
# Prepare the dataset
dataset = LineByLineTextDataset(
   tokenizer=model.tokenizer,
   file_path=text_file_path, block_size=config.max_position_embeddings - 2
)
train_size = int(0.7 * len(dataset))  # train test split
train_dataset, val_dataset = torch.utils.data.random_split(
  dataset, [train_size, len(dataset) - train_size])

# Create a data collator that randomly masks tokens. This masking is the autoencoding
language modeling task. Here it's being referred to as "masked language modelling" or
mlm.
data_collator = DataCollatorForLanguageModeling(
   tokenizer=model.tokenizer,
   mlm=True, mlm_probability=0.15  # 15% of the tokens will be masked
)
# Set training arguments
training_args = TrainingArguments(
   num_train_epochs=3,                # Number of training epochs
   ...
)
```

```
# Initialize the Trainer
trainer = Trainer(
   model=model,
   args=training_args,
   data_collator=data_collator,
   train_dataset=train_dataset,
   eval_dataset=val_dataset
)
trainer.train()  # Run our training loop
```

In Listing 9.5, “MLM” stands for **masked language modeling**. This is a synonym for the autoencoding language modeling task.

Now, let’s look at the results of our three embedding experiments.

The Final Results

We have three embedders to compare: the base embedder, the “just fine-tuned” model, and the “MLM + fine-tune” model. Figure 9.16 shows the Recall @ 10 for each of these models. We first saw the metric Recall @ 10 in Chapter 3, when we were comparing embedders for RAG. Now, it has again become useful for us.

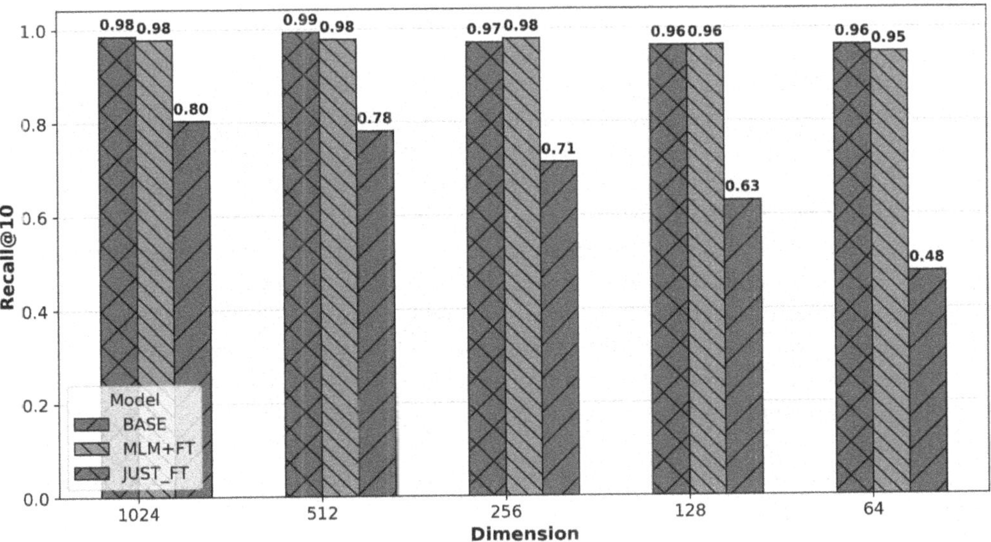

Figure 9.16 Recall @ 10 results for each model and embedding dimension. The base model’s performance drops sharply at smaller dimensions because it wasn’t trained for Matryoshka embeddings. Both the “just fine-tuned” and the “MLM + fine-tuned” models achieve nearly identical, strong performance across all tested dimensions, suggesting that additional MLM pre-training didn’t provide an extra benefit for this task.

Note a few things about the results in Figure 9.16:

- The base embedder cannot compete in lower dimensions. To be fair, though, it was not trained to provide Matryoshka embeddings.
- Both the fine-tune and the MLM + fine-tune embedders perform basically the same across all dimensions, so the MLM didn't seem to be necessary.

Regarding the last point, that's okay! Not all ideas you test in experiments will pan out. But it's important to have the mentality to try anyway, especially if you have reason to believe a specific training recipe could yield some benefit. In this case, I would argue that the reason the MLM did not help is because there likely was no underlying new terminology to learn. Thus, the act of fine-tuning against positive and negative pairs was sufficient to learn the relationships between queries and contexts, even at lower embedding sizes. If we were working in a domain packed with jargon, or doing something cross-lingual, perhaps the MLM pre-training would have added a boost. But for a classic text like *Les Misérables*, the real signal came from teaching the embedder which question matched which chunk of the book. Sometimes the simplest approach just wins out.

Case Study *N* + 1: What Comes Next?

If you made it this far, props to you! You are now well versed in the art of building, tuning, and experimenting with production-grade AI. Over these chapters, we've gone from prompt-wrangling and tool-calling to the nitty-gritty of calibration, domain adaptation, model compression, and system-level optimization. We tested, we coded, we chunked, we fine-tuned. We tried stuff that worked, and, just as importantly, we tried stuff that didn't. If you take only one message away from this book, let it be this: *The AI world rewards people who try.*

The secret sauce to successful AI products is not just accuracy, or even speed, but the ability to combine a deep understanding of your use-case with a willingness to experiment. There's no single right answer. Want to shrink your model? Try quantization. Want to speed it up? Maybe speculative decoding will do the trick. Need more control? Fine-tune the model on your own data. Need privacy? Self-host your models. Got a weird edge case nobody else cares about? Bake it into your model with a bit of domain adaptation.

But with this power comes a sense of responsibility and ownership. Every time we build a workflow, design a system, or set an agentic chatbot loose on our audience, we are making choices that affect not just the quality of the app, but the safety, privacy, and even fairness of the users' experience. We've seen throughout this book how easy it is for AI to hallucinate, to sound far too confident when it shouldn't, and to reinforce biases we never intended. That's why testing, monitoring, and a healthy dose of skepticism about what these AI models are really doing is *not* optional.

The real world is messy. Users will try things you never imagined, data will always contain some wild surprises, and even the best-laid plans will absolutely break the first time someone pastes a copy–paste prompt into your app. That's okay. The job of an AI engineer is never to be perfect, but rather to be aware, keep iterating, keep learning, and keep adapting.

Stay creative. Mix things up. Read the latest papers, but don't be afraid to build your own weird little hack to solve the problem in front of you. Lean into your experiments, your failures, and your instincts. And always keep your eyes open for the next frontier, be it multimodal, contextual, agentic, or something no one's even named yet.

AI moves fast, but the best way to keep up is to never stop learning, and never stop building.

Thank you for reading.

Index

A

B

C

D

E

F

J

K

L

M

Q

R

S

T

U

V

W

Y

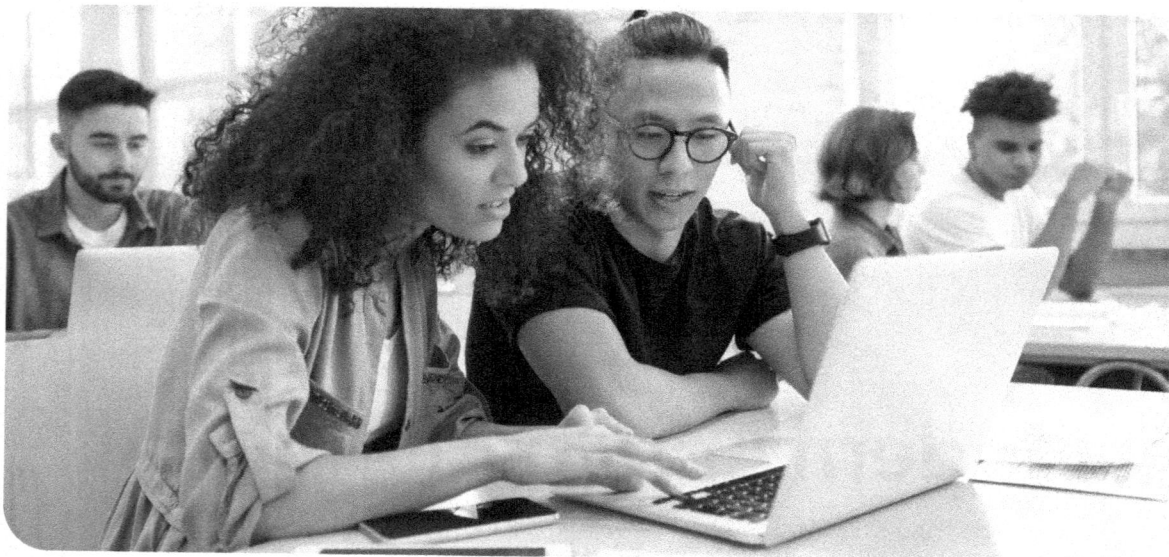